CORAL G

AN

THEIR MAGIC

A Study of the Methods of
Tilling the Soil and of Agricultural
Rites in the Trobriand Islands

—— *by* ——

BRONISŁAW
MALINOWSKI

With 3 Maps, 116 Illustrations
and 24 Figures

VOLUME TWO

THE LANGUAGE OF
MAGIC AND GARDENING

LONDON
GEORGE ALLEN & UNWIN LTD
MUSEUM STREET

BY THE SAME AUTHOR:

The Family among the Australian Aborigines, London: University of London Press (out of print), 1913.

Primitive Religion and Social Differentiation, Cracow (in Polish, out of print), 1915.

"The Natives of Mailu", Adelaide: *Trans. of the R. Soc. of S. Australia for 1915*, pp. 494–706, 1915.

Argonauts of the Western Pacific, London: Geo. Routledge & Sons; New York: E. P. Dutton & Co., 1922.

"Magic, Science and Religion", in Essays collected by J. Needham, under the title *Science, Religion and Reality*, London: The Sheldon Press; New York and Toronto: The Macmillan Co., 1926.

Myth in Primitive Psychology, London: Kegan Paul & Co.; New York: W. W. Norton & Co., 1926.

Crime and Custom in Savage Society, London: Kegan Paul & Co.; New York: Harcourt Brace & Co., 1926.

The Father in Primitive Psychology, London: Kegan Paul & Co.; New York: W. W. Norton & Co., 1927.

Sex and Repression in Savage Society, London: Kegan Paul & Co.; New York: Harcourt Brace & Co., 1927. Also French edition: *La Sexualité et sa Répression dans les Sociétés Primitives*, Paris: Payot, 1933.

The Sexual Life of Savages in North-Western Melanesia, London: Geo. Routledge & Sons; New York: Liveright & Co., 1929. Also translations into German, French, Italian, Spanish and Polish.

Mœurs et Coutumes des Mélanésiens, Payot, Paris, 1935.

PRINTED IN GREAT BRITAIN BY
UNWIN BROTHERS LTD., WOKING

INTRODUCTION TO VOLUME TWO

THE linguistic problem before the ethnographer is to give as full a presentation of language as of any other aspect of culture. Were it possible for him to reproduce large portions of tribal life and speech through the medium of a sound film, he might be able to give the reality of the culture in much greater fullness and the part played by language within it. But even this medium would not dispense him from a good deal of additional interpretation and commentary. For, as we shall see in the course of our theoretical argument and of its practical applications, language differs from other aspects of culture in one respect: there is much more of the conventional or arbitrary element in the symbolism of speech than in any other aspect of manual and bodily behaviour. Processes of tilling the ground, however much they may differ from one culture to another, have a great deal in common. A European peasant transplanted into a coral atoll or a high plateau of Central America, would still recognise what his brother husbandman is doing; he would not understand a single word of the other's speech.

In dealing with language at the pre-literate stage, the ethnographer is faced by another difficulty. The speech of his people does not live on paper. It exists only in free utterance between man and man. *Verba volant, scripta manent.* The ethnographer has to immobilise the volatile substance of his subject-matter and put it on paper. Whereas the language of literature in more highly developed communities is handed down to us on marble, brass, parchment or pulp, that of a savage tribe is never framed to be taken outside its context of situation. The speech of a pre-literate community brings home to us in an unavoidably cogent manner that language exists only in actual use within the context of real utterance.

The ethnographic approach thus demonstrates better than any other how deeply language is connected with culture. It also shows how to study language outside the framework of its cultural realities —the beliefs of the people, their social organisation, their legal ideas and economic activities—must remain entirely futile.

Language therefore must be linked up with all the other aspects of human culture. Language is not something which can be studied independently of cultural reality. To divide anthropology, as one of the leaders of our science has done recently, into three disciplines, one of which is concerned with the human frame, the other with culture, and the third with language—shows that the relation between language and culture has not been sufficiently appreciated by modern Anthropology in general. Language is intertwined with the education of the young, with social intercourse, with the administration of law, the carrying out of ritual, and with all other forms of practical co-operation. It is the function of language within these activities which is the primary linguistic problem for the cultural anthropologist—whatever the grammarian, the philologist, the logician or the aesthete may look for. As regards the anthropological problem, I found that I could not have recourse to any of the theories or methods already in existence. The grammarian—even the scientific grammarian—is still mainly concerned with the ethical aspect of the question. He teaches you how you ought to speak, what you ought to avoid, and what ought to be your ideal.

"The traditional grammarian of the old type states the rules and looks upon deviations as blunders, which he thinks himself justified in branding as illogical" (Otto Jespersen, *The Philosophy of Grammar*, p. 345)—one might almost say immoral. And Professor Jespersen, whom I have just quoted, speaks in another sentence about "that tendency to reprobation which is the besetting sin of the non-historic grammarian". The besetting sin of the historic grammarian, on the other hand, is in my opinion a tendency to reconstruction, whether it be the Indo-Germanic *Ursprache*, or Proto-Polynesian, or Fundamental Semitic. Moreover, sins or moral attitudes apart, problems of history are not problems of function. Most of the unquestionable and scientifically very valuable contributions of Indo-European philology concerning *Lautwandel* or *Bedeutungswandel*, concerning the formation of Romance languages out of Latin, or the historic birth of that supreme twin hybrid—the American and English languages—from the union of Teutonic and Romance, are not profitable to the anthropologist. Worst of all, the typical philologist, with his firm belief that a language becomes really beautiful and instructive—ethically, logically and aesthetically valuable—when it is dead, has vitiated linguistic studies in a manner so profound that no one of us has ever completely lived down the birth trauma of his grammatical categories.

The needs of the Anthropologist are entirely different, and so must be his methods. He may accept a great deal of the solid and valuable research done on comparative Indo-European linguistics and the painstaking work on modern languages (though he will always reject the sterility of the philological approach or any of the grammarian's attempts to immobilise language on paper), but he must clearly recognise that his own task is neither normative nor reconstructive nor historical. His task is to give a full description of language as an aspect and ingredient of culture. He has to do here what he has been in the habit of doing with regard to religion, social organisation, arts and crafts, or economics. And for this an entirely different approach is necessary. What this approach is will be seen in the following pages.

When the anthropologist, or more precisely the adept of the functional method, turns to the work of his predecessors in direct line—the linguistically competent missionaries, administrators or travellers—he again finds a vast material, much of which he can utilise and learn from. But here also he cannot completely rely on what others have done before him and for him. For once more the difference in aim has brought about a difference of method. The missionary or administrator who, after having mastered the intricacies of the vernacular, embodies the results of his lifelong work in a grammar and vocabulary, perhaps also in a collection of texts, thinks mainly of his successor, for whom he wants to spare labour and give a short cut to the native language. Now the practical man who deals with a native community does not need a scientific picture of that community's speech. What he needs is to use the language for his own purposes, to translate the Gospel and preach it, to educate the native in European morals, sports, handicrafts, law and arithmetic, to sell his goods and buy native labour. The vernacular serves in all this the purpose of translating the white man's point of view to the native. It is almost the reverse of what the Anthropologist aims at, whose task is to translate the native point of view to the European.

The enormous difficulties which beset the honest and clear-sighted missionary, administrator and educationalist at their respective tasks, will become increasingly clear to the reader of the following pages. They are well recognised by one class of European working among natives: the missionaries who, more than anyone else, have honestly and deliberately faced their problem during the last few years. Their point of view is well summed up in Mr. Edwin Smith's *Shrine of a People's Soul*, where especially in Chapters III and IV he comes near to recognising the "untranslatability of words" from one cultural medium into another. And the drift of most modern missionary writings on linguistics is towards the method of cultural interpretation of language which is also adopted in the present book. The missionary recognises that he is attempting to carry over to the natives a new set of ideas, a new set of values, and with this the reorganisation of the natives' own language. But all this again is at best only the counterpart of the fundamental anthropological problem, that of discovering the means of effectively bringing home the realities of native language to English readers.

In the following pages the reader will find in Part V the linguistic material presented by certain methods and devices, which as far as I know have not been extensively tried before. I mean the presentation of language, not in the form of a dictionary plus grammar plus collection of texts with annotations, but the presentation of this material woven into a continuous story. On the other hand in Parts IV and VI I had to give the justification for this method and lay down the principles on which I proceeded, and the reasons for framing these principles. In Part VII the full set of magical spells are given in the vernacular, with cultural as well as linguistic commentaries.

In tackling the specifically anthropological problem of language, I have been guided mainly by my own experiences in the field, but I have also consulted a fairly wide range of books; the work of specialised linguists on primitive languages, from Wilhelm von Humboldt to Sydney H. Ray, from Codrington to Edwin Smith; as well as theoretical disquisitions on language from Lazarus and Steinthal to John Dewey. From every one of these I have received considerable help. But not one single method or point of view could I use *in toto* as my reliable and effective guide. Those who know the modern literature of language will be able to appreciate my reasons and see the difference between the methods here adopted and those previously used.

I had originally intended to include in Part IV of this volume a critical digest of some of the most recent works on linguistic theory, such, for instance, as Jespersen's *Philosophy of Grammar*, De Laguna's *Speech*, Cournois' *La Science du Mot*, Gardiner's *Speech and Language* and—last not least—the short but important Chapter V in John Dewey's *Experience and Nature*. This would have related my own point of view to recent developments in linguistics and perhaps enabled me to bring out with greater precision some aspects of the anthropological approach to language as contrasted with that of the philologist, the philosopher or historian.

But no sooner had I drafted this critical and comparative part than I had to discard it. It would have overweighted the volume with purely theoretical and critical matter. The point of view here advanced must, therefore, be taken and judged on its merits: as the summary of an anthropologist's linguistic experiences in the field, and of his attempts at mastering the material thus collected. I think that I can claim without any presumption that every step of my argument is well founded in personal experience of linguistic work, and that it is also documented by concrete examples taken from these experiences. The theories here advanced will easily be seen to have originated in the actual difficulties of collecting, interpreting, translating and editing texts and terminologies. The approach presented has thus to a large extent been tested on the long and painful experience of learning a native language; on the practice of speaking it, of gradually acquiring fluency and that intuitive understanding which enables us, as speaker, to handle the finer shades of meaning and, as hearer, to take part in the quick interchange between several people. It took me about one year to speak easily, and I acquired full proficiency only after some eighteen months of practice, that is towards the middle of my second expedition.

But for all this it would be merely a pretence for me to claim that the theories here evolved are a spontaneous and unaided growth built by my own constructive faculty from my own experiences. I do not want for one moment to minimise my indebtedness to linguistic theory. Since I regard it as of the greatest importance always to stress the fact that only theoretical training enables us to see a sociological fact and to record and interpret it correctly, I should like to say that in no other branch of Anthropology has my reading been as extensive as in Linguistics. Up to the war, I read and digested a great many theoretical books on the psychology of language and the philosophy of grammar, and I was also acquainted with the main results of comparative Indo-European linguistics. From the newer literature I have only been able to read samples, and I certainly cannot claim to be abreast of recent developments. But even the books enumerated above well represent some of the new developments.

I hope that at some other time I shall be able to state fully and adequately my indebtedness to past work and the place which I think my contribution might be assigned in recent movements towards a more fully sociological and pragmatic treatment of language. It is well to remind the reader that this book is mainly descriptive and not theoretical. It is not a frontal attack on language, nor even a descriptive work dealing with the language of the Trobriand Islands, but only a linguistic commentary to an ethnographic work on agriculture. So that, from this point of view, a general discussion of linguistic problems had to be limited to the necessary minimum. Since the two theoretical parts (IV and VI) are very fully documented in the two parts which immediately follow them, a critical and indirect substantiation of their claims is perhaps not necessary.

CONTENTS OF VOLUME TWO

PART FOUR

AN ETHNOGRAPHIC THEORY OF LANGUAGE AND SOME PRACTICAL COROLLARIES

PART FIVE

CORPUS INSCRIPTIONUM AGRICULTURAE QUIRIVINIENSIS; OR THE LANGUAGE OF GARDENS

CORAL GARDENS AND THEIR MAGIC

PART SIX

AN ETHNOGRAPHIC THEORY OF THE MAGICAL WORD

PART SEVEN

MAGICAL FORMULAE

Page 253

ANALYTICAL TABLE
OF CONTENTS

Part Four

An Ethnographic Theory of Language and some Practical Corollaries

Homonyms: not confusion but introduction of familiar element.—
"Bush-hen mound": familiar element in magical theory.—Legal import
of homonymous uses.—Creative metaphor of magic.—Anticipatory
words.—Familiar element in *pwaypwaya*, "terra firma"; in *valu, dakuna,
kema*, etc.—Function of homonymity.—Importance of context.—Summary.

Part Five

Corpus Inscriptionum Agriculturae Quiriviniensis; or The Language of Gardens

NOTE TO READER

This somewhat detailed table of contents of the Linguistic Supplement
is meant for those especially interested both in the ethnographic and
linguistic aspect of Trobriand gardening. I had prepared it for myself,
but found it so useful in allowing me to find at a glance the place where
a word, a text or a grammatical analysis were to be found, that I decided
to reproduce it here. It is meant to be an aid to rapid orientation, hence
it was not possible to make it completely exhaustive in the sense of
including all the words; nor has any elaboration of definitions or consistency in presentation been possible.

Div. I. LAND AND GARDENS

Div. II. THE CROPS

Div. V. THE SOCIAL AND CULTURAL SETTING OF
TROBRIAND AGRICULTURE

Div. VI. THE TECHNIQUE AND OUTFIT OF AGRICULTURE

PAR

Div. VII. MAGIC

Div. VIII. INAUGURATIVE MAGICAL CEREMONIES

Div. IX. MAGIC OF GROWTH

DIV. X. THE MAGIC OF HARVEST AND OF PLENTY

Part Six

An Ethnographic Theory of the Magical Word

Literal rendering and free translation in the language of magic.
Div. I. THE MEANING OF MEANINGLESS WORDS (*Pp.* 213-218).
Abracadabra and hocus-pocus.—What is the function of a magical
utterance?—Is the spell a monologue?—The situation of magic.—The
production of *mana.*—The *vatuvi* spell and the ritual voice-trap.—Magician's voice as the vehicle of *mana.*—The beginnings of magic: its emergence from underground; *in principio erat verbum.*—Interest in the filiation
of magic.

Div. II. COEFFICIENT OF WEIRDNESS IN THE LAN-
GUAGE OF MAGIC (*Pp.* 218-223). Specific function and origin of
magical speech in native theory.—Untranslatable passages.—Specific
distortions of magic: compounds, clipped forms, pseudonyms.—Oppositions and negative comparisons.—Meaningless words made intelligible
by additional information.—Spell untranslatable without knowledge of
correlated dogma.—Untranslated words not necessarily untranslatable.

Div. III. DIGRESSION ON THE THEORY OF MAGICAL
LANGUAGE (*Pp.* 223-225). Conclusions concerning meaning of
meaningless words.—Ritual accessories contributing to weirdness and
difficulty of noting spells.—Difficulty of obtaining adequate commentaries: the special interest of these.

Div. IV. COEFFICIENT OF INTELLIGIBILITY (*Pp.* 225-231).
Intelligible elements in spells: words and phrases of common speech,
inventory words, compound expressions made up of intelligible elements,
distortions containing significant elements.—Modifications and distortions of intelligible elements.—Reason for coefficient of intelligibility.—
Magical words as attributes of man's relation to environment.—Spells
addressed to things, beings, agencies.—Coexistence of weirdness and
intelligibility.—Twofold nature of translator's task.

Div. V. DIGRESSION ON THE GENERAL THEORY OF MAGICAL LANGUAGE (*Pp.* 231-240). These pages contain suggestions rather than final conclusions.—Evolution of magical speech from nonsense to the rational or vice versa?—Child language pragmatic and magical.—Intelligible and unintelligible elements in language.—The twofold character explained by acquisition of language in childhood.—Weird Trobriand words explained by association and "sympathy".—Child's quasi-magical influence over adults.—Mastery over words side by side with mastery over things.—Defective speech identified with defective mentality.—The craftsman and the schoolman.—Citizenship and sociological terminologies.—Binding force of legal words.—Contracts and oaths: their mystical virtue.—The theory of Durkheim criticised.—Two peaks of linguistic effectiveness (magical and pragmatic) to be found in all cultures—Monsieur Coué and his Trobriand colleague.—Christian Science.—Advertising and beauty magic.—Political oratory.—The essence of magical statement.—Creative metaphor.—Freud's identification of magic with day-dreaming criticised.—Magic as supplementing human thought and knowledge.—Magic as an organising force.

Div. VI. THE SOCIOLOGICAL FUNCTION OF MAGIC AS ANOTHER SOURCE OF INTELLIGIBILITY OF SPELLS (*Pp.* 240-250). The spell: verbal communion between magician and natural objects.—The response to the spell.—Its real effect on human beings.—The magician's charter and influence.—Spells known to many Trobrianders.—The setting of the first formula analysed.—The setting of the second formula.—How far the natives know the magic.—Magician speaking on behalf of all the gardeners.—Key-words analysed.—Words of magic as creating hope and confidence.—Influence of the spell on the gardeners.—The magician as leader and organiser.—Meaning of meaningless elements in magic.—Meaning of magical word found in the effect it is believed to produce, in the manner in which it is launched, in its etymological associations and its possible sociological functions.—Explanation of the commentaries to the spells.

Part Seven

Magical Formulae

PART IV

AN ETHNOGRAPHIC THEORY OF LANGUAGE AND SOME PRACTICAL COROLLARIES

AN ETHNOGRAPHIC THEORY OF LANGUAGE AND SOME PRACTICAL COROLLARIES

This linguistic supplement owes it existence to practical considerations. Naturally I wanted to present all the linguistic material concerning Trobriand agriculture which I had collected: without it the account of gardening would remain incomplete. And yet I found that a full and clear presentation of this material became technical and unwieldy; it broke up the flow of the narrative. In order to remedy this I at first attempted to relegate my linguistic comments to footnotes. When these became too bulky I collected them into digressions. But it soon became clear that when these digressions were joined up they made a consecutive story and in that form became less tedious as well as more illuminating. Thus I found myself with no choice but to separate linguistics from description and to place it in this supplement.

The genesis of this supplement would in itself, perhaps, account for the form in which I am presenting my material. Instead of the usual glossary with texts and comments, I have woven the linguistic data—terms, phrases and texts—into a continuous narrative which, necessarily, has grown to a length almost comparable with that of the descriptive part of the book. This method of presentation, however, appears to me so much better, clearer and more readable than any other—indeed so inevitable—that I have resisted any temptation to be more concise.

In fact, in the course of these introductory theoretical reflections we shall be more and more cogently driven to the conclusion that this is the only correct presentation of any linguistic material. The method undoubtedly does entail certain hardships for the reader and writer alike. On the one hand the double account, descriptive and linguistic, submits the reader to a greater mental effort, as he will have to collate the statements from one part to the other. This method of presentation has also given the writer a considerable amount of extra work. But the double entry into the subject has compensating advantages: it allows of a much fuller control both of linguistic data and ethnographic description than could otherwise be given. I think that the material thus illuminated from two sides will stand out, so to speak, stereoscopically.

But the chief virtue of this method is that it closely follows the technique of field-work. The ethnographer has to see and to hear; he has personally to witness the rites, ceremonies and activities, and he has to collect opinions on them. The active, personal and visual side are the main concern of the descriptive chapters. The conversations, comments and grammatical apparatus are given here.

Div. I. LANGUAGE AS TOOL, DOCUMENT AND CULTURAL REALITY

In the following study of Trobriand agricultural linguistics there are several points of view which have to be kept before the reader. First of all there is the special methodological interest in the frank and full presentation of all available linguistic evidence. For language is the ethnographer's most important tool. It is through his knowledge of the vernacular and through his practical handling of native grammar and vocabulary that the ethnographer can ask clear questions and receive relevant answers. These answers he then has to interpret and comment upon before he can give them in an intelligible form to his English reader; and it is a long way from the mouth of the native informant to the mind of the English reader.

But the value of linguistic data is only in proportion to the ethnographer's own knowledge and his critical accuracy in drawing inferences; therefore he is obliged—as is every scientific worker who must present his credentials and describe the way in which he has reached his conclusions—to disclose his most important apparatus, that is, his linguistic outfit.

Thus in the study of technical terminologies and characteristic phrases—some volunteered, others obtained in answer to questions, others again repeatedly heard as traditional sayings—the reader will gain an insight into the linguistic equipment of my field-work. From the amount of terms collected he will be able to assess the range of subjects within which I could converse with the natives; from the type and structure of the statements, the difficulties of giving an adequate translation. As regards the terminologies, the reader will see that my aim is not to introduce a false precision into native ideas, but rather to ascertain precisely what a certain word means to the native and how it is used by him. About three-fourths of the statements contained in this supplement are what might be called definition texts; that is, texts in which a native either tries to define a word or uses it in a characteristic manner. As the reader will see from Divisions IV and V, such definition texts are not merely answers elicited from informants, but are an intrinsic part of the native educational process. On difficult subjects I have given several texts referring to the same word.[1]

---

[1] Texts 2, 3 and 4 (Div. I, §§ 21–23) show how a happy wording of a native statement will sometimes give a clear insight into linguistic usage. Again, such

As regards the completeness of my information, the reader will find no difficulty in judging where, for instance, one of my lists exhausts all the native forms used in that context and where it is incomplete.[1] In general the more fundamental the concept the more exhaustive is my evidence and the better is my practical acquaintance with the word and its various uses. It is hardly necessary to state that the texts and sayings here reproduced represent about a hundredth or so of the times I heard any given word used. Expressions referring to botanical characteristics, for instance, or to types of soil, I mainly learned to use and to understand in my cross-country walks. But quite often I was not able to make very full linguistic notes at the time. When an exceptionally good phrase occurred I would make a brief note of it, mental or written, and then lead my informant to repeat it, not necessarily as I had first heard it, but so as to reproduce the information it contained and its linguistic character.

Methodologically it is always interesting to know whether a statement is an answer to a direct question or whether it is a volunteered statement or a traditional saying. It is obvious that all the magical formulae, the gardening cries and ditties, are traditional, set texts (cf. Part VI). In most cases I have marked when a statement was volunteered to me. The majority of the definition texts or such little descriptive accounts as the texts concerning garden work,[2] the briefer texts on magic[3] and the fuller texts on magic,[4] were obtained in the course of ethnographic discussions. The greater part of my linguistic material was, however, obtained from my more competent informants, and with these I did not work very much by the question and answer texts as 38, 39 and 40 (Div. VIII, §§ 2 and 3) exhibit grammatical peculiarities and are juxtaposed mainly to exemplify certain difficulties with which I was faced and to account for certain apparent inconsistencies in my presentation of the linguistic material. Some really important texts—such as 33 (Div. VI, § 45) on the function of the boundary pole, 21 (Div. IV, § 13) on the aim of the *kaytubutabu* magic, 9 (Div. II, § 12), 15 (Div. III, § 24) and 19 (Div. IV, § 9) on some aspects of the growth of plants—are methodologically interesting because they show the manner in which the ethnographer has to manipulate the raw material of his linguistic evidence in order to draw his theoretical conclusions.

[1] At times, as in the lists of varieties of *yam* and *taytu* (Div. III, §§ 9 and 10), I expressly state the limitations of, and lacunae in, my materials. Again, in enumerating kinds of cultivable soil (Div. I, §§ 11 and 12) I may have missed one or two words, though the list is the result of long and repeated enquiry; but the fundamental divisions as to the type of habitat (Div. I, §§ 3 to 9) are certainly complete.

[2] Texts 29–35 (Div. VI, §§ 14, 22, 42, 44, 45, 47 and 48).

[3] Texts 38–76 (Div. VIII, §§ 2, 3, 9, 20, 22; Div. IX, §§ 6, 8–10, 13, 14, 16, 17, 20–22, 24, 28, 32, 35–37; Div. X, §§ 3–6, 8, 12 and 13).

[4] Texts 77–84 (Div. X, § 15; Div. XI, §§ 2, 4, 6, 9, 11, 13 and 14).

method. They had a clear idea of what I wanted from them and, in the course of conversations, were always keen to give me sound informative data. The line therefore between a spontaneously volunteered and an elicited statement is not always easy to draw.

The reader's methodological interest in the following analysis and the ethnographer's practical interest in language as an instrument of research both refer to language as a means to an end. But language is more than this. Although it is not correct to say that language expresses native ideas or that it embodies their concepts and categories, yet it stands in a definite relation to the life of the people who speak it and to their mental habits and attitudes. From this point of view it provides us with the most important documents illustrating types of human behaviour other than linguistic.

Take for instance two of the magical formulae which will be discussed in Part VII. When the magician in Formula 1 declares: "This is our oblation, old men, I have put it, hey"; or when in Formula 4 he says: "I cut thee—my garden site; I make thy belly blossom with my charmed axe, my garden site. It lifts and stands there, it lifts and stands here," he is definitely commenting on his actions. Now a traditional standardised commentary of this sort, which emphasises and enumerates what to the natives are probably the most relevant aspects of the ritual, has a great ethnographic value. The formulae containing exorcisms and enumerations of the most dreaded blights and pests; the formulae where fertility is anticipated in hyperbolical phrases; those where stability is insisted upon by metaphors drawn from sailing and anchoring, are one and all documents of the native attitude towards gardening. There is not a single formula in which we do not find some important piece of ethnographic information which throws additional light on the ceremony, on its function and on its meaning to the natives.

What is true of formulae is, in a way, even more true of those direct sayings and commentaries which refer to certain aspects of gardening. The series of texts, 38 to 84, which comment on the purpose, function or technique of certain practical or magical operations are, as the reader will agree, most valuable illustrations of native cultural acts. The texts—mentioned above from the point of view of methodological interest—which define the function of the boundary pole or the aim of coconut magic, or Text 37 which deals with the relation between magic and work, also illuminate the native outlook. We shall enter into this more fully in discussing the educational character of a number of texts here presented. It will be seen then that most of the sayings naturally throw light on technical, economic and ceremonial behaviour, since in native life they actually function as commentaries to these activities—and as directions and precepts given to the young (cf. Divs. IV and V). The list of terminologies, the pairs of opposites or mutually exclusive concepts, the linguistic relationship between the term *pwaypwaya* as 'fertile soil', that is, 'soil *par excellence*', and as 'land in general' (cf. Div. I, §§ 3 and 1) obviously correspond to realities of native culture and behaviour. So do also the botanical terms which show the special place occupied in the native mind by cultivable crops as against all other growth. The use of possessive pronouns and the special place given to food, more especially to vegetable crops, in this class of words, is important as indicating standards of value.[1]

Every item given in the following analysis could be considered both as a document and as a tool in ethnographic field-work. It is not necessary here to stress this two-fold orientation of interest any further. But it is necessary to insist that the function of language as a clue to mental process is by no means easy to assess. The relation between idea and word, between verbal statement and mental attitude, is a question which we shall have to consider in some detail. Words—and even more so, perhaps, phrases, sentences and texts—taken in conjunction with other types of behaviour, constitute extremely significant documents and commentaries. But there is nothing more dangerous than to imagine that language is a process running parallel and exactly corresponding to mental process, and that the function of language is to reflect or to duplicate the mental reality of man in a secondary flow of verbal equivalents.

The fact is that the main function of language is not to express thought, not to duplicate mental processes, but rather to play an active pragmatic part in human behaviour. Thus in its primary function it is one of the chief cultural forces and an adjunct to bodily activities. Indeed, it is an indispensable ingredient of all concerted human action. Here I want only briefly to indicate what I mean, as it will be necessary to enlarge on it further on (cf. Div. IV).

Let us survey rapidly the uses of language in Trobriand gardening, starting, for instance, with a group of people who after the council (*kayaku*) repair to the gardens in order to "count the plots in the bush" (*kalawa o la odila*; cf. Ch. II, Sec. 3). These people have to determine the area to be put under cultivation, to fix the boundaries, in short to make everything ready for the cutting of the boundary belt. The older men, with experience and a good knowledge of the ground, identify the fields (*kwabila*), place the boundaries by means

[1] Cf. Part V, Div. XII, §§ 3 to 7.

of landmarks and trace the lines of stone (*karige'i*). All this is done by means of a combination of speech and bodily activity. Movements, words and gestures are used to solve this practical problem. The natives search for objects such as trees, coral outcrops, or stone heaps, discuss their proper names, point out, disagree. Finally they come to a decision which is the outcome of verbal discourse, of going about, pointing and using implements; for, as they come to an agreement, they leave signs, blaze marks on trees, and cut down saplings. Such words as *kwabila, karige'i, tuwaga, baleko* or *tukulumwala*, words which define various species of trees and types of coral outcrop, the proper names of a field, path or garden plot, are used as significant actions side by side with bodily movements. Speech is here equivalent to gesture and to motion. It does not function as an expression of thought or communication of ideas but as a part of concerted activity. If we jotted down the words spoken there and treated them as a *text* divorced from its context of action and situation, the words would obviously remain meaningless and futile. In order to reconstruct the meaning of sounds it is necessary to describe the bodily behaviour of the men, to know the purpose of their concerted action, as well as their sociology. Speech here is primarily used for the achievement of a practical result. Secondarily it also fulfils an educational purpose in that the older and better-informed men hand on the results of their past experiences to the younger ones.

If we followed the group of people who usually go to cut the boundary belt we would see that they also use words in order to co-ordinate their activities, to communicate at a distance, to call out for assistance—in short to regulate their concerted work. The same would be the case also when, a few days later, after the great inaugural ceremony, they repair in a body to the garden and carry out communally the early clearing (*takaywa*). Then the bush is alive with men who call out encouragements to one another, issue commands, and co-ordinate their movements by verbal action at a distance. Their work would be impossible without speech. Speech again is meaningless without the context of the activity in which it is enveloped. The handling of poles in the erection of the *kamkokola*, the building of a fence, or the construction of a garden arbour, would each supply us with examples of speech interwoven with manual behaviour.

I want to make it quite clear that I am not speaking here only of the Trobriand language, still less only of native speech in agriculture. I am trying to indicate the character of human speech in general and the necessary methodological approach to it. Every one of us could convince himself from his own experience that language in our own culture often returns to its pronouncedly pragmatic character. Whether engaged in a technical manipulation, pursuing some sporting activity, or conducting a scientific experiment in a laboratory or assisting each other by word and deed in a simple manual task—words which cross from one actor to another do not serve primarily to communicate thought: they connect work and correlate manual and bodily movements. Words are part of action and they are equivalents to actions.

Thus put, the point which I am labouring here may appear a commonplace, something so obvious that it may well be neglected. But the neglect of the obvious has often been fatal to the development of scientific thought. The false conception of language as a means of transfusing ideas from the head of the speaker to that of the listener has, in my opinion, largely vitiated the philological approach to language. The view here set forth is not merely academic: it compels us, as we shall see, to correlate the study of language with that of other activities, to interpret the meaning of each utterance within its actual context; and this means a new departure in the handling of linguistic evidence. It will also force us to define meaning in terms of experience and situation. All this will be fully substantiated in the following sections of this book.

The pragmatic character of language has so far been illustrated only in its pronouncedly active uses; but this does not mean that other types of language, such as narratives, magical formulae, public harangues or legal utterances, lack completely the pragmatic dimension. Language is never a mere shadow of some other cultural reality. Take for instance a magical formula. The ethnographer may find in it a number of illustrative phrases. He may discover that certain words point to certain traditional attitudes and that others contain a running commentary on the manual rite. The critical reader may be interested in keeping a close methodological watch over the ethnographer's manipulation of the formula. But to the native himself a magical formula is not a piece of folk-lore, still less—obviously—an ethnographic document. It is a verbal act by which a specific force is let loose—an act which in native belief exercises the most powerful influence on the course of nature and on human behaviour. Magic, moreover, as we have seen, acts as a powerful social organising force. The utterance of a magical formula, which forms the very core of every magical rite, is to the native a very momentous and sacred act. The ethnographer who would treat it as a mere piece of verbiage containing interesting linguistic illustrations would really miss the most important point about magic—I mean its cultural and sociological significance.

The same applies to invocations of spirits, to legal utterances, such as are made at the *kayaku*; to the harangues of the magician, which are among the most powerful organising elements in native gardening; to the cries and traditional banter exchanged at a communal competitive enterprise; to expressions which accompany exchanges of gifts or of obligations. All these verbal acts are as important types of human behaviour as any manual rite.

I have tried to make clear that language is a cultural aspect in its own right, a type of human behaviour which fulfils not some sort of subsidiary function but which plays a part of its own, unique and irreplaceable. The descriptions of linguistic reality must therefore be given as fully, as minutely and accurately as those of any other fact. They have to be given, of course, as they really happen, that is, in the vernacular. With this there enters an additional difficulty into the treatment of linguistic data. In language, as has been already insisted in the Introduction, the purely conventional element is very much more pronounced than in any other human activity. Human beings have to eat, to sleep, to sharpen the point of a stick, to dig the soil and to paddle a canoe, if not on exactly the same pattern, at least in ways which are roughly comparable and have a con-spicuous common denominator. But the words which they use to describe the act of sleeping and of eating, of digging or sharpening, are based on a specific convention which must be learned for every culture. The phonetic reproduction of sounds heard in native language does not give the same direct picture to the English reader as does an account in English of what the natives are doing at a ceremony or when they carry out a piece of work in the garden.

To put it even more cogently: if we had a sound-film taken of a Trobriand gardening activity, the visual part of it would be self-explanatory or could be made so by a brief ethnographic com-mentary. But the accompanying sounds would remain completely incomprehensible and would have to be explained by a long and laborious linguistic analysis. This is the reason why we were able to condense several aspects of gardening, technological, economic, magical and sociological, into the relatively very short account of Volume I. On the other hand one aspect, that of language, is going to demand a disproportionate amount of space and attention.

We shall have in the first place to produce the texts, phrases, terminologies and formulae in native. Then we shall have to face the task of translating them. A word for word rendering is necessary to give a certain direct feeling for the language, which a free trans-lation in no way can replace. But the literal translation is not sufficient because—as you will convince yourself easily by glancing at any of the ninety or so prose texts and forty-five magical formulae which follow—such a translation simply never makes sense. The wading through the unwieldy jumble of words carries its own reward, but without an additional commentary on the part of the ethnographer, it does not lead to a clear understanding of the text. As we shall see, commentaries—and extensive commentaries at that—are necessary. But it is easy to become redundant in commentaries and by no means obvious where to draw the line between going too much into detail on the one hand and giving an insufficient and altogether too dry indication to the reader. It will be necessary, therefore, to enter more fully into the details of the task which faces us : how to achieve a full portraiture of a native language.

Div. II. THE TRANSLATION OF UNTRANSLATABLE WORDS

It might seem that the simplest task in any linguistic enquiry would be the translation of individual terms. In reality the problem of defining the meaning of a single word and of proceeding correctly in the translating of terms is as difficult as any which will face us. It is, moreover, in methodological order not the first to be tackled. It will be obvious to anyone who has so far followed my argument that isolated words are in fact only linguistic figments, the products of an advanced linguistic analysis. The sentence is at times a self-contained linguistic unit, but not even a sentence can be regarded as a full linguistic datum. To us, the real linguistic fact is the full utterance within its context of situation.

But still, as in all work of analysis, it does not matter very much where we begin. Since in the translation of texts we have to proceed by giving a word for word rendering, let us discuss this first. It will soon enough lead us into the apparently more complicated, but in reality more elementary, question of how to treat native texts and contexts.

Let me start with the apparently paradoxical and yet perfectly plain and absolutely true proposition that the words of one language are never translatable into another. This holds of two civilised languages as well as of a 'native' and a 'civilised' one, though the greater the difference between two cultures the greater the difficulty of finding equivalents.

Turning for a moment to more familiar European languages—anyone who has faced the difficulties of translating a novel or scientific book from Russian or Polish into English, or vice versa, will know that strict verbal equivalents are never to be found. Translation must always be the re-creation of the original into something profoundly different. On the other hand, it is never a substitution of word for word but invariably the translation of whole contexts.

It would be easy to skim the surface of any language for completely untranslatable terms. Such German words as *Sehnsucht*, or *Sauerkraut*, *Weltschmerz* or *Schlachtfest*, *Blutwurst* or *Grobheit*, *Gemüt* or *Gemeinheit* are not to be equated to any word in English, or, for that matter, in any other European language. Such English words as 'sport', 'gentleman', 'fair-play', 'kindness', 'quaint', 'forlorn'—to mention only a few from a legion—are never translated in a foreign tongue; they are simply reproduced. International currency has been achieved by many Italian words: *bel canto*, *basta*, *maccaroni*, *diva*, *salami*, as well as terms from music and painting. If we were to enquire why these, with certain French words referring to technicalities of love-making such as *liaison*, *maîtresse*, *au mieux*, *complaisance;* or to culinary compositions and details of menu; to fashion or to niceties of literary craft, such as *belles-lettres*, *mot juste*, *connaisseur* are untranslatable—the answer would be easy. In each culture certain aspects are more openly, minutely or pedantically cultivated: sport in England, good cooking and love-making in France; sentimentality and metaphysical profundities in Germany; music, noodles and painting in Italy.

Words referring to moral or personal values change their meaning deeply even if the form is similar: compare French *honneur*, Spanish *honra*, English 'honour', and German *Ehre*; or 'faith', *foi*, *Glaube* and *fe*; or *patrie*, *Vaterland*, 'home', and *la peninsula*. English changes east of Suez; it becomes a different language in India, Malaya and South Africa. The question whether American is English is very fruitful from the present point of view: you cannot swear in English in the U.S.A. and *vice versa*. You cannot order your food in an 'eat-house' nor 'get outside your drinks' by the same verbal symbols in a 'saloon' as in a 'pub'; while Prohibition has introduced words corresponding to the change of institutions and values surrounding drink. In brief, every language has words which are not translatable, because they fit into its culture and into that only; into the physical setting, the institutions, the material apparatus and the manners and values of a people.

With all this, it might appear that such words, however frequent, are but freaks or peculiarities. Surely, it will be contended, numerals, parts of the body, terms of relationship, conjunctions, adverbs, prepositions, words as ordinary as bread and butter, milk and meat, are simply, plainly, adequately and completely translated between any two languages of the Western cultures. A brief consideration convinces us that this is not so. Were we to aim merely at achieving some approximate indication of correspondence between two words, sufficient to order a meal, to bargain over the price of an umbrella or ask our way in the street, then even the linguistic instruction supplied on a few pages of our Baedecker, certainly a cheap pocket dictionary or an Ollendorf, will give adequate translations. But if in our scientific analysis we define words as devices used in a number of verbal and situational contexts, then translation must be defined as the supplying of equivalent devices and rules. This makes our point clearer: there is no simple equivalence between two languages ever to be found which could be used right through, replacing the German word by the English, or vice versa.

Let us take the simplest example, the numeral 'one', *un*, *ein*. They correspond closely in counting. But *un homme, ein Mann* is not 'one man' but 'a man'. 'One man one vote' could not be translated by *un homme un vote*, nor is *ein Mann ein Wort* translatable into 'one man one word'. Nor is *c'est un homme honnête* equivalent to 'this is one honest man'. As soon as we come to derived uses, to subsidiary meanings, to idiomatic handling of words, the equivalence breaks down. Translation as an act of putting 'one'=*un* appears to us at once as a matter of rough, preliminary, makeshift arrangement which has to be supplemented by a long series of additional data.

Or take the parts of the human body: we have at once to face up to the fact that the conventional restrictions, euphemisms, and twists obfuscate the meaning in English to a much larger degree than in French or in German. For instance 'belly' is not equivalent to *Bauch* or *ventre*; 'stomach' reaches almost to the knees, legs are curtailed in their upper reaches. Such words as 'breast', *gorge, sein, Brust, Busen* become untranslatable. And in English again the word 'navel', associated in a daring anatomical metaphor with an orange, shocks many a continental damsel who thinks herself absolutely protected by English prudery on this side of the Channel. 'Eye', 'hand', 'foot', and 'arm', 'mouth' and 'ears' seem so well defined and precise that here a simple = might be enough. But even here some European languages, for instance Slavonic, use the term 'hand' often to embrace the 'arm', as in Polish and Russian, where instead of having 'feet' and 'legs' we have only lower extremities. Moreover, in every European language the derived and metaphorical and idiomatic uses of 'eye', 'hand' and 'foot' are so little co-ordinated that they cannot be equated. 'My two legs' could not be set = *meine zwei Beine*; it would have to be *meine beiden Beine*. We neither eat nor sleep linguistically in the same manner: while the Englishman 'sleeps with', the Frenchman *couche avec*. As to eating, a Frenchman's *bien manger* becomes in German *gut speisen*, while the Englishman 'dines well'. As regards adverbs and conjunctions, no one brought up in a continental language will ever live down the absence of *déjà, schon, już, uże, già* or *ya*. Such German adverbs or particles as *doch, nanu, also*, the French *mais non, mais oui*—not equivalent to the German *aber nein, aber ja*—can neither be equated nor reproduced in English.

We have now whittled down our paradox to the platitude that words from one language are never translatable into another; that is, we cannot equate one word to another. If by translation we mean the supplying of the full range of equivalent devices, metaphorical extensions and idiomatic sayings—such a process is of course possible. But even then it must be remembered that something more than mere juggling with words and expressions is needed. When we pass even from one European country to another we find that cultural arrangements, institutions, interests and systems of values change greatly. Translation in the correct sense must refer therefore not merely to different linguistic uses but often to the different cultural realities behind the words. All the new systems of teaching modern languages—whether it be Toussain-Langenscheidt, Pelman or Berlitz—have in practice fully adopted this contextual theory of language and realised the untranslatability of words. In the case of words which have to be international, e.g. scientific terms, congresses have to deal with their unification; and it can only be achieved because the apparatus of science is uniform, because such arrangements as the metric system have been widely adopted and because the institutional side of scientific training, laboratory organisation and academic life is sufficiently similar.

In diplomatic documents and international treaties, which must not contain any linguistic ambiguity, we are again faced with the difficulty of finding a safe and unequivocal common denominator to untranslatable words. Whether this is mainly due to the fact that diplomatic language is used to conceal thought—according to the definition of one of the most famous diplomats of history—or whether it honestly attempts to serve its purpose, need not be discussed here.

The translatability of words or texts between two languages is not a matter of mere readjustment of verbal symbols. It must always be based on a unification of cultural context. Even when two cultures have much in common, real understanding and the establishment of a community of linguistic implements is always a matter of difficult, laborious and delicate readjustment.

When two cultures differ as deeply as that of the Trobrianders and the English; when the beliefs, scientific views, social organisation, morality and material outfit are completely different, most of the words in one language cannot be even remotely paralleled in the other.

Let us turn at once to our own special case, that of Trobriand agricultural terminology. The simplest word to be considered is 'garden'. But obviously the English term may suggest anything from a suburban plot to a park, from an allotment to a market-garden, and in none of these senses, nor yet in any of the metaphorical extensions to which this word is liable, could it be translated into Trobriand. So that at once we are faced with a serious 'gap' in the vocabulary of our Melanesian friends. For they really have no word corresponding to our general term 'garden'.

Instead they have a series of words : *bagula*, *buyagu*, *tapopu*, *kaymata*, *kaymugwa*, *baleko*, each of which describes a certain type or kind, aspect or phase of 'garden'. But to 'translate' any of these native terms by equating it to an English word would not merely be wrong, but impossible; or rather it would be impossible to find an English word exactly corresponding to any one of the native ones. Furthermore, to label the native term by even a combination of English words is at least misleading.

What then is the correct procedure? Let me exemplify it on one of the words just mentioned—the native term *buyagu*—by making a methodological reinterpretation of the technique adopted in Division I (§§ 16-26) of Part V. First we had to remind the reader of the general context of situation within which the word *buyagu* could be used: that is, to indicate the social, legal and technical arrangements by which a portion of cultivable soil is ear-marked for next year's gardens and recognised as 'the future gardens'.

Then I give the merely approximate but useful English label 'garden-site', which I have used throughout the descriptive chapters in order to avoid repeating the native term constantly. But this compound term has to be immediately redefined by fuller English circumlocutions, such as 'land under cultivation at a given season', 'the land intended for cultivation', 'all the land within the common enclosure'. These circumlocutions obviously derive their meaning from the reader's knowledge of how land is cultivated in the Trobriands; that is, tracts of land consisting of one or two fields (*kwabila*) are put under cultivation and a common enclosure is made round them, which converts the area into one communal garden. This meaning is illustrated in Text 3, where 'garden-site' and 'the garden as a whole' is defined by its economic as well as by its technical characteristics. In the definition of the term *buyagu* the reader has then to be reminded of the manner in which a garden-site is physically delimited for the natives, first by the boundary belt and later by the fence (§ 17).

Throughout its analysis we see that the word is progressively defined by reference to the ethnographic description, supplemented by additional information concerning linguistic usage. In paragraph 17 this parallelism of verbal use and real situation shows clearly: "as soon as this (i.e. the bush) is cut *buyagu,* 'garden-site' becomes opposed to *odila,* 'bush', 'all the land outside', also called *yosewo,* 'uncut bush outside the garden-site' ". It is through the opposition of the word *buyagu* to the two words *odila* and *yosewo* and, in the sentence following the one just quoted, to the words *kapopu* and *kaulaka* that the term *buyagu* is more closely defined. The relation of this term to the cognate terms, *bagula* and *baleko* (§ 20), is equally important; as well as the negative fact that one of the terms for division of land, the term *kwabila,* is never used to describe a garden in process of cultivation. Thus the definition of a word consists partly in placing it within its cultural context, partly in illustrating its usage in the context of opposites and of cognate expressions.

Turning to paragraphs 20–25 we see how the words *buyagu, bagula, baleko* are defined by placing them within a series of terms with mutually exclusive uses. It is clear that in all this the definition is partly based on the long descriptions of the main ethnographic account, but also largely on the contrast between the terms to be defined and their opposites, and also on the comparison between the respective area of each of the three terms.

It is interesting to note that, in his definition, the native informant himself reproduces the context of situation first: "When we clear the bush there remains the uncut scrub, there comes into being the garden-site" (Text 2). Here we have an indication that the term *buyagu* in its most characteristic form can be used at the clearing; that it marks the opposition between the uncut scrub and the land which is being prepared for cultivation. In the second part of this definition text: "When we stand on the boundary belt, on one side (we have) the uncut bush, on the other the garden-site," the native further defines the two terms by putting before us the concrete situation in which we can have one of the opposites on each hand. He then attaches the verbal labels to either side of the picture respectively.

The need of a clear context of situation for certain words is even more obvious in Text 3, where my informant reproduces the socio-logical as well as the physical context. We have an indication that strangers arriving at a garden would first enquire about the 'garden as a whole' (*buyagu*) and then about the 'individually owned portions' (*bagula*). In this text we find also the interesting grammatical feature that one word, and one word only, of the three expressions which we have roughly translated by the English 'garden' can be used verbally, and that this word *bagula* in its nominal form corresponds to the dynamic conception 'garden as actually cultivated'. In a full commentary on these texts a number of other grammatical points would have to be considered. For instance, the use of the possessive pronoun 'his' in Text 4 correlates a semi-economic, semi-legal claim to the whole garden site on the part of the magician with the meaning of the term *buyagu*, 'garden as a whole'; while the possessive 'his', referring to the individual owner, has a definite economic meaning and is connected with the synonymous use of the terms *bagula* and *baleko*.

We see then that it is impossible to define a word by mere equation. Translation in the sense of *exact and exhaustive definition of meaning* cannot be done by affixing an English label. Our paradoxical heading 'Translation of Untranslatable Words' is obviously based on a two-fold use of the term 'translate'. If we understand by 'translate' the finding of verbal equivalents in two different languages, this task is impossible, and the Italian adage *traduttore, traditore* holds good. Translation in the sense of *defining a term by ethnographic analysis*, that is, by placing it within its context of culture, by putting it within the set of kindred and cognate expressions, by contrasting it with its opposites, by grammatical analysis and above all by a number of well-chosen examples—such translation is feasible and is the only correct way of defining the linguistic and cultural character of a word.

Thus, while for practical reasons we have to adopt a certain rough and ready English equivalent for each native term—an equivalent which functions as an *aide-mémoire* or rough label, but lays no claims whatever to *translate* the native term—the real translation is contained in the combined ethnographic and linguistic description, which we have exemplified on the one term *buyagu*, but which will be found illustrated in the few hundred words cited in the course of Part V.

Take, for instance, the apparently simple case of a technical implement. What do we achieve in the rendering : *dayma* = 'digging-stick'? A digging-stick is not an implement familiar to an English curate or clerk, even if he happens to be an amateur gardener; he has never seen one, never heard of one, certainly never used one; and even if he knows that peoples exist who break their soil and plant their seed by means of a pointed stick, he still does not understand the term unless he also realises that the use, the type and the institutional setting of a digging-stick are not the same in every primitive culture. But to the reader the meaning of *dayma* has become real in that he knows something about its material, shape and size; the technical uses and economic associations, even the values and sentiments which the digging-stick derives from its daily employment and from the part it plays in magic and ceremonial. He is able to place it within the gardening scheme of the Trobriands. All he now needs is a general linguistic description of this word, of its various uses outside gardening, of the set of terms to which it belongs, and of its grammatical characteristics. All this the reader will find in Division VI (§ 5).

When we translate *kema* by 'axe' we have to be even more on our guard, because here we are dealing with an object which also exists and functions in our culture and it is very important not to assimilate the uses, the form and the material of the native implement with those of our own. In so far as the axe is used in gardening, I have described most of its technical functions and also its magical rôle. And the meaning of the term *kema* is in the last instance to be derived, not from the substitution of 'axe' for the native word, but from our knowledge of the rôle which it plays within native culture, here more specifically within native gardening.

All this refers also to such words as *kaylepa*, 'magical wand', *kaytukwa*, 'staff', *kali*, 'fence', *tula*, 'boundary pole'. In every case the English words merely supply a mnemonic counter, while the meaning of the native terms is given in the descriptions and through linguistic analysis. The word *kamkokola* I have only occasionally translated as 'magical prism', so far is the native word removed from anything which could be rendered by an English equivalent.

Thus it is only because we know the world of ideas, the various activities, the economic rules of Trobriand gardening that we can grasp the linguistic side of Trobriand agriculture. It is what we might call their *context of culture* which supplies us with the relevant elements whereby we can translate these words. Translation then becomes rather the placing of linguistic symbols against the cultural background of a society, than the rendering of words by their equivalents in another language.

At times it is necessary in ethnographic description resolutely to go beyond the verbal and even, as we shall see, beyond the conceptual outfit of the natives. The term 'garden', used throughout my descriptive chapters is, as we know, an example of this, for it does not correspond to any native word. At the same time I did not use this word in its English meaning, and I trust that, especially towards the end of Volume I, the word 'garden' did not conjure up to the reader a cabbage patch with a border of geraniums or pansies, but that he saw the fence enclosing yam vines, taro, some bananas and a patch of sugar-cane.

In the same way, in speaking about 'agriculture' and 'gardening', about 'labour' or the 'organisation of garden work', about 'leadership' and 'economic dependence', I was using abstract scientific terms which have no counterpart whatever in native speech, and yet have their meaning defined by facts belonging to Trobriand culture. The ethnographer has constantly to go beyond the native outlook and introduce certain categories which are not native. At the same time, in building up his concepts the ethnographer must never go beyond native facts. The question as to how far certain terminological lacunae, such as the absence of words for 'garden', 'work', *mana* (magical force), 'crops', and so on, signify the absence of native concepts, or even the absence of sociological realities, is still to be examined (cf. Div. VII of this Part).

Returning now to the mechanism of translating words, the truth of the principle that only full ethnographic description can serve as a basis for linguistic analysis becomes very evident when we deal with sociological terms.

Kayaku, whether in its more general meaning of 'sociable reunion' or in its narrower sense 'garden council'—the German words *gesellschaftliches Beisammensein* approach perhaps the native idea more closely—is obviously not at all *translated* by either English equivalent. What really supplies us with the meaning of this native term is an account of the place which the *kayaku* occupies in the scheme of gardening: the character of the deliberations, the nature of the business transacted, the legal consequences of the typical harangues, and its ceremonial and magical framework. And this applies to all magical activities, all legal acts and all the other sociological and ceremonial phenomena which we have met with in our descriptions. *Kayasa, yowota, gabu,* and so on—such meaning as these words have acquired has come from the description, not from the English label which we affixed to them for the sake of convenience.

We have found that the word *kayaku* has two different meanings: 'sociable reunion' and 'garden council'. We find a similar phenomenon in the word *towosi*, which·signifies 'garden magician' and 'garden magic' (cf. Part V, Div. VII, §§ 10–14). With the term *towosi* a formal analysis of its structure will help us to decide which meaning is primary. Such a formal analysis, which by showing certain affinities between the word discussed and others indicates probable derivations, further demonstrates the necessity of giving a special place to the linguistics of gardening over and above mere descriptions of gardening.

Multiplicity of meanings will be found a characteristic of most native words, even of such simple terms as *pwaypwaya*, 'earth', 'land', 'soil', cultivable soil', 'economically appropriated soil'; *valu*, 'village', 'place of human habitation', 'spot', 'home'; *dakuna*, 'stone', 'coral rock', 'stony soil'; *bagula*, 'area under cultivation', 'individual garden'; or, in a verbal form, 'to garden', 'to cultivate', or, in a compound adjectival form 'cultivated'; *buyagu*, 'garden enclosure', 'garden-site', 'cultivated land' as opposed to the bush. The detailed analysis of each will convince us beyond doubt that the natives do distinguish between these various meanings. If we were to index the sound we would find that the meaning of *pwaypwaya* (1) is very definitely laid down by the context in which this word occurs, and distinguished from *pwaypwaya* (2), *pwaypwaya* (3), and so on. The meaning is differentiated also by grammatical indices, by the possibility of substituting a synonymous word, by emotional tone and by circumlocutory phrases. In no case have I found any confusion in the mind of the speaker as to which of the several distinct realities he wished to indicate by the use of one homonym or another. The differentiation of meanings can be seen if we take the word, not in isolation, but in conjunction with other words, sometimes with synonyms, sometimes with opposites. Thus, as we shall see the word *odila* can be synonymous in certain uses with the word *yosewo* (Div. I, § 17) and then it can again be interchangeable with the word *baleko* (Div. I, § 15). In the first sense it is antonymous to *buyagu*, in the second sense to the body of words describing land not put under regular cultivation, words such as *dumya, rayboag, kaboma, weyka, valu*.

The contention that homonyms—that is, words which have the same sound but different meanings—should not be lumped, should not be represented as one word with a vague confused meaning, but rather as a series of distinguishable linguistic units, will be proved abundantly throughout the following pages. The extreme theoretical importance of doing this cannot be exaggerated. Carelessness in dealing with this problem, or probably a wrong theoretical attitude, has been responsible for a great deal of misleading information, sometimes on such extremely important and crucial native words as, for instance, the Melanesian word *mana* (magical force), kinship terminologies, dogmatic terms relating to such concepts as 'soul', 'spirit', 'God', and sociological appellations. To this question we shall still have to return in the course of our theoretical analysis.

We can now lay down a number of points, some theoretical and some practical, which it will be necessary to bear in mind throughout the following analysis:—

(1) The mere lexical equation of an English and a native word is necessary for practical convenience but theoretically inadequate. For practical convenience it is necessary because if we used a native term wherever possible an ethnographic book would become an unreadable jumble of native and English, of native technical expressions and sociological concepts sticking out of the grammatical framework of the English language.

(2) At times it becomes necessary to use an English term with Trobriand implications, that is, a word from our own language in a native sense. For an ethnographic description must not merely reproduce the native outlook, still less confine itself to the native linguistic compass, but must operate with general sociological concepts.

(3) The correct translation of each native term, besides its rough and ready labelling, is indispensable. This is achieved by reference to ethnographic descriptions and by the placing of the word in its context of culture, in the context of cognate words and opposites and in the context of appropriate utterances.

(4) The various meanings of a homonym must be kept apart. We have to consider the use of the same sound with several distinct meanings, not as a linguistic vagueness or lumping together or confusion, but as what it really is—a series of distinct uses.

All these considerations simply mean that language is a part, and an essential part at that, of other cultural realities. The language of agriculture enters deeply into the Trobrianders' gardening activities. Unless we know how they make their gardens we can give no sense to their terms, nor meaning to their magical formulae, nor yet develop any interest in their gardening phraseology. Without this cultural foundation linguistics must remain always a house of cards. Equally true is it that without the language the knowledge of any aspect of culture is incomplete.

This is really tantamount to saying, as we did above, that language is a cultural force in its own right. It enters into manual and bodily activities and plays a significant part in them, a part *sui generis* which cannot be replaced, even as it does not replace anything else.

What this part is, however, and in what consists the placing of a word against the context of culture, we still have not defined with any precision. It is obvious that words do not live as labels attached to pieces of cultural reality. Our Trobriand garden is not a sort of botanical show with tags tied on to every bush, implement or activity.

It will be our business to reconstruct what speech achieves in a primitive culture, or, for that matter, in a highly developed one.

But first it is necessary to realise that words do not exist in isolation. The figment of a dictionary is as dangerous theoretically as it is useful practically. Words are always used in utterances, and though a significant utterance may sometimes shrink to a single word, this is a limiting case. A one-word sentence, such as a command, 'come', 'go', 'rise', a 'yes' or a 'no', may under exceptional circumstances be significant through its context of situation only. Usually a one-word sentence will have to be explained by connecting it with utterances which preceded it or which follow. To start with single words—even if such words might occasionally be uttered in isolation —is the wrong procedure. But this I do not need to elaborate; for it is now a commonplace of linguistics that the lowest unit of language is the sentence, not the word. Our task is rather to show that even the sentence is not a self-contained, self-sufficient unit of speech. Exactly as a single word is—save in exceptional circumstances— meaningless, and receives its significance only through the context of other words, so a sentence usually appears in the context of other sentences and has meaning only as a part of a larger significant whole. I think that it is very profitable in linguistics to widen the concept of context so that it embraces not only spoken words but facial expression, gesture, bodily activities, the whole group of people present during an exchange of utterances and the part of the environment on which these people are engaged.

I have spoken several times of the *context of cultural reality*. By that I mean the material equipment, the activities, interests, moral and aesthetic values with which the words are correlated. I shall now try to show that this context of cultural reality is strictly analogous to the context of speech. Words do not live in a sort of super-dictionary, nor in the ethnographer's notebook. They are used in free speech, they are linked into utterances and these utterances are linked up with the other human activities and the social and material environment. The whole manner which I have adopted for the presentation of my linguistic and ethnographic material brings the concept of context to the fore. Not only have I tried in the definition of technical terms to show how these terms form groups of kindred entities, not only have I tried, by placing the linguistic account against an outline of real activities, to give them life and body; but the division of the linguistic material under headings which closely correspond to the chapters of the descriptive account keeps every word, every phrase and every text within its proper context of culture.

Div. III. THE CONTEXT OF WORDS AND THE CONTEXT
OF FACTS

We started the last division on a paradoxical quest: how to translate untranslatable phrases and words. Our argument, which incidentally enabled us to solve the riddle of the paradox, landed us in another apparent antinomy: words are the elements of speech, but words do not exist. Having once recognised that words have no independent existence in the actual reality of speech, and having thus been drawn towards the concept of context, our next step is clear: we must devote our attention to the intermediate link between word and context, I mean to the linguistic text.

From among the fourscore or so native utterances recorded and printed I shall choose one which, through the scope of its subject matter, the variety of its linguistic features, its grammatical interest and also through its length, is specially suitable for analysis. The free translation of this text has already been quoted in Section 1 of Chapter V, and I advise the reader first to refresh his memory by perusing it and the descriptive context in which it occurs. The tale tells us about the all-important subject of famine. The fear of famine and the hope of prosperity form, as we know, the emotional background of the whole economic life of the Trobriander. In this text, besides one or two dramatic highlights thrown upon the happenings during famine, we find an interesting account of gardening (vv. 10–12), information about economic transactions (vv. 8–9), reference to magic (vv. 6–7), legal discussion upon vendetta (v. 15) placed in the setting of the precarious existence led by inland natives on the lagoon shore (vv. 13, 14, 16). Finally, the belief, so very important in the political and tribal life of the natives, as to the causes of famine and prosperity (vv. 17–19).

The first sentence arose out of my conversation with a group of informants, in the course of which I enquired whether any one of them had himself experienced a bad famine. Tokulubakiki answered me (for abbreviations, see Introductory Note, Part V):

T. 24

1. *Molubabeba*　　　　*o gwadi-la*　　*i-gise.*
   (informant's father)　in child his　he see

Immediately after this he enlarged upon the bodily ailments associated with famine:—

2. *Iga'u*　　*i-kugwo*　　*sipsipsipwapunu*　　*i-katoula-si.*
   later on　he first　(a skin rash)　　　　they sicken

3. *Mimilisi*   *boge*   *i-kariga-si*   *tomwota*   *o la*   *odila;*   *mimilisi*   *wa*
   sundry   already   they die   humans   in   bush   sundry   in

   dumya,   *mimilisi*   *o*   *raybwaga,*   *mimilisi*   *wa*   *sopi.*
   swamp   sundry   in   coral-ridge   sundry   in   water

4. *Kidama*   *wa*   *sopi,*   *bi-lumli*   *yama-si*
   supposing   in   water   he might be moist   hand theirs

   kayke-si —   *bi-kariga-si*   *wala.*
   foot theirs   they might die   just

5. *Pela*   *molu,*   *kaulo*   *ta-kam-si*   *gala.*
   for   hunger   yam-food   we (i.p.) eat   no

Then he went on to describe the events which took place after the famine was over. It is very characteristic that first of all he turns his attention to the magical and ceremonial side:—

6. *Iga'u*   *boge*   *i-wokwe* —   *molu;*   *i-miga'i-se*
   later on   already   he is over — hunger   they magic

   leya,   *bi-pulu-se*   *valu.*
   wild ginger   they might bespit   village

7. *Oyluvi*   *bi-kaylum-si*   *boge*   *lay-kuna.*
   afterwards   they might magic-herb   already   he did rain

The subject next in importance is the quantitative measure of dearth and misery; the account of how much is paid for a basketful of seed yams. Anyone acquainted with typical European peasants, of whatever nationality, will find himself on familiar ground in this association of numerals of currency or articles of exchange with agricultural produce:—

8. *Bayse*
   this   (Here the narrator marks off a length on his forearm of about
            40 cm. = 16 in. from the tips of his fingers.)

   vaygu'a   *i-gimwala-si*   *yagogu:*
   valuable   they barter   seed yam

9. *vaygu'a*   *bwoyna,*   *luwatala*   *yagogu;*
   valuable   good   ten (basketsful)   seed yam

   vaygu'a   *kwayketoki,*   *lima.*
   valuable   small (r.b.)   five (basketsful)

Then comes an equally illuminating account of the absurdly restricted extent of gardening activities. And here again he gives numerical data and units of measurement, and the whole account is punctuated by the emotional drive: the gradual return to normality, to the state where each man makes at least one garden plot for himself.

10. *Iga'u*   *bi-sapu,*   *bi-sapu:—*   *kway-tala*
later on   he might plant   he might plant   one (r.b.)

    baleko   *luwayyu*   *tomwota,*   *gubwa-tala,*   *gubwa-tala,*
    garden-plot   twenty   humans   one (sq.)   one (sq.)

    gubwa-tala . . . .
    one (sq.)

11. *Iga'u*   *boge*   *sita*   *i-kasewo*   *yagogu;*
later on   already   a little   he plentiful   seed yam

    kway-tala   *tayyu*   *tomwota.*
    one (r.b.)   two (m.)   humans

12. *Iga'u*   *bi-kasewo*   *yagogu:*
later on   he might be plentiful   seed yam

    kway-tala — tay-tala;   *kway-tala — tay-tala.*
    one (r.b.)   one (m.)   one (r.b.)   one (m.)

After that my narrator—whom, according to the inviolable rule of field-work, I let ramble on as long as he was fluent and relevant—returns to the dramatic side of the situation:—

13. *Kulumata*   *bayse*   *bi-tamwa'u-si:*   *gala*   *waga*
(western district)   this   they might disappear   no   canoe

    bi-la   *o*   *bwarita,*   *ta-poulo.*
    he might go   in   sea   we (i.d.) fish

14. *Waga*   *bi-la,*   *i-gisay-dasi,*   *boge*   *i-katumatay-da*   *wala.*
canoe   he might go   they see us   already   they kill us   just

15. *Bi-katumatay-da,*   *gala*   *bi-giburuwa*   *veyo-da,*
they might kill us   no   he might be angry   kindred ours

    pela   *molu.*
    for   hunger

16. *Ta-supepuni*   *o*   *la*   *odila,*   *ta-gise*   *waga,*   *kay-tala —*
we hide   in   bush   we (i.d.) see   canoe   canoe one (w.l.)

    gala,   *ta-la*   *ta-poulo.*
    no   we (i.d.) go   we (i.d.) fish

Finally, he ends up by giving the 'cause' or 'reason', the *u'ula* of famine. And here we see the native mind running in its traditional groove and attributing this unusual, unnatural, intensively painful occurrence to magic inspired by retribution. However distorted its ethical value may appear to us, we have here a piece of moral metaphysics:—

17. *U'ula*   *bayse*   *waygigi,*   *boge*   *i-bulati-se*   *valu*
basis   this   drought-sorcery   already   they bewitch   place

    gweguya,   *pela*   *ta-bugwa'u*   *veyo-la.*
    chiefs   for   we (i.d.) ensorcel   kindred his

18. *Mwakenuva,*   *Purayasi*   *boge*   *i-kariga-si,*
    (dead chief)   (dead chief)   already   they die

    Numakala   *boge*   *i-bulati.*
    (last but one chief)   already   he bewitch

19. *Kidama*   *bi-karige*   *guya'u,*   *ta-bulati*   *valu.*
    supposing   he might die   chief   we (i.d.) bewitch   village

If the reader is still somewhat hazy about what I mean by context, let him reflect upon the manner in which we have framed the above narrative into its context of subject-matter. It is, alas, impossible, with the means at the disposal of a present-day ethnographer to reproduce certain aspects of the context. If I could, by a good phonographic record, counterfeit the living voice of Tokulubakiki: how it trembled with emotion when he was depicting the miseries and illnesses (vv. 2–4, 13–16); the relative rest and satisfaction of its cadences through vv. 6–12 as he described the gradual re-establishment of prosperity in the village; the accents of awe and reverence when he spoke about the dreaded and respected power of the chiefs through their magic of *waygigi* (vv. 17–19)—I should certainly be able better to *translate* the text in the sense of imparting to it its full cultural flavour and significance. Again, if by a cinematographic picture I could reproduce the facial expression, the bodily attitude, the significant gestures, this would add another contextual dimension. The gesture in at least one place (v. 8) I had to indicate because without it the words became meaningless. But please remember that the integral rôle of gesture in speech is quite as important for our understanding of an utterance as the one or two significant movements or indications which actually replace an uttered word.

There is no reason whatever why, in the future, an exact and physiological study of speech should not use the apparatus of sound films for reproducing fully contextualised utterances.

There are parts of the context of speech, however, which we shall be able to reproduce as fully as is necessary to illustrate certain essentials of language and of meaning: I refer, not to the context of gestures or of significant bodily movements, but rather to the context of associated activities. To this, however, we shall return when we have learned to understand the context of pragmatic speech, i.e. of utterances inextricably bound up with action. The contextual comments, whereby I have framed the fragments of the above narrative into their appropriate situational setting, correspond to a certain extent to such pragmatic contextualisation.

Let me, however, pass to some more technical and more elementary points with regard to the editing of native texts. Let us glance at the second line running under the native text—the word-for-word English rendering. This has been made throughout by placing what we have called "mnemonic counters" or "approximate labels" under each native word; that is, we have rendered each native word by an English one which does not purport to define the word but simply to identify it. If the literal rendering is compared with the free translation (cf. Ch. V, Sec. 1), it will be seen that a great many words are changed in passing from the one to the other. This shows that the adequate English reproduction at which we aim in the free translation could not be given in the interlineal labelling.

Let us have a look at a few of these interlineal labels. The word *iga'u*, which appears in vv. 2, 6, 10, 11 and 12, has been labelled throughout by 'later on'. But, as we shall see when we come to the commentary and free translation of the text, this word in v. 2 has a vague conjunctive sense of 'at that time', 'then'. In v. 6 it is frankly a temporal conjunction, 'when'. In v. 10 it is rather a temporal demonstrative, 'then', 'at that time'. In v. 11 it has the same meaning, something like 'as soon as', temporal correlative; in v. 12 its meaning is similar, but through its place in the context of narrative and as following the first *iga'u* it carries a stronger emphasis, something like 'and again then', 'as soon as'. Indeed the variety of meanings of such words as *iga'u*, 'later on', *pela*, 'for' (vv. 5, 15, 17), *u'ula*, 'basis' (because of) (v. 17), *kidama*, 'supposing' (vv. 4, 19), *oyluvi*, 'afterwards' (v. 7), *boge*, 'already' (vv. 3, 6, 7, 11, 14, 17, 18), is extremely great. We already know that such words as *molu*, 'hunger', 'famine', 'scarcity'; *valu*, 'village', 'place'; *odila*, 'bush', 'uninhabited land', 'uncut scrub'; *baleko*, 'garden plot', 'individual garden' and so on, have a wide range of meanings.

Now why do we make it an infrangible rule to render every native sound by the same English equivalent, only to spend a good deal of extra work afterwards in trying to indicate what exactly this equivalent represents in the given context? My aim is to show how by means of a limited number of vocal symbols the Trobriand natives arrive at expressing a very wide range of meanings. I want the reader to have as close a reproduction as possible of the bald clipped juxtapositions of the Kiriwinian language. Now it would be too great a strain on an English reader to memorise the meaning of each native term, in other words to learn the Trobriand language, before he could appreciate my collection of texts. Therefore I am using the device of identifying each native word by a rough and ready English approximation. Each such approximation, however, I want the English reader to apprehend in the native sense. Exactly as in the main ethnographic text I advised the reader to visualise the word 'garden' in the Trobriand cultural setting, so here when he reads 'hunger' for *molu*, 'barter' for *gimwali*, 'valuable' for *vaygu'a*, 'seed yam' for *yagogu*, 'garden plot' for *baleko*, 'one square' for *gubwa-tala* and so on, he must think in native though he uses English terms. And if such counters are to fulfil their main function, that is, to stand for and represent a Kiriwinian word, it is obviously necessary always to use the same English equivalent for the same native word. But after we have taken this first step to bring home the native text to our European minds two further tasks remain. The first is to establish the relationships between the words; to show how they integrate into sentences; how, by means of certain grammatical instruments, by position and by context, the various shades of meaning are produced. In other words, we must supply a grammatical commentary to each text, and redefine each term into the proper grammatical form in which it will appear in the free translation.

But the meaning of each word alters in yet another dimension. The same sound, as we know, corresponds to a variety of meanings; and each sound must be regarded as liable to function in a variety of homonymous rôles. Now the choice of the appropriate shade or distinction is not always easy, and this contextual specification of meaning constitutes our second task.

After having briefly indicated in what the general interpretation of the texts will consist, let me enumerate the practical rules observed in the interlineal rendering, in the grammatical commentary and finally in the contextual specification of meaning.

A. *Rules of Interlineal Translation.*

As we know already, the fundamental principle here is that for each native word we adopt one English *fixed meaning*. The only exception to this are accidental homonyms; that is, two or more native words that obviously have nothing to do with each other semantically and yet have by sheer accident the same sound. Thus for instance, *kam* 'to eat' and *kam* 'thine', *mi*, abbreviated from *mili* or *mini*, 'people of' and *mi* 'your', cannot be translated by the same English equivalent. Also the word *tabu* in the sense of 'grandmother', in the sense of 'maternal aunt' and in the sense of 'taboo' are accidental homonyms and I shall provide each with its own fixed meaning.

Any group, however, of cognate homonyms, that is, of words used in different but allied meanings, will be rendered by the same English equivalent. In the texts which follow the reader will find a number of words of which there is no analysis either in the preceding ethnographic description or in the linguistic commentaries to the texts. Such words as *gise*, 'to see', *kugwo*, 'to be first', *tomwota*, 'humans', *yama-*, 'arm', 'hand', *kayke-*, 'leg' 'foot', *bwarita*, 'sea', *kalasia*, 'sun', *yena*, 'fish', *sisu*, 'to sit', *la* or *lolo*, 'to go', *ma*, 'to move hither', *wa*, 'to move thither', etc., etc., are generic words which have no place in any part of this ethnographic study. They are used in all speech, whether it refers to religion, magic, economics, social organisation or arts and crafts. The full meaning of each such generic word will be understood by perusing a number of the texts in which it appears.

As to the fixed meaning for such generic words, I have tried always to choose the most usual or ordinary sense given to them by the natives. As a rule these are neither the most abstract nor yet the most concrete meanings. When the word describes a physical act, as with *gise*, 'to see', and is then in its particular contextual uses widened into the more abstract 'to experience', 'to visualise', 'to grasp mentally'; or into the more specific concrete 'to perceive', 'to discriminate', I have adopted the simple English word 'to see' as the fixed meaning. At times I was guided by practical considerations: when an exact rendering of the Trobriand meaning would require lengthy circumlocutions or compound terms I have chosen a shorter though less adequate label. In many words, such as those for the parts of the body, or for such ordinary bodily acts as to sit, to go, to lie, to sleep, to eat, there is not much difficulty.

The choice of the fixed meaning, however, is best illustrated in the divisions dealing with agricultural language and words which refer directly to gardening. At the end of each division, I am passing in review the distinctions within each group of homonymous variants. In most cases I am making an attempt to establish what I have termed the primary meaning and I have provided each derived meaning with an index number. But as will be seen, it is not always feasible or convenient to use the primary meaning as the fixed equivalent, although in most cases I have stuck to this rule. Thus *molu*, 'hunger', *malia*, 'plenty', *valu*, 'village', *pwaypwaya*, 'soil', *odila*, 'bush', are all translated by the word which we give as the primary meaning.

A glance through the texts will show that some words are rendered by a description in brackets. The first word in the text quoted above is a personal name and instead of repeating this I have described the status of the person thus named—always acting on the principle of making the text as accessible to the reader as is compatible with the principles here adopted. Certain grammatical instruments have also been rendered in brackets, but of these I shall speak more fully in our grammatical discussion (see below, B). In several texts the reader will also find the context of gesture indicated. Thus, besides the example in the above text, in Text 14 the demonstrative *bayse*, 'this', is accompanied by a deictic gesture, my informant pointing to an object in the physical context, in this case a flower. In Text 19 a similar gesture indicates the new shoot of a coconut. This type of deictic gesture, the pointing to an object instead of naming it, is as frequent in the speech of a Trobriander as in that of a Neapolitan, or for that matter, of any European. It may be rude to point, but it is often convenient. The deictic gestures in Text 15 refer to elements which are not so easily described in the language of the Trobriander; they give indications of a surface, of a severed portion of a plant, of a certain combination of vegetable anatomy for which, as far as I know, there are no native words. Here again the gesture is an integral part of language and it had to be indicated in the interlineal rendering. In the texts here quoted there are not many gestures of emotional importance, nor gestures descriptive of an action, nor yet gestures of a comical or indecent nature which are so frequently to be found in some types of Trobriand story. But every Trobriand utterance is associated with graphic gesture which, unfortunately, it would be hardly feasible to reproduce.

From all this it is clear that the interlineal word-for-word rendering is based on a great deal of antecedent work and knowledge, that it implies a detailed working out of the meaning of terms, grammatical distinctions and also certain contextual annotations. Only in so far as certain grammatical instruments are translated is anything done in it to indicate how the words are linked up, and to this we now turn.

B. *Grammatical Treatment of Texts.*

In Trobriand, as in European languages, grammatical problems can be divided into that of syntax, that is, the relationship of words to one another or the structure of sentences; into the problem of accidence, that is, the modification of certain words by formal or positional elements (cases and numbers of nouns, tenses, persons, moods and aspects of verbs, classification of nouns by gender and associated categories, and the problem of the formation of words from significant elements).

In Trobriand, also, we can legitimately divide words into parts of speech: noun, verb, pronoun, adjective, preposition, adverb and conjunction stand out as clearly as in English. Both in the choice of fixed meanings and in the general analysis of isolated words it was important to adopt a system which would clearly indicate the character of each word as a part of speech. This I have achieved by the simple device of translating a Kiriwinian word by an English noun when the root is predominantly nominal; by a verb when it is primarily an action word or one that describes a state or condition. And similarly with adverbs, adjectives and so on. Whenever for some reason this could not conveniently be done I placed behind every native word its brief grammatical description (n. = noun; v. = verb; adv. = adverb, etc., etc.).

Throughout Part V, though not in the descriptive account, the grammatical particle is set apart from the root by means of a hyphen. Such particles are principally used with verbs, adjectives and numerals, more rarely with nouns.

Without a single exception the verb must be provided with a personal pronoun. Take the word *-gis* or *gise*, 'to see': *a-gis*, 'I see', *ku-gis*, 'thou seest', *i-gis*, 'he sees', *ka-gis*, 'we two (exclusive dual) see', *ta-gis*, 'we two (inclusive dual) see'. The plural is marked by the suffix *-se* or *-si*, accompanied at times by a slight variation of the verbal root for phonetic reasons. Thus the plural of 'to see' is: *ka-gisi-se* or *ka-gisay-se*, 'we (exclusive plural) see', *ta-gisi-se* or *ta-gisay-se*, 'we (inclusive plural) see', *ku-gisi-se* or *ku-gisay-se*, 'you see', *i-gisi-se* or *i-gisay-se*, 'they see'. In the interlineal translation I have rendered each verb in its complete form by a personal pronoun and the root. In the above text, for instance, we find *i-gise*, 'he sees', *i-kariga-si*, 'they die', *ta-kam-si*, 'we (inclusive plural) eat'. Phonetically such personal verbal pronouns as well as the signs of plural are incorporated into the words. I have hyphened them off in order to make the root stand out. The pronominal prefixes never appear except in conjunction with verbs.

The reader will find two more forms of personal verbal pronoun. First, the consonant *b* is sometimes prefixed to the verbal pronoun when this is a vowel; or an extra syllable, *bu*, *ba*, may be added. Thus instead of *a-*, *ku-*, *i-*, *ka-*, *ta-*, *ku*, *i-*, we have *ba*, *buku-*, *bi-*, *baka-*, *bata-*, *buku-*, *bi-*. This sound *b* changes the character of the verb. It could be very roughly described as constituting the future tense, but in reality it is a much more comprehensive category. It conveys the idea of potentiality, past, present or future; or at times it is simply emphatic. Thus a very strong imperative, defined as a rule by gesture, context and voice, would be expressed by the prefix *bukula*, 'go away!'; on the other hand *buku* as in *bukula* might be an expression of potentiality 'perhaps thou mightest go'. As a fixed meaning distinguishing verbs thus modified by the potential *b* I have chosen the English auxiliary verb 'might'. It remains to redefine in the commentary on each text the very vague sense which we have advisedly given to this grammatical element and to give in the free translation its real and specific meaning derived from the context. Another modification of the verbal pronoun is by the sound *l*. As regards form, it is used in a manner completely analogous with the sound *b*, except that in the third singular it becomes *lay-* as in *lay-gis*, *lay-ma*. This sound imparts a tinge of definiteness; at times it places the action into a regular past, accomplished state; at times it only gives emphasis. On the whole it is best to regard it as an implement of definiteness and accomplishment. The letter *l* I have rendered by the fixed meaning 'did', *luku-gis*, 'thou didst see'. The fact that this rendering is sometimes a little un-English is rather an advantage than a drawback; for we have here to render something for which avowedly there is no equivalent in English.

Another modifier of the verbs is the adverb *boge*, rendered by the fixed meaning 'already'. This fulfils a somewhat analogous function to the *l* in personal verbal pronouns and is very often found super-imposed on them. *I-ma*, 'he moves hither', *lay-ma*, 'he did move hither', *boge lay-ma*, 'he already did move hither'. One might describe these as a series of forms of gradually increasing accomplishment. But even here, unless we know the context and very carefully assess the integral character of the utterance, it would be rash to jump to conclusions. Certainly the series has not a clear temporal meaning, and does not represent present, imperfect, preterite, perfect or pluperfect. In dealing with the Trobriand language it is best to lay aside completely the idea of clear temporal categories.

One or two more points about the use of verbs remain to be mentioned. Sometimes particles are suffixed to the verbal root: *-ki* adds direction to the meaning: *la* or *lolo*, 'to go'; *lo-ki*, 'to go there'; *sayli*, 'to put', *say-ki*, 'to put there', 'to give'; *mwoy-ki*, 'to move hither at', *woy-ki*, 'to move thither at'; *kana-ki*, 'to lie at', 'to lie by somebody'.

A difficult subject is that of reduplication in verbs. Sometimes it gives the words an iterative or durative meaning; sometimes it is employed only for emphasis. Here again one has to consider the sentence as a whole and as a part of its context, and only then proceed to the grammatical diagnosis of the word.

Nor is the distinction between transitive and intransitive verbs easy to make. Transitiveness is very clearly marked in pronominal forms only, and in these only the first and second persons have an objective case: *i-woy-gu*, 'he beat me', *a-woy-m*, 'I beat thee', but *i-woy-ye ka'ukwa*, 'he beats the dog'. The part played by a noun in a sentence, the question whether it functions as an object or as a sub-ject, is therefore not marked in any formal manner. *I-woy-ye tau* means 'the man beats' or 'he (subject implied) beats the man'. The context gives the solution. The passive does not exist.

We can deal much more rapidly with nouns. There is no plural except for kinship terms, terms for states of mind, and one or two sociological descriptions: *guya'u*, 'chief', *gweguya*, 'chiefs', *gwadi*, 'child', *gugwadi*, 'children'. Nouns are characterised, however, by two kinds of agreement: in the first place they are used with and determine the form of several types of pronouns. This point has been fully dealt with in Division XII (§§ 3–7), so I shall not enter into it here. In the second place each noun has what might be called its gender in the wider meaning. As in many Indo-European languages, notably in those of the Slavonic family, each noun is either masculine, feminine or neuter; and adjectives, ordinal numerals, pronouns and also (as in Slavonic again) certain verbal forms vary in accordance with gender, so in Kiriwinian there is a strict agreement between the class of the noun and the particle which is used to compound the adjective, numeral or demonstrative pronoun used with it.

None of these words exists in a self-contained form conveying an abstract meaning of number, quality or reference. There are no single words to express such conceptions as 'this', 'big', 'long', 'one', etc., in the abstract. Thus, for example, there is no equivalent for the word 'one', or for any other numeral. Whenever number is indicated the nature of the object numbered must be included in the word. Thus:—

(1) One man   = *TAYtala ta'u*
One woman = *NAtana vivila*
One stone   = *KWAYtala dakuna*
One canoe = *KAYtala waga* etc.

(2) Two men   = *TAYyu tau'a'u*[1]
Two women = *NAYyu vivila*
Two stones = *KWAYyu dakuna*
Two canoes = *KAYyu waga.*

Comparing the numerals in these tables, *TAYtala*, *NAtana*, etc., it can be seen at a glance that each consists of two elements, one of which remains unaltered in (1) and (2) respectively, namely, the suffix *-tala*, 'one', *-yu*, 'two', etc.; whereas the other part, *TAY-*, *NA-*, *KWAY-*, *KAY-*, etc., corresponds evidently to the objects or persons numbered.

The same holds good with regard to other numerals, as well as to demonstratives and adjectives. Such words consist of a fixed form

---

[1] *Tau'a'u*, 'men', plural to *ta'u*, 'man'. Another of the very few plurals extant in Kiriwinian.

or mould, which carries the meaning of the numeral, demonstrative or adjective, and of a variable particle which denotes the class of object to which the numeral, demonstrative or adjective is being applied. We shall call the former element the fixed part or root, and the latter one the classificatory particle or formative.

As we saw in the above example, the numerals are formed by suffixing the fixed part, which carries the meaning of the number, to the classificatory particle, which carries the meaning of the object numbered. This may be represented diagrammatically :—

Prefix denoting object numbered	Stable element or root denoting number
by means of the classificatory particle *TAY-* human	by means of the fixed numeric part *-TALA* one
TAY is the classificatory particle denoting that human beings are numbered	*TALA-* is the numeric root denoting that the number is one

The demonstratives are formed by infixing the classificatory particle into a fixed frame. This latter consists of the two syllables *ma-*, *-na*, which carry the meaning of pointing to or referring to. Thus *ma-tau-na* is used to point out a human being, 'this man'.

Root Frame	Infix	Root Frame
MA-	*-TAU-*	*-NA*
The fixed frame which of direct		conveys the signification reference.
TH-	human	*-IS*

Finally, adjectives are formed in the same manner as numerals, i.e. by suffixing the adjectival part of the classificatory particle.

Prefix denoting object qualified	Stable element of root denoting quality
by means of classificatory particle *TO-* human	by means of fixed adjectival part *-VIYAKA* big
TO- is the classificatory particle denoting that human beings are qualified	*-VIYAKA* is the adjectival root denoting that the object is big

Thus we see that the three classes of words, demonstratives, numerals, and adjectives, cannot be used *in abstracto*, but must carry in them the expression of the objects to which they refer. This reference is made, however, only in a general manner; the particle does not mention directly the thing to which it applies, but indicates only the class of object numbered, pointed at or qualified. This is why we have called them *classificatory* particles.

This is a general outline of the nature and grammatical extent of the classificatory particles in Kiriwina. It is, however, necessary for the reader, in order to follow with interest the technical details given in Part V, to familiarise himself with this linguistic pheno-menon, to get it well in hand. A good way to achieve this—to make the particles a living fact of speech—is to imagine how such an arrangement would appear in English.

Let us then transpose this peculiarity of Kiriwinian into English, following the native prototype very closely, and imagine that no adjective, no numeral, no demonstrative may be used without a particle denoting the nature of the object referred to. All names of human beings would take the prefix 'human'. Instead of saying 'one soldier' we would have to say '*human*-one soldier walks in the street'. Instead of 'How many passengers were in the accident?' 'How *human*-many passengers were in the accident?' Answer, '*Human*-seventeen.'

Or, again, in reply to 'Are the Smiths *human*-nice people?' we should say 'No, they are *human*-dull!' Again, nouns denoting persons belonging to the female sex would be numbered, pointed at, and qualified with the aid of the prefix 'female'; wooden objects with the particle 'wooden'; flat or thin things with the particle 'leafy'.

Thus, pointing at a table we should say, 'Look at *wooden*-this'; describing a landscape, '*leafy*-brown leaves on the *wooden*-large trees'; speaking of a book '*leafy*-hundred pages in it'; 'the women of Spain are *female*-beautiful', '*human*-this boy is very naughty, but *female*-this girl is good', and so on, in this Ollendorfian strain.[1]

In the interlineal rendering I have translated a compound adjective, numeral or demonstrative, by putting the specific meaning of the word underneath and its classificatory component, defined in general terms, immediately behind in brackets. Thus for the class referring to human beings, *tay- to- tau-*, I put 'human' or m.; for the class referring to persons of the female sex and animals, *na*, I put 'female—animal'; for the class comprising trees and plants, wooden things and long objects, *kay*, I put 'wooden long'; for the class referring to round bulky objects, stones, abstract nouns, *kway*, I put 'round bulky' and for that comprising objects made of leaf or fibre, or any flat, thin object, *ya*, I put 'flat leafy'. In what follows the classificatory particle will often be indicated as part of the grammatical definition of a noun. I have enlarged on this subject because it is unquestionably the most exotic feature of the Trobriand language.[2]

In all other respects the language belongs to the so-called agglutinative type of human speech; that is to say, such differences as exist in the form of verb and noun are brought about by the mere joining up of significant particles.

The real difficulty of this language consists not in the complexity of the grammatical apparatus but rather in its extreme simplicity. Its structure is on the whole what might be described as telegraphic; the relation of the words, as well as the relation of the sentences, has mainly to be derived from the context. In many cases the subject remains unmentioned, is represented merely by a verbal pronoun and has to be gathered from the situation. Of the difficulty in the modal and temporal definition of the verb I have already spoken. The relation between paragraphs and periods is often extremely erratic; abrupt transitions such as that between verse 6 and 7, 7 and 8, 12 and 13 in the text quoted are characteristic. Yet, in reality, there is no vagueness at all in the purport of speech or in its effect. When a Trobriander recounts in a long narrative some past happenings; when a group of people plan an expedition; when, in a complicated or even dangerous situation, such as a squall at sea, a hand-to-hand fight, a nightly vigil against a sorcerer or in pursuit of him—on all such occasions orders are issued and obeyed, without ambiguity or confusion. The ambiguity and confusion appear when we project the words on paper after having torn them

---

[1] Cf. *Bulletin of the School of Oriental Studies*, Vol. I, Pt. IV.

[2] A system of abbreviations has been adopted in interlineal renderings. See Introductory Note to Part V.

out of their context and tried to reinterpret them from our point of view, that is, that of an entirely different culture. As the words convey meaning within the compass of native linguistic function, the Trobriand language is an adequate instrument of communication; there are elements in their utterance and in its context which introduce as much definition as is necessary to the communicating natives. And it is a duty of the ethnographer to show where these elements which define and make precise and concrete are to be found.

C. *The Contextual Specification of Meaning.*

It results from what has been said in the two preceding sections that a great many words have to be reinterpreted when we pass from the interlineal word-for-word rendering to the free translation. This transition, however, is not arbitrary. It must be based on definite principles and the application of these principles has to be clearly although succinctly stated in a commentary to every text. In this commentary a brief 'contextualisation of meaning', as we might call it, has to be given for each sentence, for single words are affected by their integration into a significant sentence. The context supplies such grammatical data as subject and object; tense of the verb, i.e. temporal definition of action; the relation of clauses and the special meaning of the rare conjunctions. For instance, in each case we have to decide whether the *b* modifier of the verb rendered by 'might' signifies future or pending action, subjunctive mood, a command or merely potentiality. Again the suffixed *-la* may be either the third possessive person of a pronoun (nearest possession) or else an emphatic, or else almost play the part of the definite article.

But the best way of showing how this contextual specification of meaning works will be to give a full commentary on the above text. This specimen commentary must be controlled by the collation of free and interlineal translation.

(1) If we compare the literal rendering 'informant's father in child his he see' with the free translation (cf. Ch. V, Sec. 1) 'Molubabeba in his childhood witnessed a famine', it is clear that we have added the object 'a famine', changed the verb 'see' into 'witness' and given it the accomplished past tense, and slightly modified the order of the words. We were able to make these changes because we were aware of the context of situation to which this utterance belongs: i.e. we know that Molubabeba is the father of Tokulubakiki, that the subject-matter of the text is historical and concerns famine, and that the question had been asked whether anybody had himself experienced the calamity. There is one modification, however, which requires a fuller commentary: *gwadi* is the

word for 'child', male or female, but used only in describing a child without reference to kinship. 'Child' in the sense of 'so-and-so's offspring' is *latu-*: *latu-gu*, 'my child', *latu-la*, 'his child'. Nowhere is *gwadi* used with a third person pronoun of nearest possession (cf. Part V, Div. XII, Secs. 3–7). Yet it does not mean 'child of so-and-so'; for this the word *latu* would be used. Nor would such an expression fit into this context. The addition of the suffixed pronoun makes this noun into an abstract 'childhood', and thus it had to be rendered in the free translation. We see therefore that in passing from a literal to a free translation we had to modify or add four elements in this short sentence.

(2) In this sentence the adverbial conjunction *iga'u* had to be given the specific meaning 'at that time'. The main subject, which is given by context of situation, had to be added, while the subject of the verb *i-kugwo*, 'he first', which corresponds to the German impersonal *man* or French *on* or English 'one', was transformed into an adverbial expression 'with a skin disease'. To put it more precisely, the subject of 'they sicken' is just 'the people'; the subject in *i-kugwo*, 'he first', is an impersonal 'it', of which the significance here is more or less 'it first happened', so that we could pass from the literal translation, 'later on he first a skin rash they sicken', through an intermediate sentence, 'then it first happened a skin rash people sickened (with it)', to the free translation 'at that time the people became ill with a skin disease', which is the nearest grammatical and unambiguous equivalent of our intermediate link. When taking down this text I was not quite certain what the word *sipsipsipwapunu* meant, although I knew it was a rash. But I always went over such texts with some other informant and from one of my best linguistic commentators, Monakewo of Omarakana, I received the following definition:—

Sipsipsipwapunu (skin rash)	*makawala* alike	*pukuna.* pimple	*I-tuwali* he different	*pukuna* pimple
kway-viyaka big (r.b.)	*i-tuwali* he different	*i-puripuri* he break forth in clusters		*wa woulo* in body
sipsipsipwapunu. (skin rash)				

I reproduce it without further linguistic analysis as it does not directly bear on the subject of gardens and interests us here rather as a methodological device than as a linguistic document. In any case, comparing the interlineal version with the free translation, the text becomes quite clear.

Free translation: The *sipsipsipwapunu* rash is like ordinary pimples.

There is one type of pimple which is big, and another which breaks forth in clusters all over the skin; (this latter we call) *sipsipsipwapunu*.

(3) Here the commentator's work amounts merely to the choice of specific equivalents to the words given in the literal rendering. The reader is supposed to be acquainted with such words as *odila*, *rayboag*, *dumya*, so that the English equivalents 'bush', 'coral-ridge', 'swamp' bring up the correct picture. One word only had to be reinterpreted contextually: 'water' into 'water-hole'. The word *sopi*, 'water', has several sharply distinguished homonymous meanings which are not discussed in Part V, since the word does not bear directly on agriculture. The fundamental meaning of the word is unquestionably 'water', i.e. 'sweet water', for they have a special word for 'brine' —*yona*. But it can also mean 'water-hole', by an obvious derivation, and 'water-bottle'. This second meaning has to be inserted by contextual reinterpretation.

(4) Here a much fuller reinterpretation was necessary. The whole sentence has an explicative function. The conjunction *kidama*, for which the nondescript fixed meaning 'supposing' had to be chosen, has here a vaguely conditional but at the same time consecutive meaning. In the free translation I have rendered it by 'so as'. The appended clause 'they might die just' could have been translated freely 'and yet they died', 'but still they died'. On the principle, however, of not adding anything which is not clearly contained in the native utterance, I translated it 'and then they died', in which there is a vague indication of the possibilities of opposition.

(5) 'For hunger yam-food we eat not.' Here for the first time we have the appearance of the narrative *ta-*, 'we' (inclusive plural), which functions very often in Kiriwinian in lieu of the English 'one' or 'you': 'there was hunger, one had nothing to eat', 'there was hunger, you would have been starving'. The subject of these few sentences is 'people', more precisely the people affected by the famine. The grammatical expression of this subject suddenly shifts from third person plural to first person (inclusive plural) between 4 and 5. In a well-constructed narrative we would obviously have placed this sentence at the beginning, because, in a way, it is the one which contextualises the whole narrative. Its insertion as an afterthought to integrate the preceding clauses is characteristic of Trobriand speech.

(6) Here the adverbial 'already' had to be changed into the temporal conditional 'when'. To understand this sentence and the following one it is of course necessary to be acquainted with the ethnographic aspect of native life and with the fact that after a

severe famine the *vilamalia* magic would be performed (cf. Ch. VII). The word *molu* in this and in the previous sentence had to be changed from its fixed meaning 'hunger' into 'famine'. Here the word *iga'u*, 'later on', could retain its fixed meaning in the free translation.

As to the subjects corresponding to the personal verbal pronouns in *i-wokwe*, *i-miga'i-se*, *bi-pulu-se*, the first of course refers to *molu*, 'hunger'; 'it is over', 'the hunger is over'; the other two refer obviously to the magicians of prosperity who perform the *vilamalia*. It is noteworthy that the first verbal pronoun is given in a simple form: *i*. The second in the form *bi*. This second form corresponds to a certain teleological subordination of the second clause: 'they becharm wild ginger so that they might bespit the village'. The change into the past tense is obviously implied by the context of situation, though of course we could have used the historic present even in English, by straining our linguistic habits a little.

(7) The adverb *oyluvi* corresponds to the *iga'u* of the previous sentence. It means something like 'later still'; we rendered it by 'then' in the free translation. The context of situation enables us to specify the word *kaylum*, which means 'magical bundle' or 'magic-herb' according to the fixed meaning chosen (cf. Part V, Div. VII, § 26). *Boge* has a temporal consecutive meaning, 'already' being equivalent to 'and then'. It links the first part of the sentence to the second as cause to effect. Here the rare accomplished form *lay-* appears for the first time.

(8) The context of gesture, defined in the interlineal rendering, has been embodied in the free translation by an appropriate clause 'as long as a forearm'. There is a slight inconsistency between 8 and 9, as obviously the same size of valuable would not be bartered for ten and for five baskets of seed yams. But the meaning of the speaker is clear.

(9) The one outstanding grammatical peculiarity in this sentence is the use of the numeral without a classificatory particle; *luwa*, 'ten', *lima*, 'five'. Comment on this use will be found below in Division II (§ 9). The structure 'this valuable they barter seed yam' shows well the function of mere juxtaposition. We had to add the preposition 'with' in order to link up the verb 'to barter' with its two objects: barter of seed yams for valuables or barter of valuables for seed yams. In Kiriwinian you simply speak about the valuable bartering something. This, however, on the whole does not make the native wording obscure.

Finally, here once more we have a sentence without an explicit subject, though the subject understood differs from that of the preceding sentence. In vv. 6 and 7 the subject was the 'magicians', here it is 'people in general' again.

(10) The initial adverb 'later on' has a definitely conjunctional function: it links up this sentence with the previous one. 'Later on' means here 'after that had been done', or, more concretely, 'after the seed yams had been procured'. In free translation I have rendered it by the clause 'with such seed yams', in order to bring out the implicit meaning contained in such native words. It is remarkable that the word *bi-sapu* is in the singular. Here again it is probably the impersonal unspecified 'it': 'later on it became planted, it became planted, twenty men working on one garden plot'. The juxtaposition: 'one garden plot—twenty humans', and the following three-fold enumeration: 'one square, one square, one square', were rendered in free translation in as near a phrasing as possible: 'one single plot twenty men, one square each'. The correlation by mere juxtaposition in 'one garden plot—twenty men' is characteristic of the native style. In a developed European language we would say: 'twenty men working on one garden plot', or 'one garden plot being allotted to as many as twenty men'. Then again we would say something like: 'a single square being worked by each man'; the native simply repeats: 'one square, one square, one square', the rest being left unexpressed but clearly implied in the context.

(11) Is similar in structure to v. 10. Again the adverb 'later on' has a conjunctive function, correlating the previous sentence to this one in the temporal sequence: 'as soon as', or, as we put it in the free translation, 'after that, when'. Again, in the second part, correlation is achieved by juxtaposition; 'one plot—two humans'. Here the classificatory numeral shows its reference to garden plot by the use of the classificatory particle.

(12) The temporal correlative *iga'u* has, by its position, a more emphatic meaning. We translated it 'later on still, when'. The *b* modifier of the verb refers here to the past and conveys an idea of potentiality: 'would be plentiful again', as we translated it. And once more we have the direct juxtaposed correlation with classified numerals: one (r.b.) = plot: one (male) = man.

(13) Passing from v. 12 to 13 we meet a characteristic feature of native narrative. Without any verbal expression indicating it, the narrative goes back in time. Verse 12 has treated of the time after the famine is over, perhaps a year or two later when plenty is re-established. Verse 13 goes back to the famine again. The native dispenses with the special indication he could easily have found, because of his intimate acquaintance with the facts related. The speaker and his audience knew perfectly well who it was that perished in Kulumata

and when it was that this happened. In a native community the function of a narrative, however historical and real, is to call to mind, revive the memory of important deeds, rather than to impart information. In passing from the interlineal rendering to the free translation we had to add the preposition 'in', which the native easily drops. Here in fact it would not have been possible in Trobriand to say *o kulumata* or *wa kulumata*, 'in the western district'. It is not easy to explain the function of the demonstrative *bayse*: it has a spatial, pointing effect. We translated it by 'there'. The root *tamwa'u*, 'to disappear', we specified in the free translation by adding 'perish' after it. Here the verbal modifier *b* has a subjunctival meaning and is translated by 'could'. The juxtaposed single verb *ta-poulo*, 'we fish', is really a self-contained clause with the implication of reason or motive: 'so that we might fish'.

(14) Here the verbal modifier *b* gives a definite conditional flavour to the clause. 'Were a canoe to sail', as we translated it, 'then they would see us.' *Boge* again has an inferential function 'then already', translated here 'they would kill us directly'.

(15) The two verbal modifiers *b* in 'they might kill us' and 'no he might be angry' have here a conditional and potential function: 'if they would kill us', 'in case they would kill us, our kinsmen would not be angry'. It might be well to take this as an example of what I really mean by the contextual modification of meaning. This sentence on the face of it and as we have given it in the literal interlineal rendering runs: 'They might kill us, no he might be angry kindred ours, for hunger.' Now first of all this sentence is interesting because of its essential ambiguity. If the negation word were attached to the first verb the whole meaning would be opposite. It would run: 'They might not kill us, our kinsmen would be angry, because of hunger,' and the free translation would run: 'They would never dare to kill us as our kinsmen would be angry because we had been killed in famine.' In fact to the European or Christian moral sense it would seem a much greater crime to murder a famished, exhausted man in times of national disaster and because he sought for a bare subsistence than to kill the same man in times of prosperity because he was poaching. But the Trobrianders, obeying the stern law of necessity, have developed different rules. Our ethnographic knowledge, combined with the fact that punctuation was indicated by the delivery, enabled us to solve this ambiguity.

By the same means we arrive at the meaning of the two verbal modifiers. *Bi-katumatay-da*, 'they might kill us', is here obviously not the future nor the imperative. Since the verb occurs in a narrative referring to the past, it has to be projected into that time setting.

But it could still mean either 'they would kill us', a statement of likelihood; or 'they might kill us', a statement of possibility; or 'they should kill us', a statement as to moral obligation or customary rule. Taken, however, in conjunction with the second clause, 'no he might be angry kindred ours', the conditional or hypothetical meaning becomes clear, and that because the sentence, *gala bigiburuwa veyo-da*, is clearly a statement of an exceptional, extraordinary state of affairs. The fact that his kinsmen would not resent the death of a man carries with it the implication of something like 'then we would have the extraordinary case (of absence of vendetta)'. And the meaning of this sentence is given really by its ethnographic setting, which makes the first clause into: 'were they to kill us', or 'in case they had killed us', or even 'in the extraordinary event of ourselves being killed'. Here, as well as in the next clause, 'us' and 'we' (inclusive plural) functions as the impersonal *on* or the English narrative 'one' or 'you'; 'were anyone to be killed', or 'were you to be killed'.

I have given this detailed analysis of how context functions grammatically in order to justify some of our succinctly stated conclusions.

(16) Here the use of the numeral 'one' in the sense of the English indefinite article is characteristic. The use of *odila*, 'bush', in the wider sense of 'jungle', 'open nature', and the juxtaposition of clauses are very interesting. In the free translation I have almost verbally reproduced the interlineal rendering. The last clause, however, might have been placed in a more definite relation to the first ones. It is the consequence, the logical outcome, of the clause immediately preceding it. A still freer translation might render this sentence 'we hide in the bush, we look out for a canoe, (when we see one) we do not go to fish (we forbear from going out fishing)'. The sentence really expresses the anxious time, the need of precaution, even the risks which sometimes were taken. As a rule, however, even in the free translation I did not include all such contextual implications, for English prose as well as Kiriwinian has its contextual fringe, and if one started to develop all implications it would be difficult to draw the line.

(17) The noun *u'ula* is used here in the abstract sense 'basis this', 'the cause of all this'. The adverb *boge* 'already' is here what might be called an adverb of completion which, as is well known, is lacking in English to the discomfiture not only of Trobrianders but also of Poles, Germans and even Frenchmen, who miss such words as *juz*, *schon*, *déjà*.

Looking at the verbs we see that the subject of 'they bewitch' is 'the chiefs', incidentally a genuine plural. The subject of *ta-bugwa'u-si* is in inclusive plural. Here it means 'the chiefs bewitch the villages because we (meaning 'the whole lot of us', 'the commoners') have ensorcelled his (i.e. their) kindred'. The 'we' stands really for 'one among us', or 'a few among us', the chiefs being angry with the whole lot of the commoners because one of them had dared to use evil magic. It is remarkable that the term *veyo-la*, 'kindred his', is referred to in the third person singular, although the preceding noun is in the plural. Such grammatical mistakes are frequent in the native texts as I have taken them down. I do not think that this was because the natives had to speak more deliberately than was their custom when I was taking notes since, especially towards the end of my stay when I took down this text, I became able to write the spoken word rapidly and did not have to slow down the normal tempo of their speech.

(18) The same adverb *boge* has here an entirely different function, i.e. meaning. We could almost translate it by the English 'because', by reason of the temporal sense of accomplishment emphasised by its context: 'already so-and-so died, therefore another so-and-so carried out black magic'. Here, also, we could very minutely and elaborately justify these reinterpretations. But to anyone who has followed our previous arguments the grounds for them will be clear.

(19) Is really a repetition of vv. 17 and 18 in other words, the conjunction *kidama* having a somewhat general sense of temporal conditionality, which we have translated by 'whenever'. Remarkably enough, the verb 'to bewitch' is here coupled with the inclusive 'we'. Comparing v. 17 with v. 19 the inconsistency is flagrant. In v. 17 'we' were the culprits guilty of sorcery. In v. 19 'we' are the avengers punishing the commonalty. The speaker in this case probably was influenced by the fact that, as a member of the chief's village and as the son of a chief of high rank, he could identify himself with the highest nobility. But in such discriminations and corrections one constantly has to pass from grammar to context—meaning by context, native sociology, personal conditions of the speaker, verbal habits and general customs of the natives, and so on.

This specimen commentary, which will serve as a pattern for the more concise future annotations, also enables us to formulate one or two theoretical points. We see, in the first place, that the elucidation of the 'meaning' of a word does not happen in a flash, but is the result of a lengthy process. Exactly as in the field the meaning of a native term only gradually dawned on me, became clearer and finally crystallised into a manageable linguistic unit, so the English reader must pass through several stages: the rough identification of the word by means of the mnemonic counter, the subtler and more precise idea of the rôle it fulfils in a given sentence, the range of its possibilities, at times vague, at times concrete and clear, and finally its paraphrase into acceptable English. Throughout this process what really matters is to understand what the text conveys to the native. From the above commentary we see that this can be best achieved by holding constantly before our eyes the background of native culture and by showing how much the words add to it and what emphasis they place on some aspect or segment of this background.

Our scholiastic operations consist in a constant manipulation of words and context. We have to compare the word with its verbal setting; we have to interpret the occasional significant gestures, and finally we have constantly to see how the situation in which the utterance is being made and the situation to which it refers influence the structure of paragraphs, sentences and expressions.

Div. IV. THE PRAGMATIC SETTING OF UTTERANCES

Let us now for a moment consider our text as a whole. It is a narrative and it is a narrative at second-hand. That is, the man who is telling it has not gone through the experiences himself, but is recounting what was told him by his father.

It will be interesting, therefore, to enquire, first, what are the actual root experiences through which the words become significant to speaker and listener alike and, secondly, what is the function of such a narrative utterance.

Since throughout our enquiry we are trying to overcome the limitations of ethnographic apparatus and get beyond the fieldworker's notebook to the reality of native life, it will be of interest to see under what conditions such a narrative would actually occur. I heard it in the course of a conversation with a group of informants, but it is just the type of tale that might be told on some evening at a fireside, either because the conversation suggested it, or, even more likely, in appropriate seasonal conditions. The response of the natives to the atmosphere of season or circumstance is remarkable. During the lean moons, the time which is represented by the word *molu*, they will often speak about real hunger, about historical cases of sensational famine. And again in a plentiful harvest, they will remember famous examples of *malia*, 'prosperity'. Although I was told this tale in the cold blood of an ethnographic discussion, I have heard similar narratives time after time recounted, not for my edification, but to satisfy the interest of native listeners.

As with most traditionally known events, the natives are well acquainted with what happens during famine. The words which we find in our text, *molu, kaulo, kam*, are familiar to them in the sense in which they are used in their present context. In a less dramatic form hunger occurs often. The bodily discomforts associated with insufficiency of food are experienced almost every year. The emotional associations are strong, especially for children, who, moreover, connect a wide range of verbal acts with these. Words such as *ba-kam kaulo*, 'I would eat some food', *agu molu*, 'I am hungry', *magi-gu kayvalu'a*, 'I want fruit-food', are often heard during the months of scarcity when even children have to be rationed. Therefore the personally experienced reality on which the understanding of our text depends exists for every native listener. It is, moreover, systematised, i.e. associated with the rotation of seasons, with the annual yield of gardening, with excessive rain or prolonged drought. On the verbal side the use of such opposites as *molu* and *malia* (Div. V, § 3) and of such correlatives as *kaulo, kayvalu'a, gwaba* (Div. II, § 12) is consistent. In the same way with the other cycles of ideas: barter of food, the extent of gardening done in good and in bad seasons, when seed yams are plentiful or scarce, are familiar concepts to the native.

Thus we see that on the one hand the real meaning of words, the real capacity for visualising the contents of a narrative, are always derived from a personal experience, physiological, intellectual and emotional, while on the other, such experience is invariably connected with verbal acts. A narrative type of utterance is, therefore, comprehensible by the reference of the statements to past personal experiences in which words were directly embedded within the context of situation. The context of situation of words which refer to hunger, scarcity and lean seasons is obviously the time of scarcity, hunger and the lean season—the time when eating is an important act achieved with difficulty, when people clamour for food and complain about its absence, when the significance of a sentence or of a single word is driven home and extracted by the powerful pang of bodily pain.

In a narrative words are used with what might be called a borrowed or indirect meaning. The real context of reference has to be reconstructed by the hearers even as it is being evoked by the speaker. But situations in which the same words have been used with all the pragmatic vigour of a request or imperative, with all the emotional content of hope or despair, situations in which the use of a word is fraught with weighty consequences for the speaker and for his hearers, in such situations we have speech used in a primary, direct manner. It is from such situations that we are most likely to learn the meaning of words, rather than from a study of derived uses of speech. This answers our first question as to the primary experiences from which the meaning of words is derived.

But though not used in the pragmatic, i.e. primary meaning, words in a narrative have their part to play. Narratives always entertain and at times instruct, but they also fulfil a more important function. A sacred tribal tale told in justification of the social order or of morality; in explanation of a ritual, or to illuminate religious mysteries, such a tale is of the greatest importance in that it systematises belief and regulates conduct. Again a legend, an incident in tribal history may also contribute to the building up of morale. A tale, such as the present narrative, contributes indirectly to the formation of economic standards and values. For, as we have seen, it is the shadow of scarcity, hunger and famine which constitutes the most powerful incentive to work in the Trobriands. The whole system of organised work and incentives is associated with the traditional handing on from generation to generation of stories of *molu* and *malia*, of success and failure, of the importance of magic, of work and discipline in gardening. Thus, though narratives considered singly might appear idle enough, integrally their function goes far beyond mere amusement and entertainment, and those tales which centre round vital interests, such as hunger and sex, economic values and morality, collectively serve to the building up of the moral tradition of a tribe. The function of speech in them is an important cultural contribution to the social order.

The text to which we have devoted so much attention is somewhat peculiar in that it contains a multiplicity of subjects, one or two of them dramatic, and because it is a narrative at second-hand, almost legendary or historical in character. It will be profitable to consider, in a more general manner, the other texts contained in Part V, showing in the first place what part each utterance plays in tribal life and, in the second place, from what type of actual experiences its meaning has been derived.

We have one or two more narrative texts. There is one (85) which is an account of events of the immediate past, in fact the antecedents of events which were then in progress. This is a long text, and its analysis reveals very much the same features as those we found in the account of famine. The main function of Text 85 would be to keep alive the tradition concerning accumulation of food, and through this the enhancement of tribal grandeur.

It is characteristic that certain actual speeches uttered, such as a challenge or a boast or a praise of generosity, are remembered verbally and would be handed on from generation to generation. After having overheard such ceremonial and obviously important utterances as those reproduced in Texts 86, 87 and 88, I found no difficulty in getting them repeated to me, in exactly the same form, by one or two informants who had heard them with me. Some of the statements contained in these have more than a narrative function. Words which accompany gifts or which contain a challenge are usually uttered in a set traditionally prescribed form. They constitute what might be called semi-legal, semi-ceremonial set phrases. Text 94, which reproduces the verbal tribute to the traditional owners of the soil given at a *kayaku*, is typical of such sayings. Text 92 contains a number of expressions which have also a semi-legal binding force and are uttered as a request for an additional contribution from the wife's brother. Text 93 is typical of words spoken with an indirect purport, words which in a way conceal the thoughts and sentiments of the speaker rather than reveal them.

Texts 78 and 79 give us the substance of native beliefs about the effects of a magical rite which frightens away the bush-pigs and about the mythological pig which lives in the home of the bush-pigs. Such dogmatic texts are typical of the whole body of utterances on the subject current in the tribe. They would be told with an educational aim by the elder people to the young ones, or narrated in discussing the miscarriage of a magical rite, or in connexion with some damage done by bush-pigs, or in explanation of a rite given in the course of a regular training in magical lore. Their general function is obviously again the maintenance of tradition.

We have only one mythological narrative (Text 96), the function of which is largely dogmatic and to a certain extent explanatory. It is, however, not an explanation by statement of fact, but rather by correlating native interests in gardens with their geographical orientation. For this myth connects the distribution of gardening and fertility in the eastern area of our tribe with an important event of the past.

Text 82 is a set formula or ditty with a vague magical purport. The body of magical formulae collected in Part VII supplies us with rich material, to which, however, we shall devote special attention later on.

All these texts which we have so far surveyed are either narratives or fixed formulae. Some of the formulae very definitely show an effective or active side. Take utterances such as statements at a *kayaku*, or requests for a gift, or challenges which might set in motion a long series of tribal activities: each of these is a definite act which produces effects, at times on a large scale, and the function of which is obviously defined by these effects. But the effective force of such verbal acts lies in directly reproducing their consequences; and it is because there is a tribal tradition, sanctioned by various beliefs, institutions and explicit rules, that a certain challenge cannot be ignored, that a certain request must be fulfilled. The pragmatism of such verbal acts is based on the same complicated mechanism as that on which the pragmatism, i.e. the effective force, of all rules of conduct, customs and tribal laws is founded.

What is the real reason why human beings always attach such a great importance to a mere sound—to the *flatus vocis*, which in one of its aspects appears so completely futile and empty, and in another aspect has, in various human creeds and systems, been regarded as that which was at the beginning, as the force which created all things? Can we come any nearer to this problem in the consideration of the material offered by Trobriand agricultural linguistics?

Let us glance at the other texts. Most of them are shorter, more fragmentary and apparently even more remote from a direct active and pragmatic function. Take, for example, the second text in our collection, quoted in Part V (Div. I, § 21), which on the face of it is merely a definition of certain terms. The defining of terms would seem, at first glance, to be the province of a linguistically minded ethnographer rather than of an inhabitant of a coral island. Let us see, therefore, whether this text can naturally be placed within some normal context of native life. In commenting upon it above, I indicated that the speaker himself contextualised his definition and placed it within a natural situation both temporarily and spatially; 'when we clear the bush' and 'then stand on the boundary belt'. Now some such situation often occurs, because the natives have to find the boundary between the fields to be cultivated and the bush. When choosing the land for next year's garden they frequently inspect various parts of the territory. The expressions *ma-kabula-na yosewo*, 'this side uncut bush', *ma-kabula-na buyagu*, 'this side garden-site' might be actually uttered with a future anticipatory reference. Or again a stranger might thus be informed of a fact already obvious —for the natives very often comment verbally on the obvious. Or a small boy who was being instructed in agricultural lore might have a similar text given him. It is thus the informative and educational character of this text which might very well make it a linguistic actuality. Giving information to strangers and instructing children are activities which are constantly going on in Trobriand communities. Again Text 4, quoted in illustration of certain verbal uses, was given to me as a piece of information that might be given to any stranger. The direct speech reproduced in this text preserves its live and actual character and, since natives are intensely interested in the economic side of affairs, in claims of ownership, in the *towosi's* titles as master of the garden, such an utterance would pass on innumerable occasions in everyday life.

It is beginning perhaps to dawn on us that the texts which, at first blush, appear as merely artificial by-products of ethnographic field-work fit very easily as they are into the normal context of tribal life. Take for instance Text 7: 'It has no name, it is just a weed (*munumunu*)'. This phrase I have heard used time after time to children who, as is the way with children, would pick up an attractive flower or a coloured leaf and enquire its name. For Trobriand children, as do all children, take an interest in names. And again, the preceding text, defining the same word, *munumunu*, 'weed', by its inability to burn (Text 6): 'when we try to blow up a fire and it will not blaze up, this is because it is made of weeds'. Here we can easily reproduce the practical situation: a child saying, *boge a-yuvi gala bi-kata*, 'already I have blown, no it might blaze', and another child with more experience, or a grown-up, answering, *kuligaywo munumunu pela*, 'throw it away since it is a weed'. Instruction in fire-making, discussions about how to make a fire, often leading to disputes and quarrels, are as frequent in the Trobriands as anywhere else where fires are made in the open and where everybody thinks that he is a special expert in the art. Often I have heard, though I did not note down the remark, people commenting on the production of fire by friction: 'it will not catch fire because it is so-and-so (naming a wood which is not suitable); you ought to have used so-and-so (naming one or two of the plants which yield excellent material—dry, brittle and producing the fine powder which serves as tinder)', verbal discriminations, knowledge of nature and know-ledge of handicrafts are inextricably mixed up.

And this brings me to two important points: first, when speaking about the educational or instructive function of speech, I do not necessarily mean that a regular lesson is being imparted by a grown-up to a child. In the Trobriands, I should say, that more than half of the instruction was given by one child to another. In the second place, as will be amply illustrated in Part V, an interest in words and in their correct use—even in definitions—is very great indeed among the natives. They are amused at anyone, whether it be a child or a foreigner or a feeble-minded person, who does not use words adequately and in the proper sense. They regard the knowledge of words as a symptom of wisdom. The seat of *nanola*, 'mind', is located in the throat, in the larynx, because, as they say, it is from there that you speak. The word *tonagowa* is indiscriminately applied to an idiot, a feeble-minded person, a man with an impediment of speech and a hopelessly incapable or clumsy individual.

Thus the series of definition texts concerning botanical expressions (10–13) are undoubtedly exact reproductions of what is said hundreds of times every day among Kiriwinians. Again, Text 15, always accompanied by significant gestures and Text 19, both specially interesting because they contain direct speech in the form of comments, are typical instructions about the planting of taro and coconut. These and similar texts can readily be placed within the context of tribal life; and such short phrases as 16–18 are often recurring fragments of conversations.

There are a number of typical educational texts containing a direct explanation of why certain practical activities or magical ceremonies are carried out. In 29 we have a statement concerning the fertilising power of ashes, the reason why burning has to be done in the gardens. In 41 we have a very similar statement of why a magical ceremony, the first grand inaugural rite, is performed. Such brief sentences as Texts 44–77 would be used during the instruction of the young in gardening, since they include verbal definitions (58–60, 62), the correlation between magical acts and practical activities or phases in the growth of a plant (54–56, 61, 63, 69–71), and texts which state directly the effects of a magical act (44, 52, 64, 68, 72–84).

This concludes our brief survey of most of the texts presented in Part V. The reader will usually find clear indications of how each text was collected and what it represented in actual ethnographic field-work; also what it represents to us as a document in agricultural linguistics. Here I have tried to reset most of these texts into their living context, and thus to show what they mean to the natives themselves. We understand now how natives would naturally use the various types of texts, how the listeners would receive them and what the speakers normally achieve by them.

In the course of our analysis it has become increasingly clear that the contextual definition of each utterance is of the greatest importance for the understanding of it, and that this contextual reference must be two-fold. In the first place, an utterance belongs to a special context of culture, i.e. it refers to a definite subject-matter. Each of the sayings, phrases and narratives which I have here adduced belongs definitely to a certain division of our Supplement and each such division corresponds to an aspect of Trobriand gardening.

But side by side with this context of culture or context of reference, as it might also be called, we have another context: the situation in which the words have been uttered. A phrase, a saying or a few sentences concerning famine may be found in a narrative, or in a magical formula, or in a proverbial saying. But they also may occur during a famine, forming an integral part of some of those essential transactions wherein human beings co-operate in order to help one another. The whole character of such words is different when they are uttered in earnest, or as a joke, or in a narrative of the distant past. The words need not be idle in any of the cases. We have shown the function of narrative. Even a joke about a serious subject may do its part in begetting a traditional attitude—an attitude which in the long run might prove of considerable significance in tribal life, and this is the most important result of an utterance from the point of view of a scientific theory of meaning.

The pragmatic relevance of words is greatest when these words are uttered actually within the situation to which they belong and uttered so that they achieve an immediate, practical effect. For it is in such situations that words acquire their meaning.

Since it is the function, the active and effective influence of a word within a given context which constitutes its meaning, let us examine such pragmatic utterances.

Div. V. MEANING AS FUNCTION OF WORDS

All our considerations have led us to the conclusion that words in their primary and essential sense *do, act, produce* and *achieve*. To arrive therefore at an understanding of meaning, we have to study the dynamic rather than the purely intellectual function of words. Language is primarily an instrument of action and not a means of telling a tale, of entertaining or instructing from a purely intellectual point of view. Let us see how the use of words is shaped by action and how reciprocally these words in use influence human behaviour. For if we are correct it is the pragmatic use of speech within the context of action which has shaped its structure, determined its vocabulary and led to various problematic characteristics such as multiplicity of meaning, metaphorical uses, redundances and reticences.

Since it is best to investigate every phenomenon in its most pronounced form, let us enquire where the dynamism of words is most pronounced. A little consideration will show that there are two peaks of this pragmatic power of words: one of them is to be found in certain sacred uses, that is in magical formulae, sacramental utterances, exorcisms, curses and blessings and most prayers. All sacred words have a creative effect, usually indirect, by setting in motion some supernatural power, or, when the sacramental formula becomes quasi-legal, in summoning social sanctions.

The second climax of speech dynamism is to be found obviously in the direct pragmatic effect of words. An order given in battle, an instruction issued by the master of a sailing ship, a cry for help, are as powerful in modifying the course of events as any other bodily act.

Let us first consider the power of words in their creative supernatural effect. Obviously we have to accept here the intent and the mental attitude of those who use such words. If we want to understand the verbal usage of the Melanesian we must, for a moment, stop doubting or criticising his belief in magic, exactly as, when we want to understand the nature of Christian prayer and its moral force or of Christian sacramental miracles, we must abandon the attitude of a confirmed rationalist or sceptic. Meaning is the effect of words on human minds and bodies and, through these, on the environmental reality as created or conceived in a given culture. Therefore imaginary and mental effects are as important in the realm of the supernatural as the legal effects of a formula are in a contractual phrase. There is no strict line of demarcation between the signature on a cheque, a civil contract of marriage, the sacramental vow on a similar occasion, the change of substance in the Holy Eucharist, and the repulsion of bush-pigs by means of a fictitious excrement. One of the contextual conditions for the sacred or legal power of words is the existence, within a certain culture, of beliefs, of moral attitudes and of legal sanctions.

What interests us in this type of speech is that, in all communities, certain words are accepted as potentially creative of acts. You utter a vow or you forge a signature and you may find yourself bound for life to a monastery, a woman or a prison. You utter another word and you make millions happy, as when the Holy Father blesses the faithful. Human beings will bank everything, risk their lives and substance, undertake a war or embark on a perilous expedition, because a few words have been uttered. The words may be the silly speech of a modern 'leader' or prime minister; or a sacramental formula, an indiscreet remark wounding 'national honour', or an ultimatum. But in each case words are equally powerful and fateful causes of action.

Our magical formulae in Trobriand gardening produce fertility, ward off pests, guarantee the successful sprouting and growth of plants, make harvest plentiful and prevent yams from being eaten up too rapidly. All this would be simply regarded as imaginary. What, however, is very real about the words of magic is that they consolidate the morale of the gardeners, give authority to the garden magician, and thus are the main elements in integrating the whole process. This system of ideas is well known to us already and we shall be returning to analyse certain aspects of it when discussing magical formulae. Again, a word summons the help of spirits to the gardens and words are necessary to transform the material substance of food into something which is fit and appropriate for spirits to eat.

There are also ceremonial utterances with a definitely legal import. For instance, when in Text 92 the man instructs his wife to approach her brother and offer him a valuable, saying to her: "Take a valuable and untie your brother's yam-house", this utterance has a definitely contractual power. After the acts have been performed and the words have been uttered the other person has no choice but to act according to the traditional customary pattern or receive blame. The phraseology of gifts— *kam motu, kam urigubu, um pokala*—has this power, and combine ritual with legal efficacy. As we can see from Text 94, certain words must be uttered before certain fields in Oburaku may be cultivated. Equally important and equally binding are purely personal agreements: the case, for instance, of one man asking (*nigada*) another for a garden plot and the other consenting, granting (*tagwala*). In the Trobriands such an agreement, though not always absolutely quarrel-proof, is on the whole regarded as binding. The same type of pragmatic effectiveness of words is found among ourselves, where one nation boasts of *ein Mann—ein Wort*, another of 'my word is my bond', and another of the validity of its *parole d'honneur*, and all keep their promises with the same degree of sacredness as the Kiriwinians.

But in every community, among the Trobrianders quite as definitely as among ourselves, there exists a belief that a word uttered in certain circumstances has a creative, binding force; that with an inevitable cogency, an utterance produces its specific effect, whether it conveys a permanent blessing, or inflicts irreparable damage, or saddles with a lifelong obligation.

It was necessary to emphasise this point in the context of our argument, because it brings us face to face with this interesting theoretical problem: whence comes this conviction as to the creative force and pragmatic power of words?

It is this creative function of words in magical or in sacramental speech, their binding force in legal utterance, which, in my opinion, constitutes their real meaning. To record one of these sacred formulae without discussing its contextual belief, what effects it is supposed to produce and why; to quote a legal saying without showing its binding force; in short, to detach the linguistic side of sacred and binding speech from its sociological and cultural context is to sterilise both linguistics and sociology. And perhaps nothing demonstrates more clearly that words are acts and that they function as acts than the study of sacred utterances.

Of course not all religious speech, even in magical formulae, shows the character of absolute pragmatic cogency; its degree varies considerably. Glancing beyond the Trobriands we see that sacred writings, our own Holy Scriptures, for instance, use words with a function entirely different from that of prayer, sacramental speech, blessing or exorcism. Though pertaining to religion, such texts are not pragmatic in so far as they do not create sacred realities. But take certain utterances in the Holy Mass, those which within the appropriate context transform bread and wine into the Body and Blood of Our Saviour. Take again the verbal act of repentance in the Roman Catholic confession of sins, or again the sacramental act of Absolution administered verbally by the Father Confessor: here words produce an actual change in a universe which, though mystical and imaginary to us agnostics, is none the less real to the believer.

In the same way, the religious discourses of the Trobriander and his mythology; such dogmatic statements as we have in Texts 78 and 79; the parts of his magical formulae concerned with mythological similes or the enumeration of ancestral names do not exemplify pragmatic efficiency at its maximum. For this we must go to the key words of magical formulae, which we shall be discussing more fully in the comments on these (cf. Part VII.). But in Formula 2, to take only one example, such words as 'go', 'begone'; the words announcing the advent of fertility, ordering fertility to be, as in 'the belly of my garden rises, the belly of my garden swells'; exorcistic words such as 'I sweep', 'I cleanse'—these definitely represent words of magical action. The legal phraseology already mentioned, in which the utterance definitely constitutes a contract, shows the maximum of pragmatic efficiency.

Let us now turn from religious and sacred speech to utterances embedded in the ordinary life as well as in the practical concerns of man. In the free flow of speech as it passes between people who converse and co-operate, words may be bandied in joke or in gossip, formulae of politeness may be exchanged, information may be given. And then, perhaps, news of some event arrives which demands decision and starts a new line of activities. Speech immediately changes its character. Words are uttered in serious deliberation, a decision is arrived at in discourse and translated into instructions and orders. And these words are not less related with the context of action than is full pragmatic speech. They become immediately translated into activities, they co-ordinate man to man and man to his environment. The orders, the verbal instructions, the descriptions given in such circumstances show the full pragmatic effectiveness of speech in action.

If we wanted to present our point more dramatically, not to say sensationally, and emphasise the opposition between words when they are "idle" and words when they are a matter of life and death, we could take as a prototype any situation where words mean life or death to a human being. Whether it be a Trobriand canoe rapidly sailing at night over deep and stormy waves and one of the crew suddenly swept into the sea or a solitary climber in the Alps overtaken by fog and threatened by death from hunger and exposure —the reaction to the situation is the same: the signal for help, an S O S sent out mechanically, verbally or, as in an Alpine accident, by whistling. Such a signal is a compelling order, a definite force which puts all those whom it reaches under a moral obligation to render help. The *meaning* of this first signal, which we will for the moment assume to be a verbal utterance, lies in this compelling force. It has to be heard, it has to be understood and it has to convey this moral compelling force. Whence this force comes we shall see presently.

Once on the spot the rescuers have then to communicate, and here communication usually takes place by verbal means. Instructions are exchanged, some apparatus may be used; technical language, information, specification of position play their part. But the words must be heard, understood and followed. The incorrect use of a word or the incorrect interpretation of a word may be fatal.

What is the function of words here? Each of them modifies and directs human behaviour in a situation of urgency. One person acts on the organism of another and, indirectly through this organism, on the surrounding environment. The word is as powerful an act as any manual grip.

An imperative, a noun, an adjective, even an adverb, screamed from a distance in the dark might reorientate completely the movements of the rescuers or those in danger. Now what is the meaning of the word here? It is above all a stimulus to action. It is a stimulus to a very specific and determined action, a stimulus correlated to the situation, i.e. to the environment, the people and the objects they handle, and based on past experience. The efficacy of rescue action may depend on the question whether both parties are well acquainted with the technicalities of the situation and with the technical words. Hence whenever a body of people are in a situation of potential danger, they have to be instructed in the orders which will be given them, in the use of apparatus, and familiarised with their environment. Whether we consider the simple boat-drill on board a passenger steamer, the regular drill of a fire brigade, the preparedness of a life-boat crew and the corresponding preparedness of an ordinary crew of sailors, the professional drill of soldiers— they all show how essential is verbal knowledge in correlation with control over the necessary bodily movements, and knowledge of the environment and apparatus. For in all such drill the teaching of words, the explanations as to what the orders mean, exact descriptions of apparatus, environment and purpose, make linguistic and practical training inseparable. They are two aspects of the activity which we call "drill".

From what I have just said it may have become clear to the reader that the dramatic and sensational situation from which we started is not really as unique, exceptional and outside the run of ordinary events as might appear at first. Apart from drowning or being caught in deep fog on a crag in the Dolomites, we often find ourselves in a more or less difficult or dangerous situation. Here again we need not think of the recent war or political disturbances, or an encounter with kidnappers or gangsters. Few of us have passed our lives without such minor accidents as the beginning of a fire, or bodily hurts which might have serious consequences if not rapidly treated. Here very often a clear utterance, an order, or the information of what has happened may save the situation. The more correct the reference to the environmental reality, the simpler and better the co-ordination between human action, apparatus and environment, the more easily is the danger avoided and the accident prevented. The nursery is a specially usual scene of such accidents, and here also the difficulty of clear linguistic statements from children is often acutely felt by those in charge. Moreover, in all the highly complicated and at the same time essentially dangerous forms of modern transport and industrial activities, there is a strict need of symbolic communication, at times mechanical, at times verbal. In this the obedience to signs, written instructions and orders by the machine driver, leader or working man, is indispensable. In the treatment of illness words again play this fundamental pragmatic rôle. Clear verbal statement on the part of the patient makes diagnosis infinitely easier. The instructions of the practitioner are of considerable importance. Their correct comprehension and execution may be a matter of life and death.

This pragmatic speech, words which do infinitely more than impart information or tell a story, words which are meant directly to effect action and influence it, occurs to a far wider extent in our own civilisation than might at first appear. And it seems to me that, even in the most abstract and theoretical aspects of human thought and verbal usage, the real understanding of words is always ultimately derived from active experience of those aspects of reality to which the words belong. The chemist or the physicist understands the meaning of his most abstract concepts ultimately on the basis of his acquaintance with chemical and physical processes in the laboratory. Even the pure mathematician, dealing with that most useless and arrogant branch of his learning, the theory of numbers, has probably had some experience of counting his pennies and shillings or his boots and buns. In short, there is no science whose conceptual, hence verbal, outfit is not ultimately derived from the practical handling of matter. I am laying considerable stress on this because, in one of my previous writings, I opposed civilised and scientific to primitive speech, and argued as if the theoretical uses of words in modern philosophic and scientific writing were completely detached from their pragmatic sources.[1] This was an error, and a serious error at that. Between the savage use of words and the most abstract and theoretical one there is only a difference of degree. Ultimately all the meaning of all words is derived from bodily experience.

I have purposely considered the pragmatic use of words on general evidence taken mainly from our own culture. If we turn to primitive speech we can easily exemplify its pragmatic function : words have to be uttered with impeccable correctness and understood in an absolutely adequate manner in those situations where speech is an indispensable adjunct to action. In my earlier article on this subject I used the example of a fishing expedition. A small fleet of canoes moving in concerted action is constantly directed and its movements co-ordinated by verbal utterance. Success or failure depends on correct speech. Not only must the observation of the scouts be correct, but they must give the correct cry. The meaning of the cry announcing a shoal of fish consists in the complete resetting of all the movements of the fleet. As a result of that verbal symbol the canoes rearrange themselves so that the nets can be cast properly and the shoal of fish driven into them, and constant verbal instructions pass from one canoe to another in the process. Each utterance is bound up with the technicalities of the pursuit and is based on the lifelong experience of all the members of a fishing team who from childhood have been trained into the craft.

Perhaps the first time that I was struck by this mysterious power of

[1] Appendix to *The Meaning of Meaning* (Ogden & Richards), pp. 466, 474.

speech, which, as by an invisible force, moves human beings, moves even bulky objects, and forms the connecting medium for co-ordinating action, was when in complete darkness I approached one of the lagoon villages in the Trobriands with a large fleet of canoes. There was no real danger in a wrong movement, except that, with the rapidly outgoing tide, a canoe might get stuck in the mud and have to remain there the whole night. We were being directed by the local natives from the shore and the effectiveness of the instructions given, the smooth and rapid way in which they were carried out led to our fleet getting quickly into the tidal creek through the intricate channels of approach. This had a most impressive effect on me. I knew how easy it was to miss the deep punting channel which forms the only fairway and how unpleasant it may become to be caught in the deep sticky mud of the shallow lagoon.

When during illness a group of people are keeping watch over a sick person and warding off the sorcerers of whom they are afraid, they will also keep communion by words. Each man in such a watch guards an approach to the village. They signal to each other from time to time to make sure that everyone is awake, and when some suspicious signs appear, they give the danger call. Voice is used as an effective mode of concerted action. In olden days at war, scouts and watchers communicated verbally, and passed on signals of safety, of alarm or of warning against possible danger.

In all such cases the direct effect of the word, uttered as an imperative, as an environmental direction or as technical advice, is clear. The meaning of a single utterance, which in such cases is often reduced to one word, can be defined as the change produced by this sound in the behaviour of people. It is the manner in which a sound appropriately uttered is correlated with spatial and temporal elements and with human bodily movements which constitutes its meaning; and this is due to cultural responses produced by drill, or "conditioning" or education. A word is the conditioning stimulus of human action and it becomes, as it were, a "grip" on things outside the reach of the speaker but within that of the hearers.

Is this definition of meaning merely "academic"? Decidedly not: it gives us more than a different philosophic attitude towards speech.[1]

---

[1] This is not the place to enter into critical disquisitions or to buttress the importance of my point of view by comparing it with that of others. But I should like to say that, as long as we define language as "the expression of thought by means of speech sound" (Henry Sweet, *Introduction to a History of Language*, Ch. I) or a "method of communicating ideas, emotions and desires by means of a system of voluntarily produced symbols" (Edward Sapir, *Language*, New York, 1921,

Our definition of meaning forces us to a new, a richer and wider type of observation. In order to show the meaning of words we must not merely give sound of utterance and equivalence of significance. We must above all give the pragmatic context in which they are uttered, the correlation of sound to context, to action and to technical apparatus; and incidentally, in a full linguistic description, it would be necessary also to show the types of cultural drill or conditioning or education by which words acquire meaning.

Turning directly to Trobriand gardening, let us ask what forms of pragmatic speech we meet there. In actual work utterances are not as important in agriculture as in some other forms of economic pursuit, such as fishing, sailing a canoe, collecting and hunting, the building of a house or the construction of craft, because what might be called concerted work, i.e. correlated team-work, is not essential in gardening. By concerted work I mean the performance of tasks which transcend the powers of one man, which have to be done by two or more people and in which verbal instructions passing between the workers are an indispensable ingredient of success. It is only in the erection of the large yam supports, in building an arbour and sometimes in the making of the fence that two or more people must co-operate and verbally communicate. Unfortunately, I have not noted down any actual texts of such speech, being unaware

p. 7); or, if we assume with one of the latest and most acute thinkers that "the essence of language is human activity—activity on the part of one individual to make himself understood by another, and activity on the part of that other to understand what was in the mind of the first" (O. Jespersen, *The Philosophy of Grammar*, 1924, p. 17), we should never be led to the study of context, nor to the study of associated actions which is essential if our analysis is right. As a matter of fact a careful perusal of Jespersen's *Philosophy of Grammar* or of Sapir's *Language* or of some older, and still influential, books, such as Wundt's *Sprache*, shows that the whole treatment of language up till recently has neglected the effective use of context of situation. Grammatical discussions on such fundamental problems as inner word-forms, the relation between word and sentence, and the whole problem of the empirical approach to spoken language in its relation to grammar and dictionary have greatly suffered in consequence. A point of view closely akin to the one here adopted has been set forth in an excellent monograph by Grace A. De Laguna, *Speech; its Function and Development*, 1927, who follows the lines indicated by John Dewey in *Experience and Nature* (1925) and G. H. Mead in numerous articles, and expounds a general theory of language from a moderate behaviouristic point of view. Professor De Laguna critically analyses the old point of view and gives a number of additional examples of unsatisfactory definitions of meaning which will be of interest to readers of the present pages. Markey's *Symbolic Process*, London, 1928, is a book written on excellent lines but unfortunately not very clear. Compare also my earlier articles on 'Classificatory Particles' in the *Bulletin of Oriental Studies*, Vol. II, 1921; and 'The Problem of Meaning in Primitive Languages' in *The Meaning of Meaning*, by C. K. Ogden and I. A. Richards, 1923.

of the great importance of this form of utterance when in the field. I have witnessed such work dozens of times and remember quite well that it is accompanied by such simple imperatives as 'lift it higher', 'grip it from underneath', 'move it hither', 'push it there', and so on. In co-operative work, when a number of people are engaged on the same or similar tasks, they will talk and co-ordinate their movements, stimulate each other by their presence and by a sort of competition. Here the conversation would often be about the progress of the work, and sentences or phrases of the type referred to above in Division IV might well be used.

It is much more in the planning, in the discussions which precede, accompany and follow the *kayaku*, in the exhortations of the magician and in the disputes which sometimes arise, especially during cutting, that the practical value of words comes to the fore.

The most important aspects of native agricultural speech, however, would be found in education. Here again I have unfortunately not noted down the actual wording of gardening instructions though I heard them being given time after time. But many of my 'definition texts' and items of ethnographic information, as given in native, are of the type of speech used by an experienced gardener to a youthful helpmate (cf. above, Div. V of this Part). As a matter of fact I was astonished by the fluency with which information texts on the meaning of words, on technical details, on the why, when and wherefore of magical ceremonies, were given to me. One day, after I had been discussing these matters with Gomila of Omarakana, I met this informant in the garden with his little daughter, Yona'i, and to my astonishment he repeated to her almost word for word some of the explanatory texts which he had given me the same morning.

At cutting, *takaywa*, small boys, each with a minute toy axe, amuse themselves by skirmishing about the outskirts of the main body of workers. The father or some elder boy will show them how to do the work and instruct them in word and activity alike. Incidentally it is interesting that the boys use stone implements whereas their elders have completely discarded them. This 'survival' is due in the first place, I should say, to the fact that the European trader has not yet had imagination enough to supply the natives with toy steel implements, so that the boys are reduced to the use of the old material. But there is also a distinct tendency, both in child and adult, to revert to the ancient material in games. For the native, though he appreciates the greater efficiency of steel, has not yet lost his craftsman's delight in the polished stone, which appears to him infinitely more valuable and beautiful. It is on such occasions that the boys would be taught such words as *ta'i*, 'to cut', *ta-si*, 'to lop off', *ko'umwari*, 'to break the branches'. Again at the clearing of the ground, *koumwala*, boys and girls play at constructing miniature squares or assist their elders and are given instruction by means of the vocabulary found below (Div. VI, § 6). Later on little children, armed with miniature digging-sticks, are shown how to break the ground at planting and place a yam in the right position. The growth of the roots underground is demonstrated with diagrams, and by exposition on an actual example. And here as elsewhere the intense interest in the right word and in verbal distinctions is very prominent.

Another feature, which any reader of this book may already have noticed in looking at the photographs, is the interest which the children take in magic. Often when the magician goes into the field accompanied by a bevy of young boys, or boys and girls, although sometimes the girls are not quite so welcome, this interest leads them to questions and they are answered very much in the manner in which I was answered (cf. Texts 36–78). Thus as a Trobriander grows into a *tokwaybagula*, 'perfect gardener', or the average approximation to that ideal, his technical ability develops side by side with his linguistic fluency, his ideas and beliefs about magic with his knowledge of the terms of magic, his ambitions and interests with the language of boasting, of praise and of criticism. And his intense appreciation of the value and beauty of the word seems to be present from the very beginning. Indeed it appears to me that it is in the study of juvenile and even infantile uses of words that we shall find the right approach to a real understanding of the nature of these. And this leads us to one more theoretical digression on infantile uses of words.

DIV. VI. THE SOURCES OF MEANING IN THE SPEECH OF INFANTS

In order to gain a clear insight into the nature of meaning we conjured up a number of dramatic incidents in which words became a matter of dead earnest because their correct utterance in the appropriate manner and with a successful grip on the hearers was the condition of safety, comfort or even existence.

Now we could ask whether there are any ordinary situations of speech within human life corresponding to this pattern and occurring normally and usually. I think there are. The use of inarticulate and later of articulate sounds by children correspond exactly to what we have been analysing in order to establish our concept of meaning. Children react to all bodily discomforts—hunger, dampness, painful position, and so on—with a variety of physical gestures, of which vocal expression is one. These sound reactions, the crying and gurgling of infants, are a natural equipment of the young organism. They are characteristic, in that different sounds emerge corresponding to the type of emotion experienced by the child, that is, on the whole to his need or desire. Again such expressions possess a direct significance for the adults surrounding the child, especially for the mother. These sounds usually set in motion some sort of activity on the part of his surrounding adults which cuts short the emotional upset by satisfying the need or removing the cause of pain and discomfort, or, by the cuddling and comforting of the child, gives it general satisfaction and sends it to sleep. Thus a small child acts on its surroundings by the emission of sound which is the expression of its bodily needs and is, at the same time, significant to the surrounding adults. The meaning of this utterance consists in the fact that it defines the child's wants and sets going a series of actions in his social environment, and finally brings about such environmental conditions as satisfy his need.

As inarticulate sounds pass into simple articulations, these at first refer to certain significant people, or else are vague indications of surrounding objects, above all of food, water, and favoured toys or animals. These words, as were the previous pre-articulate sounds, are especially important to the child when it needs help in order to relieve some sense of discomfort or satisfy some want. As soon as words form, however, they are also used for the expression of pleasure or excitement, or they are repeated in an aimless fashion, in the same way in which a child aimlessly exercises its limbs. But even at this early stage there is a clear distinction between the manner in which the child utters these words significantly and with a purpose, and the manner in which he repeats them just for the pleasure of the sound; and it is when the words are used in earnest that they mobilise the child's surroundings. Then the uttered word becomes a significant reaction adjusted to the situation, expressive of the inner state and intelligible to the human *milieu*.

So we see that the capacity for significant utterance is the very essence of welfare, of power, nay of action, at the earliest stages of human life. The physiologically determined responses of adults, especially of the parents, to the child's clamouring; the natural expressiveness of inarticulate sounds and of semi-articulate words, combine to make the child's speech as effective as if it were real magic. The child summons the mother, the nurse or the father, and this person appears (cf. Part VI, Div. V.). When it asks for food it is almost as if it uttered a magical incantation, a *Tischlein deck dich!* Early words in childhood are a means of expression and, more

important, an effective mode of action. The child lives in a world
of effective words. While to the adult words may in certain circumstances become real forces—in so far as their utterance is equivalent
to direct bodily action—to the child they normally are so. They give
him an essential hold on reality and provide him with an effective
means of moving, attracting or repulsing external objects, and of
producing changes in all that is relevant in his surroundings. This is
the experience in which the child is immersed, and we cannot be
astonished that such experience leaves an indelible mark on human
mentality. In all the child's experience words, when seriously
uttered, *mean* in so far as they act. The intellectual function of
words probably develops later, and develops as a by-product of the
pragmatic function.

As the child grows up this conviction as to the power of words
does not weaken. It essentially grows. In the first place, as we can
see in any type of technical or moral education, instruction in the
meaning of words and in manual or intellectual skill run parallel.
In primitive conditions where every member of the community has
to master most if not all manual and technical crafts and become a
man of the world as regards social intercourse and the arts of war and
peace, the parallelism between verbal and manual technique is even
closer. I have tried to show this as between verbal and manual
technique in agriculture. In the handling of any implement or utensil
the word which signifies it becomes as familiar as the object used.
In social intercourse, after the child has learned the names and
kinship appellations of the members of his own household and
family, he has gradually to learn how to address other members
of the village community and later of the tribe, and he learns his
duties and obligations to them in association with this often very
complex sociological terminology. His knowledge of magic and of
religion is usually imparted through more or less esoteric teaching,
in which the name of the supernatural beings, a spell, a story, are
strongly bound up with the ritual *mise-en-scène*. His early magical
attitude towards words, his infantile feeling that a name conjures
up a person, that a noun sufficiently often repeated can materialise
the thing—all this receives system and body in the magical dogma-
tism which he learns.

Thus the source of the magical attitude towards words is, if the
theory developed here is correct, to be found in the use of words
by infants and children—a view to which we shall return in Part VI.
Thence also start those profoundly pragmatic ways of learning how
to use the word by learning how to use its counterpart in the reality
of behaviour.

The above is a summary of a view of language which I have already developed elsewhere,[1] or rather of that part of the position there adopted from which I have moved but little. I should also like to add, firstly, that I have here summarised the unspecialised non-quantitative observations which I made at first hand on my own three children and, secondly, that I believe this problem will have to be studied in infantile speech if we are to arrive at the most important foundations for a science of semantics: I mean the problem of how far and through what mechanisms speech becomes to the child an active and effective force which leads him inevitably to the belief that words have a mystical hold on reality.

Div. VII. GAPS, GLUTS AND VAGARIES OF A NATIVE TERMINOLOGY

Throughout our analysis the intimate relation between language and culture has become more and more prominent; and we can now appreciate how unfounded and dangerous is the assumption that language simply mirrors reality. Even more dangerous is the fallacy of "one word—one idea—one piece of reality". And let me remind you that this fallacy is by no means the laid ghost of past anthropological errors. The whole discussion about the sociological relevance of kinship terminologies, for instance, is based on the view that "Nothing gives more insight into the intimate nature of social organisation than the mode of naming relatives".[2]

We could show how untenable is this view in an abstract way, by making the generalisation that terminological distinctions cannot, by the very nature of human speech, correspond, either adequately or exactly, to real distinctions. Therefore a purely formal terminological approach to any aspect of human culture must be futile.

But let us rather examine concrete instances. Among the

[1] Appendix to *The Meaning of Meaning* (Ogden and Richards), 1923.

[2] *Notes and Queries on Anthropology*, 5th ed., 1929, p. 66. In fact one of the most distinguished social anthropologists maintains that "the way in which . . . peoples of the world used their terms of relationship was conditioned and determined by the social relations which these terms denoted", and thus "demonstrate the close relation between the terminology of relationship and social institutions"; and "the details which distinguish different forms of the classificatory system from one another have been directly determined by the social institutions of those who use the systems" (W. H. R. Rivers, *Kinship and Social Organisation*, London, 1914, pp. 18 and 19). It is impossible in this brief compass to show the errors in this point of view, but to "correlate" kinship terms with kinship facts is based on the mistaken assumption that when there is one term for two people these two people must somehow be lumped together or telescoped or united in the mind of the native, or even that they must be one and the same person.

Trobrianders nothing is so important as gardening. If sociological reality were expressed adequately in native terms we would have expressions for 'agriculture', 'crops', and 'gardens'. But there is no single native term for any of these three key concepts. Again the natives are fully aware of the importance of 'work', 'effort', 'skill' in gardening. Are there any words for these? None. The concept of magical force pervades their whole tribal life, and nowhere is it so prominent as in gardening. Now since throughout Oceania we find the term *mana* or its equivalents, we might expect such a term in the Trobriands. But it does not exist. Are we then justified in assuming that these natives have no concept of magical force? Certainly not. They have the concept very clearly and its existence can be proved.

Let me add at once that all these concepts can be expressed indirectly—by circumlocutions, metaphorical extensions and a somewhat strained or compounded use of homonymous words; but specific terms corresponding to them are absent. 'Agriculture' can be indicated in a roundabout way by one of the several terms for 'garden', such as the word *bagula* (cf. Part V, Div. I, § 18); but *bagula* does not mean either 'garden' or 'agriculture'. The European concept 'agriculture' is invariably implied in native phraseology and not expressed. In the same way the term *kaulo* can be used so as to cover 'crops'. Furthermore, this same term *bagula* may at times express 'work' or even, through such compounds as *tokwaybagula*, 'excellence in gardening', whence we see it can be translated by implication by such words as 'effort' and 'skill'.

One of the prominent characteristics of the Trobriand language is the paucity of terms which stand for general concepts and the multiplicity of words which describe particular subdivisions. In the following part the reader will find long lists of names for varieties of the main crops. We have already spoken about the several expressions covering the term 'garden' (*buyagu, bagula, baleko, kaymata, kaymugwa, tapopu,* etc.), but on the other hand such general concepts as *valu,* 'village', 'place', 'home'; *pwaypwaya,* 'soil', 'land', 'terra firma', 'cultivable soil'; *towosi,* 'garden magician,' 'garden magic', 'specific system of garden magic'; *baleko,* 'unit of gardening', 'garden plot', 'garden as cultivated by one person', are characterised by a multiplicity of homonymous uses.

To us, however, the gaps in abstract concepts and the gluts in concrete words, together with other vagaries in terminology, do not present an insoluble puzzle, for analysis has shown us that native terminology is determined by the needs and interests of everyday life. Words are necessary for the instruction of the young in gardening; they are necessary in the planning of gardens, in preparatory arrangements for gardening and in the disputes which arise about the disposition of gardens. Words are especially necessary as a means of handling things. Therefore we may expect consistent and exact vocabularies for things which are constantly handled. And this is what we find in fact. There are exhaustive, consistent and empirically sound terminologies in the inventory of native implements and for the distinctions between the various yam supports. There is an intelligent analysis crystallised in an adequate terminology of the constituent parts of the fence. The terminology for botanical distinctions is not scientific, but from the practical point of view it is adequate. The main categories of useful and useless plants are differentiated; there is a rich vocabulary for cultivable vines and taro, and an extraordinary poverty of words for any kind of irrelevant plant. Thus the terminology is pragmatically sound: it closely corresponds to the practical interests and activities of the natives, and covers the parts, varieties and peculiarities of the cultivable plants which are manipulated in conjunction with their social and economic activities. Again the minute distinctions between the functional categories of crops—between the yams to be used as seed for the future harvest, those to be offered as a ceremonial gift, and those to be kept for the household—are necessary for the co-ordination of human activities, because the various categories must constantly be referred to in planning, calculating, boasting or criticism. Similarly the exhaustive terminology referring to the series of magical ceremonies and the consistent distinctions between the varieties of human work obviously have a high practical importance. Thus Trobriand terminology in its positive aspect is determined by actual needs, and the gaps in it are accounted for by the fact that a certain type of concept is never used. A general word, for instance, such as agriculture, has no place in the typical speech situation of the Trobrianders. Since everybody has gardens, good gardeners may be distinguished from indifferent ones; but it is impossible to speak about people who do not garden at all. For the same reason it is unnecessary to speak about gardens or gardening or gardeners in general.

These considerations lead us to two conclusions as regards method. In the first place a mere collectioneering of words does not exhaust the problem of terminology. It is as essential to record phrases and sentences as the verbal settings in which these occur. Above all it is essential to study a term in a variety of situational contexts in order to elicit its full meaning or, more correctly, its range of meanings.

In the second place, we have seen that many general concepts can be expressed indirectly—by implication or by circumlocution; therefore from this point of view also a mere collection of terms with attached meanings is insufficient. And this brings me to the further question: What 'meanings' do exist in any given aspect of native culture? By 'meaning' I understand a concept embodied in the behaviour of the natives, in their interests, or in their doctrines. Thus the concept of magical force, for instance, exists in the very way in which they handle their magic. I have insisted that every magical performance which we have described shows that, to the Trobriander, it is the production, transmission and location of magical force by means of spell and rite. Every magical ceremony is, in its essence, a handling of *mana*. The nearest word for this concept is *megwa*, which, *mutatis mutandis*, covers the meaning of our word 'magic'. Also, in a way which I shall discuss in Part V, they can compensate any deficiency in their vocabulary by extending the meaning of such terms as they possess. But the problem of ascertaining that, for instance, the concept of magical force is embodied in native behaviour and in their whole theoretical approach to magic; and then of ascertaining that they certainly have no term for this concept and can only vicariously express it—this, in spite of its negative quality, is the real problem of ethnographic linguistics.

This last point leads us back to the question of homonyms. We find that a great many of the essential words in the agricultural vocabulary of the Trobrianders are used with a multiplicity of meanings. *Pwaypwaya*, roughly 'land', 'soil', has been listed under six headings; *odila*, 'bush', 'jungle', under five; and *baleko* under three; while *bagula* is used in five and *buyagu* in four definitely distinguishable classes of meaning (cf. Part V, Div. I, § 31). How comes it that important words are made to function in all sorts of subsidiary ways? In my opinion this is by no means a particularly Melanesian or primitive phenomenon. It occurs in all languages and is, in English at least, as pronounced as in Kiriwinian. But the important point is, as I said above, that the failure to distinguish the various meanings in a homonym is one of the most fertile sources of anthropological error.

For it is characteristic of the Trobriand language that the more important the term, the more pronounced is the tendency to use it over a wide range of meanings. *Ka'i*, for example, means anything from 'tree', 'plant', 'vegetable', 'wood as material', 'shrub', 'magical herbs', 'leaves', 'stick' to the abstract concept 'made of wood' or 'long object'; in this latter sense it also functions as a classificatory formative. The words *megwa*, 'magic', *taytu*, 'yam', *kaulo*, 'crops', all correspond to capital concepts and are all used in a variety of meanings, some of which are remarkably far-fetched and figurative.

When a native sits plaiting a hunk of fibre in the village and is joined by a few others, who discuss what he is doing, there is no need to inform them that he is holding a hunk of fibre, or for them to refer to it in general terms. This is given by the context of the situation. There is, as a matter of fact, no term for 'hunk of fibre' or 'fibre' in Trobriand. But it is important to be able to indicate the material from which the hunk is made, because various kinds of fibre differ in method of handling, in quality and in the purpose for which they are used. He will, therefore, define the hunk either as 'pandanus' or 'ficus' or 'hibiscus', calling it by the same name as he would use for the whole plant, for its flowers or for its fruit. The distinctions made are those which are not contained in the context of situation, and only that which is not in the context is verbally stressed. In English, too, we use the words rose, jasmine or laurel for the plant and its blossom or leaf.

I chose here the example of a hunk of fibre because the verbal identification of its kind or species is particularly important: in the form of fibre, the source of the material is not easily distinguishable by the eye, but the distinction is extremely important as regards its use. In the same way when a magician pulverises 'coral boulder' or 'bush-hen mound' for his mixture he will name these substances, defining what is no longer obvious from the context. The word *kanakenuwa*, 'sand', is used for 'beach', in the same way in which in English we speak about 'the sands', 'the pitch' or 'the turf', or in which the ancient Romans spoke about the 'arena'. The extension of the word *taytu*, which primarily means the plant and then the food derived from it and the year in which the crops ripen, is another example. It would be a commonplace to state that it is wrong either to lump these meanings together in one confused category, or to look for far-fetched explanations of such verbal uses. Yet when it comes to words such as the Melanesian *mana* or primitive kinship terms, the ethnographer does not bother to investigate their various uses, or to find out whether these are definite homonyms, that is, different words with the same sound. He lumps the meanings together, and the arm-chair anthropologist evolves confusing sociological theories out of these confused data.[1]

[1] Usually such words have been represented as indicating one concept, and their variety of uses attributed to a vagueness or confusion in the native mind which lumps meanings together without distinction, or to pre-logical mentality, or to 'poverty of language'. Thus a misinterpreted observation has been crystallised by erroneous theory.

It is clear that the homonymous use of the same word in a variety of meanings is not due to confusion. In the examples adduced we can see that this apparent 'poverty of language' or 'misuse of words' fulfils a very definite function. When a Trobriand magician describes a pinch of powder as 'bush-hen mound' he does not create confusion. On the contrary, he introduces something familiar into an undefined situation. By using this word he tells us how, wherefrom and in what way he has produced his material (cf. M.F. 2 in Ch. II, Sec. 4). In this one word he also summarises an important element in Trobriand magical theory, that is, the sympathetic use of substances. He also perhaps reminds his listeners of one or two passages in his formulae. Thus, given the context of culture, in this example familiarity with magical formulae and performances, the use of the same sound with a different meaning contributes the one element which is lacking in the situation, and yet necessary for common work or common knowledge of what goes on.

The naming of the year after the most important object in the principal economic activity points to the same conclusion. The word *taytu* underlines the most crucial aspect of the sequence of the seasons, and its theoretical, emotional and even pragmatic value is clear.

At times the use of the same sound with different meanings implies even more. When the magician describes the fields chosen for next year's gardens as 'garden-site', meaning the future garden, this anticipatory lumping does not create confusion: the natives are well aware that the bush has not yet been cut on these. But this word, officially and ceremonially uttered at the *kayaku*, lays a legal stress on the relevant aspect which is not given in the situation. It declares "we have decided on using these and no other fields for next year's garden". In the analysis of magical formulae we shall see that when the magician addresses the soil as *buyagu*, 'garden-site', in his inaugurative magic (M.F. 2), when he affirms that the 'belly of the garden rises', 'swells', 'bursts forth with fertility', the metaphor which here defines the soil as a blossoming garden has a more than legal import. It is the essence of magic that, by the affirmation of a condition which is desired but not yet fulfilled, this condition is brought about (cf. Part VI, Div. V.). What might be called the creative metaphor of magic is at the bottom of a great deal of homonymous usage. In social flattery, in the designation of people by titles which are just a little above their rank, in the incorrect and flattering use of terms of affection or kinship, we have the same principle of verbal magic. The word claims more than actually exists, and thus places upon the person addressed certain obligations, or puts him under some sort of emotional constraint.

Examples of the same thing are frequent in what might be called Trobriand legal phraseology. The presentation of a gift is always accompanied by some verbal statement which anticipates the completion of the transaction as well and indicates its nature: 'thy valuable', 'thy visiting gift', 'thy tribute'. Such ritual phrases are both subtly flattering and imply a request for a reciprocal return, thus stressing what to the Trobriander is essential in this type of legal act, namely, that a gift puts the recipient under an obligation to the giver.

This point is so important that I will add one or two more examples. Take the word *pwaypwaya*, 'soil', 'ground', 'that on which we tread and on which we labour'. Why is the word used when the crew of a benighted or strayed canoe sight terra firma? Why do they use a familiar word rather than a specific term with a meaning such as 'terra firma', or 'distant shore', or 'land and not sea'? Thus posed, the question answers itself: because they want to convey, not a fine abstract shade of meaning, but just the fact of fortunate, joyful familiarity. The crew have been in distress, hungry and thirsty, frightened of the possibility of drifting astray; they hail that which means safety and comfort by the name which is fraught with the emotional associations of 'land', 'soil', 'ground on which we usually tread'. A new word would create confusion and strain, and would be an act of pedantry incompatible with the degree of emotional stress. The word already well familiar brings intellectual and emotional satisfaction and creates also the necessary pragmatic response.[1]

The word for 'village', *valu*, designates primarily that special portion of the earth which is the most relevant and most familiar to every Trobriand native. It is obvious to us now why it is extended to mean 'place' in the abstract, and 'home', with all the emotional sociological implications of that term.

There is no abstract word for 'stone'. A coral stone, a rock, the material of which it is composed are all designated by the term *dakuna*. The natives do not lump these meanings together; but dead coral is the most familiar of this group of objects and, as it is little used for practical or technical purposes, anything made of it can thus be described without confusion. The word for stones of plutonic origin imported from the South is *binabina*. *Binabina*

---

[1] The reader who is not intelligent enough to see that here, once again, I discuss the nature of homonym, metaphor and drive to meaning in general, and not a freakish feature of Trobriand or 'savage' vernacular, will not profit by a reminder. The intelligent one does not need it, but there are always intermediate cases— *verb. sat.*

covers rocks of various types and composition, stressing only their alien origin and the non-coral character of their substance; for the significant characteristic of these is that they are not procurable in the Trobriands, but in the d'Entrecasteaux Archipelago. They are not more exactly specified because they do not play a very important part in Trobriand technology, but are mainly used for certain magical purposes, especially in the *vilamalia* magic (cf. Ch. VII, Sec. 1). In the word *kema, utukema,* on the other hand, the material is stressed—the word being applicable to all objects made of the volcanic tuff out of which the stone implements were made in the olden days. Here the word covers the rock in the mass, chips or lumps detached from it, the implement made out of it in process of manufacture, the finished blade, and the axe ready for use. This variety of meanings does not create confusion when the word is used within a well-defined context. When we speak about a man swinging an axe or cutting with it, it is obvious that he is not swinging a rock or a chip or a lump. Still less is there any confusion when the word is used within a pragmatic context. On the other hand, the similarity of the term introduces the necessary unity and gives the familiar element within the situation.

Our conclusion is then that homonymous extensions of meaning and the multiplicity of uses of each word are not due to any negative phenomenon, such as mental confusion, poverty of language, wanton or careless usage. On the contrary, homonyms add a great deal to the efficiency of language. They emphasise the familiar, or the practically important; they foreshadow legal duties and reciprocities; in the creative metaphor of magic they evoke the desired object or event.

This shows us that, in order to define a sound, we must discover, by careful scrutiny of verbal contexts, in how many distinguishable meanings it is used. Meaning is not something which abides within a sound; it exists in the sound's relation to the context. Hence if a word is used in a different context it cannot have the same meaning; it ceases to be one word and becomes two or more semantically distinguishable units.

We have therefore to index the meanings of native terms quite as carefully as is done in any good English dictionary. If possible it is important to indicate which is probably the primary and fundamental meaning and to establish the relations between this fundamental meaning and its extensions.

I think that, theoretically, the more resolutely we face this problem of homonymous and metaphorical extensions, the clearer we shall be about the magical use of words, the part played by general concepts in primitive mentality and the nature of words in their intellectual, emotional and pragmatic rôle.

Summary of Part IV:—

Why have I given this long theoretical introduction? I wanted to make clear my method of presentation and justify it. I also wanted to bring out fully the theoretical value of my material.

As to the method of presentation, I think that roundabout and explicit descriptions give a better picture of the language than a succinct and bald collection of texts with commentaries, vocabularies and grammatical notes.

. Incidentally we have been able to elicit the following principles and practical rules:

(1) The inadequacy of translating words by equating them to English equivalents and the purely provisional character of the employment of English words as mnemonic counters;

(2) We tried to show definitely that the lumping of homonyms as one word is incorrect and that to index the meanings of these is both feasible and indispensable;

(3) We made an onslaught on the idea that native terminologies represent native mental categories. It is always necessary to show where terminological distinctions are full and adequate and where they are entirely misleading;

(4) It is in the multiple uses of general terms and in the hypertrophy of concrete expressions that the greatest difficulty lies. We gave a theoretical explanation of this phenomenon and adduced a certain amount of material to back up our theoretical views;

(5) The contextualising of texts, phrases and words, the description of where such words occur and how they are used, has been a constant feature of our analysis.

But it is the insistent linking up of ethnographic descriptions with linguistic analysis which provides language with its cultural context and culture with its linguistic reinterpretation. Within this latter we have continually striven to link up grammar with the context of situation and with the context of culture. Here the distinctions between pragmatic speech, educational speech, legal and ceremonial utterances, narrative and pure gossip appears to me to furnish us with certain concepts and principles which ought to be more fully used in ethnographic work.

All this has enabled us theoretically to give and justify a definition of meaning of such concepts as 'context of situation' and the 'pragmatic reality of speech'—concepts which I have developed previously, but which the present material allows me more fully to vindicate.

I am aware that in many ways this linguistic analysis may be difficult to master as it has been difficult to compose. But theory without material is sterile and material without theory is not illuminating. And since on many points I had to struggle for a new method in my own mind and fight for it against potential misunderstanding, I should like to claim that the effort expended on the reading, and perhaps on the writing, of this part has not been altogether wasted.

PART V

CORPUS INSCRIPTIONUM AGRICULTURAE QUIRIVINIENSIS;

or

THE LANGUAGE OF GARDENS

NOTE

WITH regard to the transliteration of the texts which follow, I had to train my ear while in the field to respond to Melanesian sounds, and make a number of phonetic decisions. On the whole this was not very difficult, and for various reasons I have decided not to go beyond the elementary rules laid down by the Royal Geographical Society and the Royal Anthropological Institute of Great Britain: the vowels I have treated as they are used in Italian, Spanish, or Polish; the consonants are represented as in English.

The only difficulty I found was in the fact that *r* and *l* are interchangeable; or perhaps it might be more correct to say that the Melanesians have one sound which is a mixture of *r* and *l*, and to us sometimes appears more like an *r* and sometimes more like a clear *l*. Again the sound represented by the combined *l/r* in the North (Kiriwinian dialect) is very often represented by an *n* in the South (Sinaketan dialect). And this is further confused by the fact that the Sinaketans at times adopt the northern forms and vice versa. I adhered to the rule of writing down the sound as I heard it, and have here retained the most usual spellings found in my notes. An alternative method would have been to represent all the three sounds by the same consonant. But I think my system introduces no difficulties or confusion and it is more instructive since it shows the manifold reactions of a European to Melanesian sounds.

I must confess that, looking back on my linguistic observations, I am by no means certain that my phonetic distinctions go as far as they ought to, and I very often find in my notes two or even three transliterations of the same word. This obtains only with vowels, notably with final vowels, and mostly refers to the distinction between the *a* and the *o* sounds. But I should like to say that the natives always understood me perfectly. There are actual differences in native utterances, especially when they speak quickly and slur the vowels; and phonetic pedantry, especially when phonetics has no function in discriminating between meanings, seems to me unprofitable.

The apostrophe: the natives sometimes allow two vowels to merge into a diphthong and sometimes pronounce them independently, though there is no glottal stop between them. I have used the apostrophe to indicate that two vowels ought to be broken up.

The hyphen: this should be disregarded phonetically. It indicates certain grammatical distinctions which are fully discussed in Part IV (Div. III, B and C). The possessive suffix *-la*, however, is a special case and I have adopted the following convention with regard to it. Where a noun can be used alone or with -*la*, I shall indicate this by bracket and hyphen; e.g. *kaynavari*(-*la*). Where words are never used save in the possessive form I shall employ the hyphen only; e.g. *tama-la*. Words which are never used without the final -*la* will not be hyphened, as it is impossible to decide whether the -*la* is part of the root or a possessive, as, e.g., *u'ula*. The only criterion which can be used in the case of the parts of a plant to decide whether the final -*la*, is a suffix is found in certain magical formulae where the plant is addressed in the second person and its parts are used with the final -*m*; e.g. in Formula 17 we find *yagava-m taytu*, etc. Where a word changes its form when the possessive suffix is added both forms will be adduced; e.g. *kanawine-* (or *kaniwine-*)*la*.

Punctuation: I have followed the same rules as I would adopt in any language. Full stops mark the end of self-contained sentences; semicolons are used whenever co-ordinate and obviously dependent clauses are linked up into a bigger sentence. A comma indicates a subordinate clause or parenthesis, or the need for a slight pause; a dash or colon, a parenthesis, or a long pause marking a break or preceding an enumeration. Paragraphing follows a change of subject, which was usually marked by a longer pause in the discourse.

Abbreviations: I have made use of the following abbreviations in texts:—

e.d.—Verbal pronominal prefix of exclusive dual, e.g. *ka-sisu*, 'we two (that is, I and he, excluding person addressed) sit'.

i.d.—Verbal pronominal prefix of inclusive dual, e.g. *ta-sisu*, 'we two (that is, you and I) sit'.

e.p.—Verbal pronominal prefix, used in combination with the suffix -*si*, of exclusive plural, e.g. *ka-sisu-si*, 'we (excluding person addressed) sit'.

i.p.—Verbal pronominal prefix, used in combination with the suffix -*si*, of inclusive plural, e.g. *ta-sisu-si*, 'we (including person addressed) sit'.

n.—Noun.
v.—Verb.
m.—Man.
f.—Female.

r.b.—Round bulky (thing).
l.f.—Leafy flat (thing).
w.l.—Wooden long (thing).

These conventional signs are not used with any pedantic consistency. It is sufficient for the ordinary reader to be made aware that such distinctions exist and to give him examples of how they are used. The linguist, on the other hand, will soon learn to identify the function of *ka-* or *ta-*. Also he is advised to consult my article on "Classificatory Particles in the Language of Kiriwina" (*Bulletin of Oriental Studies*, Part IV, 1921), where a full list of these will be found.

LAND AND GARDENS

1. The most fundamental terminological distinction to be found here is that referring to 'soil', 'land' or 'habitat', on the one hand, and to 'sea', on the other. The natives define the first by the noun *pwaypwaya*, 'earth', 'ground', 'terra firma', and the other by *bwarita*, 'sea'. The term *pwaypwaya* would be used in this sense at sea to define a distant vague form as being a piece of land and not a reef or cloudbank. In description or information the natives would say:—

T. 1. *Bayse   valu   i-ka'ita   pwaypwaya,   i-sisu   bwarita.*
this here   village   he return   soil   he sit   sea

This means that 'at that spot, the land comes back (ends) and there remains the sea'. But this distinction is only distantly connected with gardening, so we cannot dwell on it.

2. Another important opposition of a general character is that between *valu*, 'village', 'place of human habitation', and *odila*, which is used for 'space outside habitation', 'land covered with vegetation', 'bush', 'jungle'. But the word *valu*, on the one hand, is used in a more general sense for 'place', 'spot'; and *odila*, on the other, in the narrower sense of 'the low, periodically cut vegetation which grows on cultivable soil lying fallow'. Thus the natives will describe any spot or place as *bayse valu*, 'this particular place'; and will oppose to *odila*, 'low bush', a number of terms designating other aspects of the jungle: *boma* or *kaboma*, 'sacred grove', *weyka*, 'village grove', and *rayboag*, 'wooded coral ridge'. The words *valu* and *odila*, used contextually and in opposition, mean 'inhabited land' and 'uninhabited land' respectively. Here, as in many other expressions, opposition plays an important part in definition. The noun *odila* is most frequently heard in the adverbial combination *o la odila*, 'in the bush', meaning 'outside the village', 'in the wilderness'; or, in certain contexts, 'outside the garden enclosure', 'in the low, periodically cut scrub'.

3. Again *pwaypwaya*, 'soil' or 'land', would be subdivided into *dakuna*, 'stony soil', 'rock'; *kanakenuwa*, 'sand'; *pasa*, 'brackish mud'; *podidiweta*, 'ooze'—all of which are uncultivable ground—and *pwaypwaya* in the narrow sense of 'cultivable soil'. In the latter sense *pwaypwaya* is opposed to any of the terms just enumerated (cf. Ch. I, Sec. 8). When I enquired directly whether there was any general term for soil on which nothing will grow, I was given two words, *sagala* and *rasarasa*, which were used in such adjectival phrases as *pwaypwaya sagala*, *pwaypwaya rasarasa*, 'barren soil', 'waste land'; but I never heard these two terms used spontaneously in a spoken context. The word *sagala* is probably a compound of *sa-*, from *sapwo*, *sopu*, 'to plant', and *gala*, 'no': 'non-plantable soil'.

4. In concrete expressions, especially when these are used as complementary or mutually exclusive terms, we find a greater definiteness in words. During a cross-country walk, such as the one described in Chapter I, Section 3, we would be informed by the natives as we pass from one type of country to another that we are now in the *valu*, 'village', now in the *weyka*, 'village grove', or *olilagala valu*, 'the surroundings of the village'. The difference between these two almost synonymous expressions is that *weyka* signifies 'the trees of the grove', 'the vegetation', and *olilagala valu* 'the site surrounding the village' which is covered with trees and rank undergrowth. The term *olilagala valu*, 'surroundings of village', is confusingly similar to *o lilaguwa valu*, 'the street running between the inner and outer ring of buildings'.

5. The 'soil of a village' has a special term, *bidivalu*, a compound of the root *bida*, which also means 'sod', 'piece of ground', and *valu*, 'village'. The soil round the village, which is usually fertile because Kiriwinian villages are generally made on such soil, is called *bidubwabwa'u*, 'black soil', in a sense synonymous with *galaluwa* (cf. § 11). This word would not be used in connexion with villages built on stony ground, such as some of the coastal villages on the western or northern seaboard, or of the villages near the *rayboag*, such as some of the southern villages, or of villages such as Wawela, which lies on the eastern side on the sandy soil of the shore.

6. As we enter the bush, the low scrub periodically cut, we are told: *bayse odila*, 'this is the bush'. An uncut piece of jungle comes in sight, which from a distance looks very much like a *weyka*, 'village grove', and we learn that this is a 'sacred grove', *boma* or *kaboma*, two synonymous words, *ka-* being merely the formative prefix (equivalent to *kay-*, cf. § 13) corresponding to 'wood', 'trees'. The word *kaboma* incidentally has another meaning, that of 'wooden dish'. 'A sacred grove' might also be described by the word *kapopu*, 'uncut forest', because there is no uncut forest on the level land of the Trobriands except round the villages and on spots tabooed by their mythological associations. While the words *boma* and *kaboma* are synonymous with each other, they are not so with *kapopu*, for this word is used sometimes even to describe the *weyka*, 'village grove', or the patches of low scrub within a garden enclosure which have not yet been cut because of the remissness of the owners (cf. Ch. II, Sec. 5).

7. We pass a swamp, a marshy part of the country, and hear that it is *dumya*. From there we come out on the coral ridge, which runs along the western shore from the village of Kavataria, all round the north and down the whole of the eastern coast to the extreme south at an average distance of about half a mile from the beach, sometimes approaching the edge of the water, sometimes receding. This is the *rayboag*, of which we have so often heard in the narrative. In the *rayboag* we are shown deep holes, *uweya*, filled with humus, or shallower ones, *kito'u*, or fairly wide stretches of soil called *waykepila*.

8. Descending from the *rayboag* to the *momola*, 'seashore', flat ground stretching down to the edge of the sea and partly under cultivation, we enter groves of coconut and betel-nut, banana, bread-fruit and mango. The *momola* joins the *kanakenuwa*, 'beach', also the word for 'sand' (see § 3). Walking along the seashore we come, from time to time, upon a beach used for bathing, where a few canoes are usually drawn up, and there is also perhaps a large boathouse harbouring a sea-going canoe, with beside it a few small huts and shelters. This is a *kwadewo*, 'stretch of sand used for bathing, starting on fishing expeditions, and the beaching of canoes'. Were we to walk round the whole island we would find that on the western, that is on the lagoon, side there is a *pasa*, 'mangrove swamp', between the *rayboag* and the sea, interrupted from time to time by a *kovalawa*, 'sandy beach between mangroves', where we almost invariably find a village. We should be informed that the open sea on the East and North is *lumata*. The adverbial expressions *wa lum*, 'in the open sea', and *wa dom*, 'in the lagoon', also define important topographical concepts.

9. Each of these nouns is very clearly defined and consistently used within the context of a topographical survey or a native narrative describing the various parts of the Trobriand landscape. But some of the terms have also, as we have said, a wider sense, which becomes almost abstract in, for instance, *valu* for 'place', *odila* for 'uninhabited land', *pwaypwaya* for 'terra firma'. Again, *boma*, literally 'taboo', can contextually mean 'uncut grove' or any of the numerous ideas connected with taboo, some of which we shall meet in Division VII. The abstract meanings are always based on a metaphorical extension (cf. Part. IV, Div. VII).

10. The term *pwaypwaya* means 'cultivable soil', 'soil under cultivation', as opposed to 'stone', 'sand', 'mud'. This meaning gives rise to another concept, for it implies 'soil economically used and legally appropriated'. The word *pwaypwaya* figures in this last meaning in such expressions as *tolipwaypwaya*, 'owner of the cultivable land', 'citizen-owner of such and such a village'; *da pwaypwaya-si*, 'our soil', meaning 'the soil belonging to a community'; *i-woye da pwaypwaya*, 'he strikes our soil', with reference to the garden magician (cf. Ch. XII, Sec. 4; see also Div. VII, § 15).

11. *Pwaypwaya*, 'cultivable land', is classified into a number of kinds, each correlated with certain crops and certain types of garden (cf. Ch. I, Sec. 8). *Galaluwa*, 'black, heavy soil', dry and perhaps best for cultivation, suitable for all crops; *butuma*, 'red light soil', found mainly near the coral ridge, not suitable for taro but excellent for all varieties of yam in a year of good rainfall; *kawala*, 'black soil near *rayboag*', very fertile and suitable for most crops, found on the inland side of the *rayboag*; *dumya*, 'greasy, swampy soil', in dry seasons good for taro, never suitable for yams, and in specially wet years useless; *sawewo*, 'earth found in the holes of the *rayboag* and on the approaches to it from inland and from the *momola*', specially suitable for the *kuvi*, 'large yams'; *mo'a*, 'dry light soil near the *rayboag*'; *malala*, 'poor stony soil', unsuitable for taro, good for hardy yams and taytu; *kwaydikudakuna*, 'very stony soil', found on the north-western side near the *rayboag*, on which some crops can be planted. This last word is obviously a reduplicated prefixed form derived from *dakuna*, 'stone'. Of all the words for varieties of soil, only the word just analysed is derived from another, and only the word *dumya* has another meaning.

12. I have already mentioned briefly the forms of ground which are unsuitable for planting: *podidiweta*, 'ooze', *kanakenuwa*, 'sand', *pasa*, 'brackish mud', and *dakuna*, 'stones' or 'rock'. Within *dakuna*, distinctions are made between *vatu*, 'boulder attached to the bed-rock', *rayboag*, 'big rock', and *kaybu'a*, 'round boulder'. It must be stated that the noun *dakuna* applies only to 'dead coral', the volcanic and plutonic stones imported from other islands having different designations, *binabina* (cf. Ch. VII, Sec. 1) and *utukema* (cf. below, Div. VI, §§ 5 and 6).

13. The term *pwaypwaya* in the sense of 'economically appro-priated land' is defined by the fact that only on *pwaypwaya* are gardens made, and any ground on which gardens are made is *pwaypwaya*. Such soil is parcelled out into large portions of unequal size, *kwabila*, 'field' or 'garden portion'. Each *kwabila* again is sub-divided into *baleko*, smaller 'plots' (cf. Ch. II, Sec. 3). The word *kwabila* governs the classificatory particle *kubila-*. Thus *kubila-tala*, 'one field', *kubilay-yu*, 'two fields', etc.; *kubila-viyaka*, 'large field'. *Baleko* and all other designations of land types govern the particle *kway-*; while *weyka*, *boma* and *odila* would have *kay-*, which is used with all words which designate plants or agglomerations of plants.

14. The division of cultivable and economically appropriated land into *kwabila* and *baleko* is permanent: the boundaries of the *kwabila*, 'large portions' or 'fields', are called *karige'i*, and of the *baleko*, 'small plots', *tukulumwala* (var. *tokulumwala*). Such boundaries are indicated by long stone heaps and other landmarks, which remain in position while the soil lies fallow. Economically each *kwabila* is apportioned to one community, and each community owns a number of *kwabila* surrounding it. The title *tolikwabila*, 'master of field', is vested in the head-man; that of *tolibaleko*, 'master of a garden plot', in the individual members of the community (cf. Ch. XII, Secs. 1 and 4). During the *kayaku*, 'council', in this context 'council for garden affairs' (cf. Div. V, §§ 17–24), decisions are made as to which field or fields are to be tilled in that year; and plots are *nigada*, 'asked for', and allotted to each gardener (cf. Ch. XII, Sec. 4).

15. The division into *kwabila* and *baleko* obtains only with regard to *odila* in the narrower sense of 'cultivable land'. The *dumya*, 'swamp', is only roughly divided into fields since it is not very easy to impose permanent boundaries on swampy soil. In certain contexts *baleko* and *odila*, in the sense of 'economically divided land' and 'cultivable bush', are interchangeable. As one of my informants volunteered, *o baleko, bwoyna, o la odila*: 'in plot, well, in cultivable bush'. In free translation: 'soil divided into garden plots, well, this is the same as cultivable bush'. The *momola*, 'seashore', is divided only into *kwabila*, 'fields'. In the *rayboag* the holes (cf. above, § 7) with cultivable soil are owned individually.

16. A new terminology comes into being as soon as land is chosen for cultivation. The portion ear-marked then becomes *buyagu*, 'garden-site', 'garden enclosure', 'land under cultivation at a given season', 'land intended for cultivation', 'all the land within the common enclosure'. In his spells the magician will refer to it as *lopou-la ula buyagu*, 'the belly of my garden' (cf. M.F. 2, Part VII), 'the soil of my garden and the crops therein contained'.

17. The *buyagu* is encircled by a *kali*, 'fence', and even before that it is marked off by the *la kali keda* or *kuduwaga*, 'boundary belt', which is cut at the inaugural rite (cf. Ch. II, Sec. 3; Ch. III, Sec. 3). As soon as this is cut, *buyagu*, 'garden-site', becomes opposed to *odila*, 'bush', 'all the land outside', also called *yosewo*, 'uncut bush outside the garden-site'. This latter term is capable of metaphorical extension to all that is useless and lifeless, that has been given up or thrown on the rubbish heap. Thus, a native explaining that the essence of personality lies in the human spirit, *baloma*, and that after death the body remains as a useless corpse, will say that "at death the soul departs; what remains is *yosewo*". The 'uncut scrub outside' is also at times called *kapopu*, though this term is also applied (§ 6) to patches of scrub as yet uncut within the garden-site and to the uncut jungle of the tabooed groves. The natives have a special term for 'fallow ground', *kaulaka*, which can be also used adjectivally, and verbally 'to lie fallow'.

18. The term *buyagu*, however, is not the most important word to describe 'garden'; it cannot be used as a verb and it does not designate the garden as actually worked. The main term for garden is *bagula*.

19. The term *baleko*, 'plot', is often extended in the general sense of 'gardens under cultivation'. It is more specifically used when a man refers to his own private garden plot, the one which he cultivates himself. Obviously he never cultivates the whole *buyagu*, and by using the term *baleko* he specifies that part on which he himself is working. The term *kwabila* is never used with reference to gardens under cultivation; it is merely a term of measurement and land tenure.

20. There exist, therefore, three terms corresponding to the English word 'garden', each of which has a fairly general meaning and wide connotation. The best way to distinguish them is to realise that *buyagu* means, in the first place, 'the enclosed garden-site', hence 'garden' in general as opposed to *odila* and *yosewo*. *Bagula* has a more dynamic and at the same time more personal meaning: it is the 'garden under cultivation', 'the garden as husbanded by one person'. Thus *ulo buyagu* will be used by the garden magician who is concerned with the gardens of the community as a whole. *Ula bagula* will be used by the individual who wants to speak of his own cultivated plots in the sense 'garden which I am working'. *Baleko* is very much used in this last sense also, that is 'garden which I am working', and in this sense is almost synonymous with *bagula* (cf. Ch. II, Sec. 3).

21. I received three very good definition texts from Navavile of Oburaku:—

T. 2.
Ta-takaywa	*odila;*	*bi-sisu*	*yosewo,*	*i-tokay*
we (i.d.) clear	bush	he might sit	uncut bush	he stand up

buyagu;	*ta-toto*	*o*	*kuduwaga;*	*ma-kabula-na*
garden-site	we (i.d.) stand	in	boundary-belt	this end

yosewo,	*ma-kabula-na*	*buyagu.*
uncut bush	this end	garden-site

FREE TRANSLATION: When we clear the bush there remains the

uncut scrub, there comes into being the garden-site. When we stand on the boundary-belt, on the one side (we have) the uncut bush, on the other the garden-site.

22. This text shows well the usage and meaning of the nouns *yosewo* and *buyagu* as terms of opposition. The next text defines the relationship of the terms *bagula* and *buyagu*:—

T. 3. *I-tuwali*   *tayta*   *la*   *bagula,*   *i-tuwali*   *tayta*
he different   one man   his   garden   he different   one man

     la   *bagula;*   *buyagu*   *kumaydona.*
     his   garden   garden-site   all

FREE TRANSLATION: One man's garden is distinct from that of another man, (but) the garden-site (the garden as a whole) (belongs to) all.

23. The most illuminating text, however, is the following one:—

T. 4. *I-kalobusi-si*   *mitawosi*   *o*   *buyagu,*   *i-katupwo'i-se:*
they arrive   visitors   in   garden-site   they ask

     "*Avayle*   *la*   *buyagu?*"   "*O,*   *ma-tau-na*   *towosi.*"
     who   his   garden-site   O   this man   garden magician

     "*Avayta'u*   *ma-kway-na*   *bagula?*"   "*O,*   *ma-tau-na,*
     which man   this   garden   O   this man

     bi-bagula   *la*   *baleko.*"
     he might garden   his   plot

FREE TRANSLATION: When visitors arrive at a garden, they ask: "Whose garden enclosure is it?" "Oh, such and such is the garden magician." "Whose is this garden?" "Oh, such and such, he gardens his plot."

24. In this text we have a clear use of the three terms *buyagu*, *bagula* and *baleko*. The first is clearly defined as the whole garden, assigned to a garden magician and 'belonging' to him. The term *bagula* is defined by its verbal use, and above all by its opposition to *buyagu*. The word *baleko* is defined as 'the plot', 'that portion of soil on which a garden is made', 'that which is cultivated'.

25. In M.F. 1, v. 3 (Part VII) we find the sentence:—

T. 5. *Nabwoye*   *ta-sunini*   *da-buyagu.*
to-morrow   we (i.d.) penetrate   our garden-site

Here the magician, speaking of the selected garden-site, describes it by the term *buyagu* with the prefixed possessive of inclusive plural: 'our garden-site', that is, 'the garden-site of the whole community'.

26. In M.F. 2, v. 3, he uses the key-words *lopou-la ulo buyagu*, repeating it with a number of verbs. Here the term *buyagu* is used in the first place as 'the garden in so far as it belongs to the garden magician'. Hence *ulo buyagu,* 'my garden'. It is also used in the very general sense of 'garden as workshop of fertility'. Probably in ordinary speech the term *bagula* would be used in this latter sense.

27. Types of garden are pretty closely distinguished in native terminology. We have the gardens of mixed crops—*kaymugwa,* 'early gardens', and *kaymata,* 'main gardens' (cf. Ch. II, Sec. 2)—in opposition to *tapopu,* 'taro garden' (cf. Ch. X, Sec. 2). *Tapopu* is exclusively devoted to taro : *uriwokwo,* 'taro it is finished', meaning 'taro exhausts all that is planted in such a garden', 'taro only', 'taro exclusively'. The etymology of *kaymugwa* and *kaymata* is somewhat difficult to trace with certainty. *Kaymata,* 'main garden', is a compound of *kay-,* classificatory formative of all wooden and woody things, and *mata.* Here *mata* may mean 'eye', in which case it would signify 'the foremost garden', 'the front garden', in opposition to *kaymugwa,* 'the old, pristine garden'. *Mugwa* can have only one derivation, 'accomplished', 'already established' or 'finished'. The *kaymugwa* is planted first, therefore, though 'earlier' it is also 'later', 'at a later state', 'more advanced', because, at the time when the *kaymata* is planted, the *kaymugwa* is already in full swing. *Mata* could of course also be the word for 'dead', 'asleep', 'lazy', 'slow', meaning here perhaps 'the gardens which ripen later', therefore more slowly. Again *mamata,* 'to wake up', might give us 'wide awake', 'main' garden, but I think the interpretation of *mata,* 'eye', is the most plausible.

28. *Kasisuwa* is the name for some of the gardens on the *momola,* made by the eastern villagers of the South part of the island (Ch. X, Sec. 5).

29. *Ligabe* is the term for 'garden during harvest', 'deserted garden-site', which has not yet become bush (cf. Ch. V, Sec. 5).

30. All the nouns descriptive of the various kinds of garden take the classificatory particle *kay-.* The same element *kay-* appears also as a formative in the words *kaymata* and *kaymugwa.* The prefixed formative *ka-,* as in *kasisuwa,* or *kaboma,* is derived from *kay-.*

31. We can now index the principal words analysed in this Division. (For the importance of indexing homonyms cf. Part IV, Div. III, A.)

    1. *bagula*   1. 'garden under cultivation'.
                        2. 'garden'.
                        3. 'individual garden'.
                        4. 'to garden', 'to cultivate'.
                        5. 'cultivated'.
                        6. 'to be an agricultural community' (verb; cf. Div. V, § 1).
                        7. 'workshop of fertility' (= *buyagu*).

2. *baleko*   1. 'garden plot'.
    2. 'individual garden'.
    3. 'garden under cultivation'.

3. *boma*   1. 'taboo'.
    2. 'sacred grove'.
    3. 'war magic'.

4. *buyagu*   1. 'garden site'.
    2. 'land intended for cultivation'.
    3. 'garden as a whole'.
    4. 'workshop of fertility' (magical use, cf. Part VII, M.F. 2).

5. *dakuna*   1. 'stone'.
    2. 'material of dead coral'.
    3. 'coral rock'.
    4. 'stony soil'.
    5. 'rock' in general.

6. *kaboma* = *boma* (2).

7. *kaboma* = 'wooden dish'.

8. *kanakenuwa* 1. 'sand'.
    2. 'beach'.

9. *kapopu*   1. 'uncut scrub'.
    2. 'uncut garden patch'.
    3. 'uncut forest'.
    4. 'sacred grove'.

10. *odila*   1. 'low bush'.
    2. 'cultivable soil'.
    3. 'economically divided land'
    4. 'uncut bush'.
    5. 'wild' (adj.).

11. *pasa*   1. 'brackish mud'.
    2. 'mangrove swamp'.

12. *pwaypwaya* 1. 'soil', 'earth'.
    2. 'cultivable soil'.
    3. 'terra firma'.
    4. 'floor', 'bottom'.
    5. 'economically appropriated land'
    6. 'magically amenable soil'.

13. *valu*   1. 'village', 'place of human habitation'.
    2. 'particular place', 'spot'.
    3. 'own village', 'home'.

14. *yosewo*   1. 'uncut scrub'.
    2. 'anything useless or lifeless'

THE CROPS

1. There is no abstract name to designate 'garden produce' or to represent the idea of 'crops' (cf. Part IV, Div. VII). There are a number of expressions which enable the native clearly to distinguish in linguistic usage between those plants which he grows in his garden, on which he is dependent and round which a great deal of his life interests are centred, together with certain wild plants, and the undifferentiated rest of the vegetable world and from one another.

2. Perhaps the most general noun referring to the vegetable kingdom is *ka'i*, 'plant', 'tree', 'shrub', 'wood', 'stick', 'magical leaves'. This word furnishes also the classificatory particle *kay-*, used in connexion with all plants, all things made of wood, all things which are long and thin, or which are thought of as implements. In a narrower sense the word *ka'i* means 'tree' as opposed to *munumunu*, 'weed', and *wotunu*, 'creeper'. *Munumunu* is any plant which is neither a tree nor a creeper; a plant, that is, which has no woody stem and which does not wind round a support or creep along the soil. The word has an economically derogatory meaning referring to any small plant which is useless, of no special value. The distinction between *munumunu* and *ka'i* also turns upon whether a plant has any woody parts which can be burned. As the natives put it to me:—

T. 6.
Sitana	*ta-yuvi*	*kove,*	*gala*	*bi-kata,*	*munumunu*
little bit	we blow	fire	no	he might blaze	weed

pela.
for

FREE TRANSLATION: When we try to blow up a fire and it will not blaze, this is because these are weeds.

3. *Munumunu* always signifies a plant which is not cultivated in the gardens, nor grown in the village, nor round the houses, nor on the *baku*. Very often when I enquired the name of some plant which interested me for one reason or another they would say:—

T. 7.
Gala	*yaga-la,*	*munumunu*	*wala.*
no	name his	weed	just

FREE TRANSLATION: 'It has no name, it is just *munumunu*.' The aromatic or decorative herbs grown in the village, above all *borogu*, 'croton', and *kwebila*, an aromatic plant, *sulumwoya*, another aromatic plant with a mint-like scent, would not be called *munumunu*.

4. *Wotunu*, 'creeper', would be defined as a plant with *matala*, 'tendrils', which *i-kwari*, 'catch hold of', *i-tavine*, 'twine round', and *i-mwoyne*, 'climb up', some tree or artificial support. The natives would not speak of the cultivated creepers, the various kinds of yam, as *wotunu*, but would call each by its specific name, but they realise that these are creepers, *wotunu*. Besides these they cultivate one creeper, the *tuva*, the roots of which supply the poison for fish. A number of wild creepers from the jungle are of economic importance, notably *wayugo*, a creeper used for the lashing of canoes (cf. *Argonauts of the Western Pacific*, pp. 136–139).

5. I have given this general native classification because it is important, linguistically as well as concretely and pragmatically, that the terminology referring to crops stands out in precision and detail from that applying to other plants. To repeat, the cultivated creepers are never called creepers but always *taytu*, 'small yam', *kuvi*, 'large yam', or, even more concretely, by one of the specific terms which designate the varieties of cultivated yam. The less important a plant, the fewer its economic, ritual or aesthetic uses, the more would it be called by some such generic term as *ka'i*, 'tree', 'shrub', *munumunu*, 'weed', *wotunu*, 'creeper'.

6. Another couple of words which indirectly serve to distinguish the cultivated crops from other plants are our old friends *odila* and *bagula*. They would be used in simple opposition to mark the distinction between things which grow wild and things grown by human effort. As a matter of fact, in collecting information about certain magical herbs or aromatic herbs used in armlets, I found that the natives naturally distinguish between *ka'i odila*, 'leaves (from the) bush', *ka'i i-susina o valu*, 'plant sprouting in village', *ka'i rayboag*, 'plant (from the) coral ridge', *ka'i wa weyka*, 'plant in village grove', *ka'i momola*, 'plant (from the) seashore', and finally *ka'i wa bagula*, 'plant in garden'.

T. 8. *Bita-bagula*   *bayse*   *ka'i.*
    we (i.d.) might garden   this here   plant

The opposition implicit here is between *odila*, 'everything that grows wild', and *bagula*, 'everything which is cultivated' (cf. the opposition between *odila*, 'jungle', and *valu*, 'human habitation' Div. I, § 2).

7. The two cultivated vines, that is *taytu* and *kuvi*, are further set apart by the use of the classificatory particle *tam-*,[1] derived from *tamula*, *tamla*, *tamna*, all phonetic variants of the same word meaning

[1] The reader will find that this particle has been omitted from the list of classifiers published in the article already referred to in Part IV (Div. III, B).

'stalk of cultivated creeper'. It is used with numerals, as *tamtala*, 'one vine' (taytu or yam), *tamyu*, 'two vines', *tamtolu*, 'three vines', etc. As far as I was able to ascertain, this term would not be used even in the enumeration of the cultivated vine, *tuva*, nor of any creepers growing in the bush and utilised for practical purposes.

8. The generic term nearest to our 'crops' is *kaulo*, pronounced in the southern dialect *kauno* or *kanuwa*. This term embraces in its widest meaning 'vegetable food in general', but, if used in distinction from other forms of vegetable food, it acquires the meaning of 'staple food', that is, *taytu*, 'small yam', *kuvi*, 'large yam', and *uri*, 'taro'. Still more specifically *kaulo* is a synonymous expression for the tubers of the 'taytu', a word incorporated into the current English vocabulary of this book (cf. Div. V, §§ 9-12). The taytu, as we know, is not only the staple food of the natives, but is that part of it which is accumulated in large quantities and most extensively handled in exchange, gifts and ceremonial presentation (cf. Part I, Sec. 10 and Chs. V and VI). The word *kaulo* would never be used of the garden crops *in situ*, that is, it never refers to the plants as they are growing; but as soon as the tubers are taken out of the soil they become *kaulo*. They are designated by this name when they are stored in the *bwayma*, they are called by it when they are accumulated in any of the receptacles for transport or ceremonial offering, and they still retain this name when they are cooked and served on a wooden platter. *Kaulo* is a noun and cannot be used in any other form. A derived form is used in conjunction with possessive pronouns as what might be called a possessive noun, *kagu*, 'my food', *kam*, 'thy food', *kala*, 'his food', and so on through all the persons. In this form the word has a wider meaning: *kala*, 'his food', does not necessarily mean taytu or even any of the three staple crops, but refers to any food; except again when a distinction is drawn between the staple tubers and meat or wild fruit. Here, at the cost of a brief digression, I may conveniently exhaust the whole matter of prepared food. There is no general term for meat, and a meat dish would be called by the name of the animal from which it is derived. There is a word for flesh, *viliyona*. Cooked fish would be called by the same term as fish in general, *yena* or *ilia*.

9. *Kaulo*, 'accumulated taytu', enjoys another linguistic privilege: when loaded in baskets it governs what might be called paradoxically the absence of any particle. No other noun can be counted by the naked numerals *tala*, *yuwa*, *tolu*, *vasi*, etc., except basketsful of taytu (cf. Part IV, Div. III, B). A basketful of taytu is, indeed, the main unit of value, and one of the most important items in all forms of exchange. The large yams, as well as individual tubers of taytu, would be counted by the particle *kway-*, which refers to any rounded or bulky object; while taro governs the particle *kway-* if the tuber be mainly considered, *kay-* if the whole plant be counted. When counted in bundles it governs the specific particle *umwa-*. Empty baskets have the prefix *ya-* : *peta ya-tala*, 'one empty basket'. Baskets filled with other stuff would be numbered with *kway-* : *kway-tala peta*, 'one basketful'. It may be mentioned that *kuvi*, 'large yams', are too bulky to be carried in baskets, while taro is usually transported in bundles.

10. Besides the three main crops, *taytu*, *kuvi* and *uri*, a number of minor crops are grown in the garden: *pempem*, 'peas', *yaguma*, 'pumpkins', *to'u*, 'sugar-cane', *viya*, a variety of taro with big elongated roots, *bisiya*, 'arrowroot' (?), sometimes *usi*, 'banana'.

11. The white man's importations—maize, called by the natives *ma'isi*, and sweet potatoes, *simsimwaya*, a term which sounds native but whose origin I could not ascertain, are also now grown in the gardens (cf. Ch. X, Sec. 5).

12. All these minor products might be called *kaulo* at times, and at times they might be called by the term *kavaylu'a*, 'wild fruit'. This term is as a rule opposed to *kaulo*. From the culinary point of view, the natives distinguish between *kaulo*, 'staple food', 'basic food', *'pièce de résistance'*; *kavaylu'a*, 'wild fruit', 'something which gives pleasure rather than fills the belly', 'any food which is eaten over and above the *pièce de résistance'*; *gwaba*, 'dainty', 'morsel', 'flavouring' (the German *Leckerbissen*), something which is eaten with stodgier food in order to make it go down more easily. There is a definite lubricatory feeling in the meaning of the term *gwaba*. Thus the natives will say about a piece of meat kept over for the next day, or more especially a piece of fat:—

T. 9. *Kala gwaba ka-gu.*
    his   dainty staple food mine

'its lubricatory addition to my staple food'.

13. We turn now to the expressions used for parts of cultivable plants and for the processes of their growth; and here one or two complications must be mentioned. In the first place with regard to the grammatical use of words, certain terms, as we have said, can be used as verbs and also as nouns. As a matter of fact the concepts for 'flower', 'branch', 'fruit', are more often used verbally in the sense of 'to flower', 'to put out branches' or 'to have branches', 'to produce fruits', than nominally. On the other hand the word for 'root' cannot be used except as a noun.

14. A further complication arises from the fact that, in Kiriwinian, the parts of any component whole can be used either in an independent form or else in a relational form. Later on, when we discuss the ideas of relation and possession (Div. XII, §§ 3–13), we shall have to deal more fully with the several classes of possessive pronoun. Here it must suffice to say that a part of a plant may be described by reference to the whole with the suffixed possessive -*la*, or with the prefixed pronoun *kala*. Thus 'root' can be used independently, *kaynavari*, or else in the form *kaynavari-la*, or in the southern dialects *kaynavari-na*. Fruit may be described as *uwa* or *kayuwa* or else *kayuwa-na*. The independent and the relational forms are, as regards meaning, equivalent. *Kaynavari* might perhaps be translated as 'root', *kaynavari-la* as 'root his', 'root of it', 'root of the plant'; the sense being 'the root of', 'its root'. But such a rendering in English would lay too much stress on a difference which is purely formal. To the native the possessive carries perhaps a slightly greater emphasis, and in some instances the relation of the part to the whole may be felt.

15. Again, some of the terms can be used as a type of classificatory particle with suffixed numerals. Thus *sisila*, 'branch', forms the compounds *sisi-tala*, 'one branch', *sisi-yu*, 'two branches', and so on—expressions which, however, are not numerals but self-contained nouns, combining the description of the object and its number. *Sisi-tala*, moreover, is very often used instead of *sisila*—a phenomenon not unlike the use of 'one' in the function of indefinite article in French and other Romance languages, and in German.

16. I would like here to remind the reader that he will find the conventions adopted with regard to the presentation of the possessive suffix explained in Part IV (Div. III, B).

17. Certain words are what might be called terms of general botanic native description and are used with reference to any plant. Thus *kaynavari(-la)*, 'root', *lala'i*, 'branch', 'forking of a tree', *sisi-la*, 'bough', 'twig', refer to wild plants as well as to cultivated crops. Other words again are used differentially: the term *kaytone-na*, 'stem', is not used with regard to the two cultivated vines, the stalks of which are called *tamu-la*, *tam-la* or *tam-na* (see above, § 7).

18. The distinction between *u'ula*, 'basis of trunk', *tapwana*, 'main part of trunk', *dabwana*, 'top of trunk or of plant', and *dogina*, 'tip', refers to all plants alike. It has a wide range of figurative and metaphorical extensions. It is applied in the tri-partition of magical formulae, where the first part is called *u'ula*, the main part *tapwana*, and the last part *dabwana* or *dogina* (cf. Part VI). *U'ula* is used for 'cause' or 'reason' or 'foundation' of any argument, arrangement or principle (but cf. also Div. XII, § 10), and *tapwana* for the body or middle part as well as for the surface of things.

19. The aerial or buttress roots of trees are called *ninasa-na*. Those of the pandanus have a special name, *im*; a word used also for the fibre made out of them, and for the string and rope produced from such fibre.

20. The noun *sisi-la*, 'bough', governs the particle *sisi-*, as in *sisi-tala*, 'one bough', while *lala'i*, 'branch', 'forking', is counted with *lila-*, *lila-tala*, 'one branch'.

21. *Yagava-na*, 'leaves', of any tree or weed or creeper, are spoken of as *ka'i* when they are used as magical herbs, and as *yewesi* (Sinaketan dialect) or *yakwesi* (Kiriwinian) when they are prepared for cooking or cooked.

22. The word *yagava-na* furnishes the classificatory prefix *ya-*, which refers to leaves, fibres, objects made of leaves or fibre, and to all flat and thin objects. Specific words are used for certain leaves: *yoyu*, 'coconut leaf', *yobu'a*, 'areca palm leaf', *yokum*, 'bread-fruit leaf'. *Kalawa* is the term for a leaf used for counting, usually a leaf of *sisiye'i*, 'bracken', or of the cycas tree (cf. Ch. V, Sec. 5).

23. *Kapo'u-la*, 'midrib of a leaf', is also used for the human spine and for the human back in general. *Kapagana* means the 'flaps' or 'wings of a leaf', and *visiyala* 'veins of a leaf'. A budding leaf is called *kokopa*, which in a narrower sense applies to its lower butt-end, while *pagana* designates its twirled-in, budding end.

24. *Lala*, 'to flower', *kaylala*, 'flower', are words used to describe the process and product of flowering when there is a pronounced corolla, pistil and stamens. For these component parts of a flower there are no native terms.

25. *Sisi-la*, in its primary meaning 'bough', is the noun for 'sprays', 'flowers in boughs', 'frondescent flowers', such as those of the mimosa and certain other trees. I was given the following, obviously botanically erroneous, text:—

T. 10. *Ka'i   kayketoki   i-lala,   ka'i   kayviyaka   i-sisi.*
     plant   small   he flower   plant   big   he flower-frondesce

26. The verb 'flower-frondesce' may not be usual in English, but it had to be coined as the appropriate label for the native word, which is very difficult to render. In free translation, 'a small plant flowers with a corolla, a large tree flowers in sprays'. Even the informant who gave me this generalisation admitted, on being confronted with facts, that it was but a very rough-and-ready distinction, since many of the large trees have regular *kaylala*, while some small shrubs and even weeds have *sisi-la*. The coloured leaf-petals of the poinsettia (*kakuraypaka*) and other trees are also called *lala*. *Sisi* can be used verbally even as *lala*.

27. Small inconspicuous flowers which neither form sprays nor show a pronounced corolla are called at times *yovilu*, 'flowerlet', a word also used in verbal form. *Uwa*, literally 'to fruit', is also used to describe small flowers, similar in shape to the fruit into which they develop. *Kayuwana* (variant *ka'uwana*) would be the corresponding noun, 'small undeveloped flower'. *Luwa'i*, *luluwa'i* is the term for 'bud'. The following short texts illustrate the use of some of the words :—

T. 11.

Kum	*bi-yovilu*	*bi-uwa;*	*momyaypu*
bread-fruit	he might have flowerlet	he might fruit	papaya

bi-lala	*bi-uwa;*	*tuvata'u*	*i-lala,*
he might flower	he might fruit	marigold (?)	he flower

gala	*bi-uwa;*	*waywo,*	*menoni*	*i-sisi,*
no	he might fruit	mango	(fruit tree)	he flower-frondesce

bi-uwa.
he might fruit

The following brief saying sums up the relation between buds, flowers and fruits: *i-luwa'i, i-lala, i-uwa,* 'he buds, he flowers, he fruits'.

28. Whether the term *uwa* refers only to a fleshy fruit or to any fruit, and whether seeds are also called by this term, is not easy to determine. I pointed out to my informant, for instance, that *tuvata'u*, a plant with flowers like the marigold, reproduces from *weytunu*, 'seed', and that a seed is a fruit, to which he agreed :—

T. 12.

Mokita	*boge*	*bi-uwa.*
truly	already	he might fruit

'Yes, it is true that it does fruit.' But I feel that on this point I did not reach a full knowledge of linguistic usage.

29. As to the relation between *weytunu, weytuna* or *weytune-na*, 'seed', 'kernel', *kanawina, kaniwine-la*, 'skin', 'fleshy parts', I received the following definition text :—

T. 13.

Orokayva	*kanawina,*	*onuwanay-na*	*natu,*	*o*	*lopou-la*
in top	skin	in middle his	(fruit-tree)	in	belly his

weytune-na.
kernel his

Here we have the noun *kanawina*, 'skin'. without the possessive pronoun, and *weytune-na*, 'kernel', with the affixed possessive 'his', which is also added to the prepositional expression *onuwanay-na*, 'in middle his', 'inside of it'. It would be incorrect to lay too much stress on this distinction, but perhaps it might be said that, since we are starting from the outside and taking the skin, so to speak, as the system of reference, the use of the preposition *onuwanay-na* refers to the previous noun. 'On top we have the skin, in the middle of it, inside it, the fruit called the *natu*, and inside this again its kernel.'

30. The flesh of the fruit is described here by the term which is applied ordinarily, not merely to the fruit itself, but also to the whole tree. Since it is the flesh, the edible part, which is of primary importance, it is described here by the specific name of the plant from which it comes. In free translation and bringing out all the implications, this text could be rendered: 'Outside we have the skin, in the middle there is the flesh of the *natu* fruit, inside remains the kernel.'

31. The relation between seed, fruit and flower brings us to the problem of reproduction. There is no idea whatever about the sexual function of flowers, any more than there are names for the component parts of a flower, or interest in their meaning.

32. The following text from Gigi'uri of Sinaketa contrasts the reproduction of plants with that of animals :—

T. 14. (i) *Ka'i*   *i-tuwali,*   *gala*   *makewala*   *tomwota,*   *bulukwa,*
     plant   he different   no   like   humans   pig

     ka'ukwa: *bi-kayta-si,*   *i-sumay-se,*
     dog   they might copulate   they become pregnant

     i-valulu-si.
     they give birth

      (ii) *Tatoulo*   *i-nanamsa,*   *i-matutile,*   *i-kapusi,*   *i-ma*
        self   he consider   he ripe   he fall down   he come here

      o   *pwaypwaya,*   *boge*   *i-susine.*
      in   soil   already   he sprout

     (iii) *Bayse* (pointing to a flower)   *iga'u*   *bi-matutile;*
        this here   later on   he might be ripe

      boge   *i-kapusi,*   *mokita*   *i-valulu,*   *boge*
      already   he fall down   truly   he give birth   already

      i-sisu   *weytuna*   *o*   *lopou-lo.*
      he sit   seed   in   belly his

FREE TRANSLATION: (i) Plants are different and not like human beings, pigs and dogs, which copulate, conceive and give birth.

(ii) The plant itself makes up its mind, ripens, falls down, enters the soil, and then it sprouts.

(iii) This here (pointing to a flower) will presently ripen, it will fall down and truly give birth, because there is already a seed in its inside.

33. COMMENTARY: the second sentence expresses in a concrete manner the idea that in the plant the reproductive process is quite spontaneous. 'Self it considers'—the verb *nanamsa*, 'to consider', 'to make up one's mind', refers probably to the fact that at times a seed will not ripen, at times it will. This text is remarkable, because it is one of the two native statements which might seem to point to a somewhat clearer knowledge of human and animal reproduction than the native really has. The same informant, when I cross-questioned him about what he said here, made it quite clear to me that he did not imply in his first sentence any definite causal relation between the copulation, conception, pregnancy and bringing forth, but that rather in human beings and animals copulation was one of the necessary conditions. Animals and human beings must mate before they reproduce. In plants there is nothing analogous to it. This probably adequately sums up the native belief.

34. In some species the natives distinguish between the male and the female plant, saying that one of them has fruit and the other is *bwita wala*, 'just a flowering tree'. The word *bwita* is specifically used for a large tree with beautifully scented white blossoms, which are classed as *lala*, and which play a part in native decoration and festivities. This tree apparently has no fruits, which means its fruits are very inconspicuous. I think they used the terms *kaymwala* and *kayvivila* for male and female plants. They know that certain plants grow only out of seeds, others from cuttings. The verb *susine*, 'to sprout', describes the process of germination and development in general. *Sakapu*, *sunapulo* or *kounapulo*—all verbs—are used for 'the coming out of the ground'.

35. The swelling of roots and the growth of fruit they describe by the verb *kabina'i*, 'to grow'. The verb *puri* or, in reduplicated form, *puripuri*, describes 'the bursting forth of fruits or root tubers into a multiplicity of clusters'.

36. The principal words with homonymous meanings encountered in this division are:—

1. *bwita*	1. 'a tree'.
= dialectic *butia*	2. 'flowering tree in general'.
2. *dabwana*	1. 'head his', i.e. 'top of plant'.
	2. 'foliage of creeper'.
	3. 'third part of magical formula'.
3. *dogina*	1. 'tip'.
	2. 'end part of magical formula'.
4. *ka'i*	1. 'tree'.
	2. 'plant'.
	3. 'wood'.
	4. 'magical herbs'.
	5. 'stick'.

5. *kapo'ula*   1. 'midrib of leaf'⎫ not clear which meaning
                             1. 'human spine' ⎭   is primary

6. *kaulo*   1. 'vegetable food'.
                             2. 'staple food'.
                             3. 'taytu' as opposed to other vegetable food.

7. *kavaylu'a*   1. 'wild fruit'.
                             2. 'any food eaten for pleasure rather than sustenance'.
                             3. 'slow-growing yams'.

8. *kokopa*   1. 'budding leaf'.
                             2. 'lower butt-end'.

9. *sisila*   1. 'bough', 'twig', 'branch'.
                             2. 'flowers in boughs'.

10. *tapwana*   1. 'main part of trunk'.
                             2. 'body or middle part'.
                             3. 'taytu tuber'.
                             4. 'body or middle part of magical formula'.
                             5. 'surface'.

11. *u'ula*   1. 'basis of tree'.
                             2. 'cause', 'reason'.
                             3. 'first part of magical formula'.
                             4. 'organiser'—as of ceremonies or enterprises.

12. *uwa*   1. 'fruit'.
                             2. 'small flowers'.

THE CROPS: STAPLE PRODUCE OF THE GARDENS

1. With the background of this general terminology of plants, we can pass to the listing of words which refer to the growth and build of those plants in which the main interest of the natives lies, and with regard to which they have developed their most detailed terminology; I refer to their cultivated crops. Let me start with the small yam, taytu, bearing in mind that whatever is said about this plant refers also to *kuvi*, 'large yams'.

2. The cycle of taytu development begins at the moment when the *yagogu*, 'the small tubers selected for seed', which have remained in the storehouse for four or five months, are planted (cf. Ch. IV, Sec. 2). The whole tuber is placed horizontally in the ground (see Fig. 6). The word *tapwana*, 'trunk', designates its main body. The tapering end is called *sibu-la*,[1] 'bottom his' (Fig. 6). At this end there still remains the *koga*, 'old stalk', by which the tuber was attached to its mother plant. The opposite rounded-off end, called *mata-la*, 'eye his', *i-susine*, 'he sprout', or *i-tavise*, 'he cut through', and, working its way up underground, *i-sunapulo*, *i-sakapu* or *i-kounapulo*, 'he emerge'. The verb, *kabina'i*, 'to grow', 'to swell', refers more specifically to the swelling of roots and the growth of fruit, but can also be used to describe the whole process of growth and most of its phases (cf. Div. II, § 35).

3. Underground the first tendril, *sobula*, has grown into a strong stalk, and from this and from the old seed tuber new underground shoots emerge (cf. Fig. 7). While they are young and flexible, and before they have produced new tubers, these are called *silisilata*. After the *bwanawa*, 'new tuber', have sprouted from them, they are called *gedena*, a word also used to designate any maturer roots growing out of a young tuber. The roots of the plant as a whole are named *kaynavari*, which is the generic term for roots.

4. Glancing at the analysis of Magical Formulae we can see that the names of some of the rites and spells as well as their wording reproduce a good many of the technical expressions of growth. Thus *ta-tavisi*, 'we make cut through', or *ta-katusakapu*, 'we make come out', are the names of two spells of growth magic. The term *ta-vaguri*, 'we wake up', is alternatively used for the magical production of the first tender sprout.

---

[1] Note that the resemblance between *sobula* and *sibu-la* s merely accidental.

5. As the young sprout, *sobula*, 'grows', it becomes the main stem of the vine, called *tamu-la*, *tam-la* or *tam-na* (see Div. II, § 17). As the plant grows and develops there are changes over-ground and underground. Over-ground the vine forks are called by the term *lalavi* or *lala'i* (n. and v.), 'fork', 'bifurcation', used with the possessive pronoun *kari lala'i* or, in magical address, *kam lala'i*. These are also described by the term *salala*, *kari salala*. The noun *salala* is probably composed of *sa-* signifying pendants and pendent things, things which radiate brush-wise or in tufts and wisps, and *lala* probably from the same root as *lala'i*, 'fork'. Sometimes a secondary stalk grows out of the same root, emerging independently from underground, and this is called *towabu*, *kalu towabu*.

6. When the forking takes place near the root, 'secondary shoots' or 'lower lateral branches' grow out of the stalk and are called *posem*, *kalu posem*, or *yawila*. These have a tendency to grow downwards and enter the earth, forming aerial roots. The English rendering therefore could be either 'secondary shoot' or 'aerial root'. The natives try *katukwani*, 'to train them up', to prevent this. *Yosi-la*, 'small branches', sprout from the higher forks. The generic term for the foliage of the taytu is *dabwa-la taytu*, and the leaves are called *yagava-na*. The tendrils at the end of the twining branches are called *mata-la*, 'eye his', and the term *dogina* can be used also for them, though it usually is reserved for very highest tendrils (cf. Part VII, M.F. 17 and 21 for all these terms).

7. The above-mentioned words, *koga*, 'stalk', of a 'fruit' or of a 'tuber', *sibula*, 'bottom', *mata-la*, 'eye', 'tendril', *tapwana*, 'body', 'surface', *lala'i*, 'forking', 'branch', *yagava-na*, 'leaf', *dabwa-la*, 'head', 'foliage' of a creeper, are all terms which can be used of any plant. The only words which can be used specifically of a vine are *towabu*, 'secondary stalk', *posem*, *yawila* and *yosila*. The only term which I am certain is specific to taytu and yams is *tam-la* (see Div. II, § 17).

8. The 'old tuber' or 'spent tuber' is called *gowa(-na)*, or *go'u*. This is surrounded by *bwanawa*, 'new tubers', which sprout on the *silisilata*. As I have said, as soon as a *bwanawa* has formed on a *silisilata* the latter changes its name to *gedena*. The part of the *gedena* adjoining the *bwanawa* is called *koga*. The word *bwanawa* may be used with suffixed pronouns, when it receives the form *bunem-*, *bune-la* (cf. Part VII, M.F. 23, v. 4). Another synonymous expression for the new tubers as a whole is the term *kabina-va'u*, 'the new growth'.

9. The following lists contain a few names for varieties of taytu and *kuvi* respectively.

A. NAMES FOR TAYTU VARIETIES.

imkwitala	lupisayse	bomatu
katumyogila		kalasamwayna
tirimwamwa'u	kwaymwasia	diduwakayviyaka
		susu
kwayma	titula'uya	tukuluwedi
nabugwa	titudobu	bwadu'a
nakoya	tituboya	gibulaki
sakaya		nutunatu
nonoma	udaweda	tomwaya
	weynu'a	mwaredi
lupilakum	pupwaka	molugotana

10. B. NAMES FOR KUVI VARIETIES.

kwibanena	kuvisayda	tubwebegila
kuvisaku	komuri	
kuvibwaga'u		mogunam
kuviborogu	boyawulu	maya'u
kuvipwawa	bo'utuma	marada
kuvipunaya	na'ovala	masiku
kuvitayumila	vivila	muku
kuvibaba	tayvivila	danuma
kuvibuya'i	ilumteulo	yama
kuvidubwadobwa		yamsa
kuvigerena	todu'i	mwedomweda
kuvisiye'i	tobigabage	pwadum
kuvidi'agila	torara'i	nisinosi
kwiyatam	tobabana	vatila
kuvidubwaneta	to'urabakana	bwalage

11. These lists are by no means exhaustive. Working with the natives in the gardens, I began one day to question them about the varieties of taytu and, surrounded as I then was by a large group, I was simply appalled by the volley of names in answer to my question. When I had noted some twenty or more, I stopped writing. The full list numbered over a hundred. It seemed to me worthless then to write them down, but I reproduce such of them as I noted. In order to estimate the value of this terminology it would have been necessary to discover how far native distinctions correspond to real botanic variations, what the native terminology expresses, and why they have such a great variety of names. The results of such an enquiry would have been interesting, but as a sociologist I was more interested in other aspects of agriculture. As far as I was able to ascertain, from repeated though not systematic enquiries, the native names really represent actual botanical varieties, of which, therefore, there is an enormous number in the district. The varieties show a differential adaptation to soil, moisture, rainfall, and practical requirements. Some of them are good but difficult of growth, others are very prolific and hardy in drought, others thrive in rainy seasons and on somewhat swampy soil. Some produce large tubers suitable for show, others small tubers which are good for keeping, and so on (cf. Part VII, commentaries on M.F. 12, 13, 16, 19 and 20).

12. I should like to observe that, when obtaining my original list from a group of natives somewhat early in my ethnographic career in the Trobriands, I noted down a few words such as *bwanawa*, *kakawala*, *taytukulu*, *unasu* among taytu varieties. These words distinguish entirely different aspects of the taytu, which might be described as functional sociological aspects, and to these we shall return. They are words which afterwards I learned to know and understand perfectly well. It would, however, be wrong to say that the natives do not discriminate between botanical and sociological distinctions, or that they confuse pathological categories due to disease or blight with natural characteristics.

13. But like most untutored minds they do not readily grasp a purely theoretical enquiry. They know that the ethnographer is after words which describe distinctions in taytu, and unless they are clearly told, they give as many names as they can. Nor is it easy for the ethnographer to explain to them exactly what he wants. The confusion is born therefore of the contact between ethnographer and informants. Try to enter into a technical discussion with a member of the London Stock Exchange or a Roumanian peasant or any specialist engineer showing you round his works, and you will find exactly the same confusion. I have presented this fragmentary evidence on purpose, for my early difficulties and mistakes make this point clear: that the Trobriand language is neither more nor less consistent than any other type of speech, or rather that familiarity with context and usage is as necessary for its proper understanding.

14. Returning to Table A, it will be seen that the first nine entries give names and varieties which are mentioned in magical spells and commentaries. The first three entries I did not, in fact, obtain in the list written in the gardens. They are to be found in M.F. 13. *Lupilakum*, the ninth entry, is one of the favourite varieties of taytu, appreciated because of its size, the clear creamy colour of its flesh and the excellence of its taste.

15. Some of the names are obviously figurative or descriptive expressions. *Pupwaka* is from *pupwaka'u*, 'white'. *Bomatu*, 'north-east wind', may refer to the season in which this taytu ripens or to the north-east corner of the island where perhaps it has been cultivated. *Susu* is the Southern Massim word for 'milk'. *Nutunatu* is probably derived from the name of the fruit tree *natu*. *Tomwaya*, literally 'old man', might express the wrinkled appearance of this taytu. Three names, *titula'uya*, *titudobu* and *tituboya*, are obviously compounded of the prefix *titu-*, standing for taytu and other roots. *Dobu* would then refer either to the island of that name or else to the edible part of the young coconut tree, 'palm cabbage', the lower, fleshy substance of its young sprouts. But all this is etymological guess-work.

16. In the matter of *kuvi* varieties (Table B), I am even more embarrassed by inadequate information. I do not know, for instance, where the line of demarcation comes between the class of *kuvi*, on the one hand, and those kinds of yam which are not *kuvi*, on the other. *Kwanada*, *baluluwa*, *kasiyena*, *mumwalu* and *bubwaketa* are, to my knowledge, yams but would not be classed by the natives as *kuvi*. Taytu also, in all its varieties, is of course a yam. The natives explained to me that *baluluwa* are 'like *kuvi*'.

17. The first sixteen entries are compounded of *kuvi-* or *kwi-*, its equivalent, and various nouns, some of which can be identified with plain words of ordinary speech. Thus, *-banena*, 'finding', 'the found yams'; *-bwaga'u*, 'sorcerer', 'sorcerer's yam'; *-borogu*, 'croton yam'; *-pwawa*, 'elephantiasis yam', probably 'very large yam'; *-tayumila*, 'returning yam' or 'scooping yam'; *-baba*, 'yam with elongated ramifications' (?); *-buya'i*, 'blood', 'the blood-coloured yam' with reference to its pink flesh; *-dubwadobwa*, 'cave' (?), 'yam with large cavities'; *-siye'i*, 'bracken', 'the bracken-shaped yam'; *-sayda*, 'yam like a *sayda* nut'.

18. One group of names beginning with *to-*, *tu-* is thereby classified as a 'male group'; the other beginning with *bo-*, *na-*, *ilu-*, all three feminine prefixes, is thereby marked as 'female'. The noun *vivila* signifies 'woman'. The feminine prefix is found also in one or two names of taytu: *na-koya*, *na-bugwa*.

19. Let me pass now from these ill-digested and incomplete enumerations of variety names to a class of word on which my information is better. The few words *taboula*, 'taytu with rotten patch', *nukunokuna*, 'blighted taytu', *bwabwa'u*, 'black', i.e. bad taytu (a term also used for the ripe taytu, cf. Div. X, § 6), *pupwaka'u*, 'white', i.e. good taytu, refer to the condition of the tuber, healthy or diseased (see, e.g., M.F. 13). We deal elsewhere with the word *kavaylu'a* (literally 'wild fruit,' cf. Div. II, § 12), which is used to describe slow-growing, difficult varieties. The natives would distinguish between kinds of yam which are *mwa'u*, 'heavy', and *nanakwa*, 'quick'. They speak also of varieties which have *kakata matala*, 'sharp spines', referring to the *unu'unu*, 'spiky hair covering taytu', and they consider the sharper and stronger the hair, the better the taytu.

20. The verbal distinctions made concerning the uses and handling of taytu are the most important, because they are those most intimately associated with human work, the grouping of human beings, and agricultural interests. As we know (Chs. V and VI), a terminology emerges with dramatic suddenness and completeness at harvest or a little earlier. When the soil is first opened at *basi*, the 'thinning' or 'preliminary taking out of taytu' before the harvest (cf. Ch. IV, Sec. 3), the natives begin to distinguish between *bwanawa*, 'young tubers', 'supernumerary tubers to be taken out', and *go'u* or *gowa-na*, 'decayed seed tuber', 'spent tuber', both of which are removed. What remains is taytu, the crops proper. After these have ripened they are taken out at the harvest proper, and then new terminological distinctions, which correspond to real categories, appear. As opposed to *bwanawa*, 'unripe supernumerary tubers', all these tubers are called *taytuva'u*, literally 'new taytu', or *kalava'u*, 'new yam-food'. *Taytuva'u* is 'that part of the crops which is eaten directly after being taken out of the soil', as opposed to *taytuwala*, 'the tubers stored in the yam-house and only subsequently eaten' (cf. Ch. V, Sec. 3). In *taytuwala*, the second root, *wala*, means literally 'just'; the word therefore signifies 'just taytu', 'real taytu', 'genuine taytu'. The tubers stored in the *kalimomyo*, 'garden arbour', are divided into heaps; those stacked in the main heap are called simply *taytu*, sometimes also *taytuwala*, all the rest are designated by the generic term *unasu*, 'all inferior taytu'. The main heap is also called by its sociological destination, *urigubu*. *Yagogu*, 'seed taytu', is put in a smaller heap somewhere in the corner of the arbour. *Kakawala*, 'small seed yams', might be stacked in yet another heap. Some tubers called *unasu* in the narrower sense (equivalent to *taytukulu* or *ugu*, 'inferior taytu', which is not seed taytu), may be shown in the arbour, but most of it is taken immediately to the owner's storehouse. These can never be used for an *urigubu* gift. *Ulumdala*, 'gleaned taytu', are the tubers which are accidentally, or often on purpose, left behind at the main taking out, *tayoyuwa*. These various classes are, first of all, based on real differences in the tubers. The main heap of *taytuwala*, taytu *urigubu*, or simply taytu, contains the best and biggest tubers. As such it is sometimes also described as taytu *kavakayviyaka*, 'taytu very big'. *Yagogu* are sound tubers smaller in size. *Unasu* (*taytukulu*, *ugu*) would be somewhat misshapen, perhaps blighted, but edible. If there is a great quantity of first-rate taytu, more than the gardener is prepared to give as *urigubu*, he will leave a generous quota in the ground to be gleaned as *ulumdala*, or take it out early in the proceedings and carry it, more or less surreptitiously, to his yam-house, in which case it would probably be described as *taytuva'u* or *kalava'u* (with reference to the terms analysed in this paragraph, cf. Ch. V, Secs. 3 and 4; and Ch. VI, Sec. 1).

21. I do not think any of these functional distinctions would refer to *kuvi*. As far as I know, there is no distinction even between *kuvi* tubers used for seed and those used for eating.

22. We pass now to the terminology of *uri*, 'taro', which, in some aspects, is even fuller than that for the taytu and yam. In an early attempt to find out the names for different types of cultivable plant, I named the taro, and was greeted with such an outburst of terminological distinctions that I subsided and did not even start writing them down. But the number of taro varieties seemed to be unquestionably greater than that of either taytu or kuvi, though I only recorded the two or three which appear in M.F. 15. On the other hand the distinctions between the parts of taro and the terminology for its growth are, perhaps, a little simpler than those for taytu: the taro leaf is called *nayta*, the lower part of the leaf *kokopa*, which is also a generic term (cf. Div. II, § 23), the stalk of a leaf *kwaynuta*, the fleshy lower part *sikwaku*. The tuber, being the main part of the plant, is called by the term *uri*, 'taro'. Distinctions are made between the various parts of the tuber: *sibu-na*, 'bottom', called also sometimes *pwa-na*, 'buttocks' or 'fundament', or *kayke-na*, 'legs'; *tapwana*, 'body', 'main part'; and *dabwana*, 'head', 'top'.

23. The following text illustrates the use of some of these words and adds one or two new expressions. It was given me by Nabigido'u of Sinaketa during a walk through the gardens at the time of taro planting. A number of men and women were digging holes in the soil, the superficial little holes which are made for taro, and inserting into each a taro top (cf. Ch. X, Sec. 2). The question arose how the plant developed after it had been placed in sufficiently humid and fertile soil.

24. Holding a taro top in his left hand and demonstrating with the fingers of the right, Nabigido'u explained to me the procedure:—

T. 15. (i) *Bayse* (pointing to surface at 1 in Fig. 15)   *bi-sunapulo,*
this here   he might come out

        bi-ma   *bayse* (measures distance from 1 to 3)
        he might come   this here

        pwa-na   *uri,*   *kayke-na*   *uri.*
        buttocks his   taro   leg his   taro

    (ii) *Bayse* (shows the stalk of the taro top, 2)   *bi-pulupolu*
this here   he might burst forth

        yasina —   *natu-na*   *uri.*
        new sprout   children his   taro

What follows refers to the new sprouting *uri* :—

   (iii) *Bayse   otanawa   kanagi-na,   bayse   orokaywa   yasine-na.*
         this here   below   basis his   here   in top   new sprout his

   (iv) *Bayse* (pointing to old leaves and stalk) *bi-pwamata,*
         this here   he might rot away

      boge   i-uritana   yasina,   boge   i-pwamata
      already he stand up (?) new sprout already he rot away

      uri.
      (old) taro

25. COMMENTARY: This text is a good example of how necessary it is to reproduce the context of gesture as well as the full context of the situation. Half the meaning of each sentence was conveyed by pointing to different parts of the truncated root and leaves. In the first sentence Nabigido'u pointed to the cut surface and

TARO PLANT

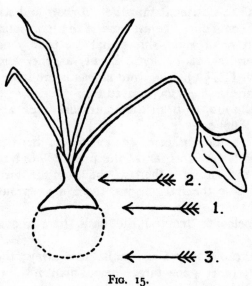

FIG. 15.

informed me that there the process of growth begins, the roots developing gradually till they form a new tuber as big as the old one. The old tuber, which the natives call *woma*, 'stale root', 'spent root', does not, of course, regenerate into a new one; but a number of new roots sprout from it, one of which grows into a tuber and gradually becomes the main taro and produces the new plant (see Fig. 15). This main tuber is called *ina-la*, 'mother'. Other new roots grow beside it, presumably out of the *woma*, and produce secondary plants, called *latu-la*. Those which sprout first would be called *tuwa-la*, 'older sibling', and the later ones *bwada-la*, 'younger sibling'. Thus a whole family terminology is reproduced by the growing taro underground.

26. Let us now comment on the text: (i) would have to be elaborated as follows: "From surface 1 new roots emerge. Growing independently they reach the size of the old tuber and come as far as the bottom or leg of the taro."

In the second sentence Nabigido'u told me that new leaves grow out from the top of the stalk. This also would probably have to be amended in the sense that it is from the new roots or the sprouting part of the old root that the new plant springs.

iii. is a terminological statement giving the names *kanagi-na*, the same as *kaylagi-la*, 'foundation', 'basis', for root, and *yasina*, in a possessive form *yasine-na*, 'new sprout', for the new plant above the surface of the soil.

iv. contains the statement that the old roots and stalks rot away and new ones come out. The use here of the term *yasina*, which is a Sinaketan variant of *yosila*, shows that the term *yosila*, used with regard to lateral shoots of taytu, is only a general term for 'new shoot' (cf. Div. III, § 7). The word *uritana* is probably a compound of *uri*, 'taro', and *tana = tala*, derived from *toli* or *tolo*, 'to stand up'. The free translation, with all the contextual implications inserted, would run as follows:—

(i) From here, the surface of the cut tuber, there comes out the new root, which grows as far as the present lower surface of the tuber. This is the bottom of the taro, the leg of the taro.

(ii) Here, where the stalk begins, there now sprouts the young plant, the child of the taro.

(iii) Here below is (comes) the basis, here above the young plant.

(iv) This, the old leaves and stalk, rots away; the new plant stands up, it becomes a new taro. The old plant rots away.

27. When the taro is harvested, the rotting remains of the old plant, the *woma* as it is called while it is sending out new roots, is still to be found underground. It is called *bam*, 'afterbirth'.

28. There are not many homonymous meanings that need be noted in this division.

1. *bwabwa'u* 1. 'black' extended by reason of their colour to
          2. 'bad taytu'.
          3. 'ripe taytu' (cf. Div. X, § 6).

2. *bwanawa*   1. 'new tuber', 'unripe tuber'.
          2. 'taytu taken out at *basi*'

3. *mata-na*   1. 'eye his'.
          2. 'round end of the taytu'.
          3. 'tendril'.

4. *sibu-la*   1. 'bottom-his'.
          2. 'tapering end of taytu tuber'.

DIVISION IV

THE CROPS: TREES AND PLANTS OF THE VILLAGE GROVE

1. The two principal cultivated trees are the *nuya*, or *luya*, 'coconut', and the *bu'a*, 'areca palm' (cf. Ch. X, Sec. 3). We will consider them side by side, as their structure is homologous in some respects, and also because this method brings out certain characteristics of native terminology. Roots, stem, leaves, branches are, of course, designated by the generic terms, but they also have specific descriptive names which are more often used. Thus for the leaves of the coconut we have the special term *yoyu*, though the generic term *yagavana* may also be applied. In fact the natives would define *yoyu—yagavana luya* '*yoyu* is the name for the leaves of a coconut'. In the same way *yobu'a* would be used to describe the leaves of the areca palm. *Yo-* is formative of leaf, *bu'a*, 'areca palm'.

2. Both palms grow by producing young shoots in the middle of their top bunch of leaves, which enclose budding leaflets and bunches of young fruit. In the case of the coconut, these have the specific name *kaykapola*, a term with which we are familiar in garden magic, where dried *kaykapola* are used as torches (cf. Ch. III, Secs. 1 and 2). To the natives this part of the coconut represents the quintessence of fertility. The analysis of the word shows that it is compounded of the formative *kay-*, and the root *kapola*, from the word *kapwari*, 'to wrap up', 'to enclose', used in a nominal form as *kapwala*, 'wrapped-up bundle', 'parcel'. *Kapwa-* is the classificatory prefix for any bundle or parcel. We might interpret the word *kaykapola* as 'the vegetable bundle'. In the areca palm this same part is called *mwaykena*; *mway-*, formative probably derived from *mo'i*, 'mat', and *kena*, 'spatula'. *Kena* is used with reference to the human ulna when ceremonially employed as betel spatulae, and it also means spatulae in general. Why this part of the areca palm should be associated with 'spatula' I cannot explain. I never came across the *mwaykena* being used in a ceremonial manner.

3. Within the enclosed bunches the budding leaves and fruit develop. Incidentally the natives are not aware that the coconut or the areca have flowers:—

T. 16. *Nuya,*   *bu'a*   *i-uwa*   *gala*   *bi-lala.*
      coconut   areca-nut   he fruit   no   he might flower

When the fruit forming in the fertilised flower reaches to about the size of an egg, it is called *kapuwa*, a compound of prefix *ka-*, *kay-* and *puwa*, which is probably an apophonic variety of *po'u*, 'egg'. The areca-nut at the same stage is called *bubuwana*. When it is larger, but not yet fully developed, the coconut is called *talapem*. When the fluid has formed, but the flesh still remains a sweetish jelly, the natives call it *bwaybwaya* or *bwaybwa'i*, to which the colloquial expression of tropical English 'green coconut' corresponds. The areca-nut at this stage is described as *kikiya*. When the coconut is almost ripe, but not quite, it is described as *sagola*; *sa-* formative found in several expressions referring to coconut and areca-nut; *gola* perhaps related to the noun *gwara*, a form of taboo specially connected with the ripening of coconuts. *Gwara* is not used in the Trobriands to describe the coconut palm taboo, but is found over a wide area among other Papuo-Melanesian tribes (cf. *Argonauts of the Western Pacific*, p. 346, and monograph on *The Natives of Mailu*, pp. 580, 659, *gwara*). Areca-nut at this stage is called *viliyona ku'iga*.

4. The ripe coconut is simply called *nuya* or *luya*. This agrees with the general usage whereby the most important part of a plant is, in its fully developed condition, designated by the same word that signifies the plant as a whole. We found this in taytu, *kuvi* and *uri*, and it holds good with regard to banana, coconut, areca-nut, mango, and most other fruit trees (cf. T. 13, Div. II, § 29). The statement:—

T. 17. *Nuya   boge   i-yagi.*
       coconut   already   he ripen

expresses the fact that the young nut has developed into a *nuya*. The verb *yagi* is also used to describe the process by which fruit and leaves ripen in the sun, or by which leaves, browned in front of a fire by toasting, change colour and become strong and tough. It defines the change of colour from green to brown and the change in consistence. With regard to the areca-nut, another expression is used:—

T. 18. *Bu'a   boge   i-lalava.*
       areca-nut   already   he becomes brown and ripe.

I do not know why *yagi*, which has more or less the same significance—'becomes brown and ripe'—should not be used. It is almost a synonym of *lalava*. A ripe coconut is also called by the compound *numatutile, numatatile*; the formative *nu-*, from *nuya*, and *matutile*, 'ripe', 'sere'.

5. When a ripe coconut is left out of the soil it produces a *variga*, 'sprout' from one of its 'eyes'. The natives call the sprouting end of the nut *kwoymata-na*, 'eye-side' or 'top of coconut', from *kwoy-*, *kway-*, formative of round, bulky things, and *mata-na*, 'eye his'. The other side of the shell is called *kwoysibu-na*; *kwoy-* formative and *sibu-na*, 'bottom his'. As the sprout develops outside, the fluid dries and a spongy substance forms. This sponge, remarkably enough, is also called *variga*, simultaneity in development being, as far as I can see, the only common denominator of this and the sprout. The sprout of the areca is also called *variga*.

6. The 'fibre' of the coconut is called *kwaysanu* or *kwoysalu*, 'coconut fibre', and it is used for many purposes. The corresponding part of the areca is called *kuku* or *baykuku*, 'areca-nut fibre', *bay-* being no doubt a derivative of *bu'a*. The shell of the coconut is called *viga* or *kwoyviga*, 'coconut shell', sometimes pronounced *ku'iga*. The meat, the fleshy part, is called *luya*, 'coconut meat', the fluid, *sopi luya*, 'coconut milk'. The meat is sometimes grated, mixed with water, and the mess squeezed out. The resulting fluid, 'coconut cream' as we might call it, is named *bulaya*. After it is boiled, or the whole mess boiled with water, the 'coconut oil', which separates then, is called *bulami*.

7. The coconut is broken by slashing the *tapwana*, 'outer surface', an act called *kulami* or *takulami*, and then breaking the shell, *bolu* or *utubolu*, 'to break', 'to make a hole'.

8. The special name for a whole 'bunch of coconuts' is *samaku*, and for that of areca-nut *saleku*. The first governs the classificatory particle *bukwa-* (Kiriwinian), *bikwa-* (Sinaketan). Bunches of areca-nut are counted and adjectivally described by means of the classificatory particle *sa-*. Bunches of four coconuts or four areca-nuts are counted and described by means of a classificatory particle, *yuray-*, as are also four eggs, four water-bottles, etc.

9. In Chapter X (Sec. 3) I have described the process of planting a coconut, the wastefully greedy, penny-wise pound-foolish method used by the natives. The following text gives the native account of this :—

T. 19. (i) *Ta-sayli*   *ya-mwaydona*   *iga'*   *i-susina*,
we (i.d.) put down   all (l.f.)   later on   he sprout

ta-gise   *boge*   *i-viyaka:*
we (i.d.) see   already   he big

(ii) *"Ku-woki*   *nuya,*   *ku-maye*
thou approach there   coconut   thou bring here

ta-kalilavay-se   —   *ku-na,*   *ku-vala*   *kada*
we (i.p.) plant coconut   thou go   thou plant   our (i.d.)

nuya-si."
coconut

(iii) *Bayse*   *i-kounapulo*   *variga.*
this here   he emerge   sprout
(Here the speaker points to the new shoot coming out of an actual sprouting coconut)

Ta-gesi   *ma-pila-na,*   *ta-gesi*
we (i.d.) push away   this (part)   we (i.d.) push away

ma-pilawe-na,   *kwoysanu*   *deli*   *variga*
this other (part)   coconut husk fibre   together   sprout

bi-sisu   *deli*   *kaynavari.*
he might sit   together   root

(iv) *Nuya*   *ta-kome,*   *variga*   *ta-kome,*
coconut   we (i.d.) eat   sprout (spongy kernel)   we (i.d.) eat

ku'iga   *ta-lava;*   *kwosysanu*
shell   we (i.d.) make go (throw away)   coconut husk fibre

deli   *variga,*   *deli*   *kaynavari*   *ta-vala.*
together   sprout   together   root   we (i.d.) plant

(v) *Tuvayle*   *ta-vaulo*   *deli*   *moroba'u,*
another   we (i.d.) plant   together   (native lily)

(vi) *ta-keli*   *pwaypwaya*   *i-wokwo,*   *moroba'u*
we (i.d.) dig   soil   he is over   (native lily)

nuya   *ta-sayli*   *ta-dubwani.*
coconut   we (i.d.) put down   we (i.d.) cover up

(vii) *Iga'u*   *kaynavari-na*   *moroba'u*   *kaynavari-na*   *nuya*
later on   root his   (native lily)   root his   coconut

boge   *bi-peulo,*   *boge*   *bi-susine*
already   he might be (make) strong   already   he might sprout

nuya.
coconut

For the free translation of this text, see Chapter X (Sec. 3).

10. COMMENTARY: (i) *Ta-sayli*, 'to put down', means here 'to leave'; and *ya-mwaydona*, 'all', with the 'flat, leafy' particle *ya-*, 'all of the coconut'. An object like a coconut can sometimes take the prefix *kway-*, the most abstract and generic classificatory particle of the language, but in preference *ya-* is used, reference being made here to the thin flesh of the coconut.

(ii) The verb *kalilava* I met only in this text. It was explained to me by one informant as a specific verb used for the planting of coconut and areca-nut. The informant who gave me the text, defined it to me as follows:—

T. 20. *Ta-turatura*   *so-da,*   *gala*   *i-ma*
we (i.d.) wait   companion ours (i.d.)   no   he come here

ta-kaybiga: "*Bwoyna,*   *bogwo*   *ta-ulilava,*
we (i.d.) speak   good   already   we (i.d.) ulilava,

ku-ligaywo   *ma-tau-na."*
thou throw away over   this (m.)

He uses the synonym *ulilava—valilava* and insists that it is synonymous with *kalilava*. From this text we might translate the word *ulilava* as 'write off a bad debt', 'close up a matter', 'leave it on one side'. Such a verb could of course be a metaphorical expression for planting, that is, putting away and closing up the soil on something. In the words *kalilava* and *valilava* we would have the effective and causative prefix *ka-*, *va-*, and the partially reduplicated root *lava*, 'to throw', 'to effectively throw' or 'throw over', 'to leave on one side', 'to plant'. But this analysis is merely tentative. *Vala* is the specific term for planting; it is used with regard to seedlings or tops of plants such as taro, or to kernels, all of which only have to be superficially placed in the soil.

(iii) The words literally translated 'this here he emerge' must be taken in the context of my informant's gesture. They must be understood: 'look at this point where the sprout emerges'—and then the next phrase means: 'we tear off this part', that is, the part which my informant was by then holding in one hand, the actual sprout. 'Then we tear off the other part,' and he pointed to the lower end on which the sprout does not appear. The 'coconut fibre' here really means the large chunk of fibre which 'remains together with the sprouting twig and with the roots' as well as with a portion of coconut meat, that is, the small rootlet formed at the bottom of the coconut. This third sentence therefore states the fact that, before planting, the coconut is severed into two parts.

(iv) Here we have the explanation of what happens to the parts. The wording is perfectly clear; the most interesting linguistic phenomenon is the use of the same word in two contextually different meanings, the homonym *variga*. This and similar terms should be indexed in anthropologically edited texts as: *variga* 1, 'sprout', *variga* 2, 'sponge'. From the linguistic point of view it is paradoxical that the definition of the term *variga* in the first phrase, *variga ta-kome*, is given by the verb *ta-kome*, though *variga* must be understood before the verb *ta-kome* has any sense. The paradoxical character of sentence (iv) is very largely due to the fact that here a native is speaking to someone who is an apprentice in both language and the collateral situation, so that he has at the same time to define both, one by the other. *Ku'iga* is equivalent to *kwoyviga*.

(v) Here we have an apophonic variation of *vala*, *vali*, 'to plant', in *vaulo*. The adverb *tuvayle*, literally 'another', means here 'besides', 'together with', that is the coconut with the native lily.

(vi) This is a characteristically circumstantial description of planting. *Keli* is the general term for making a hole, whether for planting, digging a grave, burrowing as molluscs or insects do, or any other similar activity. *Dubwani*, a verb connected with the noun *dubwadebula*, 'cave', corresponds best to the English term 'vault', 'to form a cavity'. Here of course there is no cavity from our point of view, only the covering over. But to the natives there is the feeling of a cavity when you plant something and leave it underground.

(vii) As already mentioned in Chapter X, I was never able to find out whether the planting of a lily with the coconut is a practical measure providing a substitute manure or substance for nourishment to the new palm, or whether it has a merely magical or pseudo-magical significance.

11. With regard to the terminology of the *kaytubutabu* (cf. Ch. X, Sec. 3), this term is in itself of great interest because, so far as I know, it is about the only term in Kiriwinian which contains the root *tabu* in the sense of something 'sacred'. I am not certain whether the word *tabu* was ever used in old days in the sense 'forbidden'. I have heard the natives use it, instead of the more usual *tage*, in the meaning 'do not', 'I forbid you to'. The ordinary word in such a context would be *boma-la*, 'prohibition his'; used in the second person *boma-m*, 'prohibition thine', 'forbidden to thee'. Sometimes also the word *tabu*, 'grandfather', is used when speaking of totemic animals; but whether this simply means that the totemic animals are regarded as ancestors or ancestors by courtesy, or whether the term is used in the sense 'forbidden animal', I could never discover. The use of the word *tabu* in the sense of 'forbidden', 'sacred', 'ancestral', is perhaps due to the influence of European missionaries and Fijian teachers, who, I think, have introduced the Polynesian word into the language of religious instruction. Missionary influence had been established for about a quarter of a century in 1918, and a quarter of a century is quite long enough for natives as susceptible as the Melanesians to acquire a new word and give it a genuine native ring. Certain terms of the white man's culture such as *palati*, 'bloody', *sanapapiti*, 'son of a bitch', *pokiyo'u*, 'f—— you', are now good currency as well as having a beautiful Kiriwinian sound.

12. Another term associated with the *kaytubutabu* is *gam*, the band of coconut leaf tied round the trunk of a palm. The contraption itself is almost identical with the *kaypaku*, a coconut leaf girdle tied round trees for protection against theft and with a conditional curse attached to it. I am unable to analyse these terms further.

13. The following text refers to the aim of the *kaytubutabu*:—

T. 21. (i) *Ta-sisu,*   *bita-sagali,*   *bita-vitawo*
       we (i.d.) sit   we (i.d.) might sagali   we (i.d.) might set up
       kaytubutabu.
       kaytubutabu

(ii) *Ta-miga'i,*   *bi-nanakwa,*   *bi-sagu,*
    we (i.d.) charm   he might be quick   he (?)
    bi-bawa,   *bita-sagali.*
    he might abound   we (i.d.) might *sagali*

For free translation, see Chapter X (Sec. 3).

14. COMMENTARY: The verb *vitawo,* 'to set up', has also got the meaning of 'inaugurating', 'opening up', as the physical setting up of the stick. The aim of the *kaytubutabu,* as is expressed in this short text, is to produce plenty of coconuts for an approaching distribution. The text shows that the essence of the whole institution is magic: 'we charm; the coconuts ripen quickly, they abound, so that we may use them for a *sagali*'.

15. *Usi* is the generic term for the banana tree, for a bunch of bananas and for the individual fruit; it governs the classificatory particle *kay-,* 'long', 'wooden', 'instrumental'. A 'hand' of bananas, as it is called in French regime, that is, the dozen or so fruit hanging on the main stalk from the same lateral stem, is counted with the prefix *kila-, kila-tala,* 'one hand', *kila-yu,* 'two hands', *kila-viyaka,* 'big hand', etc.

16. The natives distinguish a number of varieties of banana, of which the following are amongst the most important:—

wakaya: a tall tree with large leaves from which the fibre used for women's petticoats is made; it has a stout trunk which bulges as it nears the earth; and it is used in various forms of gardening and fertility magic. The fruit is small, sugary, yellow in colour, without much flavour and not specially favoured by the natives.

kabulukusa: a large, squashy variety, soapy in texture, strongly coloured magenta or red, eaten when well *monogu,* 'ripened'.

usikela: a yellow long fruit, pleasant in flavour, though somewhat sugary and dry. According to mythological tradition this banana came once upon a time from Kaytalugi, a country inhabited by sexually rabid women, who copulate to death any man shipwrecked there or any male child born there (cf. *Sexual Life of Savages,* p. 356).

kuli: similar in shape to the previous variety and nicely flavoured.

kanitopera-mwateta, usiyawiwi: both well-flavoured eating varieties.

usimauna: a great favourite with the natives; short and yellow with a sugary fruit.

wowo'u: a large fruit, rounded off at the ends, of a soapy texture.

mokinana: a very good eating fruit (to both European and native taste); especially when baked.

siguni: is eaten half ripe.

memekwa: is eaten raw.

ulapeula: is cooked when half ripe.

17. The following is an alphabetical list of all those fruit trees and industrially exploited plants which grow in the village grove, in the jungle of the *rayboag*, on the *momola* and in the bush, with as much information as I obtained about them. The list is far from complete, since my material here is most deficient.

bokaykena: creeper growing in *odila*, 'bush'; in fruit all the year round; eaten only in *molu*, 'hunger season'; taboo to chiefs.

bubwaketa: yam growing in *odila*; eaten in *molu*.

buraku: fruit tree growing on *momola*, 'seashore'; ripens all year round; not taboo.

gutaguta: tree with edible leaves; growing in *weyka*, 'village grove', *rayboag*, 'coral ridge' and *momola*; young leaves boiled or baked.

gwadila: fruit tree growing in *weyka*; flowers in moon of *Yakosi* and fruits in moons of *Yavatam* and *Gelivilavi*; fruit eaten, also the kernels, which are called *kanibogina* (see below).

kakayluva: tree with fruit in pods 'like *pempem*' (native peas); not taboo, and tribute of it was brought to chief by Kaulagu and Tilakayva in olden days.

kanibogina: kernels of *gwadila* fruit tree; taken out of fruit and cooked.

kikirodu: tree with edible leaves; growing in *weyka*, *rayboag* and *momola*; young leaves boiled or baked.

kukupwa: fruit tree growing in *rayboag*; fruit grows on stem.

kukuva: creeper growing in *odila*; fruits all year round; eaten in *molu*; not taboo.

kum: 'bread-fruit'; grows in *weyka* and on *momola*; ripens in winter in the moons *Ilaybisila* to *Milamala*; eaten unripe, boiled or roasted in the embers, and ripe, baked on hot stones; the seed (*kweta*) is also eaten.

kwa'iga: kernel of *vivi* fruit; taken out of fruit and cooked.

kwanada: yam growing in *odila*; eaten in *molu*.

kwoymalesi: tree growing in *weyka*, *momola* and *rayboag*; leaves edible all the year round; young leaves boiled or baked.

lawa: fruit tree growing in *weyka*, *momola* and *rayboag*; large, round, nicely scented fruit but tasteless; ripens in the moons of *Kuluwotu* to *Ilaybisila*; kernels called *sasana* also eaten.

lokwa'i: tree growing in *weyka*, *momola* and *rayboag*; leaves edible all year round; young leaves boiled or baked; taboo to chiefs.

luweta: small fruit tree growing in *weyka*; fruits all year round; edible leaves also eaten boiled or baked; taboo to chiefs of Kiriwina.

menoni: fruit tree growing in *weyka*; ripens during *Yavatam* and *Gelivilavi*; juicy, aromatic fruit eaten raw to quench thirst; no taboo.

mokakana: tall tree growing in *weyka*; flowers in moon of *Milamala* and fruits in moons of *Yakosi* and *Yavatakulu*; no taboo.

mokolu: 'Malay apple'; fruit tree growing in *weyka*.

mumwalu: yam growing in *odila*; eaten in *molu*.

natu: large fruit tree growing in *weyka*; ripens during taytu harvest; small fruit highly valued and not taboo.

noku: small tree growing in *odila*; fruits all year round, and in times of *molu* principal staple food.

nori'u: plant creeping on ground of *odila* with green fruits resembling small pineapple; fruits all year round and staple food in times of *molu*; no taboo.

nunuri: fruit tree growing in *momola*; fruits all the year round.

pipi: fruit tree growing in *dumya* (swamp); fruits all the year round; small fruits like olives, extremely acid and popular in *malia* as well as *molu*; no taboo.

sasana: kernels of *lawa* fruit; taken out of fruit and cooked.

sayda: kernel of tall tree growing in *rayboag* and also occasionally in *weyka* and *momola*; the only nuts eaten raw; kernel enclosed in strong husk.

saysuya: small fruit tree growing in *odila*; ripens during *pwakova* (weeding) season; eaten during *malia* as well as *molu*; no taboo.

seuse'u: tree growing in *weyka*, *momola* and *rayboag*; leaves edible all year round; young leaves boiled or baked.

tumatama: fruit tree growing in *momola*; taboo to chiefs and only eaten by commoners during *molu*.

utukwaki: seeds of *youmwegina* fruit; taken out of fruit and cooked.

vadila: fruits of a pandanus species growing in *odila*; sucked in hot weather.

vidaveda: roots found in *dumya*, eaten only in *molu*; taboo to chiefs.

vivi: fruit tree ripening in the moon of *Yavatam*; the fruit, roasted or baked, is a favourite with the natives; kernels called *kwa'iga* also eaten.

wawolu: creeper growing in *odila*; ripens all year round; eaten in *molu* only; no taboo.

waywo: 'mango' tree growing in *weyka* and *momola*; ripens in moons of *Yavatakulu*, *Yakosi* and *Toliyavata*; fruit is eaten raw and cooked, and is of some economic importance; no taboo.

yokakayluva: tree growing in *weyka*, *momola* and *rayboag*; leaves edible all year round; young leaves boiled or baked.

youmwegina: tall fruit tree growing in *weyka*, *momola* and *rayboag*; no special season; fruits eaten all year round; kernels called *utukwaki* also eaten.

18. We have found few words with a variety of homonymous meanings in this division.

1. *kaykapola* 1. 'coconut shoot'.
2. 'magical torch'.

2. *nuya* 1. 'coco palm'.
2. 'ripe nut'.

3. *usi* 1. 'the banana tree'.
2. 'the bunch of fruit'.
3. 'the fruit itself'.

4. *variga* 1. 'sprout of the coco and areca-nut'.
2. 'coconut sponge'.

THE SOCIAL AND CULTURAL SETTING OF TROBRIAND AGRICULTURE

1. No abstract terms exist in Kiriwinian corresponding to such concepts as 'husbandry', 'agriculture' or 'cultivation' (cf. Part IV, Div. VII). There are, however, some expressions denoting, on the one hand, the importance of gardens and, on the other, certain general ideas which characterise gardening as a whole and serve to contrast it with other activities and aspects of culture. One of them already discussed (Div. II, § 8) is *kaulo*, 'staple crops', 'accumulated crops'. Another word is *bagula*, which means 'garden' in its nominal form but is, perhaps, even more important in its verbal use for the delimitation of activities (cf. Div. I, § 18). When the natives wish to characterise a certain community as 'agricultural', they would refer directly to their gardens, saying that:—

T. 22. *Ma-tau-si-na   si   bagula   bi-kugwo.*
these (m.)   their   garden   he might be first

This means: 'these people their gardens they are first', 'they excel'. The most general word in fact to define all agricultural activities is the verb *bagula*. It would be specifically opposed to the verb *poulo*, 'to fish':—

T. 23. *Yakamaysi   ka-bagula-si,   ma-tau-sina   i-poula-si.*
we (e.p.) ourselves   we (e.p.) garden   these (m.)   they fish

or vice versa. In this sentence 'we garden' is used in the sense 'we are an agricultural community'. In the nominal form, people speaking of their cultivation would say: *da-bagula-si* (inclusive plural), politely admitting the stranger into a possessive relation to the object of their pride and glory. There is an expression for a 'fisherman', *toluguta*, and for a 'landlubber', *tokwabu*. The *tokwabu* are usually also agriculturists, though there is no term describing this economic status. *Tokwaybagula*, as we know, means 'good gardener' and not 'gardener' in general.

2. Another general term in connexion with gardening is *towosi*, 'garden magician', 'garden magic'. When speaking about the agriculture of one community and their system of gardening as opposed to another, *towosi* would be the word most frequently used; it would naturally occur to a native when speaking of the gardening of his own community (cf. Ch. I, Sec. 5 and App. I).

3. Another couple of words of general connotation connected with agriculture, though not meaning anything like 'agriculture' in general, are the words for prosperity and famine, *malia* and *molu*. These two words stand in clear contrast to each other; *malia* means 'plenty', 'prosperity', and *molu*, 'dearth', 'hunger', 'famine'. *Malia* in its most fundamental meaning defines 'the well-being due to prosperity' (cf. Ch. V, Sec. 1); in its derived meanings it stands for 'plenty of food', 'a season or a year in which there is plenty', as in such expressions as *wa malia*, 'while we had a superabundance of food in such and such a year', or else 'during the season when there is usually plenty'. In this sense natives speak about *tubukona malia* (native moons *Utokakana* to *Yavatakulu*, and especially *Kuluwasasa* to *Yakosi*), when food is usually plentiful. The word *malia* is thus used nominally and adverbially, and also in the adverbial phrase *wa malia*. It is never used verbally.

4. Venturing here on what I regard as an entirely unsupported, and therefore unscientific speculation, which may, however, provoke further researches, I should like to add that the word *malia* fascinated me because the *l* and *n* are interchangeable and the sound *li* is sometimes replaced by *l*. Thus I received the impression that the word might be cognate with the Oceanic term *mana*, with its multiplicity of meanings. Another speculative question which troubled me, though I was never able to answer it, was whether *malia* was etymologically cognate with *Milamala*, the name for a season and month which is always the peak of prosperity, and also for the *palolo* worm which appears at that time.

5. This would be plausible only if the primary meaning of the word were 'season of plenty', and if the use of this term for the *palolo* worm were derived by association. If *Milamala*, probably a reduplicated form of *mala*, and *malia* were connected, this would strengthen the argument for regarding *malia* as a variant of *mana*.

6. The counterpart of *malia* is *molu*. Its fundamental meaning is 'hunger', and from this derive 'dearth', 'the temporal or seasonal determinants of hunger', and, yet more abstract, 'conditions of hunger', 'famine'. The word *molu* is also used to define certain seasons, *wa molu*, *tubukona molu*, exactly as with *malia*. The following text, noted down from statements made by Tokulubakiki, gives us a description of what happened during a big *molu* (for Commentary, see Part IV, Div. III; and for free translation, see Ch. V, Sec. 1):—

T. 24. (i) *Molubabeba*   *o*   *gwadi-la*   *i-gise.*
(informant's father) in   child his   he see

(ii) *Iga'u*   *i-kugwo*   *sipsipsipwapunu*   *i-katoula-si;*
later on   he first   (a skin rash)   they sicken

(iii) *mimilisi boge i-kariga-si tomwota o la odila, mimilisi*
sundry already they die humans in bush sundry

wa dumya, mimilisi o raybwaga, mimilisi wa sopi.
in swamp sundry in coral ridge sundry in water

(iv) *Kidama wa sopi, bi-lumli yama-si,*
supposing in water he might be moist hand theirs

kayke-si, bi-kariga-si wala.
foot theirs they might die just

(v) *Pela molu; kaulo ta-kam-si gala.*
for hunger yam-food we eat no

(vi) *Iga'u boge i-wokwe molu; i-miga'i-se*
later on already he is over hunger they magic

leya, bi-pulu-se valu.
wild ginger they might bespit village

(vii) *Oyluvi bi-kaylum-si, boge*
afterwards they might make magic-herb already

lay-kuna.
he did rain

(viii) *Bayse* (here the narrator marks off a length on his forearm)
this here

vaygu'a i-gimwala-si yagogu;
valuable they barter seed yam

(ix) *vaygu'a bwoyna, luwatala yagogu.*
valuable good ten (basketsful) seed yam

Vaygu'a kwayketoki, lima.
valuable small (r.b.) five (basketsful)

(x) *Iga'u bi-sapu, bi-sapu kway-tala*
later on he might plant he might plant one (r.b.)

baleko — luwayyu tomwota, gubwa-tala, gubwa-tala,
garden plot twenty humans one (square) one (square)

gubwa-tala . . .
one (square)

(xi) *Iga'u boge sita i-kasewo yagogu,*
later on already a little he plentiful seed yam

kway-tala tayyu tomwota.
one (r.b.) two (m.) humans

(xii) *Iga'u bi-kasewo yagogu: kway-tala —*
later on he might be plentiful seed yam one (r.b.)

tay-tala; kway-tala — tay-tala.
one (m.) one (r.b.) one (m.)

(xiii) *Kulumata*   *bayse*   *bi-tamwa'u-si:*   *gala*
(western district)   this here   they might disappear   no

     waga   *bi-la*   *o*   *bwarita,*   *ta-poulo.*
     canoe   he might go   in   sea   we (i.d.) fish

(xiv) *Waga*   *bi-la,*   *i-gisay-dasi,*   *boge*   *i-katumatay-da*   *wala.*
canoe   he might go   they see us   already   thcy kill us   just

(xv) *Bi-katumatay-da,*   *gala*   *bi-giburuwa*   *veyo-da,*
they might kill us   no   he might be angry   kindred ours

     pela   *molu.*
     for   hunger

(xvi) *Ta-supepuni*   *o la*   *odila,*   *ta-gise*   *waga*   *kay-tala* —   *gala,*
we hide   in   bush   we see   canoe   one (w.l.)   no

     ta-la   *ta-poulo.*
     we go   we fish

(xvii) *U'ula*   *bayse*   *waygigi:*   *boge*   *i-bulati-se*   *valu*
basis   this   drought-sorcery   already   they bewitch   village

     gweguya,   *pela*   *ta-bugwa'u-si*   *veyo-la.*
     chiefs   for   we ensorcel   kindred his

(xviii) *Mwakenuva,*   *Purayasi*   *boge*   *i-kariga-si,*
(dead chief)   (dead chief)   already   they die

     Numakala   *boge*   *i-bulati.*
     (last but one chief)   already   he bewitch

(xix) *Kidama*   *bi-karige*   *guya'u,*   *ta-bulati*   *valu.*
supposing   he might die   chief   we bewitch   village

Definition of word *sipsipsipwapunu* (Monakewo informant, Omarakana) :—

T. 25.   *Sipsipsipwapunu*   *makawala*   *pukuna.*   *I-tuwali*   *pukuna*
(skin rash)   alike   pimple   he different   pimple

     kway-viyaka,   *i-tuwali*   *i-puripuri*   *wa*
     big (r.b.)   he different   he break forth in clusters   in

     woulo   *sipsipsipwapunu.*
     body   (skin rash)

Definition of word *lu'um'li:*—

T. 26.   *Bi-lu'um'li:*   *ta-doki*   *ta-la*   *wa*   *sopi,*   *ta-kakaya,*
         we deem   we go   in   water   we bathe

     ta-doki   *bita-kidumkini* —   *ta-kariga:*   *sopi*   *bi-lu'um'li,*
     we deem   we might swoon   we die   water   he might be moist

     bi-tula.
     he might be cold

7. A text given to me as a definition of a term referring to the trading of food rather than to gardening must be adduced here because it refers to drought and to the plague in the gardens.

Navavile of Oburaku was describing to me the failure of gardens, caused by continual drought and too much sun.

T. 27. (i) *Bi-kala*　　　　*kalasia,*　*bi-woye*　　　*leria.*
he might scorch　sun　　he might hit　plague

(ii) *Makawala*　*da*　*leria*　*tomwota,*　*makawala*　*kala*　*leria*
alike　　　our　plague　humans　　alike　　　his　　plague
bagula.
garden

(iii) *Ta-sayki*　*so-da*　　　　　　*vaygu'a;*　*ma-tau-na*　*kaulo*
we give　companion ours　valuable　this man　yam-food
bi-yousi;　　　　*ta-vem.*
he might get hold　we barter yam-food for valuables

FREE TRANSLATION: (i) When the sun scorches and burns our gardens, they will be struck with plague (blight) too.

(ii) Exactly like our human plague, so is the plague of the gardens.

(iii) Under such circumstances we give to our companion a valuable; he takes some yam-food, we barter the valuable for the yam-food.

8. COMMENTARY: (i) is a mere juxtaposition of two statements which, however, are bound up by temporal conditionality. 'When the sun scorches (all the vegetation), the plague would strike.'

(ii) An interesting *rapprochement* between the plague in the gardens, which really means drought and general blight, with an epidemic which strikes human beings.

(iii) Here we come to the real subject-matter of this text, a definition of the barter of valuables for yam-food.

The first two statements really describe the situation in which such trading would take place, a situation analogous to the one described in T. 24.

9. One more word, which has become very familiar to us, must be mentioned while we are discussing the terms and linguistic features which indicate the importance of gardens in Trobriand culture: I mean the word *taytu*; and as we are here dealing with the word as an object of linguistic interest, it must be italicised in this and the succeeding paragraphs. At the very beginning of Chapter I, I mentioned that the word *taytu* also means 'year', and I have shown how this figurative or metaphorical extension derives naturally from certain linguistic usages: that is, from the description of successive years in terms of successive annual crops. In its various more or less figurative uses the word *taytu* is important because we can assign its primary meaning and follow some of its derivations more clearly than is the case with any other term. Whether the primary meaning of *taytu* should be conceived as 'the taytu plant' or 'the taytu tuber' is perhaps not possible to decide. But these two meanings are so cognate that we are not obliged to come to a conclusion. It is, however, important to be clear that even here the natives never use the word in a careless or confused manner, as meaning either the edible tubers or the plant as a whole, because such a confusion might lead to very serious pragmatic inconvenience. But in any given statement it is always clearly indicated by the context of situation, gesture and common knowledge, whether *taytu* means 'tuber' (or 'tubers' in the plural; the singular and plural being always discriminated contextually in Trobriand speech), or whether it means 'the whole plant', 'the vine'. Note that the word *taytu* is never used for any other part of the plant; the leaves would be described simply as *yagavana*, 'leaves' or, if it were necessary to specify the leaves of a particular plant, *yagavana taytu*. It is only the important part of the plant which can be simply designated by the term *taytu*. If a native wants to speak of the tubers after they have been dug up, emphasising their various uses at this stage, he would use the term *kaulo*. Or if the tubers are in the ground though severed from the plant, or if they are still unripe, they call them *bwanawa*. At an earlier stage still the natives speak about *kaynavari-na*, 'root his', 'the roots of the *taytu*'.

10. Sometimes such expressions occur as *taytu kalava'u*, 'the newly harvested tubers'. Obviously derived is the use of the term to describe a special class of selected tubers. *Taytuwala, taytu kavakayviyaka*, synonymous with *taytu*, mean, in this narrow and derivative sense, 'the selected tubers of taytu', such as would be used for *urigubu* (cf. also Div. III, § 20 and Ch. VI, Sec. 1).

11. We can follow the process whereby the word *taytu*, 'year', derived in linguistic usage from its prototype 'the plant with edible tubers'. *Taytu* stands to the natives for garden produce in general, being economically the most important garden produce. They very often speak about *taytu* when they mean all other cultivated plants. Thus, talking of a year's crop, they would say *taytu*. Since their interests in the future and in the past are chiefly associated with the crops, and since they measure time by the gardening seasons, the derivation of *taytu*, 'recurring cycle of gardening activities', 'recurring cycle of periodic events', 'year', is not difficult to follow. The following phrase shows *taytu* used in this meaning :—

T. 28. *Tuta-la   taytu   o   mata-dasi*
      time his   taytu   in   eye ours

'the time of the next taytu crops', 'next year'.

12. We can therefore distinguish at least five meanings of *taytu*: (1) 'tuber', (2) 'plant', (3) 'selected tubers', (4) 'crops' as a *pars pro toto* figure of speech, (5) 'year'. There is no confusion in the use of these terms; the series is really a series of homonyms, each of them invariably well indexed in actual usage by the context of speech and of situation, and sometimes, though rarely, of gesture. Whenever any doubt or ambiguity could occur, there are further ways of distinguishing meaning in such synonymous expressions as *kaulo*, *kalava'u*.

13. The term *tokwaybagula*, 'good gardener', has already been mentioned above (§ 1). Its meaning from 'efficient husbandman' to 'perfect gardener', whose *butura*, 'renown', resounds over the whole district, never expresses being occupied in gardening—all Trobrianders are more or less gardeners—but rather excellency. It is, of course, formed from the personal prefix *to-*, the root *bagula*, together with the infixed word *-kway-*, which is a colourless formative perhaps derived from the word *kwa'u*, 'to take', 'to wield'; in this context, 'man-wield-garden'. There is thus no verbal element expressing excellency or perfection in the composition of the word. Its opposite *tobugumata*, strictly 'poor gardener', in a wider sense 'lazy', 'indolent person', is more easily analysable. *To-*, personal prefix, *bugu* from *bagula*, 'garden', *mata*, 'to be dead', 'to be weary'; 'man-garden-weary'. This word again conveys a moral judgment. The opposition between *tokabitam*, 'carver', 'expert in manual pursuit', and *tobekam*, 'non-expert', 'incompetent', has a somewhat more limited and defined character. *Tobekam* may, in certain contexts, as a rule jocular, mean 'duffer', 'bungler', 'fumbler'. A man would frankly speak of himself as *tobekam*, or others may so speak about him without giving offence. In the same way the term *tokwabu*, 'non-fisherman', 'landlubber' (used in opposition to *toluguta*, 'fisherman'), carries no stigma with it. But *tobugumata* is definitely a term of serious reproach and might, under some circumstances, be deeply resented and taken as a great insult. It is also characteristic that this is the generic term for 'lazy person', 'ne'er-do-weel', 'generally useless individual'.

14. Thus perfection in gardening is the general index to the social value of a person. To exhaust the remaining terms connected with the glory and competitiveness of gardening, we have the expressions *yakaulo*, 'to admire', *yakala*, 'competitive challenge' (cf. Ch. II, Sec. 5), *kayasa*, 'contractual enterprise' (cf. Ch. VI, Sec. 3). All these terms have also a wider connotation and are not only applied to gardens. *Buritila'ulo*, on the other hand, is specifically a gardening challenge and competition (cf. Ch. V. Sec. 6).

15. The distinctness of gardening from other pursuits is further marked by a special term for theft or thieving from gardens; theft of crops from the ground or from the yam-house. The terms *vayla'u*, 'to steal vegetable food', *tovayla'u*, 'food thief', are distinct from *kwapatu*, 'theft of any other goods or chattels'. The act of *vayla'u* is regarded as more despicable than *kwapatu*. *Vayla'u* is a verbal root which I cannot further analyse. *Kwapatu* seems to be compounded of *kwa-*, 'to get hold of', and *patu*, 'to close', 'take—foreclose' = 'steal'.

16. What might be called the professional terminology relating to gardens is restricted, as far as I know, to one term only, *towosi*, 'the garden magician'. In discussing gardening we had to introduce an abundant sociological terminology referring to kinship distinctions, chieftainship, clan differentiation, and relationship-in-law (cf. esp. Ch. VI). But these terms do not in themselves throw any light on gardening, or on the grouping of human beings during their garden work, or on the organisation into what might be called gardening teams.

17. *Kayaku*, 'social gathering', is a generic term which is used in a specific and important sense in the context of gardening (cf. Ch. II, Sec. 3). It acquires the meaning of 'council for the discussion of gardens' when used in the context of gardens and of gardening deliberations, or as a term of time-reckoning. Thus when an event is described as happening *o kayaku*, at the time, though not neccssarily during the sitting, of the council, the natives know that the garden *kayaku* is meant. Primarily this term has the wider meaning of 'social gathering', '*gesellschaftliches Beisammensein*', 'conversational sitting', 'forgathering for deliberations', and in this sense it is generally used. It can only be used to mean 'garden council' with contextual indices or else in one or two stock phrases or topical contexts. At the council the *kalawa*, 'counting' or 'enumeration', of the *baleko* and their allotment takes place. The verb *kalawa* means primarily 'to prepare the tally leaf by plucking the leaflets' (cf. Ch. V, Sec. 5). Most likely the verb itself is derived from the noun *kalawa*, 'tally leaf'. I am not quite certain, but I think that here again we have a derived meaning, and that the root meaning is cycas leaf. But once or twice in my notes I find this plant described as *kalatuba* and, while in the field, I did not ascertain whether *kalawa* is primarily 'cycas leaf' or 'counting leaf'.

18. It seems probable that the word *kweluva*, 'time-count', 'seasonal sequence', 'calendar', is derived from *kalawa*. The term *kalawa* is not a specific garden term, but the counting of plots at the *kayaku* and of crops at harvest are its two most important uses. The use of *kweluva* is illustrated in the following text, which will be found freely translated in Chapter II (Sec. 5), and which needs no commentary.

T. 28a. *Gala*   *bi-yousise*   *kweluva!*   *Ma-tau-na*
        no   they might catch   time-reckoning   this (m.)

        bi-kugwa   *bi-sopu,*   *bi-yousi*
        he might be first   he might plant   he might catch

        kweluva,   *boge*   *bi-kabinai.*
        time-reckoning   already   he might grow

19. The following text referring to the *kayaku* in Teyava will be found in free translation in Document VII.

T. 28b. (i) "*Gugwadi,*   *magi-mi*   *ku-may-se,*   *ku-livala-se:*
           boys   desire yours   you come   you speak

           a-ma-kubila-na   *bita-wa'i-si?*
           what this field   we (i.p.) might hit

     (ii) *Kayne*   *ma-kubila-na*   *wa*   *waya,*   *kayne*   *ma-kubila-na*
          whether   this field   in   creek   whether   this field

           rayboag?"
           coral ridge

           (Here the *towosi* mentioned several names of garden fields, after each of which one or other of the men would say:—)

   (iii) "*Gala*   *bayse,*   *bi-sisu*   *ma-kubila-na.*"   (or)
          no   this here   he might sit   this field

   (iv) "*Ka-pakay-se*   *ma-kubila-na.*"   (or)
          we (e.p.) refuse   this field

   (v) "*Ma-kubilawe-na*   *bi-simwo.*"
          this field,   he might sit here

          (The *towosi* then mentioned the field of Odabayabona, and all the men agreed in chorus, saying:—)

   (vi) "*M'tage!*"   "*Bwoyne!*"   "*Mokita!*"   "*Magi-ma-si*
          well   good   that's right   desire ours (e.p.)

          ka-takaywa-si   *ma-kubila-na!*"
          we cut   this field

          (At last the *towosi* agreed, saying:—)

  (vii) "*Magi-mi*   *ma-kubila-na Odabayabona. Bwoyne,*   *nina-mi.*"
         desire yours   this field   good   your mind

         (He then enumerated the plots, beginning with the *leywota*:—)

 (viii) "*Leywota*   *bi-takaywa*   *ma-tau-na*"
         standard plot   he might cut bush   this (m.)

         (mentioning a name. He then proceeded to the fence plots, describing or naming one after the other, and the men would call out:—)

(ix) "*Ma-ko'*   *yaygu*   *ba-pali!*"
this (r.b.)   I (or myself)   I might choose

(x) "*Ma-kwoy-na* *yaygu* *ba-yousi!*"   "*Ma-kwoy-na*   *yaygu* . . ."
this (r.b.)   I   I might take   this (r.b.)   I

(and so on. After which the magician said:—)

(xi) "*Boge*   *ta-sagali-se*   *kali,*   *la-mwala* *bi-sisu.*"
already   we (i.p.) distribute   fence inside   he might sit

20. COMMENTARY: (i) *A-ma-kubila-na: a*—interrogative pronominal prefix; *kubila*, derived from *kwabila* (cf. Div. I, § 13); *ma- — -na*, demonstrative pronominal frame. *Bita-wa'i-si:* derived from *woye*, 'to hit', which stands for 'magically to hit the garden', 'to magic the garden in general' (cf. Div. VIII, § 7). (v) *Bi-simwo:* is a compound of the verb *si* (*sisu*), 'to sit', and the adverbial formative *-mwo*, 'here', 'thither'. 'Sit here' means 'remain quiet', 'remain put'. It will be noted that in (iv) and (vi) the members of the garden team use the exclusive plural, as is natural when they are putting themselves in contrast of discourse to the garden magician.

(ix) *Mako'*=*ma-kwoyne*, demonstrative 'this'. *Pali:* a verb here translated by the word choose, may be a metaphorical use of *pali*, 'to barter'.

(xi) *Sagali:* literally 'ceremonial apportionment', is here used metaphorically for apportionment. The elliptic construction 'we apportion fence' is characteristic of native speech. The plots adjoining the fence are obviously meant. *La-mwala:* 'inside', nominal form of the prepositional *olumwolela*, 'in the inside'.

21. The following text I noted down in Sinaketa. It was a conversation held during the *kayaku* between To'udawada, chief and garden magician of one of the component villages, and the members of his community.

ỉ . 28c. (i) CHIEF: "*Avayle*   *o*   *kalapisila?*"
                           Who   in   stile

     HIS SON: "*Yaygu.*"
                         I

     CHIEF: "*I-sekeli?*"
                         he follow

     A COMMONER: "*Yaygu.*"
                         I

(ii) CHIEF: "*Bwoyne. Ta-livala-si,*   *ta-mwaya-si*
                         good   we (i.p.) speak we (i.p.) come here
                         wa pasa.   *Avay-ta'u*
                         in   mangrove swamp. which man
                         i-sakaywo?"
                         he follow there

A COMMONER: "*Yaygu.*"
            I

CHIEF: "*I-sakaywo?*"
            he follow there

A COMMONER: "*Yaygu.*"   (and so on)
            I

(iii) CHIEF: "*Boge   ta-ma   o   wokunu.*
            already   we (i.d.) come   in   garden corner

            Avay-ta'u   bi-kivila
            which man   he might turn round

            wokunu?"
            garden corner

A COMMONER: "*Yaygu.*"
            I

(iv) CHIEF: "*Avayle   mako   karibudaka   bi-pari?*"
            who   that   garden side   he might choose

A COMMONER: "*Yaygu.*"
            I

(v) CHIEF: "*Wokunu   i-wokeya*
            garden corner   he come thither

            Bwadela?"
            (village name)

A COMMONER: "*Yaygu.*"
            I

(vi) CHIEF: "*Avayle   bi-bagula   Ogayasu?*"
            who   he might garden   (name of plot)

A COMMONER: "*Yaygu.*"
            I

The last question was repeated with other plot names of which I noted the following: Wabusa, Okaybu'a, Omwadogu. For free translation, see Chapter II (Sec. 3).

22. COMMENTARY: (i and ii) This text exemplifies the amount of words implied in native speech. Thus in the literal 'Who in stile?' we have the following implications: the verb 'will make' and the noun 'his garden'. The brief 'he follow' means 'who will cultivate the following plot', and so on throughout. Comparing (i) and (ii), we see that the verb *sekeli*, 'to follow', appears in (ii) with the suffix of thither motion *-wa*.

(iii and iv) show the use of the technical terms referring to garden lay-out (*wokunu, karibudaka*) and the way in which the natives can define the position of the plots by their names.

(v) Shows a characteristic use of the verb *woke* in the meaning of 'to return'. 'The corner which returns (see free translation) from

Bwadela' (the village immediately to the south of Sinaketa) is a figure of speech obviously built on the idea that the village lands 'return' (stretch back) from that point.

(vi) All the plot names are built on the pattern of *o*, 'in', prefixed to a noun denoting a tree or natural feature of the plot. *Gayasu* is a tree with edible leaves; *o gayasu*, 'in or at the *gayasu* tree', where the *gayasu* tree grows. *Kaybu'a*, as we know, means 'coral boulder'; *busa* is a large tree; *mwadogu* is the name of a variety of mangrove (cf. M.F. 16, Part VII).

23. Towards the end of my stay, about the middle of July, 1918, I visited several times the village of Obweria, while the *kayaku* and the preliminary ceremonies were taking place. The summary of the proceedings in a brief chronological survey was given to me by Modulabu, head-man and garden magician of Obweria :—

T. 28d. (i) *Ka-kaykuwosa-si* — *bi-kumuli* *kaulo*,
we (e.p.) garden council he might bake yam-food
bi-maye *ta-kam,* *ta-kayaku.*
he might bring here we (i.d.) eat we (i.d.) garden council

(ii) *Ta-kalawa* *kali,* *ta-tavine* *ta-tapatu,*
we (i.d.) count fence we (i.d.) go round we (i.d.) join up
ta-tokay.
we (i.d.) rise

(iii) *Ta-kaymola:* *ta-kalawa* *lopou-la*
we (i.d.) fetch back we (i.d.) count belly his
buyagu — *lay-wokwe.*
garden-site he was over

(iv) *Ta-vawo'i* *ula'ula* — *towosi*
we (i.d.) present oblation garden magician
bi-vapupula *digadaga.*
he might cause breaking forth bracken

(v) *Kayne* *bi-vagi* *burakema* — *ta-talala;*
whether he might do (magical rite) we (i.d.) make flower
kayne *bi-lolo* *o* *kaylepa* —
whether he might walk in garden magician's wand
kumaydona *yowota.*
all (magical ceremony)

(vi) *Nano-la* *towosi:* *kayne* *magi-la*
mind his garden magician whether desire his
bi-vagi *burakema,* *kayne* *magi-la*
he might do (magical rite) whether desire his
bi-woye.
he might hit.

For free translation, see Chapter II (Sec. 8).

24. COMMENTARY: (i) The term *kaykuwosa* is synonymous with *kayaku*. It is very seldom used and I did not ascertain whether it was just a local expression used in Tilataula or whether it was a rare synonym. Etymologically it may be the compound of *kayaku* and *wosa*. The latter root, reduplicated in the form of *waywosi*, means 'to linger', 'to rest'. *Kaykuwosa* might then mean 'we meet and linger', 'we meet deliberately'. The subject of the second clause is implied by the cultural context. Everybody knows that the person who bakes food and brings it to the garden councillors is the wife of the *towosi*. The juxtaposition of the three verbs 'she might bring, we eat, we garden council' implies contextually the purposive relation between the first and second verb and a temporal co-ordination between the second and third. In free translation, the wife would 'bring (the yam-food) so that we eat while sitting in council'.

(ii) The expression 'we count fence', etc., means, by context of situation, 'we count the plots lying along the fence' or 'we count following the fence'. 'We go round, we join up' is an idiom (see free translation). The verb 'to rise' means here 'to adjourn'.

(iii) The verb *kaymola* may be either a specific expression denoting the second day; more likely it is a dialectic variant of *kaymali*, 'to fetch back', in the sense of 'to bring up the matter again', 'to return to the subject'. The expression *lay-wokwe* is the accomplished mode of *i-wokwe*, 'he is over'. It might mean 'this ends the proceedings', or more likely as given in the free translation 'until it is over'.

(iv) The verb 'to present' is probably the word *woy*, 'to bring there', with the formative prefix of completion. The expression *vapupula digadaga* or *vapopula digadaga* is a technical name for a magical rite (see below Div. VIII, § 11). The relation between the two clauses is that of temporal sequence, or even consequence: *first* we present the oblation to the spirits *and then* the *towosi* carries out the rite.

(v and vi) The interpretation of these sentences is only possible against the background of the ethnographic information given about the two variants of the *yowota* inaugural rite (Ch. II, Sec. 8).

25. The expressions denoting the various gifts or payments offered to the garden magician are also not specific. The terms *sousula*, *sibugibogi* and *ula'ula* are not exclusive to garden magic. *Sousula* means 'gift of ordinary possessions' (*gugu'a*) or of 'valuables' (*vaygu'a*) presented by a member of the community to the garden magician. *Sibugibogi* is a large gift offered at night (cf. Ch. I, Sec. 6). *Ula'ula*, 'oblation to ancestral spirits', in the first place, and derivatively 'gifts offered to the magician from the community in order to provide the wherewithal for such an oblation', is used also in one or two other cultural contexts. But the gardening *ula'ula* is the most important, and also the oblation which inaugurates the gardening season is probably the chief ritual act of that name. The term also applies to the 'first-fruit offerings' deposited on the graves of the recently deceased. When thus used it has the slightly different sense of first-fruit offering (cf. M.F. 1, Part VII, where the invocation uttered at this rite is analysed; especially vv. 1 and 2).

26. We have encountered the following important homonymous meanings in this division:—

1. *kayaku*
    1. 'social gathering'.
    2. 'garden council'.

2. *kayasa*
    1. 'contractual enterprise'.
    2. 'competitive food enterprise'.

3. *malia*
    1. 'plenty'.
    2. 'annual season of plenty'.
    3. 'prosperity'.

4. *molu*
    1. 'hunger'.
    2. 'famine'.
    3. 'the annual lean season'.
    4. 'general destitution', 'lack of food'.

5. *taytu*
    1. 'tuber'.
    2. 'taytu plant'.
    3. 'selected tubers'.
    4. 'the garden crops in general'.
    5. 'year'.

6. *tobekam*
    1. 'non-expert'.
    2. 'duffer'.

7. *tobugumata*
    1. 'poor gardener'.
    2. 'ne'er-do-weel', 'lazy person'.

8. *ula'ula*
    1. 'oblation'.
    2. 'gift to magician'.
    3. 'first-fruit offering'.

THE TECHNIQUE AND OUTFIT OF AGRICULTURE

1. Here as elsewhere the general abstract concepts are not expressed linguistically by any specific terms (cf. Part IV, Div. VII). There is no name for 'work' in Kiriwinian. The distinction between technical or practical activity and magical activity cannot be made by the use of two mutually exclusive terms: and there is no word describing craftsmanship or skill in gardens specifically. The natives have to fall back on the term *bagula*, 'garden', which in its verbal form, as we know, denotes the entirety of agricultural activities and, in the compound *tokwaybagula*, is both a term of praise and, to a certain extent, a term of definition, 'skill in gardening', 'knowledge of gardening', 'competence in gardening'.

2. To such terms as 'labour', 'work', 'craftsmanship', there correspond the various verbs defining concrete activities such as *bagula*, 'to garden', *poulo*, 'to fish' (with nets), *banyi*, 'to fish for shark with a large hook', *ginigini*, 'to carve', *yowari*, 'to twine ropes and strings', *wayga*, 'to hunt', etc.

3. On the other hand there is, as we know, a wealth of concrete words which describe the component activities of gardening, such as the cutting of the scrub, burning, cleaning of the soil, planting, and the setting up of the various supports for the growing vine. There is an even richer terminology for the various components in what might be called the lay-out of the garden. This terminology has already been discussed and defined in relation to the activities and objects to which it applies in Chapter III (Secs. 3, 4 and 5). Here we need only enquire whether a given term is specific, that is, used only in the context of garden-making, or whether it is a general term which acquires a specific meaning by the context of speech or situation.

4. Our analysis falls into three parts: the first is concerned with the limited apparatus of tools and gardening implements, the second with gardening activities, and the third with the details of the lay-out of the gardens.

5. The implements used in gardening are the *dayma*, 'digging-stick', *kema*, 'axe', *ligogu*, 'adze', *kaniku*, 'mussel shell', *kayeki*, 'mother-of-pearl shell', and *yama-*, 'the human hand' (cf. Ch. III, Sec. 5). This is an exhaustive list of the Trobriander's "garden tools". The noun *dayma*, 'digging-stick', is a specific word designating any stick from about one to two metres in length, sharpened at one end and used for digging the soil. The definition of a *dayma* is functional rather than formal, it refers rather to the use of the stick than to its shape. The short *dayma* used by a woman or a child might quite as well be used for a stake in the fence, in which case it would be called *gado'i*. I do not think that the shape would be distinguishable. Again, save that the end would be blunt, a long *dayma* might serve as part of a *tula*, 'boundary line of the garden square'. Again an impromptu pole picked up and used on the way to the gardens as a staff could be sharpened and employed as a *dayma*. *Dayma* is a generic term for any digging implement: graves, trenches to drain off the water when a village is flooded, holes for laying the foundations of a house or yam-house are all dug with the *dayma*. Thus the word *dayma* means 'digging-stick' and not 'garden digging-stick'. But the use of the *dayma* in the gardens is so immensely more important than any other use that the word *dayma* brings the gardening context immediately to the mind of the native. I do not know of any metaphorical or symbolic uses of the word, representative of gardening activities in general, nor am I able to relate it linguistically to any other expressions. It is not used, as far as I know, in any other but the nominal form, nor does it enter any compounds.

6. The term *kema*, 'axe', has a wider application. It is the word for the finished, sharpened, mounted and trimmed implement. It is also used to designate one special shape of the finished blade, as opposed to the *ligogu*, 'planing blade', *kavilali*, 'chisel', *beku*, 'ceremonial blade' (cf. Part IV, Div. V). It is applied to the material from which the Trobriand stone implements are made, the volcanic tuff obtained on Woodlark Island and imported into the Trobriands. In this sense any implement made of this stone might be called *kema* or *utukema*; *utu-*, prefix associated with implements used for breaking or cutting. The classificatory prefix of sharp cutting implements is not *utu-*, however, but *kavi-*. Thus one axe would be counted *kavi-tala*; *kavi-yu*, 'two axes', *kavi-tolu*, 'three axes', and so on.

7. I am not able to decide whether, to the natives, the primary meaning of the word *kema* is 'volcanic tuff' or 'axe'. However that may be, the word has two distinct meanings. One refers to the material used, thus distinguishing all implements made of tuff from Woodlark Island from those made of obsidian or conus shell or *binabina*, 'volcanic stone', from the d'Entrecasteaux archipelago; and, since the vast majority of implements are made of tuff, *kema* is sometimes a generic term for any stone implement. The other differentiates an axe-shaped implement, of whatever material, from implements different in shape and function from the axe.

8. *Ligogu* is a specific term for the adze, that is for an 'implement consisting of a flat, well-polished blade, mounted transversally to the plane of striking'. The *ligogu* is, on the whole, less important than the axe and is used at planting for cutting out roots found in the soil and sharpening the digging-stick; later for pruning, thinning out the tubers and at harvest.

9. The mussel shells come into prominence at harvest, when they are sometimes used to cut the roots as well as to scrape the hair off the tubers to make them look nice (cf. Ch. V, Sec. 4). The terms used to designate the two shells as implements are not functional, but define them as natural products. The mussel shell (*kaniku* or *kaybomatu*, which is a larger variety) is used as it comes out of the sea; the pearl shell (*kayeki*) is usually polished on the *simata*, 'polishing coral boulders'.

10. Turning now to the terminology of gardening activities, we have already discussed the word *kalawa*, 'to count', in the sense of 'enumerate', 'finding out' (cf. Div. V, §§ 17 and 18, and also §§ 23 and 24): *kalawa o valu*, 'counting in the village', *kalawa o buyagu*, 'counting on the garden-site'. The cutting of the boundary belt round the chosen garden-site is described by the expressions: *ta-ta'i kuduwaga* or *ta-ta'i la kalikeda*, 'we cut the *kuduwaga*', 'we cut of the fence its road'. The noun *kuduwaga* seems specifically to designate the belt of cut scrub, translated 'boundary belt' in Chapter II (Sec. 3); I do not know of any other context in which it is used. Etymologically I am tempted to regard it as a compound of *kudu-* derived from *keda*, 'a road', and *waga*, 'canoe'; 'the road of the canoe', 'a canoe passage'. I did not come across it among the nautical expressions of the natives, but then I put no definite question on the point. Remarkably enough the other noun, *la kalikeda*, 'his (of) fence road', which obviously has a primary meaning referring to gardens, is used with regard to sea-passages, entrances into reefs or deep channels in the lagoon. There is no feeling of a metaphor when this word is used with reference to sailing, and the two expressions, whatever their etymology may be, are, as now used, regarded as homonyms (cf. also the word *tokeda*, Div. XI, § 5).

11. Sometimes the same action is described by the expression *ta-vali-se kali*, 'we plant the fence'. The verb *vali*, 'to plant', is here used in the figurative sense 'prepare the ground for', as the fence is made at a much later stage (cf. Ch. III, Sec. 3). This use of the word is a typical example of what I have called creative metaphor (Part IV, Div. VII).

12. *Takaywa*, 'to clear the scrub', is the first large-scale activity in the garden cycle (cf. Ch. II, Sec. 5). Etymologically this word is probably compounded of *ta-*, from *ta'i*, 'to cut', *-kay-* from *ka'i*, 'tree', and *-wa*, the suffix of 'thoroughness', 'accomplished action'. *Takaywa* would thus mean 'cut-tree-completely'. This, I should like to add, is a tentative etymology, but I think it is correct. It fits the meaning 'to clear the bush'. The verb is used for any clearing away of small bush, *odila*, as, for instance, when the natives prepare their fighting-ground in war, or cut a part of the bush for a preliminary settlement, or clear a small patch in order to play some game. But here again the clearing of the bush for gardens is by far the most important clearing. The actions involved in the process would be *ta'i*, 'to cut', *guya*, 'to prune' those saplings which are left standing, *ko'uwari*, 'to break with the hand', and *katu'uwari*, 'to break off with a stick', that is, to break off some of the branches of the larger trees.

13. *Gabu*, used nominally and verbally for the burning of the scrub, is a generic term for burning (cf. Ch. III, Sec. 1). The drying of the bush after it has been cut is described by the expression *i-kali i-matutile*, 'he dries in the sun', 'he becomes sere' (cf. also Div. VIII, §§ 15 and 16).

14. Motago'i, one of my best informants, discussing the burning of the leaves on the ground, volunteered the following statement:—

T. 29.

Kidama	*gala*	*ta-gabu*	*yovesi*	*o*	*pwaypwaya,*	*bogwo*
supposing	no	we burn	leaf	in	soil	already

i-ula,	*gala*	*i-simasimla.*
he sterile	no	he fertile

For free translation, see Chapter III (Sec. 1).

15. COMMENTARY: The verbal expression *i-ula*, which I translated here by 'to be sterile', I have not found in any other context. In other contexts *ula* means 'foulness', and is associated with human excrement. The natives have a deep conviction that human excrement renders the soil useless. Perhaps the verb here does not so much denote barrenness as a bad or foul quality of soil which makes it impossible for food to grow. But I could not obtain any helpful commentary from my informant. *Simasimla* is an expression for fertility in soil and for the condition of smoothness or mellowness in substances prepared for food, 'the state of being prepared'.

16. *Koumwala* (cf. Ch. III, Sec. 3), 'to clear the soil of weeds, refuse, stones', is a term which I have never met except in gardening, as indeed the activity itself would hardly be carried out in other cultural contexts. *Koumwala* consists in *nene'i*, *ninene'i*, 'to sweep the ground' with the hands or with a *kaytane'i*, 'small broom', made of leaves tied together; *kabi*, 'to pick up stones', 'to collect stones with the hands'; *tubwalasi*, 'to collect small sticks and refuse'; *katununuma*, 'to gather the rubbish together'; *yolukula*, 'to place the refuse into heaps'; *vakalota*, 'to set the heaps on fire'; *supi*, 'to feed the fire with new sticks'. The *yogulamaysi*, 'dead burnt leaves'. and *kaynunubwa*, 'half-burnt sticks', have very often to be collected from the cold embers and relit next day.

17. As far as I know, all these expressions have a generic meaning, that is, they do not refer only to activities carried on in the gardens. Thus *nene'i* is the ordinary term for 'to sweep', and I have heard the expressions *vakalota* and *supi* a hundred times when natives were kindling a fire. The nouns for small embers or burnt leaves are generic. The verb *yolukula*, 'to make heaps', I have not often come across, but it is not specific. The verb *katununuma* is compounded of *katu-*, prefix of completion, and *nunuma*, probably the same root as *lumlum*, 'heap of small sticks and leaves' or 'bundle of magical leaves'. I am not sure which of these two meanings is primary.

18. The *koumwala* is closely associated with the subdivision of garden plots into squares, the linguistic technicalities of which we shall analyse below in §§ 28, 39, 45 and 46.

19. The most generic term connected with planting is the verb *keli*, 'to dig', closely associated with the noun *dayma* (cf. above § 5). It is used in the same general way as *dayma* for any act of digging. *Keli* is not used for burrowing in the soil with the hands; this is denoted by the verb *yeni*. But it is used in speaking of animals burrowing in the ground, such as crustaceans, worms and insects.

20. Apart from this generic term, however, the natives have certain specific expressions. Thus the verb *sopu*, *sapwo*, 'to bury in the ground', is used most naturally for the planting of taytu. But it may also be applied to the planting of *kuvi*, and I am not able to say whether the use of this verb is determined by the nature of the crop or by the mode of activity. It must be remembered that whereas taytu is buried completely, taro is only loosely laid in the ground. This action is called *vitawo*, 'to set up', a verb which is also employed with reference to a number of inaugural acts, all of which have the meaning of 'to set up' in the physical sense, and 'to institute', 'impose' (as a taboo), 'inaugurate' in the figurative sense (cf. also analysis of verb *vatuvi*, M.F. 2, Comm. 1). The planting of a tree or vegetable from a seed is called *vala* or *vali*. With reference to the large yams the verb *sopu* is also employed. The expression *sopu malaga* (cf. Ch. III, Sec. 4) is used with regard to the planting of the main crops. I am not able to trace the etymology of either *sopu* or *vali* further.

21. *Pwakova*, 'to weed', is a specific term for uprooting a weed (cf. Ch. IV, Sec. 2). It is used of weeding done at any stage in gardening. *Sapi*, used for the pulling out of smaller weeds and the more minute work of clearing the soil round the sprouting crops, is a special application of a verb which means 'to scratch'.

22. *Basi* is a generic term meaning 'to pierce' (cf. Div.III, Sec. 20). This verb has two or three specific applications, which have become so standardised and have acquired such a definite meaning that, within their special context, they hardly even suggest the more general meaning. Thus when used in connexion with this stage of gardening (cf. Ch. IV, Sec. 3), *basi* signifies the whole process of opening the soil, taking out the superfluous roots, and leaving the good ones. Here is a short text describing the *basi*:—

T. 30 *Ta-kelikeli   i-wokwo,   ta-liya   ta-sasi.*
           we dig on   he is over   we lift (the roots)   we pluck

           Bwanawa   ta-kam;   ta-mwoye   o   valu   ta-kome.
           unripe tuber   we eat   we bring here   in   village   we eat

           Taytu   ta-saymwo,   iga'u   bi-kabina'i.
           taytu   we put there (leave)   later on   he might grow.

23. COMMENTARY: The reduplicated (cf. Part IV, Div. 3) *kelikeli*, 'to dig and dig', 'to dig on', describes the first stage of the *basi*; the soil has to be opened. The expression 'we dig on he ends' means 'we dig on till the roots are exposed'. Then, according to the text, the roots have to be lifted and plucked. *Sasi*, equivalent to *sasa*, means 'to make holes in something', 'to sunder', here 'to make breaches in the roots by taking out (the tubers)'. The text goes on to explain that the unripe tubers taken out are brought into the village and eaten, while the taytu, here used in the special sense of 'good tubers', are left to mature.

24. Leaving the terminology of yam supports till we discuss the lay-out of the gardens, we come to harvest, described generically by the word *tayoyuwa*, used verbally and nominally—in the latter function to denote the various activities of the period, and in the adverbial phrase *o tayoyuwa*, 'at harvest'. Here again the natives would use the word *keli*, 'to dig', for the process of getting at the roots, but afterwards they would distinguish between the various types of harvesting. The taytu, they say, *ta-kava'i*, 'we take out'. The verb *kava'i* I have not met in any other context, but I do not think it is specific to harvest. Moreover, though it can be used with regard to taytu and taytu only, the general term *ta-tayoyuwa*, 'we harvest', would be much more frequently used when describing the harvesting of taytu. The verb *kopo'i*, literally 'to take into one's arms', would be used with regard to the harvesting of the *kuvi*, 'large yams'. This word is used for the hugging and nursing of a little child. Whether it is used here with any consciousness of the figurative derivation, or whether we have two homonyms with independent meaning, I cannot say.

25. *Kousisuwa* is a verb used for the taking out of certain large yams which are very long or have very branchy roots, notably the *baluluwa*. I cannot analyse this verb any further.

26. As to taro, the natives would not use the word *keli*, 'to dig', with reference to its harvesting. The ripe taro is simply pulled out of the soil without need of digging. The verb *lulu*, 'to lift', 'to pull out', to lift out', used also for the pulling of an axe out of wood, or for the lifting of any object which can simply be taken out, is applied to the harvesting of taro.

27. The following is a list arranged in alphabetic order of the cries which accompany gardening activities, especially during communal labour:—

dodo'u—ta-dodo'u-si taytu—literally 'we call out at the taytu'. A melodious scream uttered during the planting of the taytu (cf. Ch. III, Sec. 5).

kabwaku—special cry belonging to the *dodo'u* class, the first part of which imitates the cry of the *kabwaku* bird (cf. Ch. III, Sec. 5).

katugogova—shrill intermittent sound made by clapping hand against mouth, uttered during *kaytubutabu* ceremony, etc. (cf. Ch. X, Sec. 3).

ta'ukuwakula—scream during communal labour of cutting the scrub (cf. Ch. II, Sec. 5).

tilaykiki—intermittent yell, generic term in connexion with screams at gardening. Uttered when men bring fish to village for the *ula'ula* 'oblation' (cf. Ch. II, Sec. 4).

sawili—high intermittent scream uttered during harvest while *urigubu* carriers run from garden to village (cf. Ch. V, Sec. 5).

28. Passing now to the lay-out of the gardens, we may start with a brief restatement of the permanent frame-work (cf. Ch. II, Sec. 3). All the cultivable lands of a community are divided into large portions of unequal size with fixed boundaries. These are called *kwabila*, and their boundaries *karige'i*. These large portions are subdivided into *baleko*, 'small plots', with boundaries, *tukulumwala*. Generally the boundaries are marked by long heaps of stone. Conical heaps of stone in fields are called *tuwaga* and the open spaces between them *sapona*. The *buyagu*, 'garden-site', comprising usually one or at most two fields, is first marked off by the boundary belt, *kalikeda* or *kuduwaga*, and usually divided in half by a road. Into this garden site small in-roads are sometimes made, an action described in Vakuta by the expression *i-yowota-si lopou-la buyagu*, 'they cut road through the inside of the garden-site'.

29. The most important point in the garden-site is where the road from the village meets the road through the garden. This, called in anticipation of the stile which will appear there (another example of creative metaphor, cf. Part IV, Div. VII), *kalapisila o valu*, 'the stile on the village side', is surrounded by a piece of ground which will be called *mile'ula*, literally 'clean of pollution': *mile-*, 'clear', 'clean of', *ula*, 'excretory matter'. Starting from this point, we have on the right and left the four or six 'representative plots', *leywota*. Beginning with the ones nearest the village these have the individual names—on the right: *reutau'la o kakata*, *vaboda o valu* or *vaboda emaymo*, *vaboda o la odila* or *vaboda ewaywo*; and on the left: *reuta'ula o kikivama*, *sigeya'i o valu* or *sigeya'i emaymo*, *sigeya'i o la odila* or *sigeya'i ewaywo*. All these words, starting from the word *mile'ula*, are specific to gardens.

30. I am not certain about the derivation of the word *leywota*. The root *wota* might be derived from *wota*, 'net', in which case the etymology baffles me, or else it might be from *wotu*, *utu*, 'to cut', 'to cut off', 'to break off', 'to slice off', a verb used in connexion, for instance, with the breaking of boughs and branches for firewood. In this context it might mean something like 'the clearing of bush', 'the preparing of bush'. The verb *yowota*, found in the phrase *i-yowota-si lopou-la buyagu*, 'they cut road through inside of the garden-site', fits this explanation. *Yowota*, *yo-*, 'to make', 'cause', *wota*, 'to cut', 'to clear', to 'make clear', would have the meaning of 'to cut clearings'. Again the same verb appears as we know in the magical ceremony of *yowota*, where again the noun *yowota* or *kayowota*, 'the positive', 'beneficent sapling', might symbolise the clear garden in opposition to the *kaygaga*, which is thrown into the bush and symbolises *yosewo*, 'the uncut, useless scrub' (cf. Div. VIII, §§ 9 and 10).

31. If my etymology is correct, the word *yowota* would stand for the well-cleared, well-trimmed part of the garden. *Leywota* might be the verbal form 'already cleared' in an attributive form as past tenses sometimes are; *baleko leywota*, 'plot already cleared', 'plot perfectly cleared', and from this we would get the attributive word used nominally as *leywota*, 'perfectly cleared plot'. All this, however, is speculation, which I am giving here because, in the hands of some scholar in Oceanic linguistics, it might prove fruitful, even if in its present form it proved erroneous. The noun *reuta'ula*, on the other hand, is unquestionably a contraction of *leywota o u'ula*: 'the fundamental *leywota*', 'standard plot at the beginning'. I think that the similarity between *mile'ula* and *reuta'ula* is accidental, even as the words *u'ula*, 'foundation', 'beginning', and *ula*, 'excretory matter', show an accidental resemblance.

32. *Vaboda* is literally 'the closing up,' from *va-*, causative prefix, and *boda*, *bwadi*, 'to close up', 'to enclose'. *Sigeya'i* I cannot analyse into any simpler elements or place in any etymological scheme.

33. The ordinary garden plots are designated by the terms *o gayala kaylepa* and *kaymwila*. The first word I received in Kiriwina, the second in the South. The noun *kaylepa* in the first expression means 'magical wand', but otherwise I was unable to analyse the structure of this phrase further.

34. The terminology for the constitution of the garden-site is fully defined and illustrated in Chapter II (Sec. 3), and needs here only a brief linguistic commentary. The corners of the garden, *nunula*, literary 'breast', 'nipple', used in a figurative sense for angles or corners, are also designated by the term *wokunu*, not found in other contexts. The expression *kalibudaka* for the two sides of the garden is obviously a compound of *kali-*, 'fence', and *budaka*, literally 'board of a canoe', 'built out gunwale of a canoe'. I have no doubt, though I can only offer my Kiriwinian linguistic feeling in support, that the fundamental sense of the term *budaka* is the one derived from the canoe, and that it is extended figuratively to the lateral aspects of the garden as well as of the yam-house (see Ch. VIII, Sec. 4).

35. There are no specific terms for the paths of the garden, so far as I am aware. The word *keda*, general term for 'path', 'road', is used.

36. The *kali*, 'fence', consists of *gado'i*, 'upright stakes', thrust into the ground, and *kalibala*, 'horizontals', laid between two rows of *gado'i*. *Gado'i* is the name given to any stake planted vertically. *Kalibala* is literally 'the horizontal of the fence'; *kali*, 'fence', *bala*, 'horizontal stick, log or beam'. The term *kali* is used only for a fence in the garden, the small fences in the village are called *yokonikan*, which is probably a cognate word compounded of prefix *yo-* and the reduplicated form *koni-kani*, *konikali*.

37. Passing now to what I have called 'the magical wall', which is described in Chapter III, Section 4, we come to the term *lapu*, 'stout pole', used also verbally 'to procure stout poles' in such phrases as: *lagayle mi Omarakana i-lapu-si*, 'to-day the people of Omarakana procure (go and bring) their *lapu*'. From these are constructed the *kamkokola*, 'prismatic structures', the other ornamental structures and yam supports, which are described and photographed in the same chapter. The vertical pole of these is also called *kamkokola*, the two slanting poles *kaybaba*. A verbal distinction is made between the real *kamkokola*, the one over which magic is performed in each plot, and

the ones in the three remaining corners, which are called *kaynutatala.*
Karivisi, 'boundary triangles', are the triangular structures bounding
each plot.

38. As regards the derivation of these words, *kamkokola* contains
the root *kokola,* which is a generic term for 'foundation pillar', but
I do not know what the prefix *kam-* might mean, and so would be
chary of describing the structure as 'magical pillar'.

39. I cannot further analyse etymologically the words *tula,* 'partition stick', and *gubwa-tala,* 'squares into which the plots are divided
by means of these sticks'. *Gubwa-tala* is a numeral noun compounded
of the classificatory formative *gubwa-* and the numeral roots *-tala,*
-yuwa, and so on (cf. Ch. III, Sec. 3). The erecting of the various
uprights connected with the magical fence is described by the verb
keli, 'to dig', 'dig in' (already analysed in § 19). The verbs *lova,* 'to
throw', and *vitawo,* 'to set up', refer to the magical acts connected
with the *kamkokola* rather than to the technical procedure (cf. above
§ 20).

40. We pass now to the 'supports', for which there is a generic
term *kavatam,* probably compounded of *ka-,* formative for all wooden
things, *va-,* causative or effective, and *tam,* from *tamna,* 'stalk of taytu';
'the wood for the stalk'. The generic term *kavatam* covers several
kinds of vine support, verbally distinguished according to their
function, a description of which will be found in Chapter IV,
Section 1. Where possible the seed yam is planted at the foot of a
sapling. Such a 'stem left over from cutting' is called *kamtuya.* If a
kamtuya is not available, a 'small stick' called *kaygum* or, when it is
very slender, *yeye'i,* is supplied. A generic term for such very small
sticks is *kaytosobula,* literally 'stick-stand-sprout', stick to keep the
sprout up'. *Tamkwaluma* is another term used sometimes, almost
synonymous with *kaytosobula,* the etymology of which is obscure to
me. The *kaybudi* is a support leant against a larger tree as a bridge
between this and the young shoot. Although all supports might be
called generically *kavatam,* in the narrower sense this word means
'large yam support'. Very large poles are differentiated from smaller
ones by the specific name *kayvaliluwa,* compounded of *kay-,* 'tree',
-va-, causative, *liluwa,* perhaps from *luluwa,* 'to flare up', 'to develop';
'tree made for developed taytu', here 'pole made for developed
taytu'.

41. *Kaysalu,* 'tree with several branches left over from cutting',
or else such a tree planted as a support, is a word sometimes used. I
cannot give its etymology.

42. *Kwari,* 'to catch', 'to get hold of', is used to describe the grip of
the vine round the support. The verb *tetila* means 'to creep up';

yokeli, 'to twine round'; *mwayne*, 'to climb up'; *tavine*, 'to encircle'. The following texts illustrate some of these expressions:—

T. 31. *Boge i-kanabogwo kamtuya; oluvi taytu*
already he lie-of-old support-tree afterwards taytu

ta-sapu, i-mwayne. Kidama ta-sapwo gala
we plant he climb up supposing we plant no

kamtuya, iga'u ta-ta'i ka'i kekewoni kaygum,
support-tree later on we cut tree slender small-support

ta-katukwari. Iga'u ta-ta'i ka'i kaduvana'u kavatam,
we make coil later on we cut tree long yam pole

ta-woye, ta-katukwari.
we hit we make coil

For free translation, see Chapter IV (Sec. 1).

43. COMMENTARY: *i-kanabogwo* is compounded of the root *kana*, 'to lie', 'to remain', *bogwo*, 'of old', and it means in this context 'to remain from a previous occasion', 'to be already there'. In *katukwari* the root *kwari* means 'to catch hold of', the prefix *katu-* giving an effective sense. The whole word means 'to make coil'. The verb *woye*, literally 'to hit', 'to strike', is used here in the somewhat vague metaphorical sense 'to put up', 'to set up'.

44. Another short sentence describes the arrangements made to train the vine from a small support on to a larger one:—

T. 32. *I-mwayne o kaygum, ta-woye kavatam,*
he climb up in small stick we hit yam pole

bi-luvapela o kavatam.
he might throw-jump in yam pole

For free translation, see Chapter IV (Sec. 1).

45. The following is an interesting comment on the function of the partition squares:—

T. 33. *Ta-saytula pela bagula bi-nana'u.*
we lay boundary stick because garden he might be quick

Ta-sopu gubwa-tala, bi-wokwo, ta-luvapela
we plant one garden-square he might be over we throw-jump

gubwa-tala; ta-sopu, ta-sopu, bogwo
one garden-square we plant we plant already

bi-wokwo.
he might be over

For free translation, see Chapter III (Sec. 3).

46. COMMENTARY: *saytula*, compounded of *say-*, 'to place', and *tula*, 'boundary stick', is a verb used for the action of laying a boundary stick. The analysis of the subjective feelings of people at work: 'we plant one square, it is finished; then we change over to another one; we plant, we plant', is of interest. The double repetition of 'we plant' means that each time 'we plant' on one square, the work goes quickly (cf. Ch. III, Sec. 3).

47. Concerning the taboo mentioned in Chapter IV, Section 4, the natives told me:—

T. 34. *Boma-la*   *ta-sikayla-si*   *o*   *tula.*   *Kidama*
taboo his   we sit-at   in   boundary stick   supposing

tay-tala   *bi-sila*   *bi-kapwawo.*   *Vivila*
one (m.)   he might sit   he might get elephantiasis   woman

makawala,   *kway-viyaka*   *puwa-la.*
alike   big (r.b.)   labia his

For free translation, see Chapter III (Sec. 2). The expression 'to sit at' is a euphemism for sexual intercourse (cf. also Div. XI, § 5).

48. I shall adduce here a brief text which refers to garden activities in general as well as to what we have called the functional classification of crops (Div. III, Sec. 20).

T. 35. (i) *Kidama*   *ta-sapwo*   *taytu,*   *i-vagi*   *gowa-na;*
supposing   we plant   taytu   he make   dead tuber his
oluvi   *i-kabina'i.*
afterwards   he grow

(ii) *Gowa*   *bita-tayoyuwa*   *bita-lava,*
dead tuber   we might harvest   we might throw away
bi-ma-ga   *kanuwa,*   *bata-waye*
he might come instead   yam-food   we might bring there
bata-sayli   *wa*   *gugu.*
we might put   in   heap

(iii) *I-kabina'i:*   *i-tuwali*   *kabine-na,*   *i-tuwali*   *yagogu-na,*
he grow   he differ   growth his   he differ   seed yam his
i-tuwali   *kakavala,*   *i-tuwali*   *ugu,*
he differ   minor seed yam   he differ   inferior taytu
i-tuwali   *taytu*   *kavakay-viyaka.*
he differ   taytu   very big (w.l.)

49. FREE TRANSLATION: (i) When we plant taytu, it (the seed tuber) (turns into) the dead tuber, while (at the same time) it grows (into a new plant).

(ii) The dead tuber at harvest we throw away; yam-food we keep, we bring (to the village), we put it in a heap.

(iii) (The plant) grows, a different (part of the plant) are the roots, a different part the seed yams, a different part the minor seed yams, a different part the inferior tubers, a different part the taytu, the very big ones.

50. COMMENTARY: (i) describes the fact that the old seed taytu becomes on the one hand the dead or spent tuber while at the same time the new plant grows out of it.

(ii) tells us that, at harvest, the spent tuber is thrown away while the yam-food 'comes', that is, is brought into the village and ceremonially made into heaps. The word *tayoyuwa* is used here in a loose way for 'to take out'; the correct term would have been *basi*. The word *kanawa* is a dialectical variety of *kaulo*, 'yam-food', for which see Div. II, § 8.

(iii) probably refers back to the word *kabina'i* as used at the end of (i), where it signifies the plant's growth. It enumerates those parts of the plant which are the most relevant to the natives, that is, the roots (literally described here as 'growth'), the seed yams, the minor seed yams, the inferior tubers and taytu in the narrow sense of 'show tubers.'

51. The following homonymous meanings may be noted in this Division:

1. *basi*	1.	'to pierce'.
	2.	'to thin'.
	3.	'the period of thinning'.
2. *kabwaku*	1.	'a bird'.
	2.	'planting cry' (in imitation of the bird).
3. *kalawa*	1.	'cycas' ⎱ I am not clear which meaning
	1.	'tally leaf' ⎰ is primary.
	2.	'to prepare the tally leaf'.
	3.	'to count'.
4. *kamkokola*	1.	'magical prism'.
	2.	'the central pole' of this.
	3.	'the rite' of this name.
5. *kavatam*	1.	'yam-pole' in general.
	2.	'large yam-pole'.
6. *la kalikeda*	1.	'road of the fence' ⎱ I am not clear which mean-
	1.	'sea passage' ⎰ ing is primary
7. *lopou-la*	1.	'belly' 'inside'.
	2.	'earth and plants therein'.
8. *nunu-la*	1.	'breast'.
	2.	'corner of garden'.
9. *yowota*	1.	'to cut clearings'.
	2.	'the rite' of that name.
	3.	'sapling'.

DIVISION VII

MAGIC

1. Some of the words used for garden magic are not specific, but refer to magic in general. We shall have therefore to go somewhat beyond the scope of our present subject in order to show where the specific vocabulary of garden magic begins. The word *megwa* (n.), to which the English noun magic corresponds in a remarkably adequate way, is the most generic term. It means 'the body of magical practices', that is, 'the body of magical rites and spells'; all the magic known to the islanders, all that is magical as opposed to any other form of human activity. In this sense they would predicate *bayse megwa*, *bayse gala megwa*, 'this is magic, this is not magic'. In its sense of 'body of magical practices' the natives would speak of *megwa towosi*, 'magic of the garden magician', or *megwa bagula*, 'garden magic'; *megwa bwaga'u*, 'magic of sorcery'; *megwa poulo*, 'magic of fishing'; *megwa kabilia* or *kabilia la megwa*, 'magic of war'. In some such phrases the specific name of a type of magic can be used without the addition of the noun *megwa*. Thus 'garden magic' will be called simply *towosi*, 'war magic' *boma*, 'black magic' *bwaga'u*, and so on.

2. *Megwa* in a narrower sense means 'magical virtue', 'magical force', 'magical influence', as in the expression:—

T. 36.

towosi	i-miga'i	o	wado-la,	megwa
garden magician	he magic	in	mouth his	magic

bi-la	o	pwaypwaya.		
he might go	in	soil		

For free translation, see Chapter I (Sec. 5).

3. In a concrete sense *megwa* might represent a special system, as when the natives speak about *da megwa-si*, 'our magic'; *ma-tau-si-na si megwa*, 'the magic of these people'. I need not repeat here that this noun has not one vague meaning but a series of clear meanings, so that, when in actual use, the word is contextually indexed and yields a definite meaning. The noun *megwa* can also be used with possessive pronominal suffixes, mostly of the third person, and then it changes its form into *migava-*. Thus we find *migava-la yena* side by side with *megwa yena*, 'fish magic'; *migava-la bagula*, 'magic of gardens', side by side with *megwa bagula*, 'garden magic'. Such expressions with the suffixed pronoun of nearest possession (cf. Div. XII, § 3) mean always the magic of something in the sense of 'magic pertaining to something', the magic which controls an object or a natural force.

The legal or economic possession of magic is always expressed with the pronouns of ownership (cf. Div. XII, § 7): *ulo megwa*, 'my magic'; *da megwa-si*, 'our magic'. Thus Bagido'u would speak of *boma-la ulo megwa*, 'taboo of my magic'.

4. The verb *megwa*, *miga'i*, means 'to make magic' or 'utter a spell': *towosi i-miga'i bagula*, *towosi i-megwa bagula*.

5. When it is necessary to express the fact that the utterance of a spell is concentrated on something, the verb *yopo'i*, *yopwi* is used (noun *yopa*, 'spell'). *Towosi i-miga'i*, *i-yopwi ka'i*, 'the garden magician magics, he charms over herbs'. Thus in the expression *i-miga'i o wado-la*, 'he magics by mouth', the verb *miga'i* cannot be replaced by *yopo'i*.

6. When the evil character of a magic is to be emphasised, its name is *bulubwalata*, verbal form *bulati*. *Ma-tau-na i-bulati bagula*, *i-keulo bulubwalata*, 'this man bewitches the garden, he recites black magic'. The verbs *keulo* (literally 'to carry', 'to sail') and *ka'u*, *kwawo* (literally 'to take') are at times used to describe the act of reciting. I cannot say whether there is a feeling of metaphor in these two extensions of meaning, but the two verbs are so often used in the context of magic and so formally associated with the nouns 'magic' and 'spell' that to my feeling the figurative sense has disappeared.

7. *Kariyala*, 'magical portent', describes the natural event or convulsion which, in native belief, is a by-product of magic (cf. Ch. III, Sec. 4). I can suggest no derivation for this word.

8. Another general term closely connected with magic is *boma-la*, 'taboo'. It is a noun used with possessive pronouns, *boma-gu*, 'my taboo', 'a taboo to be observed by myself'. *Boma-la*, however, mentioned with the object or a person means 'taboo to be observed because of something or with reference to something'. *Boma-la ulo towosi*, 'taboo of my garden magic'; *boma-la buyagu*, 'taboo of garden'. Here again the uses are multiple, but the context always makes the meaning definite. The noun can sometimes be used without possessive pronouns, but not in the sense of taboo. *Boma*, 'tabooed grove' (cf. Div. I, § 2 and, for an example of it, Ch. IX, Sec. 2), is generally found in the form *kaboma*, with the formative of tree, wood. *Boma* also means 'war magic', and *kaboma* also means 'wooden dish' (probably 'piece of wood surrounded with observances') and 'taboo imposed on gardens'.

9. As regards the delimitation of magic from other aspects of culture, the natives have a number of expressions by which they can define certain acts as magical; and they have never any doubt as to what is magic and what is not (cf. Ch. I, Secs. 5 and 8). Whenever I have to confess to a certain confusion in my own mind, that is due to the inadequacy of my enquiries or to the inadequacy of an individual informant, not to the natives' incapacity for distinguishing between magic and practical work. With regard to the *kamkokola*, for instance, I received the following in answer to my question:—

T. 37. *Megwa wala, gala tuwayle si koni wa bagula.*
     magic just no other their task in garden

'They are only magical and have no other task in the garden.' Another general expression which one of my informants once uttered spontaneously and which I found extremely useful in my enquiries, was the distinction between *megwa la keda* and *bagula la keda*, 'the road of magic' and 'the road of garden work'. Substituting for *bagula* the word for any other activity, I was able to make my informant rapidly define any activity as technical or magical.

10. So far we have been concerned with the generic terminology of magic. The noun *towosi*, which was one of the linguistic leitmotivs of the descriptive chapters, as it will be of Part VII, is the principal word with which we have to deal. *Towosi* means 'garden magician', 'garden magic', 'the concrete system of garden magic used in a community'.

11. It is not possible to decide which is the fundamental meaning of this word. The prefix *to-*, which characterises the word as being originally applied to a human being, would point, from the formal point of view, to the meaning of 'garden magician' as the primary one.

12. *To-*, 'man', 'human being'; *wosi*, 'song', 'song and dance', is a tempting etymology. *Towosi* would mean the man who sings, the man who chants, 'the chanter'. But this is only a hypothetical etymology, for I was not able to detect any real cultural affinities between dancing and any form of magic, still less between the magic of gardens and the dances and chants which are called *wosi*. Only once, I think, was a certain formula connected with love-magic and appearing in a myth described by the term *wosi*. So that the interpretation of *towosi* as 'chanter', if it has any value, is merely an historical and reconstructive one. There is no living affinity between the two terms.

13. But apart from formal analysis, the noun *towosi* in the sense of garden magician occurs more often and fits more naturally into the various contexts of speech, so that I have no hesitation in adding the semantic verdict to the formal one, and in regarding 'garden magician' as the meaning of the noun *towosi*. When, therefore, the word *towosi* is used to describe the ritual of the gardens it should be understood as 'the magic of the *towosi*', the 'magic performed by the hereditary officiating *towosi* of a community'.

14. *Towosi* in the sense of the given system of magic pre-eminently connected with a village community, is but a narrow application of this term in its meaning of garden magic.

15. The expression: *avayle la kaylepa*, 'whose garden magic wand is it?' would be equivalent to *avayle towosi*, in enquiring who is the garden magician of a community. *La kaylepa Bagido'u* would mean 'the magic wielded by Bagido'u', the manner in which the system practised by Bagido'u runs. Another corresponding expression is: *ma-tau-na i-woye da buyagu*, 'this man strikes our garden'; *ma-tau-na i-woye da pwaypwaya*, 'this man strikes our soil' (cf. Ch. II, Sec. 4).

16. The verb *woye*, 'to strike', is often used in the general sense of carrying out garden magic. It is a *pars pro toto* figure of speech, defining the whole garden magic by one act (cf. Div. VIII, §§ 6 and 7).

17. Another general term for performing the rites is *lova, lava*, or *lavi*, 'to throw'; in the southern dialect *louya*. *I-lova kamkokola*, 'he carry out the *kamkokola* rite'; *i-lova kaydabala*, 'he carry out the *kaydabala* rite'. Whether this verb has the meaning of physically putting up, 'throwing', placing of an object', or is frankly figurative, 'throwing' = 'casting', and refers rather to the magical virtue of the spell than to the physical act, I cannot say (cf. for examples of its use Div. VIII, § 20; Div. IX, §§ 6, 8, 24, 27 and 37; M.F. 17).

18. There are one or two other activities which are typical of the office of garden magician: the gathering of herbs; *towosi i-yo'udila ka'i*, 'the garden magician collects-in-the-bush magical herbs'; *towosi i-sulubulami*, 'the garden magician boils the herbs in coconut oil', which is done only in Vakuta (cf. Document VI); *towosi i-ula'ula baloma*, 'the garden magician presents oblation to the spirits'. Spirits are named at this oblation, at the harvest offerings, and several times in the spells, but it is the magical virtue of their generic name or of the specific names of ancestral predecessors in the office of magician which, in native belief, produces the magical effect.

19. The reader will remember that I have constantly spoken about 'acolytes', 'helpers', 'junior magicians'. There is no word for these functionaries, though their rôle and their office is real enough. Sometimes, in the carrying out of some special activity, the magician's assistants receive a temporary functional designation. In Kurokayva magic the men who put the *bwabodila*, 'charmed leaves', on the *kamkokola* are called *to-bwabodila* (cf. Ch. IX, Sec. 2). The people who carry the two or three adzes in the *tum* ceremony are called *to-kwabi-la ligogu*, 'wielder of adze'. I have heard the helpers who put up the *kamkokola* described as *to-kelikeli-la kamkokola*, 'men who dig in *kamkokola*'. But all such expressions are merely functional designations and at times, as in the case of *to-bwabodila*, may not designate the real 'junior magicians', the two or three young kinsmen of the magician, but certain acolytes chosen for the occasion.

20. Besides the *towosi* magic we have come across three other types of magic in dealing with agriculture: private garden magic, *vilamalia*, *kaytubutabu*. The system of *vilamalia*, 'magic of prosperity', literally 'village prosperity', whose wielder is called *tovilamalia*, contains the rites of the *kaytum-la bubukwa*, 'pressing of the yam-house floor', and of the *basi valu*, 'piercing of the village' (Omarakana), or *bibila valu*, 'exorcising of the village' (Oburaku). (For Omarakana System, cf. Ch. VII, Secs. 1–3; for Oburaku, Sec. 6.)

21. The second named magic is *kaytubutabu*, the magic of the coconut, a term which we have analysed when we were speaking of this palm (Div. IV, § 11). Lastly there is *momla*, an inaugural rite of thinning (cf. Ch. IV, Sec. 3), which is also found in Sinaketa (Ch. X, Sec. 1). A nameless type of magic consists of the private spells of the garden and the village grove: the magic of bananas; and perhaps of the bread-fruit, though I had only vague statements about the existence of this last. Individual acts of such magic may be called by names used also for rites in the official system: e.g. *momla* (Ch. IV, Sec. 3), *bisikola* (Ch. III, Sec. 1), but there is no generic word to describe such magic throughout the district.

22. With regard to the terminology of magical paraphernalia, a catalogue of the terms gives us a good survey of the actual reality, therefore it will be helpful to list the words and divide these into classes corresponding to the classes of things. I shall, then, enumerate first the implements of magic, that is, objects produced *ad hoc*, used and kept as indispensable elements in rites. In the second place, I shall list the contrivances and erections constructed in the gardens as parts of ceremonies. They are distinguished from the first class in that they are not part of the permanent magical outfit, but are seasonally made and allowed to perish; and, as a rule, are the objects on which and round which the rite of the magic is performed, and not implements used in the rite. In the third place, I shall list the substances of magic, that is, certain natural products, mainly leaves, which are impregnated with magic in the rite and afterwards applied to the object which ultimately has to be charmed. Such substances differ from both the previous classes in that they are vehicles of magic and are consumed or destroyed in the rite; and, though they are in a way instruments, stand in a special relation to magic in that they are always being the recipients of the magical virtue.

23. A. IMPLEMENTS OF MAGIC.

kaylepa: 'the magical wand used in striking the gardens' receives naturally the place of honour. It is symbolic of the magician's office, and can be used figuratively for the whole magic. I am not able to analyse its root *lepa*; the prefix *kay-* is obvious. We find the word in the expression *o gayala kaylepa*, the name given to the plots which are not standard plots, and in the *bulukaylepa*, the name of one of the component ceremonies of the Omarakana *yowota* (cf. Ch. II, Sec. 8). *Kaylepa* is, as far as I know, a specific name exclusively reserved for the magical wand used for striking the garden. Both word and object are specific, but the object might be confused with any short staff or walking-stick, the sacred wand of Omarakana not even being decorated with any carvings.

kaytukwa: 'staff', is a generic name for any walking-stick. One is used by the garden magician on certain occasions, especially when chanting growth magic and at the *okwala* ceremony (cf. Ch. V, Sec. 3).

kema: 'axe', generic name. The object is used as a magical implement in the first inaugural rite, where the magician and all the gardeners carry axes with medicated herbs round the blades (cf. Ch. II, Sec. 4). The word figures in the compound *burakema*, the name given in Omarakana to a partial rite of the *yowota* first inaugural ceremony. The axe, however, becomes a specific magical implement when, as in Kurokayva, the magician carries the large ceremonial axe. In this context the implement can be labelled *beku*, 'ceremonial blade', though it may also be called *kema*.

ligogu: 'adze' used in the *tum* ceremony to cut through the stalk of the taytu (cf. Ch. V, Sec. 3). The word and the implement are not specific, but they acquire a ceremonial character when they are medicated and the herbs wrapped round the blade.

kaykapola: 'magical torch'. The generic meaning of this as well as its linguistic analysis has been given above (cf. Div. IV, § 2).

katakudu: a compound of *ka-*, prefix 'stick', *-ta-*, derived (?) from *ta'i*, 'cut', *kudu*, 'tooth'—etymology not clear; 'small stick' made of *kayaulo* (iron-wood palm?) chanted over at the *vilamalia* rite and used for making holes at the *basi valu* (cf. Ch. VII, Sec. 3).

dimkudukudu: etymology unknown. Another name for the same object.

moyluma: a special word given to 'the mat in which the *kaykapola* torches, magical herbs, and axes are wrapped up (cf. Ch. II, Sec. 4). As far as I am able to judge the word is specific, and is used only for mats when magically employed. But whether it is specific to garden magic I cannot say. The word is composed of the prefix *moy-*, from *moi*, 'mat'; and *luma*, probably connected with *lumlum*, 'magical bundle', or 'heap of small sticks and leaves' (cf. below, § 26).

kwoylabulami: the generic term for a pot used for the cooking of coconut oil. It is used in the preparation of herbs for the first ceremony in Vakuta (cf. Document VI). A special pot would be set aside for this magical purpose.

kaybomatu: the generic name for any large mussel shell. It is used to scrape some calcareous stuff from a coral boulder, an ingredient in certain magical mixtures.

This, together with *moyluma* and *kwoylabulami*, is not a primary magical implement: these three never figure in any rite, but are used and traditionally defined as instruments for the preparing or cutting of magical substances.

24. Passing now to the substances used in *vilamalia* and *kaytubutabu* magic, we have:—

binabina: stones left on the floor of the *bwayma* over which the first ritual of Omarakana *vilamalia* is performed (cf. Ch. VII, Sec. 1). The rite is called *kaytumla bubukwa*, 'the pressing of the yam-house floor', and the stones are also called by the same expression, which then means 'the pressers of the yam-house floor'. *Binabina* is a generic name for stones of volcanic origin imported from the d'Entrecasteaux archipelago.

ta'uya: 'conch shell' (generic), is used in the *kaytubutabu* magic and in the *vilamalia* magic of Oburaku (cf. Ch. X, Sec. 3, and Ch. VII, Sec. 6).

urinagula: 'hearthstone' (generic), is perhaps not a magical implement but a part of a magical outfit. On them the magician deposits the oblation to the ancestral spirits. On them also a rite of the *vilamalia* magic in Oburaku is performed (cf. Ch. II, Sec. 4, and Ch. VII, Sec. 6).

25. B. MAGICAL ERECTIONS.

si bwala baloma: 'house of the spirits', the miniature hut constructed at one of the component rites of the *gabu*, 'burning' ceremony in Omarakana (cf. Ch. III, Sec. 1).

gado'i baloma: 'stake of the spirits', a few sticks or a miniature fence associated with the ancestral spirits, made in Oburaku at one of the *kamkokola* rites (cf. Ch. X, Sec. 1).

kayluvalova: a small stick put up to indicate that work in the gardens is taboo during the performance of a ceremony (cf. Ch. II, Sec. 4).

kaydabala: a stick indicating taboo on work put up at one of the rites of growth magic (cf. Ch. IV, Sec. 2).

kaykubwaya: small sticks put up round a *kamkokola* or *kavatam* in Vakuta, having a magical and also perhaps a practical significance (cf. Doc. VI).

26. C. Magical Substances.

Here I shall first give a few terms of more general connotation, defining the magical substances functionally; that is, by the place where they are put or by the part which they play within the rite, rather than by their substance.

boda (n.) : literally 'closing up'; leaves which are put at the foot of the *kamkokola* in Oburaku during the inaugural rite (cf. Ch. X, Sec. 1).

bwabodila (n.): reduplicated form of *boda* with the third possessive *-la* attached, 'his covering'. Herbs inserted under the lower end of the *kaybaba*, 'slanting pole', in the *kamkokola* rite of Kurokayva (cf. Ch. IX, Sec. 2).

lumlum: 'heap of debris' made on garden plots and ritually burned in *gibuviyaka* rite (cf. Ch. III, Sec. 1). As mentioned already (Div. VI, § 17), I am not certain whether the primary meaning of this word is a heap of debris or such a heap in so far as the magical bundle of leaves is inserted in it, or whether it means the magical bundle of leaves alone. Judging from the expression *moyluma*, 'magical mat', 'mat for magical bundles' (cf. § 23), the latter assumption seems to be the more probable one.

kavapatu: literally 'leaves which close up'; inserted at the foot of the *kamkokola* in Omarakana and in Kurokayva (cf. Ch. III, Sec. 4, and Ch. IX, Sec. 2).

kaypaku: literally 'leaves that stick'; band of coconut leaf used at the *kaytubutabu* magic in Omarakana (cf. Ch. X, Sec. 3).

paku: 'closing leaves' put under the *kaybaba*, 'slanting pole', of a *kamkokola* in Oburaku (cf. Ch. X, Sec. 1).

27. I am now listing the various substances used in magic in so far as I recorded their names in the commentaries I made on this subject. Obviously it is but a fragmentary list, and had I been able to survey all the other systems of garden magic the list would have swelled indefinitely. I am giving first the list of herbs and leaves employed in magic, and then the very brief list of three entries in which substances other than vegetable are enumerated. This numerical proportion, or rather disproportion, is evidence of the extremely preponderant rôle played by vegetable matters in Trobriand magic.

borogu: 'croton', used in Vakutan *gibuviyaka*.

boyeya: small prolific plant used in *kaytubutabu* magic.

bulabula: small stout tree with penetrating roots, growing to a great age; used in Oburaku *vilamalia* and Kavataria *gabu*.

busa: tree whose wood is used for the *kaytubutabu* pole, and its leaves in the ceremony.

dadam: reed growing in swampy soil used in Vakutan *yowota*.

gegeku: tree with edible fruit, leaves used in Oburaku *vilamalia*.

gipware'i: 'lalang grass' tied to *kaykapola* in *gibuviyaka* rite of Omarakana. It also imposes taboo before *tum* in Teyava.

gutaguta: tree with edible leaves, used in Vakutan and Teyavan *yowota*.

gwadila: tree with edible fruit, used in Oburaku *vilamalia*.

ipikwanada: creeper with luxuriant foliage resembling taytu, used in Omarakana *yowota* magic.

kaga: ficus tree, used in Vakutan *yowota*.

kakema: dwarf tree with powerful roots, used in first act of Omarakana *vilamalia*.

kaluluwa: herb used in Kurokayva *kamkokola* rite and in Vakutan *yowota*.

kaluwayala: hibiscus flower used in Kurokayva *kamkokola* rite.

kasiyena: a species of yam used in Kurokayva initial ceremony and Teyava *tum*.

kavega'i: tree of stunted growth with leaves spreading wide on ground, used in Oburaku *vilamalia*.

kaybwibwi: species of pandanus with fragrant white flowers, used in Omarakana *yowota*. (See below *modigiya*.)

kaytagem: leaves used in Kurokayva *kamkokola* rite, and also in *yowota*.

kekewa'i: leaves used in Oburaku *isunapulo*.

kirima: ficus tree used in Vakutan *yowota*.

kotila: herb used in Teyavan *yowota*.

kubila: plant with scented flowers or leaves, used in Omarakana *yowota*.

kwanada: species of uncultivated yam used in *kalimamata* rite of Omarakana.

kwaygagabile: tree with large pods whose leaves are used in *kaytubutabu* ceremony.

lawa: tree with scented, tasteless fruit, whose leaves are used in Vakutan *yowota*.

lewo: stunted tree reaching to very old age, used in second act of *vilamalia* of Omarakana.

leya: wild ginger used in second act of Omarakana *vilamalia*.

lileykoya: plant with aromatic leaves, used in *tum* of Omarakana, in Vakutan *yowota* and in *tum* of Teyava.

lubiyayaga: herb used in Teyavan *yowota*.

makita: creeper with strong, sweetish smell used in *kaytubutabu* magic.

menoni: tree with edible fruit, used in Oburaku *isunapulo* and *vilamalia*.

modigiya: dried leaves of the *kaybwibwi* pandanus (see above), used for *kaytubutabu* pole.

noku: tree with edible but despised fruit whose leaves are strewn on *baleko* during *okwala*.

noriu: plant from *odila*, used in *kaytubutabu* magic.

nunuri: tree whose leaves are used in Kurokayva *kamkokola* rite.

peraka: herb used in Vakutan *gibuviyaka*.

sasari: plant used in Omarakana *isunapulo*, placed on *kamkokola*.

sasoka: tree with very large fruit used in Omarakana *yowota* magic.

sayda: nut tree, leaves used in Oburaku *vilamalia*.

saysuya: tree with edible fruit, leaves used in Oburaku *vilamalia*.

setagava: tough weed with strong roots used in first act of Omarakana *vilamalia*, and in *kaytubutabu* magic.

seuse'u: tree with edible leaves used in Vakutan *yowota*.

siginibu: dried banana leaf used in Omarakana *yowota*.

silasila: herb used in Teyavan *yowota*.

sisiye'i: 'bracken', common rank weed used in Kuroyava *yowota*.

sulumwoya: aromatic mint-like plant used in Oburaku *isunapulo* magic.

tuvata'u: plant used in Oburaku *isunapulo* magic.

ubwara: small bush plant with long white tubers used in Omarakana *yowota* magic, and in *kaytubutabu* magic.

vayoulo: acacia tree used in Omarakana *gibuviyaka* rite.

wakaya: largest variety of banana, whose leaves are used in Omarakana *yowota*, *isunapulo* and *tum*.

wokubila: herb used in Kurokayva *yowota* and *kamkokola* rites.

yayu: casuarina leaves used in Omarakana *kamkokola* and *kaytubutabu* magic.

yokunukwanada: creeper with luxuriant foliage resembling taytu used in Omarakana *yowota* magic.

yokwa'ula: creeper with luxuriant foliage resembling taytu used in Omarakana *yowota* magic.

yonokiu: tree whose wood is used for *kaytubutabu* pole, and leaves in the ceremony.

youla'ula: creeper with luxuriant foliage resembling taytu used in Omarakana, Teyava and Vakuta *yowota* magic.

youlumwala: bush plant with large tubers used in *kamkokola* rite of Omarakana.

yoyu: coconut leaf used in Omarakana *yowota*.

NON-VEGETABLE SUBSTANCES

ge'u: enormous mounds made by bush-hen for brooding purposes; used in Omarakana and Teyava *yowota*.

kabwabu: large round hornets' nest used in Omarakana *yowota* magic.

kaybu'a: large coral boulder used in Omarakana and Vakuta *yowota* magic.

28. The homonymous meanings to be noted in this Division are few but important.

1. *kaylepa*	1.	'wand'.
	2.	'garden magic wielded' by someone.
2. *kaytubutabu*	1.	'coconut magic'.
	2.	'The pole which is the chief symbol of this magic'.
3. *megwa*	1.	'magic', 'body of magical practices'.
	2.	'magical virtue'.
	3.	'special system of magic'.
	4.	'to utter a spell'.
4. *towosi*	1.	'garden magician'.
	2.	'garden magic'.
	3.	'system of garden magic'.
5. *woye*	1.	'to hit'.
	2.	'to carry out garden magic'

INAUGURATIVE MAGICAL CEREMONIES

1. In this division we shall deal, as succinctly as the material allows, with the various names given to magical performances, and, in the course of our survey, certain points must be borne in mind. We shall have to distinguish between the names of a rite, a spell or a whole inaugural ceremony—not always easy apart from the context. We shall have also to distinguish between names that refer to one specific magical act, and generic descriptions. For example, such nouns as *kamkokola*, *kaylepa*, verbs such as *yowota*, *talala*, *vakavayla'u*, seem to be genuine technical terms of magic. Each of them denotes and is the proper name for one object or act, or for both; each of them is used so as to exclude all other denotations. On the other hand, such a word as *gabu*, which is invariably used to describe the second big compound ceremony of garden magic, is not a specific name, but merely defines what is happening in the course of this ceremony. Similarly, the various verbs by which some activities are described, *lova*, 'to throw', *vitawo* or *vita'u*, 'to inaugurate', *vapatu*, 'to close up', *woye*, 'to hit', are not specific terms of magic but generic terms used in this context in a consistent and discriminating manner.

2. Another point which must be made clear is the variety of forms in which the same root may appear. To take the word *gabu* again. It may be used nominally; and then, in one context, means 'the burning of the gardens', or in another context, 'the magical ceremony which includes the burning of the gardens' or 'the act of wholesale burning', for which the specific term *vakavayla'u* is also used. Or again *gabu* may be used verbally. The magician speaking of himself may say:—

T. 38. *Naboye   ba-gabu,   da   buyagu-si.*
to-morrow   I shall burn   our   garden-site

Or he may say: *a-gabu buyagu*, 'I am burning the garden-site'. Very often when obtaining my information from the magician himself I noted his use of the first person in speaking of garden rites.

3. The form changed when other men gave information, for they would speak in the third person:—

T. 39. *Towosi   i-gabu   buyagu.*
garden magician   he burn   garden-site

or:—

Towosi   i-woye   pwaypwaya.
garden magician   he hit   soil

And again the first person plural inclusive, *ta-*, is used in the following as in many other descriptive statements:—

T. 40. *Ta-gabu-si   da   buyagu   Yakosi, Yavatakulu.*
      we burn   our   garden-site   (in the months of *Yakosi* and
                                            Yavatakulu)

This inclusive plural tends to be used in Kiriwinian almost as an impersonal verbal form, corresponding to the German *man* or the French *on*. It also tends to be used in dual form, without the suffix -*si* at the end of the verb. Thus when natives tell you: *ta-bagula, ta-gabu, ta-woye pwaypwaya*, it should be translated probably by the expression 'it is customary to do so', 'one does so', 'everyone does so'. Thus in the verbal forms the root only is invariable and the person does not matter very much. Every verb which is given here can be used in any of the verbal forms which the language possesses (cf. Part IV, Div. III, A).

4. Again, some of the verbal roots receive a nominal form by the addition of one of the formative prefixes, especially *kay-*, the instrumental prefix. Thus if the magical action be described by the verb *sayboda* or *vapuri*, the spell, which in a way is the instrument of this action, is called *ka-sayboda, kay-vapuri*, the difference between *ka-* and *kay-* being merely phonetic. The effective prefixes *va-, katu-, vaka-* are also sometimes found with the root. As a rule I shall list the root and give the various prefixes together with the usage to which I have found the root submitted.

5. It was necessary to make this digression on the various forms in which we find verbal roots used in the context of magic, because it is in the terminology of magic that the greatest variety of such forms occurs. This is partly because magic is handled in an exclusive manner by the garden magician, hence the first and third person singular; partly because in magic figurative speech is very prominent; partly because in magic words are more important in themselves— because of their effective and pragmatic significance in spells—than in any other cultural activity.

6. Let us turn to the nomenclature of the *towosi*, 'garden magic', taking this in chronological order. It is interesting that there is no specific name to designate the first big inaugural ceremony (cf. Ch. II, Sec. 4). It is simply described by one of its component acts. According to context, the expression *i-woye buyagu* or *i-woye pwaypwaya* may mean either the one partial rite of striking the ground or the whole ceremony. Also, as we know, this expression may stand for the whole magic of gardens, for the exercise of the office of garden magician (cf. Div. VII, §§ 15 and 16). *Yowota*, which is the name of a component ceremony, the rubbing of the ground, is at times also used to designate the performance as a whole. The same is the case with *talala*. We will now analyse these words one after the other.

7. *I-woye buyagu* means literally 'he hits the garden-site'. The verb can be used in any person or tense. It describes the act, which consists of striking the ground, using two words of ordinary speech. The same holds good, of course, of the expression *i-woye pwaypwaya*, 'he hits the soil'.

8. *Talala* (v.) describes the cutting of two saplings, the *kaygaga*, literally 'bad tree', and the *kayowota*, 'the *yowota* tree'. The verb *talala* can be analysed into *ta-*, probably from *ta'i*, 'to cut', and *lala*, 'flower'; 'to cut into flower, to make blossom by cutting'.

9. The verb *yowota* designates the rubbing of the soil under the *kayowota*, the *yowota* sapling. We discussed it in analysing the term *leywota*, 'standard plot' (Div. VI, § 30) and the expression *i-yowota-si lopou-la buyagu*, 'they cut road through the inside of the garden-site'. We arrived there at the conclusion that the verb *yowota* has the meaning of 'to make clear', 'to prepare the soil.' In the present context *yowota*, the act of rubbing the soil, would have the meaning 'to make the ground clear' (for the coming gardens). This fits well into the native belief that this ceremony makes the ground soft. This is a short text given me by Bagido'u:—

T. 41.

Yowota,	*ba-miga'i*	*pwaypwaya,*	*bi-simsimla*
yowota	I might magic	soil	he might soften
makawala	*dumya.*		
alike	swamp		

For free translation, see Chapter II (Sec. 4).

10. Let us compare the spell accompanying the act (M.F. 5). In the first part we have the statement that in a tabooed grove, the grove of Yema, the magician and two mythical personalities sit and bless and anoint with coconut cream, making the taytu grow quick and straight. Then in the second part (repetition of strophe 3, M.F. 2) there is the magical affirmation of fertility, of specific fertility of yams, 'the belly of my garden lifts', etc. All these data point to the same conclusion: the verb *yowota* designates an act which magically makes the soil soft and fertile (cf. Div. VI, §§ 30 and 31).

11. Another expression used, but only very rarely, to describe this action is *ta-vapopula digadaga*, literally 'we cause the breaking forth in clusters of sere bracken'. *Vapopula* consists of the causative prefix *va-*, *popula* from *puri*, *puli*, 'to break forth into clusters'. Why the production of sere bracken should be a figurative expression of fertility I am not certain; probably at that time the bracken naturally turns brown in dry weather, and dry weather is desirable until after the burning.

12. We have encountered two more expressions connected with the first inaugural rite (cf. Ch. II, Sec. 8). *Bulukaylepa,* the longer and more elaborate form of this ceremony, taking four days, and *bulakema,* the shorter form used by Bagido'u, taking only one day. The second parts of these expressions, *kaylepa* and *kema,* have well-established meanings, 'magical wand' and 'axe'. The prefix *bulu-, bula-* might refer to the root *bwala,* 'house', or *bulukwa,* 'pig'. If the former, then there might be some historical reason, not expressed in the present ritual, by which the magical wand was charmed in the *bwala,* 'house', in the first form of the rite, and the axe only in the second. If the prefixes refer to pigs, the meaning would be the exorcism of pigs by means of the magical wand and axe respectively. Both explanations are conjectural.

13. As will be seen from a glance at the comparative table of Omarakana and Vakuta gardening magic (Document VI), and also from references to other systems (cf. especially Chs. IX and X), such terms as *ula'ula, yowota, talala, kaylepa, kaygaga* are of universal occurrence. The expressions *bulukaylepa* and *bulakema* I obtained in Omarakana and did not check elsewhere.

14. The following text, concerning the proceedings at the *yowota* in Teyava, will be found in free translation in Document VII.

T. 41a. (i) *Kumaydona   mi   kema   tomwota   ku-mayay-se,   o-gu-bwala*
             all   your   axe   human   you bring   in my house
         bi-kanukwe-nu.   (The magician then referred to his evening rite
         he might lie   over the axes:—)

    (ii) *Iga'u   bogi   ba-kapula   kema.   Kumaydona*
         Later on   night   I might wrap up   axe   all
         kema   ba-miga'i.
         axe   I might magic

The following comment was made by my informants on the need for rapidity on the magician's part in gathering the herbs:—

    (iii) *Kidama   bi-sisu,   bi-waywosi —   boge   i-woya-si*
          supposing   he might sit   he might rest   already   they hit
          baloma,   bi-katoulo.
          spirit   he might be sick

COMMENTARY: (ii) The verb *kapula* is another form of *kapwari,* 'to wrap up'.
(iii) The subject shifts in the three clauses: in the first it is the

magician, in the second, the spirits and in the third, the magician again.

15. Passing now to the second main ceremony of gardening (cf. Ch. III, Sec. 1), we find the one word (noun and verb) *gabu* to describe this rite, which really begins in Omarakana with the charming of the torches at the previous harvest, though actually the first direct act is the wholesale burning, *vakavayla'u*. Four more rites follow, which extend over three or perhaps only two days according to the system. The word *gabu* I have already alluded to (Div. VI, § 13). *Vakavayla'u* is, as far as I know, a specific expression denoting the act of setting fire to the cut and dried bush by means of medicated torches. It can be used as a verb as well as a noun. The action of carrying the torches is also described by the verb *suluwa*, which in ordinary speech means 'to err', 'to walk about aimlessly'. I could not discover why this verb is used in this context. The analysis of *vakavayla'u* has not yielded at my hands any definite results. It might either be composed of the causative *vaka-* and the root *vayla'u*, which means 'to steal'; 'to cause stealing'—an analysis which does not seem satisfactory either semantically or formally. Or else the word might be composed of *va-* causative, *kova*, 'fire', *la'u*, 'to be carried'; cause fire to be carried. This makes sense but is uncertain.

16. The second partial rite of the *gabu* is called *gibuviyaka*, literally 'big burning', perhaps here meaning 'thorough, final burning'. It is also done by means of *kaykapola*, 'coconut shoots', in this case 'torches', a word analysed elsewhere (cf. Div. IV, § 2). The heaps to which fire is set ceremonially are called *lumlum* (cf. Div. VII, § 26).

17. The names of the rites which follow, *pelaka'ukwa*, *kalimamata* and *bisikola* (cf. Ch. III, Sec. 1), are linguistically interesting. *Pelaka'ukwa* is undoubtedly a compound of *pela*, a formative derived from *pwala*, 'excrement', and *ka'ukwa*, 'dog'. I suggested in Chapter III (Sec. 2) that this term is applied to the medicated taro in a magically pejorative sense. It disguises the planted tuber by representing it as something which should become unpalatable to the bush-pig against which this magic is directed. We see that the object of the rite, the text of the spell and the symbolism of taro or stone all fit into this explanation. The ceremony is meant to frighten bush-pigs away, and this is done by verbal exorcism and derogatory naming of the taro itself.

18. Linguistics, ritual and context do not fit so well in the next ceremony, *kalimamata*. The name, which here designates rite and spell together, means on the surface 'wakening of the fence'; *kali*, 'fence', *mamata* (v.), 'to awaken'. Of course it could also mean some-

thing like 'eye of the fence', *mamata* being a reduplicated form of
mata, 'eye'; or if *kali* were an apophonic form of *kala-*, formative of
kaulo, it might mean 'the wakening of food'. Contextually this last
explanation would be the most plausible, for the ceremony is
performed over a variety of yam, *kwanada*, and the spell is directed
towards the crops, exhorting them to grow luxuriantly.

19. *Bisikola* is a charm and rite uttered over taro and associated
in Omarakana with the construction of a miniature 'house for the
spirits', in Vakuta (cf. Doc. VI) with a miniature fence. The word
is a compound of the prefix *bisi-*, which is often found in words
designating magical ceremonies. It may be derived from *basi*, 'to
pierce', in the sense of 'open up', 'inaugurate'. *Kola* is probably
derived from *kwari* = *kuri*, 'to get hold of'. In this context, therefore, it
might mean 'the inauguration of a getting hold of', probably of
taking root by the crops. On the other hand *kola* might be an
apophonic variety of *kali*, 'fence', as with *kokola*, 'wooden pillar used
as a foundation', *kamkokola*, 'magical prism'. This last word brings us
to the next big complex of rites.

20. The noun *kamkokola* designates primarily the whole structure
described in Chapter III (Sec. 4) more particularly the upright pole
(cf. also Div. VI, §§ 37 and 38). It is not used verbally, a number
of verbs being associated with the noun to describe the act. *I-vagi
kamkokola*, 'he makes the *kamkokola*'; *i-miga'i kamkokola*, 'he magics
the *kamkokola*'; *ta-woye kamkokola*, 'we hit (put up) the *kamkokola*';
ta-vitawo kamkokola, 'we set up, inaugurate the *kamkokola*'; *i-vapatu
kamkokola*, 'he (the magician) closes up the *kamkokola*'. These
are the phrases which, as I find in my notes, were actually used by
natives when referring to the processes of erecting and charming a
prism. Each verb either refers to part of the rite or describes figuratively some aspect of it. One verb was most frequently used—*towosi
i-lova kamkokola*, 'the garden magician throws the *kamkokola*'. In this
connexion the verb (cf. also Div. VII, § 17 and the references there
given), with its southern variants *i-louya*, *i-lavi*, refers more especially
to the casting of the taboo associated with the rite, but also to the
act as a whole. The first meaning I have documented in this text:—

T. 42. *Bi-lova*	—	*bi-tasi*	*ka'i*	*kayketoki*,
he might throw		he might pare	wood	small (w.l.)
bi-lavi		*o nunula,*		*bi-sisu.*
he might throw		in magical corner		he might sit

21. We find here characteristically the verb 'to throw' in two forms,
lova and *lavi*, with identical meaning; the verb *tasi* represents the
action of trimming a piece of wood by lopping off the branches. In

free translation: "When the magician throws (i.e. *kamkokola*), he trims a small piece of wood, he throws it (inserts it) in the magical corner, it remains there."

22. A special expression is used for the first putting up of the *kamkokola*, *vitoboge* from *vitawo*, 'to inaugurate, set up'; *boge* is the same root as *bogwo*, 'already', 'of old', 'first'; hence 'to erect first'.

T. 43. *Ta-vitoboge*   *ta-keli kamkokola o leywota.*
        we erect first (*kamkokola*)   we dig   *kamkokola* in standard plot

23. Further expressions connected with the magical prisms are: *kayluvalova*, the small stick referred to in Text 42, literally 'the stick of throwing', 'the stick of casting' (probably casting a taboo associated with the making of the *kamkokola*); and *kaybaba*, the slanting poles of the *kamkokola*. But we need not enumerate the other elements, as they were linguistically analysed in Div. VI, § 37.

24. *Kiya* (v.), 'to rub', 'to polish', is used of the magical action of rubbing the *kamkokola* pole with leaves before insertion. The verb *lola*, 'to moor', 'to anchor' (trans.), occurs in a great many spells and it is also used to describe the act of cutting or striking with the axe in the form *talola*, where *ta-* probably refers to the act of striking, *ta-*, from *ta'i*, 'to cut', being the formative of cutting implements and acts of cutting. *Kavapatu*, 'the leaves of closing', *kavaboda*, 'the leaves of covering', designate the herbs buried at the foot of the *kamkokola* and put on its fork. The verbs *patu*, 'close', and *boda*, 'cover', are of course generic terms, *va-* effective formative and *ka-* formative of leaves and wood. *Vakalova*, the name of a small ceremony distinctly exorcistic in character, is composed of *vaka-* causative prefix and *lova*, 'to throw'; 'to cause the throwing off'.

25. The spells associated with the *kamkokola* rite have no special names in any of the systems of magic that I have recorded.

26. The rite connected with *pwakova* (v. and n.), 'weeding', is described by the natives as *kariyayeyla sapi* (cf. Ch. IV, Sec. 2); *kari-* formative with the meaning 'through', *yayeyla* verbal root, probably reduplicated form of *yeyla* or *yeni*, a verb which means 'to scoop out', as one does with the hands or an implement. *Sapi*, literally 'to scratch' (cf. Div. VI, § 21), is another verb figuratively denoting weeding, and it appears in this expression in a nominal, that is gerundial or infinitival form. The expression would therefore mean 'he (the magician) scoops through the scratching'. The expression seems pleonastic, but I cannot analyse it further.

27. *Momla* is the name given to an inaugural rite of thinning, etymology unknown (cf. Div. VII, § 21).

MAGIC OF GROWTH

1. The nomenclature of the various spells and rites in growth magic is simpler, more direct and more lively than that in other parts of our subject. The verbs are usually borrowed directly from ordinary speech, they stand in perfect accordance with the aim of the spell and its meaning and with the stage of growth to which the magic refers.

2. The reader will do well in comparing the various analyses to glance occasionally at Documents VI and VII (garden magic of Vakuta and Teyava), at the information given about other systems in Chapters IX and X (Sec. 1), at the description of growth magic in Omarakana given in Chapter IV (Secs. 2 and 3), and at the commentaries on the Magical Formulae there referred to.

3. The first expression which we meet is *vaguri sobula*. The word *vaguri* means 'to wake up', the expression therefore means 'to wake up the sprout', to start it on its growth (cf. Ch. IV, Sec. 2, and M.F. 13, Comm. 1 in Part VII). Both verbs belong to the vocabulary of ordinary speech. For *sobula*, see Div. III, Sec. 5.

4. The next rite is defined by the term *katusakapu* or *vasakapu*, a word often heard in everyday language: *va-* or *katu-* causative, *sakapu*, 'to emerge'; hence the compound verb 'to cause emergence'. The verb *sakapu* is used as leading word in the spell (cf. Ch. IV, Sec. 2 and M.F. 14, Comm., Part VII).

5. The two words can also be used in a nominal sense, *kayvaguri-na sobula*, 'the act of wakening the sprout', and similarly *kayvasakapu-la sobula*. We find here a complete agreement between etymology, the aim of the magic and the state of growth to which it refers.

6. *Ta-lova kaydabala*—an Omarakana rite (cf. Ch. IV, Sec. 2, and M.F. 16) also mentioned to me in one of the southern villages (cf. Ch. X, Sec. 1)—is a linguistically clear expression: 'we throw the head-wood'; *lova*, 'to throw', *kay-* prefix, 'woody', 'pertaining to a tree', *daba-la*, 'head his' (cf. also M.F. 17, v. 6). I received the following elucidatory text (cf. also §§ 36 and 37 below) :—

T. 44. *Ta-lova*   *kaydaba-la,*   *bi-vagi*   *yagava-na*
we throw   head-wood his   he might make   leaf his

sene   *bidubadu.*
very much   many

7. Another form in which I found this rite described is *kaylavala kaydabala*, 'the throwing of the head-wood'. Only one point needs comment: What does 'wood' mean in the compound 'head-wood'?

As a matter of fact the natives put up a little stick in this magic which they call *kaydabala*. At the same time the rite refers to the foliage which is also called *kaydabala*. Probably the stick symbolises the foliage and we have here a magical pun (cf. Ch. IV, Sec. 2).

8. *Ta-lova dabana* (or *dabwana*) *taytu*, or *kaylavala dabana taytu*, is a rite of which I obtained the spell (M.F. 17, cf. Comm. D.) and which has been described in the growth magic cycle (cf. Ch. IV, Sec. 2).

The following text comments on this rite:—

T. 45.
Ta-lova	*daba-la*	*taytu* —	*bidubadu*	*tuvayle*	*yagava-na,*
we throw	head his	taytu	many	still	leaf his

makawala	*bogwo*	*bi-vagi*	*silisilata.*
alike	already	he might make	underground shoot

FREE TRANSLATION: 'We throw the head foliage of the taytu, another instalment of leaves; and also this magic already produces underground shoots.'

9. The equivalence of the two foregoing rites is expressed by the interesting comment which I received in a southern village:—

T. 46.
Ta-siway-yu	*bayse*	*megwa*
we time two	this here	magic

'We repeat this magic', which really means here: 'one magic is another instalment or counterpart of the other'.

10. *Ta-sayboda* or, in its nominal form, *kasayboda* refers to the magic by which the final exuberance of foliage is produced (cf. M.F. 18). *Sayboda* means 'to cover completely', from *say*- formative of *sisu*, 'to 'sit', 'to remain', and *boda*, *bwadi*, 'to cover'; hence *sayboda* (lit. to 'sit-cover'), 'to cover up definitely or completely'. This is a short comment I received:—

T. 47.
Ta-sayboda	*i-saybwadi*	*taytu.*
we close up	he close up	taytu

'We perform the *sayboda* magic, and foliage closes up.'

A longer commentary runs:—

T. 48.
Ta-sayboda	*taytu,*	*i-sayboda:*	*bi-vagi*	*sisi-tala,*
we close up	taytu	he closes up	he might make	one (branch)

sisi-yuwela,	*sisi-tolula.*
second (branch)	third (branch)

This means that the *sayboda* charm produces branch after branch till everything is closed up. In the South there is an alternative expression for this charm, *kaykaduba* in its nominal form; *kaduba* (*ta-kaduba*) in the verbal. *Ka*- is instrumental prefix, *duba* probably from *dubwadebula*, 'cave'.

T. 49. *Ta-kaduba*   —   *kuyawa-la*   *taytu*   *bogwo*
    we perform *kaduba* rite   root his   taytu   already

    bi-la   *o*   *pwaypwaya.*
    he might go   in   soil

11. The word *duba* here would refer to the entering of the roots into the soil as into a cave. This spell thus has a two-fold character: it refers to the foliage on the one hand and to the roots on the other, a parallelism clearly recognised by the natives.

12. *Vapuri* consists of *va-* causative, and *puri*, 'to break forth in clusters'. This verb has been fully analysed in the commentary to M.F. 19, Comm. D. It means 'to produce a cluster of tubers underground'.

13. *Kammamalu* is the name of a rite and a spell (cf. M.F. 20, Comm.). The aim was described to me thus:—

T. 50. *Ta-kammamalu*   *bi-puri*
    we perform the *kammamalu* rite   he might break forth in clusters

    tuvayle.
    still

The name signifies the 'fetching back' (of taytu).

14. *Kasaylola*, compounded of *ka-* instrumental, *say-* particle of permanence, *lola*, 'to anchor'—'the spell of anchoring', 'fixing' (M.F. 21, Comm. D.)—was thus defined:—

T. 51. *Ta-saylola*   —   *ta-lola*   *silisilata,*
    we perform the *saylola* rite   we anchor   underground shoot

    bi-lola   *bi-la*   *o*   *pwaypwaya.*
    he might anchor   he might go   in   soil

15. The following data refer mainly to the magic of Vakuta. Since I did not obtain any formulae there or see any rites performed the value of what follows is almost exclusively linguistic and not ethnographic.

16. Glancing at the comparative table of Vakuta and Omarakana magic (Doc. VI, IV), we see that the names of several rites of growth magic are identical. Thus we find *vaguri*, *vasakapu*, *vapuri* in both lists. As regards *vasakapu* or *katusakapu* I was told in Vakuta:—

T. 52. *Ta-vasakapu,*   *bi-sakapu*   *taytu,*
    we make the *vasakapu* magic   he might emerge   taytu

    bi-sabusi   *o*   *pwaypwaya.*
    he might sit-pierce   in   soil

'When we make the *vasakapu* ceremony, the taytu would emerge, it would come out of the ground while it remains there.' The compound *sabusi*, *sa-*, 'to sit, 'remain', *busi*, 'to come out', is a verb which expresses the fact that while a part of the plant comes out of the soil most of it still remains underground.

17. The third Vakutan entry (Doc. VI) is *gilulu*, defined by the expression:—

T. 53. *I-gilulu*   *kay-tala*   *o*   *nunula.*
he puts up (?)   one (w.l.)   in   magical corner

This act is apparently closely connected with the magic of the *katusakapu* or *vasakapu*. I was told:—

T. 54. *Ta-katusakapu*   *sobu-la*   *deli*   *i-gilulu.*
we make emerge   sprout his   together   he '*gilulu*'.

This means that the rite of emergence coincides with the magician's making *gilulu*. The magician himself told me:—

T. 55. *A-gilulu* — *a-gibaba*   *ka'i*   *kayketoki* *o* *kabulu-la*
I gilulu   I place slanting wood small   in nose his
kavatam,   *a-waya'i.*
yam pole I hit

'When I make the rite of *gilulu*, I place a small slanting stick against (at the side of) a *kavatam*, I put it up.'

18. COMMENTARY: The root *baba* we know already; it appears in the compound *kaybaba*, 'slanting pole of the *kamkokola* erection'. The verb *waya'i*, accomplished form of *waye* or *woye*, 'to hit', is often used in a figurative form to describe the accomplishment of an act. The ritual of *gilulu*, which apparently is not accompanied by any spell, consists in the placing of small slanting sticks round a *kamkokola* or a *kavatam*. (For the function of these, cf. Doc. VI.)

19. I was also given another name for these sticks, *kaykubwaya*, etymology unknown.

20. *Kala'i* (Doc. VI, 4th entry) consists of rubbing the ground with herbs while a spell is recited. The name *kala'i, kalova=kalava*, is probably an apophonic form of *kalavi*, 'to throw at'. The act itself was defined to me thus:—

T. 56. *Ta-kala'i* — *ta-waye* *ka'i*   *o*   *pwaypwaya.*
we *kala'i*   we hit   wood in soil

'The act of *kala'i* (throwing) consists in rubbing the soil with leaves.'

21. The verb *kala'i*, as a matter of fact, can also mean 'to throw away', as when the natives speak about—

T. 57. *Ta-kala'i-si* *kalabogwo* — *ta-pakay-se* *kalabogwo.*
we throw   old food   we refuse old food

This refers to the rite in which the garden magician breaks his taboo and eats new food (cf. Ch. V, Sec. 2).

22. *Vakwari* (5th entry) was thus commented upon:—

T. 58. *Taytu   bi-kwari   wa   ka'i,   bi-mwoyna.*
taytu   he might catch hold   in   wood   he might climb up

FREE TRANSLATION: 'The *vakwari* rite makes the taytu catch hold of (its support) so that it might climb up on the pole.' *Kwari* is a well-established verb in the Kiriwinian dictionary, in fact one of the most usual words of everyday life. *Vakwari* is a perfectly transparent compound 'to make catch hold'.

23. *Lasawa* (6th entry), on which I received only the comment, *ta-lasawa, taytu bi-lasawa*, is a word which I cannot further analyse. Perhaps it is compounded of *la-*, the root 'to go', and *sawa*, 'to put there', 'to settle'—'to make settle', 'to proceed to the settling down of the tuber'. This etymology would be in accordance with the stage of this rite and with its aim, which is directed towards the production of tubers.

24. *Valuvalova* (7th entry), a spell creating abundance of foliage, is obviously a reduplicated form of *lova*, 'to throw', with a causative prefix. The two terms *yo'uribwala* and *yobunatolu* (8th and 9th entries) refer to the foliage of the taytu:—

T. 59. *Yo'uribwala   i-vagi   taytu   yagava-na   migamaga;*
the rite of *yo'uribwala*   he make   taytu   leaf his   plentiful

yobunatolu   boge   bi-dudubile   lopou-la
the rite of *yobunatolu*   already   he might darken   belly his

buyagu.
garden-site

Thus the *yo'uribwala* rite produces abundance of foliage, while the *yobunatolu*, a second instalment with the same object, darkens the inside of the garden. Both words start with the prefix *yo-*, 'leafy', and contain the root *bwala = bula*, 'house', 'interior' (cf. also the fact that at this rite a diminutive 'spirit hut' is created, Doc. VI). The word *yo'uribwala* has the infixed *-uri-*, which is found in one or two magical expressions. Thus *urikuna* refers to the magic of making rain. *Uri* would have the meaning of 'making', 'producing'. It might perhaps be connected with the root *u'ula*, 'cause', 'basis'.

25. *Yobunatolu* (9th entry) has *-buna-* (equals *bula*) infixed, a derivative of *bwala*. *Tolu* might come from *tolo*, 'to stand up', 'to stand erect'; *yobunatolu* being thus 'the leafy house standing erect'. I have assumed here that *yo-* is the prefix denoting foliage, but it might also be the general causative *yo-*. Both *yobunatolu* and *yo'uribwala* are

words mainly used in a verbal form, but they appear in a gerundial
nominal form without verbal prefixes.

26. The names *tata'i tageguda* and *tata'i tamatuwo* (entries 10 and 14),
'we cut the unripe-thing-that-is-cut' and 'we cut the ripe-thing-
that-is-cut', fit the explanation suggested in Document VI, that
these ceremonies refer to the cutting or trimming of the yam supports
for young shoots and for mature ones respectively. The prefix *ta*-
in *tageguda* and *tamatuwo* is derived from the verb *ta'i*, 'to cut', and is
here translated as 'thing-that-is-cut', 'something cuttable'.

27. The expression *i-lova kaluvakosi* (11th entry), 'he throw the
final stick', is fairly clear. It refers probably to the slender stick used
as a bridge between the young plant and a large support, which
enables the taytu to *kayopela*, 'jump to another wood'; *kay*- prefix
'leafy', 'wooden'; *yo*- causative or 'leafy' (?); *pela*, 'to jump'.

28. *Vapuri* (12th entry) is the same word which we met with in
Omarakana. The following commentary obtained in Vakuta
throws additional light on the meaning:—

T. 60.
Vapuri —	*boge*	*i-sunapulo;*	*bi-pulipuli*
the *vapuri* rite	already	he emerge	he might break forth in [clusters

kalwo,	*bi-sunapula-si.*
staple food	they might emerge

'The *vapuri* rite, after the plant has sprouted, makes the tubers
break forth in clusters, they would come to the surface.'

29. Here we have the direct indication that *puri* in *vapuri* refers to
the forming of clusters of tubers. The word *kalwo* is a dialectic
Vakutan apophony of *kaulo*.

30. *Vapwanini* (13th entry), the name of a spell referring to the
size of taro roots, is etymologically obscure and was not commented
upon.

31. *Ta-sasali* (15th entry) describes the act of putting a stick at
the foot of the *kamkokola*; etymology unknown.

32. Concerning the two ritual acts, specific to Vakuta, of eating
fish and eating taytu, I obtained the following comment:—

T. 61.
Ta-vakam-si	*yena;*	*bi-keli-se*	*kuvi,*	*uri,*	*ta-ula'ula*
we eat ritually	fish	they might dig	yam	taro	we oblate

baloma.	*Ta-vakam-si*	*taytu;*	*ta-mwoye*	*da*	*bwala;*
spirit	we ritually eat	taytu	we bring here	our	house

ta-ula'ula,	*ta-kam*	*taytu.*
we oblate	we eat	taytu

FREE TRANSLATION: 'We eat fish ritually; then they are allowed
to dig yams, taro, and we make oblation to spirits. We eat taytu

ritually; we bring it home to our houses, we make oblation (to spirits), we eat taytu.'

33. COMMENTARY: The effective prefix *va-* in *vakam-si* I have translated by the adverb 'ritually'. *Vakam* means in this and similar contexts 'to eat effectively' in the sense 'to inaugurate by eating', 'to set up a precedent', 'to break a taboo'. In Vakuta there is an oblation to the ancestral spirits associated with this when the whole village eat fish, after which taro and yams may be eaten.

34. Similarly at the harvest of taytu there is a ritual eating of this staple food, each man eating in his house. This is associated with an oblation, and after it new taytu may be eaten.

35. It remains now for me to comment on one or two expressions from other communities. In Sinaketa (cf. Ch. X, Sec. 1) we find hardly any new words except that there seems to be some specific magic of the yam pole called *ta-lova-si kayke-la kavatam*:—

T. 62. *Ta-lova   kayke-la   kavatam,   kavatam   ta-waya'i.*
       we throw   foot his   yam pole   yam pole   we hit

This means: "The magic which we call the casting of the foot of the yam pole consists in hitting (putting up, making) the *kavatam*."

36. About *kaydabana* magic I was told there:—

T. 63. *Bi-lova   kaydaba-la,   bi-pwakova-si   vivila.*
       he might throw   head-stick his   they might weed   woman

This means that there the 'throwing of the head-stick' is weeding magic.

37. Again, about *ta-lova dabana taytu*, I was told:—

T. 64. *I-kayosi   dabwa-na   taytu — bi-nanakwa   taytu.*
       he get hold   head his   taytu   he might quicken   taytu

This means: 'The magical getting hold of the taytu foliage makes it grow more quickly.'

THE MAGIC OF HARVEST AND OF PLENTY

1. The amount of ethnographic information which I was able to obtain concerning certain rites, and the need of commenting on them linguistically, might almost be said to stand in inverse ratio. This is not quite so paradoxical as it appears because, with regard to such ceremonies as those to which we are now passing, the ceremonies of *isunapulo*, of *okwala* and *tum* described in Chapter V (Secs. 2 and 3), I was able to incorporate a great deal of my linguistic information into the analysis of magical texts and into the ethnographic descriptions, so that not very much is left to purely linguistic commentary and etymological speculation.

2. The harvesting rites can be classified under three heads, *isunapulo*, *okwala* and *tum*. The first of these stands apart, since it concerns the harvest of *uri*, 'taro', and *kuvi*, 'large yams', while *okwala* and *tum* are two correlated ceremonies of the *tayoyuwa*, 'taytu harvest'.

3. About *isunapulo* I obtained the following text in Omarakana :—

T. 65.
O	isunapulo	towosi		bi-miga'i		kayeki
in	isunapulo	garden magician		he might magic		pearl shell

wa	bwala,	bi-la	o	buyagu,	bi-si'u
in	house	he might go	in	garden-site	he might sever

yagava-na	uri,	i-sagi	o	mitakwabu	wa	bwala.
leaf his	taro	he thrust	in	thatch-frame	in	house

This statement gives a succinct description of the rite of *isunapulo* but does not add to our knowledge of the linguistic nature of the verb. *Sunapulo*, however, is a well-known word of daily life and means 'to come out', being almost synonymous with *sakapu*. As to its composition, *suna* may be derived from the verb *suluwa*, 'to err', 'to look for one's way', and *pula*, 'to arrive', 'to search one's way for arrival', 'to come out effectively'. Perhaps there is just this distinction between the word *sunapulo* and *sakapu*, that *sunapulo* is less definite than *sakapu* (cf. Div. IX, § 4).

4. The word *okwala* may be an expression compounded of *o*, 'in', and *kwala* from *kwari*, 'to get hold of'; 'at the time of getting hold of'. But this does not fit very well into the context. As the natives put it, commenting upon the aim of the rite :—

T. 66.
Okwala	—	bi-kabina'i	mokita,	bi-matuwo.
the *okwala* rite		he might grow	truly,	he might ripen

"The *okwala* rite is made so that the taytu might truly, i.e. really, grow, so that it might ripen."

5. Again in Sinaketa I was told :—

T. 67. *Okwala* — *taytuva'u* *bi-ma* *o* *valu.*
the *okwala* rite   new taytu   he might come   in   village

This means : "The *okwala* rite is performed so that the new taytu might be brought into the village."

6. *Tum* is the real rite of harvesting. The word itself has a clear vocabulary meaning, 'to press down', 'to weigh down'. The same word, as will be remembered, appears again in the magic of plenty, when it figures as *tum bubukwa*, 'the pressing down of the yam-house floor' (cf. Ch. VII, Sec. 1). I was told in Omarakana :—

T. 68. *Tum* — *bi-bwabwa'u* *tapwa-la* *taytu*
the rite of *tum*   he might darken   body his   taytu

bi-tabwa'u *taytu.*
he might become black   taytu

This means : "We make *tum* so that the surface of the taytu might blacken, so that the taytu might get a black surface." In still freer translation, this means that the final rite of harvest makes all the tubers black, in this context 'dark-coloured', 'ripe'. The same word 'black' we have met in other contexts (cf. Div. III, § 19) as 'bad', 'diseased' taytu as against *pupwaka'u*, 'white', 'good', 'healthy' taytu. In the one case the adjective refers to the surface of the taytu, in the other to its inside.

7. In the word *tabwa'u*, the prefix *ta-* is probably not from *ta'i*, 'to cut', nor from *ta-*, 'to stand up', but a contraction of *tapwa*, 'body', 'surface', hence *tabwa'u*, 'surface blackness', 'black surface'.

8. Concerning the rite of *tum*, I obtained the following statements :—

In Vakuta—

T. 69. *Tum,* *ta-miga'i* *ligogu,* *ta-kapituni* *kayo-la* *taytu*
(at) *tum*   we magic   adze   we cut off   throat his   taytu

o *kamkokola.*
in   *kamkokola*

In Sinaketa—

T. 70. *Towosi* *i-tum* — *i-kapituni* *wotunu* *taytu,*
garden magician   he make *tum*   he cut off   creeper   taytu

tamu-la; *bi-tum* *tamu-la* *deli* *ka'i.*
stalk his   he might press   stalk his   together   wood

In Teyava—

T. 71. *Tum* —   *ta-miga'i*   *ligogu,*   *ta-kapituni*   *tam-la*
the rite of *tum* we magic   adze   we cut off   stalk his
taytu.
taytu

9. COMMENTARY: These three texts are a good example of how time after time one receives the same answer from different informants belonging to different communities. Perhaps, unfortunately, I did not usually take down statements which I found merely duplicated information already noted. In this case the metaphorical expression *kayo-la taytu*, 'the throat or neck of the taytu', is paralleled by the concrete expressions *tamu-la taytu*, 'the stalk of the taytu', in the other texts. The second text gives a clear reference to the act of pressing down the cut stalk together with weeds by means of a stone, a rite described in Chapter V (Sec. 3) with regard to Omarakana. In Teyava some weeds are pulled up and pressed down by means of a split yam of the *kasiyena* kind. In two of these texts we have the mention of the *ligogu*, and in all we have the stress laid on the ritual cutting of the vine, which seems thus to be the essential element in this ceremony.

10. The *vilamalia*, described in Chapter VII and there freely translated 'magic of prosperity', is etymologically *vila-*, from *valu*, 'village', *malia*, 'plenty'—'the magic of village plenty'. It consists of two ceremonies. The name for one of these, *basi valu*, 'piercing of the village', describes one of the component rites in which little holes are made in the village soil and magical herbs inserted (cf. Ch. VII, Sec. 3). In Omarakana another expression, *u'ula valu*, 'the basis or foundation of the village', is also used, the reference being probably that by this rite a foundation is laid for village prosperity.

11. The insertion of the leaves between the logs of the yam-house, which is part of this rite, has been described to me as *kubisakavata bwayma*, the prefix *kubisa-* being perhaps derived from *kubisi-*, 'partition of the yam-house' (cf. Ch. VIII, Sec. 4). *Kavata* may be *ka-* causative, *vata* the same as *vatu* (?), 'boulder', 'making the partitions firm as boulders'—but this etymology is only conjectural.

12. *Tum bubukwa* (cf. Ch. VII, Sec. 1), on the other hand, used verbally, *bita-tum bubukwa*, 'we might press the yam-house floor', or nominally, *kaytum-la bubukwa*, 'the pressing of the floor', has a clear vocabulary meaning. In this rite the magician does press down the floor of the yam-house and this action is named in the title. The following texts illustrate the aim of *vilamalia* magic :—

T. 72. *Gala   ta-vagi   vilamalia   lopou-la   sene*
no   we make   (magic of prosperity)   belly his   very much

bulaboula,   sene   i-uwaya'u.   Ta-basi   valu
big hole   very much   he flighty (?)   we pierce   village

lopou-la   bogwo   i-tubwo.
belly his   already   he satisfied

For free translation, see Chapter VII (Sec. 4).
The term *uwaya'u* is, I believe, a reduplicated form of the root *yova*, 'to fly'; other variations: *yuvayova, uvayova.*

T. 73. *Vilamalia   bi-vagi   kaulo   deli*
(magic of prosperity)   he might make   yam-food   together

lopou-dasi;   sene   kasa'i.   Ta-kam   ututana
belly ours   very much   hard   we eat   one (cut piece)

bogwo   i-tubwo   lula.
already   he satisfied   stomach

For free translation, see Chapter VII (Sec. 4).

13. As to the herbs used in Omarakana at the rite of pressing the yam-house floor, I received the following information:—

T. 74. *Setagava —   kasa'i;   ta-lulu,   sene   peulo.*
(a weed)   hard   we pull out   very much   strong

This means: "The *setagava* is a very hardy (weed); we try to pull it out, it is very strong (resistant)."

T. 75. *Kayaulo   —   gala   ta-ko'uwari,   gala   ta-katuni.*
iron-wood palm (?)   no   we wrench off   no   we break off

Wa   kema   ta-taye   wala.
in   axe   we cut   just

'The *kayaulo* tree—we cannot wrench off any of its branches, we cannot break off any of its boughs. Only with an axe can we cut it.'

T. 76. *Kakema   makawala   kayaulo.*
(a tree)   alike   kayaulo

'The *kakema* tree is like the *kayaulo*.'

14. As regards private garden magic, there is no generic term to describe it. It would be simply spoken of as *migava-la bagula*, 'magic his garden', if a generic term were necessary; but most likely the natives would just name each rite by its object—*megwa yagogu*, 'magic of seed yams', *megwa tula*, 'magic of dividing sticks'; or else *sodayma, sokema*, 'the magic of the digging-stick', 'the magic of the axe'. The linguistic affinities of the prefix *so-* I am not able to give.

15. A magic of *basi* which seems to be private was once spoken of by one of my informants under the name *kabidabida*; *bida* meaning 'sod', 'soil' (Div. I, § 5), this would be the 'charming of the soil'.

T. 77. *Kabidabida* — *ta-bisibasi,* *ta-dubwari* *taytu*
the spell of the soil   we pierce   we cover over   taytu

deli *pwaypwaya.*
together   soil

This means: 'The *kabidabida* spell is uttered when we make the *basi* (thinning out the roots), and then we cover over the remaining tubers with soil.'

16. In this division we need only note the homonymous meanings of:—

kayo-la   1. 'throat'.
2. 'stalk'.

A FEW TEXTS RELATING TO GARDEN MAGIC

1. In order not to interrupt the sequence of the names of spells and rites, I have relegated the following texts to this place, especially since they are not what might be called 'definition texts', but rather items of ethnographic information in native speech.

2. The following series of statements were given to me by Motago'i of Sinaketa and refer to the rite of *pelaka'ukwa*, which as we know is carried out in Sinaketa over a stone:—

T. 78. (i) *Bi-gisay-se*   *dakuna,*   *boge*   *bi-lou-si*   *kwayta*
they might see   stone   already   they might go   one (r.b.)

vanu,   *Tepila,*   *bulukwa*   *si*
village   (mythical home of bush-pigs)   pig   their

valu.
village

  (ii) *Bi-miga'i-se*   *buyagu,*   *bi-yoba-si*
they might magic   garden-site   they might drive away

bwalodila,   *bi-na*   *Tepila.*
bush-pig   he might go   (mythical home of bush-pigs)

  (iii) *Kwaytala*   *si*   *valu*   *bwalodila*   *Tepila,*
one (r.b.)   their   village   bush-pig   (mythical home
                                        [of bush-pigs]

kwaytala   *Lukubwaku;*   *Giribwa*
one (r.b.)   (mythical home of bush-pigs)   (village)

ewaywo,   *emayma-ga.*
that side   this side however

  (iv) *Bi-yabay-se*   *bunukwa,*   *bi-lou-si*
they might drive away   pig   they might go

Lukubwaku;
(mythical home of bush-pigs)

  (v) *Boge*   *bi-ma*   *bunukwa*   *gado'i —*   *minana*
already   he might come   pig   stake   this (f.)

pila-vasi   *tayga-na,*   *yayyu*   *yeyu-na.*
four (portions)   ear his   two (f.l.)   tail his

  (vi) *Bi-yabay-se*   *kumaydona,*   *bi-lou-si*
they might drive away   all   they might go

Lukubwaku,   *minana-ga*
(mythical home of bush-pigs)   this (f.) however

bi-yamata   *kali,*   *pela*   *bulukwa*   *gado'i.*
he might guard   fence   for   pig   stake

(vii) *Migava-la   i-kateta-si   towosi   pela   si*
      magic his   they know   garden magician   for   their

      bunukwa.
      pig

(viii) *O   si   valu   mokita,   tomwaya,   tomwaya,   tomwaya,*
       in   their village truly   old man   old man   old man

       bi-sisu-si   wala.
       they might sit   just

For free translation, see Chapter III (Sec. 2).

3. COMMENTARY: (i) The connexion between the two clauses, 'they might see stone', 'already they might go', is the typical contextual expression of conditionality. 'When they see the stone, then they go', or 'if they see the stone, they go'. *Kwata*, 'one' (r.b.), is here used almost in the sense of the indefinite article, 'they go to a village, by name Tepila'. This text shows well the equivalence of *n* and *l*, the same word appears as *valu* and *vanu*. I noted these phonetic discrepancies carefully. This noun appears also with two meanings: first, as place—'they go to a place, Tepila, the home of pigs'; second, as 'village', the particular place to which the pigs pertain, their 'home'.

(ii) This is really a repetition of the first sentence. The second clause is explanatory of the first. A subjunctive meaning is contained in the relation of the clauses. 'When the magicians charm the gardensite, they drive away the bush-pigs, and then these go to Tepila.'

(iii) The two words *kwaytala*, 'one' (r.b.), are given here in the sense of 'one—another'. In the second clause of this sentence we have the somewhat clumsy way of expressing spatial relations. In order to state 'this side of Giribwa', they have to use the round-about and lengthy expression: 'Giribwa is on the other side; on this side'; to which must be mentally added by the hearer, 'on this side there remains Lukubwaku'.

(iv) We have here the somewhat puzzling diversity of subject in the two adjoining clauses—'they might drive away pigs, they might go to Lukubwaku'. The subject of the first clause is of course the garden magicians; of the second, the pigs.

(v) This sentence is connected structually with the previous one. We would express it thus: 'When the magicians drive away the pigs, they go to Lukubwaku and (on the other hand) there would come the pig of the stake.' In native all this is expressed by juxtaposition. *Pila-vasi*, 'four portions', one of the compound numerals, corresponds here to the English 'four-fold'. *Yay-yu*, 'two' (f.l.), is a simple classified numeral: 'The pig with four-fold ears and two tails'.

(vi) This is both grammatically and semantically a repetition of (v).

(vii) A clearly constructed sentence with a causal clause.

(viii) This consists of three clauses. The first and the last 'in their village truly' and 'they might just remain' belong together; the middle clause consists of a three-fold repetition of the word 'old man'. The meaning of this is 'in the memory of old men'; and the three-fold repetition expresses the length of duration. Thus the whole sentence might be thus translated: 'In the village truly—as old, old, old men remember—they just remain.'

4. A text referring to black magic, also received from Motago'i of Sinaketa, runs as follows:—

T. 79. (i) *Bi-vata'isi*   *tomwota:*   "*Iga'*,   *ba-bulata*
they might contend   humans   later on   I might bewitch
buyagu!"
garden-site

(ii) *Bi-miga'i*   *dakuna,*   *bi-katutuwani*   *kali,*
he might magic   stone   he might throw across   fence
bi-mayay-se   *bulukwa*   *Lukubwaku*
they might come   pig   (mythical home of bush-pigs)
bidubadu,   *bi-koma-si*   *kaulo,*   *bi-wokwo,*
many   they might eat   yam-food   he might be over
bi-bulatay-se   *buyagu.*
they might bewitch   garden-site

(iii) *Kayne*   *gala*   *bi-bulatay-se,*   *gala*   *bi-may-se*
if   no   they might bewitch   no   they might come
bulukwa.
pig

(iv) *I-katupwo'i-se*   *tomwota:*   "*Avaka*   *pela*   *iyam*
they enquire   humans   what   for   day by day
bi-ma   *bulukwa,*   *iyam*   *bayse?*"
he might come   pig   day by day   this here
"*I-sikay-se*   *tokeda!*"
they sit at   garden-way

For free translation, see Chapter III (Sec. 2).

5. COMMENTARY: (i) Here the *bi-* form expresses conditionality— 'when people quarrel'. There follows a quotation in direct speech without any announcement, as is characteristic of Trobriand; the threat: 'Just look out, I shall bewitch your garden.' *Iga'* = *iga'u*, the *u* being elided.

(ii) This is a description of what the magic consists in as well as of its effect: 'The man charms a stone, throws it across the fence, pigs will come (from) Lukubwaku in great numbers and eat the yam-food. It might be over.' Between 'food' and 'it might be over' we would insert some such word as 'until'. The last clause is an after-thought giving the general description or definition of the substance of (ii).

(iii) Here the same vague conjunction *kayne* has the temporal conditional sense, 'when there is no black magic, bush-pigs will not come'.

(iv) This treats of another subject. It is an expression of the taboo which forbids people to have sexual intercourse near the gardens. The statement is couched in the form of a question: 'People would enquire: "Why day after day will pigs come here?"' To this the answer would be: 'They sit at the garden way.' *Si* means 'to sit'; the transitive suffix *-ki* or *-kay* gives 'sit at', 'sit over'. *Tokeda* is an expression denoting the immediate neighbourhood of the garden; *to-* the root meaning 'to stand', *keda*, 'road'; 'the road of standing', perhaps 'the way of the standing uncut bush', in which case it would be synonymous with *yosewo*. The expression 'sit at the garden way' is a euphemism for 'they copulate in or near the garden' (cf. Ch. III, Sec. 2 and Div. VI, § 47). I received the same expression *i-sikay-se tokeda* with the same meaning and in a similar context from another informant in a different community; so it must be a fixed phrase.

6. There seems to be a taboo on reciting garden magic outside the garden during the time when the crops ripen. Whether this is unimpeachable information or due to the fact that Navavile, the garden magician of Oburaku, did not want to give me his garden magic, does not essentially impair the linguistic interest of his statement. The grammar of lies is as good as the grammar of truth.

T. 80. (i) *Kidama   ba-keulo   megwa o la odila, o   valu,*
supposing I might recite magic   in   bush   in   village
gala bi-kabina'i   taytu.
no   he might grow   taytu

(ii) *Kidama   oyluvi   ta-dodiga-si bwayma,*
supposing afterwards we load   yam-house
ba-keulo   megwa, bi-gagabile,   gala sita
I might recite magic   he might be light no   one bit
boma-la.
taboo his

7. FREE TRANSLATION: (i) 'Were I to recite magic in the bush or in the village (now), the taytu would not grow.'
(ii) 'When we have filled the yam-houses, I would recite magic, this would be a light (i.e. good) thing. There is no taboo then.'

8. COMMENTARY: (i) The conjunction *kidama*, which indicates the hypothetical nature of a clause, could be translated here by 'if' or simply by the English word order 'were I', with the verb first. In the second clause the word *kidama* has much more definitely the conditional meaning, and I might have translated it by 'if'.

(ii) The pause after *oyluvi*, which my informant made, indicated that there was a temporal conditional meaning, so that the translation might run: 'If afterwards, when we have', etc. The verb *ba-keulo* has, in Trobriand, a directly future reference, so that the free translation should be, 'then I shall recite magic'. The verb *gagabile*, 'to be light', has the meaning of 'absence of taboo', as is explicitly stated here in the clause that follows. It is one of the few Trobriand words with a distinct moral flavour to it.

9. I wish to give here two texts referring to gardens and magic in general. The first is the amusing comment on European gardening magic which I received in a conversation held in Omarakana with Kayla'i and Gatoyawa:—

T. 81. *I-livila-si   misinari: "Ta-taparoro*
    they say   missionary   we *taparoro* (make Divine Service)

    boge   i-kabina'i   buyagu."   Sasopa   wala.
    already   he grow   garden-site   lie   just

10. This is the characteristic way in which native statements render in a condensed form at times quite complex ideas. In free translation (Ch. I, Sec. 5) I have added in brackets the conjunctive clause which, in English or any other European language, would be indispensable. We would also probably make a clear distinction between the quotation of the alleged missionary opinion, 'we make Divine Service and as a result of this the garden-site already grows', on the one hand, and the direct opinion of the speaker on the other, 'lie just'. We would say, 'The missionaries say so-and-so; we of course know that this is just an imaginative statement.' The native word *sasopa* covers anything from a purely accidental mistake, a *bona fide* flight of imagination, to the most blatant lie.

11. The second text refers to the vague influence exercised on gardens by the recital of fairy-tales. It is the native text of the ditty or rhythmic standardised saying which each speaker utters after he has recited his *kukwanebu*, 'fairy-tale'.

T. 82. *Puripuri*   *kasiyena,*   *labayse*   *kweluva*
    break forth in clusters   (species of yam)   this here   time-count

    i-yari   i-yapu.   *A-sulu   mone,*
    he cut   he grows round   I cook   taro-pudding

    i-kome (personal name of a distinguished person present).
    he eat

A-lilami   *bu'a,*
I break off   betel-nut

i-kome (another name of a distinguished person present).   *Um*
he eat   thy

kwatayayle   (name of next speaker).
return payment

For free translation, see Chapter IV (Sec. 4).

12. COMMENTARY: The verb *puripuri* has been analysed in the Part VII, M.F. 19 (Comm. 1). The form *labayse*, 'this here', refers probably to the *kasiyena* yam: 'This is the season (time-count) of the *kasiyena* yams.' The noun *kweluva* designates the sequence of seasons, the system of counting them, as well as the season pertaining to a certain event. The term *yari* refers to the cutting through of new tubers. (Cf. the use of the term *tavisi* in M.F. 13, a spell of growth magic.) *I-yapu*, 'he grows round', has been analysed in the commentary to M.F. 41 (Comm. 9). The reference to three men present creates a sort of social feeling. It has got no deeper or more symbolic meaning that the natives could explain to me. The name of this ditty, *katulogusa*, I was not able to analyse more fully.

13. In commenting on the vague influence of the recital of fairy-tales on the growth of taytu, my informants told me:—

T. 83. (i) *Kurava-la*   *kalava'u — kukwanebu.*
       magical stimulus his   new crops   fairy-tale

    (ii) *Bi-puri*   *kasiyena,*
       he might break forth in clusters   (species of yam)

       bi-matuwo   *kaulo.*
       he might ripen   staple food

    (iii) *Lili'u gala kurava-la*   —   *ta-livala wala.*
       myth   no   magical stimulus his we talk just

For free translation, see Chapter IV (Sec. 4).

14. COMMENTARY: (i) *kurava-la* has a general meaning of something which spurs on, which influences magically. I translated it here 'magical stimulus'. I have not found it in other contexts, but obtained the following brief definition:—

T. 84. *Kurava-la — bi-vagi*   *bi-matuwo,*
     kuravala   he might make   he might ripen

which means, 'it makes the crops ripen'; 'an influence which produces ripening'. Etymologically the word is perhaps a compound of *ku-*, and *lava*, 'to throw'. *Ku-* again might be derived from *kwa'u*, 'to take'; 'take-throw', 'something which casts an influence', 'gets hold of'. The prefix *kwa-* with the possessive suffix -*la* would be easily reduced to *ku-* simply.

(ii) is contextually dependent upon the previous phrase. If we were to drag out all the implications, the sense of this sentence would be as in Chapter IV. It will be noted that there the sentence "as the yam breaks forth into clusters, so the staple food matures", is implied in the native text but not spoken.

(iii) This needs an ethnographic rather than linguistic comment. 'Myth no magical stimulus his' obviously means that myths have no magical influence. By this the natives wish to say that the myth does not exercise a direct magical influence on the plant. The relation of myth and magic, which belongs to the universe of discourse of theoretical anthropology, would not be stated directly by the natives though no doubt they recognise it vaguely.

15. Only two words with homonymous meanings need be noted in this division:—

1. *gagabile*   1. 'to be light'.
               2. 'to be without taboo'.
2. *kweluva*   1. 'sequence of seasons'.
               2. 'time count'.
               3. 'a particular season'.

THE TERMINOLOGY OF THE LEGAL AND ECONOMIC ASPECTS OF GARDENING

1. Since I hope to deal with the general economic and legal conditions of the Trobriands in a subsequent publication, I shall only briefly enumerate and analyse the terms and expressions which refer to ownership, production, distribution of crops, and the appreciation of value—terms which must be classed as economic (cf. Part I, Sec. 10). Again terms, expressions and texts which illustrate native ideas of ownership, in so far as this is safeguarded and sanctioned, might be called legal; legal also are the words or phrases which refer to contractual obligations, duties and privileges.

2. There is no word to render the abstract concept of ownership in the widest sense, that is, of the right of use and disposal by man over things, but there are a number of linguistic instruments which allow of describing these relations between a human being and a thing or a portion of environment.

3. Thus all possessive pronouns obviously serve to describe that relationship, and in Kiriwinian we have already found significant distinctions which convey a certain amount of economic information. There are four types of possessive, the distinction between which could roughly be described as closeness or intimacy of relationship. The closest possession is expressed by pronouns suffixed to the word. This possession or dependence is used only with regard to parts of the human body, terms of kinship and certain qualities or parts of human personality in the abstract sense. 'My hand' is described by the Trobriander as *yama-gu*; 'my father', *tama-gu*; 'my mind', *nano-gu*; 'my desire', *magi-gu*. A somewhat more distant relationship, as that to articles of clothing or states of mind, is expressed by the pronouns *agu*, *kam*, *kala*, etc. (for complete list, see below, § 7). Thus, *agu dagula*, 'my dancing feathers'; *agu wakala*, 'my belt', etc. Two articles of apparel only accept the suffixes of nearest possession: the man's 'pubic leaf', *yavi-gu*, and the woman's 'fibre skirt', *daba-gu*. These are regarded as so intimately associated with the human body that they are grammatically used with the particle of nearest possession. The second nearest possessive, *agu*, etc., is also applied to certain moods and mental dispositions, *agu laviya*, 'my anger', *agu sibula*, 'my sensation of cold', *agu kokola*, 'my fear'.

4. Most articles of food, in so far as stress is placed not on their being the object of human consumption, but on possession, also belong to this class. *Agu kuvi*, 'my yams'; *agu taytu*, 'my stored and owned taytu'; *agu kavaylu'a*, 'my fruits'. In the magical formulae we find, among other enumerated parts of the yam-house, the expression *agu liku*, 'my log-cabin', in the sense of 'the contents of my log-cabin'. While all the other parts of the yam-house take the pronouns of most distant possession, this one part takes the second nearest possessive.

5. A special class of possessive is that which refers to food as an object of immediate consumption, *kagu, kam* and so on. This possessive, if used alone, has got a nominal meaning, designating 'my yam-food'. The word *kagu*, 'my yam-food', emphasises the aspect of accumulated stores as a means of sustenance, 'yam-food on which I am living'. Thus *gala kam*, 'no yam-food thine', one of the most insulting expressions which can be levelled at a Trobriander, signifies 'you have nothing to eat', 'you are a hungry beggar', as we might say (cf. below § 34, and Ch. V, Sec. 4).

6. The pronouns *kagu, kam, kala* might be used, however, not only with yam-food but with any food to be consumed. Thus *kagu kavaylu'a* might be used side by side with *agu kavaylu'a*. The first means 'the fruits which I am about to eat', the second, 'the fruits which I own'. There is no doubt that these two types of possessive pronoun are distinguished from each other, though in form only the first person singular differs, all the others being identical. The imperfect formal distinctions are compensated by contextual differentiation of meaning.

7. The fourth class of possessives, those of furthest possession or of real economic possession as we might call it, is expressed by the possessive prefixed pronouns *ulo*, 'my', *um*, 'thy', *la*, 'his', *ma*, 'our' (e.d.), *da*, 'our' (i.d.), *ma—si* (e.p.), *da—si* (i.p.), *mi*, 'your', *si*, 'their'. This is really the most important class used with regard to such relationships as the full or legal ownership of land, houses or movable possessions; the citizenship in a village, the actual working of a plot of ground, and the legal claims on crops from such grounds. Here is a list of possessives:—

POSSESSIVES

NEAREST PARTS OF BODY AND KINDRED	DRESS AND FOOD AS OWNED	ENGLISH	FOOD FOR CONSUMPTION	FURTHEST
-gu	agu	my	kagu	ulo
-m	kam	thy	kam	um
-la	kala	his	kala	la
-ma	kama	our (e.d.)	kama	ma
-da	kada	our (i.d.)	kada	da
-masi	kama-si	our (e.p.)	kamasi	ma—si
-dasi	kada-si	our (i.p.)	kadasi	da—si
-mi	kami	your	kami	mi
-si	kasi	their	kasi	si

In plural (first person, inclusive and exclusive) the possessive pronouns of Columns 2 and 5 would imply the suffix -si attached to the noun to which they refer. Thus while in dual we would have *kama dagula*, 'the dancing feathers of us (e.d.) two', or *kada kavaylu'a*, 'the fruit of us (i.d.) two'; in plural it would be *kama dagula-si*, 'the dancing feathers of us (e.p.) many', *kada kavaylu'a-si*, 'the fruit of us (i.p.) many'. The expressions of Column 4 are used nominally as equivalent to 'yam-food'. Thus *kagu*, 'yam-food mine'; *kamasi*, 'our (e.p.) yam-food'; *kadasi*, 'our (i.p.) yam-food', are self-contained.

8. The most important noun to describe general claims of ownership is the prefix *toli-*, 'master', 'owner', 'organiser', 'supervisor', 'master of ceremonies'. The English word 'master' is perhaps the most appropriate label for this term. The prefix *toli-* is very much the equivalent of the possessive pronouns *ulo*, etc. Thus a man might say: *bayse ulo baleko*, 'this is my garden-plot', or *toli-baleko yaygu*, 'I am the master of the plot'.

9. The expression *to-kabi*, 'wielder of', is sometimes used to describe not so much ownership as the technological grip of an artisan on his implement, or of a functionary on his appurtenances. *To-kabi-la ligogu* would describe the man who, in a ceremony or in an activity, is using the adze. *To-kabi-la dayma* would be 'wielder of the digging-stick'. The infixed particle *-kway-*, probably derived from *kwa'u*, 'to take', in the same way as *kabi* is simply the verb 'to catch hold', is used to form certain derived personal nouns. *To-kway-bagula*, 'the perfect gardener', is the most important of such compounds. Sometimes nominal words of position or function are formed by the simple prefixing of *to-*. Thus we have come across such words as *to-bwabodila*, 'the man who carries the *bwabodila* leaves' (cf. Ch. IX Sec. 2, and Div. VII, § 19).

10. The word *u'ula* as a noun of possession is somewhat hard to define. Literally it means 'the basis of a trunk or post or tree'. It has also the meaning of 'cause', 'reason', or 'motive'. It is also sometimes used to describe, in a very vague sense, the economic or legal relationship of a man to an object or an act. Especially during a ceremonial performance the man who is 'the wielder' or 'master (or organiser) of ceremonies' would sometimes be described as *u'ula*. This word would regularly be used, for instance, to define the master of a *kayasa*, 'contractual ceremonial enterprise'. It might also be used to define the rôle of a garden magician in certain cases, as, for example, if somebody enquired: "Who is the 'master' (*u'ula*) of this ceremony?" Such a question would be answered by naming the garden magician (cf. Div. II, §§ 18 and 36).

11. Whether a relationship defined by any of these words is specifically economic or legal, or whether it is just a vague statement of some more or less nominal claim, can be gathered only from context of speech and very often only from the context of situation. By consulting Chapters XI and XII (especially XI, Sec. 3), it will be easy for the reader to reconstruct the linguistic usage of such a term as *toli-* with reference to ownership of land (cf. also below T. 94, § 36). A native speaker would need to add no qualifying words to the noun *toli-* in describing To'uluwa's claim to the land of Omarakana as against the claims of Bagido'u, or against those of any villager, or the head-man of the Katakubile sub-clan or of the Yogwabu sub-clan. His audience know the cultural context and all its implications.

12. The expression *toli-pwaypwaya*, which might be replaced by the assertion by any member of the community *ulo pwaypwaya*, 'my ground', *ma pwaypwaya-si*, 'our ground', or *u'ula bayse pwaypwaya akamayse*, literally 'basis this soil ourselves', would define the combined mythological, economic and legal claims to their soil (cf. Ch. XII, esp. Sec. 1). *Toli-kwabila*, 'master of the field', would be a title bestowed on the eldest member of the owning sub-clan; in a slightly different sense, on every member of that sub-clan; and in a still different sense, on every resident in the village which gardens it. In still a different sense it would be used by the magician, if he were not the same person as the headman. *Kwabila*, let us remember, is a 'field' or a 'body of fields' in its topographical as well as its economic sense. Topographically they are units named, delimited and forming the larger part of the political and the natural territory of a community. Economically they are owned in a nominal manner by the whole community and by the headman as its representative.

13. The expression *toli-baleko* would have a much more limited application, each plot being assigned to one man. Such ownership, as we know, has little economic significance, because, if the owner does not reside in the village so that it is not convenient for him to garden his own plot, he will garden somebody else's and lease or, more correctly, loan his plot. For on a simple *nigada*, 'request', the plot has so to be loaned. The arrangement is made before the *kayaku*, 'garden council', but the transaction is formally or legally sealed by being discussed during it (cf. Ch. II, Sec. 3, and Ch. XII, Sec. 4). The gifts and counter-gifts connected with such a loan or lease—*kaykeda*, *takola* or *takwalela*, *karibudaboda* or *vewoulo* are also discussed in Chapter XII (Sec. 4, cf. also § 17 below).

14. As regards production, there are of course no general terms corresponding to such concepts as 'capital', 'labour'. There is no generic word for 'work' as we know, no expression for 'output' or 'yield', no terminology referring to hours of labour or times of work. The expressions for the various types of communal labour are discussed in Chapter IV (Sec. 5).

15. As regards payments for labour, we meet the two terms *vakapula* or *vakapwasi*, 'cooked food given to workers', and *puwaya*, 'refreshments given during the work' (Ch. V, Sec. 5).

16. As regards distribution the terminology is much richer. I have discussed such expressions as *gubakayeki, taytumwala, urigubu* fully in Chapter VI (cf. the table in Sec. 1). From the linguistic point of view, the term *gubakayeki* consists of *guba-*, probably from *gebi*, 'to lift', 'to take up', and *kayeki*, 'mussel shell'. This term means 'plots cultivated for one's own use'. The mussel shell is used in harvesting (cf. Ch. V, Sec. 2), and the etymology of the word might mean something like 'plot cultivated by means of a mussel shell', that is, 'plot where I myself am using the mussel shell'. This etymology is purely conjectural, and is somewhat discredited by the fact that in the South (south of Kwabulo), where taro gardening is more important than in the North, the own taro plots are not called *gubakayeki* but *kubuna yamada*, meaning 'the *kubuna* of our hands'. *Kubuna* (= *kubula*) is probably equivalent to *kwabila*; hence the expression means 'the fields of our hands'. In the South the term *urigubu* refers only to taro or taro plots cultivated for the sister's husband. The analysis of the word conforms well with this meaning. *Urigubu* is literally 'taro to be lifted out', and in the South the taro gardens destined for the sister's husband are not harvested by the cultivator but by the sister's husband (cf. Ch. X, Sec. 1). Taytu given to the sister's household is called *taytumwaydona*, 'taytu altogether' (cf. Ch. X, Sec. 1). In the North, where the most important *urigubu* gift is in taytu, the term *urigubu* refers to taytu primarily, and only secondarily to the minor crops given to the sister.

17. A rapid survey of the various expressions referring to the harvest gift with a brief linguistic commentary when possible must suffice (cf. also Ch. VI, Sec. 1).

> *Taytupeta*—literally 'taytu basket', 'taytu given in baskets'—small gift of *kaulo*, 'yam-food' in baskets, offered as between two kinsmen or from a man to his kinswoman. In the wider sense *taytupeta* may be used of any gift given in baskets.

> *Kovisi* (etymology unknown)—almost synonymous with the previous, and having also the meaning of gift offered from kinsman to kinsman or more rarely from friend to friend.

Likula bwayma—literally 'untying of yam-house'—present given to wife's brother in order to make him give an additional present at harvest. The gift is taken from the brother's storehouse.

Dodige bwayma—etymology simple, *dodige*, *didagi* is the root of 'filling out', as a canoe with cargo, a yam-house with food, a basket with goods, or any hollow object with its contents.

Takola—a generic term meaning payment in objects for uncooked food; linguistically it is probably derived from the root *kwari*, 'to catch hold of'; *ta*—effective prefix—'the clinching gift'.

Karibudaboda—from *kari*—a prefix of completion, and *budaboda*, from *bwadi*, 'to meet', 'to close up'; 'the final payment'—a gift in repayment of a *takola*, and usually consisting of yams, sometimes taytu and *uri*, and at times even of cooked taro in the form of *mona*, 'taro pudding'. It is also a generic term not restricted to payments in garden produce. A valuable may also be given as *karibudaboda*. This, for instance, is the form of repayment for transporting and storing away the *urigubu* gift used in Vakuta, where it is not the duty of the man to 'fill his sister's husband's *bwayma*' though it is his duty to provide food wherewith this is done (cf. Ch. X, Sec. 1). Many of these expressions are vague; definiteness of meaning accrues from the context.

18. The following text refers to a legal term which has not yet been mentioned in this section, the *kayasa* or 'contractual enterprise'. Linguistically I cannot further analyse *kayasa*. The text concerns the big *kayasa* harvest which took place in Omarakana in 1918:—

T. 85. (i) *Siva-tala   ku-sisu,   gala   kayasa,   pela*
        time one   thou sit   no   contractual enterprise   for

        gala   vata'i.
        no   quarrel

   (ii) *Lagayla   tuta,   pela   u'ula   vata'i.*
        to-day   time   for   basis   quarrel

  (iii) *I-tuwali   mi   Kwaybwaga,   i-tuwali   mi*
        he different   people   (village)   he different   people

        Liluta   deli   mi   M'tawa   i-vata'i-se.
        (village) together   people   (village) they quarrel

   (iv) *I-wokwo: "Bwoyna,   ta-latova,   ta-vagisay-se*
        he is over good   we continue   we make

        kayasa   o   tayoyuwa,   ta-kovaysa-se
        contractual enterprise   in   harvest   we make a *kovaysa*

        Omarakana."
        (village)

(v) *Iga'*   *bi-wokwe*   *To'uluwa*   *la*
later on   he might be over   (paramount chief)   his

mwamwala,   *bi-lousi*   *o*   *si*   *valu,*
ceremonial distribution   they might go   in   their   village

bi-kovaysa-se   *tuvayle*   *bi-mwala-si*   *o*
they might *kovaysa*   another   they might distribute   in

si   *valu.*
their   village

(vi) *I-tuwali*   *mi*   *Liluta,*   *i-vagi-se,*   *i-tuwali*
he different   people   (village)   they make   he different

mi   *Kwaybwaga;*   *i-kam-si*   *bi-wokwo.*
people   (village)   they eat   he might be over

(vii) *U'ula*   *la*   *keda*   *kayasa,*   *tay-tala*
basis   his   way   contractual enterprise   one

bi-peulo,   *kakata*   *la*   *megwa.*
he might strengthen   sharp   his   magic

(viii) *I-wokwo*   *gogebila,*   *bita-kateta:*   "*Yoku*   *ambayse*
he is over   carrying   we might know   thou   where

i-ka'ita?"   *O*   *kalawa*   *i-vitulokay-da:*   "*Si*   *kalawa*
he return   in   count   he explain us   their   count

i-sisusi!"
he remain

(ix) *Tuta*   *o*   *mata-dasi,*   *bi-wokwo*   *gogebila*   *taytu,*
time   in   eye ours   he might be over   carrying   taytu

bi-wokwo   *kayasa,*   *bi-wokwo*
he might be over   contractual enterprise   he might be over

si   *vata'i.*
their   quarrel

(x) *Kidama*   *tuvayle*   *bi-vata'i-la,*   *bi-tokay*
supposing   another   he might quarrel   he might stand up

tuvayle   *kayasa.*
another   contractual enterprise

(xi) *Ma-tau-si-na*   *i-vata'i-si*   *pela*   *kiliketa.*
these (m.)   they quarrel   for   cricket

(xii) *Mi*   *Kwaybwaga*   *i-lou-si*   *Mtawa*   *i-kiliketi-se.*
people   (village)   they go   (village)   they play cricket

(xiii) *I-kiliketi-si,*   *i-wokwo,*   *i-kalawa-si;*   *i-kalawa-si*
they play cricket   he is over   they count   they count

i-kaybiga-si: "*Avayle*   *bi-kugwo?"*
they speak   who   he might be first

(xiv) *I-kaybiga-si mi   Kwaybwaga,   i-livala-si   mi*
they speak   people (village)   they say   people

M'tawa: "Ku-sasopa-si,   ka-kugwa-si   yakamayse!"
(village) you lie   we (e.p.) first ourselves (e.p.)

"Gala   mokita   ku-kugwa-si!"
no   truly   you are first

(xv) *I-vata'i-si: "Bwoyne,   baka-woy-mi!"   I-wo'i-si*
they quarrel   good   we (e.p.) might hit you   they hit

lewo,   i-bokavili-si   mi   Kwaybwaga,
throwing-wood   they drive off   people   (village)

i-mayse   o   si   valu.
they get here   in   their   village

(xvi) *"Bwoyne,   boge   bu-kovilay-ma-si;   nabwoye,*
good   already   you drive off us (e.p.)   to-morrow

buku-wayse   Omarakana,   baka-woymi."
you might get there   (capital of Kiriwina)   we might hit you

(xvii) *Iga',   i-mayse,   i-tokaya-si   mi*
later on   they get there   they stand up   people

Kwaybwaga,   i-mapu-si,   i-yogagay-se,   kayala,   vayoulo.
(village)   they repay   they hurt   spear   shield

(xviii) *I-sakauri-si,   i-lousi   o   si   valu   i-livala-si:*
they run   they go   in   their   village   they say

"Boge   ta-vata'i-si —   ta-vagi-se   kayasa,
already   we (i.p.) quarrel   we make   contractual enterprise

ta-gisay-se   avayta'u   bi-kugwo   bi-bagula."
we see   which man   he might be first   he might garden

(xix) *U'ula   kayasa   Kwoyavila,   Liluta.*
basis   contractual enterprise   (personal name)   (village)

(xx) *Tokunabogwo   makawala,   bi-vata'i-si,   boge*
long ago   alike   they might quarrel   already

bi-tokay   kabilia;   iga'u   i-tokay
he might stand up   war   later on   he stand up

kayasa.
contractual enterprise

(xxi) *Vata'i —   pela   vivila,   baleko,   kaulo.*
quarrel   for   woman   garden plot   yam-food

For free translation, see Chapter VI (Sec. 3, cf. also Doc. II).

19. COMMENTARY: (i) *Siva-tala* is one of the numerical compounds corresponding to the English of 'one time', French '*une fois*', German '*einmal*', meaning 'one temporal occurrence', 'one occasion'. In this context it means 'the one time you remained', 'on your first visit here'.

(ii) *Lagayla tuta*, 'to-day time', 'the time of to-day', 'now'; the word *lagayla*, abbreviated sometimes to *laga*, means 'now', but its main meaning is 'to-day'. The structure of the second clause, *pela u'ula vata'i*, 'for its cause quarrel', is cumbersome. Usually sparing of conjunctions, the natives sometimes heap them up too lavishly. *Pela*, 'for' or 'because'; *u'ula*, 'cause'; 'because the cause'.

(iii) Describes the division of the two competing parties: the two words *i-tuwali* express 'on the one hand and on the other'.

(iv) The term *ta-latova* has a vague sense of futurity. I do not know exactly whether it is compounded of *ta-* first person plural and the root *latova*, 'we wait and see'; or whether it is a fixed form meaning just 'later on' or 'in the future'. Another word of interest is the expression *ta-kovaysa-se*. *Kovaysa* may be identical with *kovisi*, 'a gift', one of the harvest gifts, but it certainly has a different meaning. *Kovaysa*, in a ceremonial sequence, is the opening gift whereby the organiser of an enterprise puts all those who partake in it under an obligation to carry the enterprise through.

(v) Explains the details of the proceedings. First of all there is the paramount chief's *mwamwala*, 'small ceremonial distribution', after which the local headmen return to their own villages and make there another *kovaysa*. Thus first the paramount chief, who will benefit by the harvest, puts the headmen under an obligation to himself. Then each of the headmen puts his own subjects under an obligation to work for him by a similar distribution of food.

(vi) We are here told that both parties carry out their own distribution independently of one another.

(vii) is an interesting document in that it states directly that the real strength of gardening lies in magic. We have here two words used in a metaphorical manner: *u'ula*, literally 'trunk', and *la keda*, 'his road'. The first, used in an abstract sense here, means 'cause', 'reason for'. *La keda* figuratively means 'the custom of', 'the mode', 'form', 'manner', 'fashion': thus here "the *raison d'être* or 'motive' of the ways of a *kayasa*", showing we can use the English word 'way' in the same figurative sense as in Kiriwinian. The absence of conjunctions makes the linking up of the two sentences somewhat difficult. We would say: 'The *raison d'être* of the ways of the *kayasa is so that we can see* whether one man is stronger *than another*, his magic sharper.' The italicised clauses are absent in Kiriwinian. Contextual juxtaposition is as expressive to the natives as our accumulation of conjunctions and comparatives is to us.

(viii) Describes the proceedings of comparing the tally. I suspect the verb *vituloki* of having developed under European missionary influence, but it may be native. It has an abstract sense 'to explain', 'to make clear'. It is compounded of *vitu*, 'to set up', and *loki*, probably the transitive of 'to go': 'set-up-get-there', 'show how to get there', 'make clear', 'explain'. The whole phrase has here to be contextually completed. In the first place the native speaker and listener have the proceedings before their mind's eye: when the taytu is brought in baskets, a tally is taken; hence "at bringing we would know". Then follows a clause in direct speech of which the reader knows neither the subject of the speech (the speaker) nor the person addressed. The narrator here identifies himself with the impartial observer, who asks: "Where does thy tally go back?" or as we should say: "How far does thy tally go—to what figure does it mount?" And commenting on this, the narrator adds "at the tally taking they'd explain (it would be explained to us): 'Their tally sits (i.e. is) at such and such a figure.'" This observation implies the question would be asked of either side, the data compared and the conclusion drawn as to who was the winner. All this is omitted in the narrative, but taken as said by the narrator.

(ix) Gives the native statement of the function of the *kayasa*. Here again we have the juxtaposition of co-ordinated sentences where we could add an explanatory conjunction. 'Time ahead of us'—'*when* the carrying of the taytu is over, *then* the *kayasa* is over, *and then also* the quarrel is over'.

(x) Here the statement is made that were the quarrel still to continue, another *kayasa* would have to be made.

(xi and xii) The next sentences deal with the cause of the quarrel. (xi) is a plain statement: 'these men quarrel because cricket'.

(xiii) and (xiv) are important documents as what might be called a cultural and moral translation of sporting ethics from English into Kiriwinian. In (xiii) we have the painful process of counting and counting again, with the inconclusive question: "Who has won?"

In (xiv) the unvarnished assertion is made by the people of Kwaybwaga that they were ahead, and the affirmation that the M'tawans are liars. The structure of certain transitive sentences is typical: 'They take word people of Kwaybwaga, they say to people of M'tawa.'

In (xiv) and (xv) the European reader has almost to count on his fingers the subjects of address, answer and repartee. At times I felt that the native audience followed the changes in person of speaker with ease; in this case this might well be so, as the narrator was present at the quarrel and probably quoted phrases actually exchanged, and the listeners could guess from characteristic utterances who was supposed to be speaking.

In (xv) it is obvious that there are four verbs which have a different subject in each case. The subject of the verb 'to quarrel' is probably the Kwaybwaga people; the subject of the verb 'to hit' is all the villagers present at the quarrel; the third verb, 'to drive off', has for subject the people of M'tawa, and as object the people of Kwaybwaga, who were those driven off. In the fourth case the object changes into the subject and the people of Kwaybwaga are those who had to seek refuge in their own village.

(xvi) is an address of the vanquished, the people of Kwaybwaga, containing a challenge to the people of M'tawa to meet in Omarakana and have a fight. The two verbs *wayse* and *woymi*, which have a similar sound, but different meanings, are here in close proximity. The first means 'to get there' and the second 'to hit'.

(xvii) Describes the fight in a somewhat confused manner. Here it is very difficult to ascertain the subject of the four verbs occurring. The subject of the first, 'they, get there', is probably the two parties in the quarrel; that of the second one, 'they stand up people of Kwaybwaga', is clear; with the third we must assume that it is the previously vanquished, that is, the people of Kwaybwaga, who 'repay' what they received; the fourth, 'they hurt', 'they inflict injuries', probably refers to both fighting sides.

(xviii) refers probably also to both villages reciprocally, so to speak. We are left without a very definite idea as to who ran away in this second contest. Probably from the context of (xix) we can assume that this time the Kwaybwaga people had the upper hand, because it is usually the vanquished who challenge to a competition, and here the headman of Liluta, a community associated with M'tawa, became the leader of the *kayasa*.

20. The reader will note that the temporal references as between several succeeding clauses are of such a nature that in English we should have to mark them by a definite change in tense or by some adverbial indication. Thus, for instance, (viii) is a general statement about custom, while (ix) refers to the incident in question. (x) is again a general statement about custom, while (xi) returns to the narrative. (xix) gives a particular fact about the *kayasa* described, while (xx) is a statement about the custom in general.

21. This is the original of the text given in free translation in Chapter VI (Sec. 3).

T. 86. (i) *Bi-kugwo*   *i-livala*   *Kaniyu,*
        he might be first he say   (headman of Liluta)

        i-kaybiga,   *i-luki*   *mi*   *Kwaybwaga.*
        he speak   he tell   people   (village)

(ii) "*Ba-sakay-mi*   *kuvi*   *deli*   *bu'a*   *deli*
I might give you   yam   together   areca-nut   together

bunukwa,   *gala*   *buku-mapu-si.*
pig   no   you might repay

(iii) *Iga'u,*   *Liluta*   *gala*   *buku-wakay-se*   *sene*
later on   (village)   no   you might get there at   very much
bidubadu!"
many

(iv) *I-giburuwa*   *Tokunasa'i,*   *i-lawa,*
he angry   (headman of Kaytagava)   he did get there

i-mapu   *la*   *biga:*   "*Kaniyu,*   *ku-livala*
he repay   his   speech   (head-man of Liluta)   thou say

bu'a,   *bulukwa,*   *kaulo.*
areca-nut   pig   yam-food

(v) *Nabwoye*   *kway-yu*   *liku*   *buku-kwa'u,*
to-morrow   two (r.b.)   log-cabin   thou might take

kway-tala   *bulukwa,*   *kway-tala*   *bu'a.*   *Kumayye*
one (r.b.)   pig   one (r.b.)   areca-nut   thou bring

ba-gis!"
I might see

22. The most important linguistic comment on this text refers to verse v, where the noun 'pig' is used with the numerical classifier *kway* instead of the usual *na*. *Na* refers to all things female and to animals (cf. Part IV, Div. III, B). A pig can be used with the most abstract and comprehensive particle *kway* when the stress is laid on its bulk and its destination for food. *Liku* here means 'crate'.

23. The following text—a conversation overheard at the same *kayasa* (i and ii) and the *kolova,* 'loud calling out of names', which followed our return to Kwaybwaga (iii–v)—will be found in free translation in Chapter VI (Sec. 3).

T. 87. (i) "*Boge*   *i-wokwo*   *taytu?*"   "*Gala,*   *bi-sisu.*"
already   he is over   taytu   no   he might sit

(ii) "*Nani,*   *ku-lokay-se,*   *ku-gabi-se,*   *bi-wokwo,*
quickly   you approach   you carry-on-head   he might be over

kami   *puwaya*   *bulamata!*"
your   refreshment-during-work   pig for killing

(iii) "*Mi*   *Omarakana,*   *kami*
people   (capital of Kiriwina)   your

puwaya   *luya!*"
refreshment-during-work   coconut

(iv) "*Mi   Tilakayva,   kami   puwaya*
     people   (village)   your   refreshment-during-work
     bu'a!"
     areca-nut

(v) "*Kumaydona,   kami   puwaya*
    all   your   refreshment-during-work
    bulamata!"
    pig-for-killing

24. The following texts concern the *buritila'ulo* (cf. Ch. V, Sec. 6).

T. 88. (i) *I-vata'i-si   wa bagula;   bi-livala*
               they quarrel   in garden   he might say
               so-da: "*Yoku,   bi-simwo*
               companion ours (i.d.)   thou   he might sit here
               kam?   Gala   kam!"
               thy food   no   thy food

(ii) *I-kaybiga:* "*Ku-ma   ta-bulitila'ulo.*"
     he speak   thou come here   we make *buritila'ulo*

(iii) *I-kugwa-si   biga   mina-Kabwaku,   i-kaybiga-si:*
      they are ahead   speech   people (a village)   they speak
      "*Gala   kam!*"
       no   thy food

(iv) *I-kaybiga-si   mina-Wakayse:*   "*Iga'u,   baka-waya-se*
     they speak   people (a village)   later on   we might get there
     kuvi; kayne   buku-waya-si?"
     yam   whether   you might get there

(v) *I-kaybiga-si   mina-Kabwaku:*   "*Bwoyna!*"   *boge*
    they speak   people (a village)   good   already
    i-waya-si.
    they get there.

(vi) *Lowa   mina-Wakayse,   lagayla   mina-Kabwaku*
     yesterday   people (a village)   to-day   people (a village)
     i-mapu-si,   i-wokwo; tuwayla   i-keula-si   kala mata,
     they repay   he is over   still   they transport   his eye
     i-sakay-se   mina-Wakayse.
     they give   people (a village)

(vii) *Tokunabogwo,   kidama   i-sakay-se   kala mata,   boge*
      long ago   supposing   they give   his eye   already
      i-giburuwa-si   mina-Wakayse,   boge   i-tokaye
      they angry   people (a village)   already   he stand up
      kabilia.
      war

For free translation, see Chapter V (Sec. 6), where this particular *buritila'ulo* is described. Cf. also Plates 66–71.

25. COMMENTARY: (i and ii) The introductory two sentences give a general outline of the custom and the conditions under which this is practised. The change of subject is characteristic. 'They quarrel in the garden'. Then by the inclusive dual -*da* the personal element is introduced, while in direct speech a representative individual—who in this case is the narrator himself—is addressed in the second person.

(iii) Here the narrative passes to the actual occurrence of the moment, giving concrete details as to who started the *buritila'ulo*. The set expression *gala kam*, which is always used in the singular, 'no food thine', is here obviously an insult offered by one community to another. The expression 'they are ahead speech' is equivalent to 'they started the talk' or 'they were ahead as regards the palaver or quarrel'.

(iv) The adverb *iga'u*, literally 'later on' or 'afterwards', is often used in the sense of 'Go slow. Do not hurry.' We translated it in the free version by 'wait a little'. Here the meaning is "This will be decided later on; let us bring in and show you our yams, or would you prefer to start?"

(v) In this sentence a great deal of contextual implications had to be brought out in the free translation. The people of Kabwaku agree, which means that the first suggestion is accepted. Hence the subject in the last clause is the people of Wakayse. The mere juxtaposition of the penultimate and the last clause conveys a sense of consequence which in the free translation is expressed by 'upon which the people of Wakayse already fetched yams'.

(vi) In this context the adverb *tuwayla*, 'still' or 'besides', has here the meaning of 'over and above'; *mapu* expresses here not a commercial repayment but the concept of equivalent; the noun *mata*, 'eye', has the meaning of something which is ahead, which protrudes. It will be remembered that *mata* is used to describe tendrils or tips (cf. Div. III, § 6). Here it means 'something in excess', 'over and above' the full measure.

(vii) Here the concrete case of the people of Wakayse is given as an example and has a general meaning. The word *tokaye*, 'stand up', is used in the abstract sense 'to come into being'.

26. These are the words used by the chief Moliasi to anger his opponents and cast contumely on their gift.

T. 89. (i) *"Avaka-pela   ku-mayay-se   bu'a   Kaybola,   Kwaybwaga!*
　　　　what for　　you bring　　areca-nut　(a village)　(a village)

　　(ii) *Ku-kaymalay-se   bu'a   Kwaybwaga,   Kaybola;*
　　　　you bring back　areca nut　(a village)　　(a village)

　　a-payki   yaygu!
　　I decline　myself

(iii) *Ku-banay-se   mi-bu'a   Wakayse!"*
      you find   your areca-nut   (a village)

For free translation, see Ch. V (Sec. 6).

27. COMMENTARY: (i) The juxtaposition of the two village names with the word for areca-nut expresses the possessive or derivative relation, 'the areca-nut of Kaybola, of Kwaybwaga'.

The same formation is found in (ii) and (iii).

28. These are the boastful words of the Kabwaku men quoted in Chapter V (Sec. 6), as they were reproduced for me by one of my Omarakana informants:—

T. 90. *Mimilisi   i-livala-si: "Ta-ligaymwoy-se   ma-kwoy-na;*
        sundry   they say   we throw away over   this (r.b.)

ta-koya-se   kway-va'u,   ta-karisa'u-se   mini-Wakayse.
we (i.d.) take   new (r.b.)   we (i.d.) exceed   people (a village)

29. COMMENTARY: In this context the demonstrative *ma-kwoy-na* as well as the adjective *kwaywa'u* refers to the large wooden *liku* or crate. The verb *koya* is here an apophonic variety of *kwa'u*, 'to take', the forms *ta-kwaywoy-se* and *ta-koya-se* being interchangeable though the latter is less usual. The verb *karisa'u* is one the meaning of which I was never quite able to ascertain to my satisfaction. It may mean 'exceed' or 'to beat back', or 'to dwarf'.

30. I obtained a definition text of the word *kokouyo*, 'distribution of food to the onlookers' (mentioned above in Ch. V in the account of *buritila'ulo*):—

T. 91. (i) *Kumaydona   sagali,   kayasa   —*
            all   ceremonial distribution   contractual enterprise

ta-sayki   kokouyo   togigisa.
we (i.d.) give   kokouyo   onlooker

(ii) *I-tuwali   u'ula yakida,   i-tuwali   kokouyo.*
     he different   basis ourselves   he different   kokouyo

FREE TRANSLATION: (i) "At all the ceremonial distributions and contractual enterprises we give a *kokouyo* to the onlookers. (ii) It is different when we ourselves are the *raison d'être* of the distribution; it is different when there is a *kokouyo* (for the onlookers)."

31. COMMENTARY: (i) Here the preposition 'at' or an adverb such as 'during' is implied. Mere juxtaposition of words contextually expresses the relationship between the first clause: 'at' or 'during' all the ceremonial distributions and contractual enterprises; and the second clause: 'we give the distribution to the onlookers'.

(ii) Here a great deal has to be added to bring out the meaning which is implied to the natives in this context. The bare statement 'it is different basis ourselves, different *kokouyo*' appears incomplete to a European reader. We have to add some such conjunction as 'when the basis' and also some such explanatory phrase as 'the basis of this performance' or 'of this transaction'.

32. The following text concerns the custom of *likula bwayma*, 'untying of the yam-house', or *tatunela woya'i*, 'the snapping of the rope'.

T. 92. (i) *Boge   i-dodiga-si   ulo   bwayma   ulo   vayva'i:*
already   they load   my   yam-house   my   relations-in-law
i-kasewo.
he plentiful

   (ii) *Iga'u   bi-ma   lu-gu-ta,   i-gis*
later on   he might come here   sister mine   he see
bwayma   boge   i-kasewo.
yam-house   already   he plentiful

   (iii) *I-kaybiga,   i-lokaye   la-mwala.   Ma-tau-na   i-kaybiga:*
he speak   he go at   her husband   this (m.)   he speak

   (iv) *"Kwa'u   vaygu'a,   ku-liku   la   bwayma*
thou take   valuable   thou untie   his   yam-house
lu-mu-ta."
brother thine

   (v) *Minana   i-keulo   i-sakay-da;   iga'u*
this (f.)   he transport   he give us (i.d.)   later on
ta-lupisawo   kabisi-tala.
we lift-and-spill   one yam-house compartment

   (vi) *Kidama   kaviy-yu   i-sakay-da*
supposing   two (sharp)   he give us (i.d.)
kabisi-yuwela.
second yam-house compartment

   (vii) *Biga: liku-la   bwayma;   i-tuwali;   tatune-la*
speech   untying his   yam-house   he different   snapping his
woya'i — i-tatuni   woya'i,   i-taleyku-si   bwayma.
rope   he snap   rope   they untie   yam-house

For free translation, see Chapter VI (Sec. 1).

33. COMMENTARY: We need only comment on the following verses: (v) The persons become mixed as usual, and instead of the subject being in the first person singular as in (i) and (ii), it changes into the inclusive dual, which has the impersonal feeling of French *on*, German *man*.

In (v) and (vi) the economics of the transaction are given—for each valuable one compartment of the yam-house would be given.

In (vii) we have the characteristic way in which the word *biga*, 'speech', 'language', 'linguistic usage', is employed to explain that this is the way in which a certain effect is linguistically defined. The second part of the sentence even makes an attempt to bring home the *raison d'être* of the expression: "The custom is called 'snapping of the rope' or 'untying of the yam-house' because, as it were, the rope snaps, the yam-house is being untied." The expressions about 'untying' and 'snapping the rope' are purely figurative, as no rope or other fastening is used to secure the yam-house; the restrictions on removing taytu being purely customary.

34. The following text was uttered by a commoner in a chief's village, and in the presence of some of the chief's dependants.

T. 93. (i) *Gala, gala kagu;   gala taytala   i-bagula.*
        no   no   yam-food mine   no   one (m.) he garden

    (ii) *Bogwo   i-bagula-si   ka-la   To'uluwa.*
        already   they garden   yam-food his   (Paramount Chief)

For free translation, see Chapter V (Sec. 4).

35. COMMENTARY: (i) Here we have the rare words *gala kagu*, 'no yam-food mine'. The abjectness of the humility expressed in this phrase can be gauged by comparing it with *gala kam*, 'no food thine', which, as we know, is the most deadly insult that can be levelled at a man.

(ii) Explains this verbal humility in the affirmation that the paramount chief's richness in yams is at the expense of the speaker's poverty.

36. Here is a text on land ownership, containing in a few statements a number of most important points concerning ideas of ownership, mastery and the value set on purely nominal and ceremonial claims.

T. 94. (i) *Toli-kwabila — toli-valu.*
        master of field   master of village

    (ii) *I-sibogay-se   veya-la*
        they remain of old   kindred his

        Mosagula Doga   Oburaku.
        (headman of indigenous sub-clan)   (village)

    (iii) *Sene   bidubadu   tomwota   si   baleko*
         very much   many   people   their   garden plot

        Wagwam,   ma-tau-na   toli-kwabila.
        (division of Oburaku lands)   this man   master of field

(iv) *O   kayaku,   osisuna   Navavile,*
in   garden council   in outskirts   (garden magician)

     i-katupwo'i   Navavile: "Amakawala   nano-m?
     he asks   (garden magician)   what like   mind thine

     Ta-ta'i-se   um   kwabila?"
     we cut   thy   field

(v) *"Bwoyne,   ku-woye   ulo   buyagu!"*
    good   thou hit   my   garden-site

For free translation, see Chapter XII (Sec. 1).

37. COMMENTARY: In (i) we meet the typical compressed statement by mere juxtaposition: 'master of field, master of village'. The natives thus express what we have to put in a somewhat cumbersome way. It is a direct equation, 'the master of fields is the same as the master of village', in which of course the predicate concept follows the subject concept.

(ii) The verb *sibogwo*, here in the form *sibogay*, expresses the privilege of length of residence.

38. In the text given below we have a direct affirmation of the commoners' fear in olden days of making a large storehouse, and of the sanctions against it.

T. 95. (i) *Tokunabogwo   tokay   gala   bi-kwani*
long ago   commoner   no   he might catch hold
     kway-viyaka   bwayma   bi-kariya'i.
     big (r.b.)   yam-house   he might set up

(ii) *Pela   mita-si   gweguya: i-kokola-si.*
for   eyes their   chiefs   they fear

(iii) *Bi-kariya'i-si,   boge   bi-bwabu-si   liku*
they might set up   already   they might cut across   log-cabin
     gweguya.
     chiefs

FREE TRANSLATION: (i) "In olden days it would not be fitting for the commoners to set up a big storehouse. (ii) That was because of the eyes of the chiefs of which their commoners would be afraid. (iii) Were they to set up a big storehouse, the chiefs would cut up the beams."

39. COMMENTARY: (i) The verb to 'catch hold' has a metaphorical meaning, reaching into the abstract 'to be appropriate', 'to be fitting', exactly as the English 'to fit' is used in an abstract metaphorical way in the same context and with the same significance.

(ii) The strange construction here is characteristic of Trobriand: 'Because eyes chiefs; they fear.' The sentence should not read: 'Because they fear the eyes of the chiefs', but rather 'The reason is the eyes of the chiefs. This is why they (the commoners) fear.'

40. I am giving here the native text of the myth which has been quoted in free translation in Chapter I (Sec. 7). It is a fair sample of what might be called traditional speech.

TUDAVA MYTH

T. 96. (i) *Tudava*   *Kitava*   *valu*   *bi-vagi*
(mythological hero) (an island) village   he might do

      bwoyne; i-la   *o*   *valu,*   *i-sapwo*   *kuvi,*   *taytu,*
      good   he go   in   village   he plant   yam   taytu

      uri,   *viya;*   *valu*   *i-bubuli.*
      taro   (an arum species)   village   he shine

     (ii) *I-vagi*   *sene*   *bwoyne wala Kitava:*   *gala sita'*
          he do   very much   good   just   (an island)   no   one bit

       yayana,   *kuvi*   *kava-kay-viyaka o*   *valu,*   *ola odila,*
       bitter   yam   very big (w.l.)   in   village   in   bush

       o   *raybwaga*   *bwoyne; kuvi*   *kaba-la*   *wala.*
       in   coral-ridge   good   yam   seat his   just

   (iii) *I-tavine*   *valu*   *wala, i-tapatu — i-sila,*
        he come round   village   just   he close up   he sit down

       boge   *i-vina'u Kitava,*   *boge*   *Kitava*
       already   he finish   (an island)   already   (an island)

       i-bubuli   *valu,*   *boge*   *i-wokwo.*
       he shine   village   already   he is over

   (iv) "*Ba-kewo,*   *ba-la*   *Iwa*";   *Iwa*
        I might sail   I might go   (an island)   (an island)

       i-kota,   *i-kammaynaguwa, i-sapwo kuvi o*   *valu,*
       he anchor   he go ashore   he plant   yam   in   village

       taytu i-sapwo,   *iga'*   *i-kammaynaguwa,*   *bi-la*
       taytu   he plant   later on   he go ashore   he might go

       mwada ola odila, i-sopu.
       perhaps   in   bush   he plant

    (v) *I-kaybiga-si:* "*Tudava,*   *um-maga*   *boge*   *i-kuluwa,*
       they speak   Tudava   thy canoe   already   he drift

       ku-loki   *um-maga,*   *ku-biyasi!*"
       thou go at   thy canoe   thou pull

   (vi) (*Ku-gise,*   *gala i-sapwo*   *ola odila — yayana, o*   *valu*
       thou see   no   he plant   in   bush   bitter   in   village

       wala.)
       just

  (vii) *I-loki:* "*O, gala, boge*   *ba-kewo,*   *desi-la*
       he go at   O   no   already   I might sail   enough (emphatic)

       o   *valu*   *boge*   *la-sapwa.*"
       in   village   already   I did plant

(viii) *I-kewo   Digumenu,   i-may-se   mi-Kwaywata*
      he sail   (an island)   they come   people (an island)

      torey-simla,   i-bokaylalay-se: "Ma-simla-si,   gala
      master of island   they drive off   our (e.p.) island   no

      buku-sili   Tudava!"
      thou might sit down   (mythical hero)

(ix) *I-bokaylalay-se,   i-luki: "Bayse   valu   Digumenu,*
    they drive off   he tell   this   village   (an island)

    a-doki   kuvi   ba-sapwo,   taytu   ba-sapwo,
    I deem   yam   I might plant   taytu   I might plant

    usi   ba-sapwo . . . pela   boge   ku-bokaylalo-gu-si —
    banana   I might plant   for   already   you drive me off

    luya   wala   ba-sakaymi,   ba-sila   Kwaywata."
    coconut   just   I might give   I might sit down   (an island)

(x) *I-sila,   i-la   Kwaywata,   Kwaywata   i-vakoupa*
   he sit down   he go   (an island)   (an island)   he make fast

   waga,   i-kotakota,   i-kammaynaguwa — i-kammaynaguwa,
   canoe   he anchor   he go ashore   he go ashore

   i-sapwo   uri,   taytu,   kuvi   o   valu,   i-bokaylaloy-se;
   he plant   taro   taytu   yam   in   village   they drive off

   i-luwapela   Gawa.
   he move over   (an island)

(xi) *Gawa   i-kammaynaguwa,   i-sapwo   kuvi   o   valu,*
    (an island)   he go ashore   he plant   yam   in   village

    i-sapwo   usi,   viya,   taytu,   uri i-sapwo.
    he plant   banana   (an arum species)   taytu   taro he plant

(xii) *Iga'u   bi-loki   mwada   ola   odila,*
    later on   he might go   at   perhaps   in   bush

    bi-sapwo,   bi-bwoyna   valu   kumaydona —
    he might plant   he might good   village   all

    i-bokaylaloy-se.
    they drive off

(xiii) *I-sila,   i-sila,   i-kewo*
     he sit down   he sit down   he sail

     Bovagise;   Bovagise
     (village on Woodlark Island)   (village on Woodlark Island)

     i-sapwo   uri,   i-sapwo   yabiya,   taytu — i-yobwali
     he plant   taro   he plant   sago   taytu   he like

     Bovagise   —   yena   i-sayki,   i-kewo
     (village on Woodlark Island)   fish   he give   he sail

     Wamwara.
     (village on Woodlark Island)

(xiv) *I-la,   i-siwo,   i-vagi:* "*Mini-Wamwara,*
he go   he sit there   he do   people (village on Woodlark Island)

ba-sapwo   kuvi,   taytu,   uri,   ba-sapwo   valu
I might plant   yam   taytu   taro   I might plant   village

kumaydona,   bi-wokwo   ba-katubiyase
all   he might be over   I might put order into

mi-valu."
your village

(xv) *I-tagwalay-se,   valu   i-sisapwo,   i-wokwo,*
they consent   village   he plant (emphatic)   he is over

i-sila   ola   waga,   i-kewo,   i-la
he sit there   in his   canoe   he sail   he go

Nadili.
(Laughlan Island)

(xvi) *I-kota,   i-kota   wala,   i-tokayamay-se,*
he anchor   he anchor   just   they arise hither

i-bokaylalo-si;   i-setuni   kabula-tala   i-tomo
they drive off   he break   nose one   he stand here

kway-ta   valu,   kala-sibu   la-waga   Tudava.
one (r.b.)   village   his bottom   his canoe   (mythical hero)

(xvii) *I-la   wa   luma,   i-sakauli;   i-tavina-si   mwada'*
he go   in   open sea   he run   they come round   perhaps

bi-woya-si,   i-setuni   kwayta'   valu,   kway-wela,
they might hit   he break   one (r.b.)   village   second (r.b.)

karikeda   o   luwalay-la.
sea passage   in   middle his

(xviii) *Bi-setuni   valu   kway-tolu: kway-tala   yaga-la*
he might break   village   three (r.b.)   one (r.b.)   name his

Obulaku,   kway-tala   Bugwalamwa,   kway-tala   Budayuma.
(a village)   one (r.b.)   (a village)   one (r.b.)   (a village)

(xix) *I-livala:* "*Sene   gaga   yokwami   mina-Nadili!*
he say   very   bad   yourselves   people (Laughlan Island)

Ba-katubiyase   mi   valu,   bi-bwoyna,
I might put order into   your   village   he might good

kuvi   ba-sakay-mi   taytu,   usi,   uri;   m'tage
yam   I might give you   taytu   banana   taro   indeed

pela   ku-yogagay-gu-si,   luya   ba-sakaymi."
for   you make bad me   coconut   I might give

(xx) *I-kewo,   i-lawa   kinana,   Nadili*
he sail   he go there   strange land   (Laughlan Island)

o   sibu-la   i-la   i-simwo;   i-sisu   o   sibu-la,
in   bottom his   he go   he sit there   he sit   in   bottom his

Nadili,   *tay-tala*   *i-binibani*   *kala*
(Laughlan Island)   one (m.)   he fish with shark-hook   his

yena kwa'u.
fish shark

(xxi) *I-sakawala*   *kwa'u*   *kala*   *bani*   *touyo;*   *i-la*   *kinana,*
he run   shark   his   find   own   he go   strange land

i-katulagwa,   *i-vagi*   *Tudava:*   "*Avayta'u*   *yoku?*"
he set ashore   he do   (mythical hero)   what man   thou

(xxii) "*O,*   *yaygu*   *tolay-gu*   *Nadili.*
O   myself   owner mine   (Laughlan Island)

A-binibani   *kwa'u,*   *i-sakawalay-gu,*   *a-ma*
I fish with shark-hook   shark   he run me   I come here

um-malu."   *I-siwoy-se.*
thy village   they sit there

(xxiii) *I-kaybiga*   *Tudava:*   "*Lubay-gu*   *yoku,*
he speak   (mythical hero)   friend mine   thyself

ba-ta-bagula   *ka-da-tayyu!*" —   *I-bigubagula-si.*
we (i.d.) might garden   we (i.d.) two together   they garden

(xxiv) *Boge*   *i-wokwo*   *kala*   *tubukona,*   *i-kaybiga:*   "*Yaygu*
already   he is over   his   moon   he speak   myself

ba-la   *o-gu-valu.*"   *I-kaybiga*   *Tudava:*
I might go   in my village   he speak   (mythical hero)

"*Ta-yuwari*   *um-maga,*   *bu-kwaydodige*   *ka-m.*"
we lash   thy canoe   thou might fill   food thine

(xxv) *I-kaybiga:*   "*E . . .*   *nabwoye*   *ba-la.*"
he speak   (narrative interjection)   to-morrow   I might go

I-didagi   *la*   *waga*   *Tudava,*   *i-kaybiga:*
he fill   his   canoe   (mythical hero)   he speak

"*Boge*   *i-wokwo;*   *ku-ma'i,*   *a-miga'i*   *um*
already   he is over   thou come here   I magic   thy

leya."
wild ginger

(xxvi) *I-miga'i,*   *i-kapwari*   *kapwa-yu;*   *i-kaybiga:*   "*Ku-sisu*
he magic   he wrap up   bundle two   he speak   thou sit

ba-wola-ga!"
I might paddle however

(xxvii) *I-tokaye*   *Tudava:*   "*Ku-ulawola*   *o*   *bwarita;*
he stand up   (mythical hero)   thou paddle   in   sea

kapwa-tala   *ku-kome,*   *ku-kwasu*   *um-malu,*
bundle one   thou eat   thou ritually bespit   thy village

bi-simarita;   *ku-sivila,*   *ku-kwam*   *kapu-yuwela,*
he might clean   thou sit change   thou eat   bundle second

ku-kwasu   ulu-valu,   bi-tamwa'u   —
thou ritually bespit   my village   he might disappear

ba-sisu,   gala   avayla   bi-gisay-gu.''
I might sit   no   who   he might see me

(xxviii) I-ulawolaga,   i-kwasu   valu   Tudava,
         he paddle   he ritually bespit   village   (mythical hero)

         i-tamwa'u;   Nadili   ga   i-kwasu
         he disappear   (Laughlan Island)   however   he ritually bespit

         i-milakarita.
         he clean

(xxix) I-ulawola   ola   valu   boge   o   mamada,
       he paddle   in his   village   already   in   ebb

       i-beku   pela   kaysa'i;   i-talagila,   kalwo   kumaydona
       he founder   for   breakers   he flow out   food   all

       i-la   o   bwarita,   doga,   i-kapusi.
       he go   in   sea   boar's-tusk pendant   he fall down.

(xxx) (Tudava   kala-doga,   i-sayki
       (mythical hero) his boar's-tusk pendant   he remain

       ma-tau-na   la-vaygu'a,   o   bwarita   ta-gise   i-numanamile.)
       this (m.)   his valuable   in   sea   we see   he flash

(xxxi) Gugu'a   kumaydona   i-kapu-si   o   bwarita;   ma-tau-na
       chattels   all   they fall   in   sea   this (m.)

       i-la   ola   valu,   i-siwo.
       he go   in his   village   he sit there.

41. COMMENTARY: (i) In the first phrase a comma might be
inserted between Kitava and valu. For the sentence should run:
'Tudava in Kitava made the whole countryside good (from the
agricultural point of view).' The word valu is first used in the abstract
sense of 'place', 'countryside', in the second it is used in the specific
sense of 'village', 'place of human habitation'. In the third it again
means 'countryside'. The expression valu i-bubuli has probably the
noun valu as its subject: 'the countryside it shines'; in the free
rendering, 'the countryside was made bright'.

(ii) In the first clause the vague expression 'very good' conveys
within the context the clear idea of agricultural excellence which
has been incorporated in our free translation. After the colon there
follow the detailed explanations of how the hero made the crops
good. Sita' obviously is an abbreviation of sitana. The expression
yayana, 'bitter', is a general word for inferior, ill-tasting tubers. In
the last clause the noun 'seat' is used in a metaphorical meaning of
'home of' (cf. Div. XI, § 4, Text 79, 'home of bush-pigs'). In the
expression ola odila it is to be noted that the preposition ola is equiva-

lent to *o* or *wa*, 'in'. The change of *o* into *ola* is for euphonic reasons only; *o odila* or *wa odila* being difficult to utter for the natives. The expression *ola odila* is undoubtedly built on the pattern of *ola waga*, 'in his canoe' (cf. (xv) of this text); *ogu valu*, 'in my village' (cf. (xxiv)); *ola valu*, 'in his village' (cf. (xxxi)). In these latter expressions the appended syllable is a possessive pronoun. In *ola odila* it is merely an expletive syllable.

(iii) The two verbs *i-tavine*, *i-tapatu* are used to express completeness; the first signifying an encircling movement, the second the meeting of two ends or closing up. The verb 'to sit' has here an abstract meaning 'to rest' or 'to stop', almost comparable with the Creator's cessation of activities on the seventh day. The penultimate expression presents the same difficulties as its inverted form in verse (i), as it is uncertain whether the subject is the mythical hero or the village of Kitava. A compromise version was adopted in the free translation.

(iv) As often in a narrative, the speaker of the direct speech is not specified, but is obvious. In the free translation this has been made explicit. In the second clause the sequence of verbs 'he anchored, he went ashore, he planted' replaces to a certain extent the poverty of temporal modifiers of the verbs as well as of adverbs. We would say here: 'After he had anchored he went ashore, and then planted.' In the penultimate clause the adverb *mwada* has been rendered by 'so that he might'.

(v) The possessive pronoun *um*, 'thine', influences the first consonant of the noun, and where this happens the two words are run together in speech. Hence they have been hyphenated here. In the penultimate clause we have the directed formative *la*, 'to go', with the formative *-ki*, 'go at, get there'.

(vi) This, as indicated by brackets, is a narrator's aside. The two last clauses depend to a great extent on the context of the narrative. The expression 'bitter' refers obviously to the crops in the bush, hence to the last word of the previous clause. 'In the village just' obviously refers to the foregoing verb 'he planted', and it also implies an opposition to the adjective 'bitter'. Hence in the free translation it has been rendered by an explicit phrase 'only in the village (did he plant and there it is sweet)'.

(vii) The direct speech of the culture hero illustrates certain vaguenesses of native speech. The *gala*, 'no', implies either a change of mind on the part of the culture hero or a discussion with some other people. As it stands it is not unambiguous.

(viii) The verb *bokaylalay* is a variant of *bokavili*, a verb expressing the attack and routing together. The prefix *torey-* is a variant of *toli*.

The verb *sili*, translated here by 'to sit down', is the iterative and durative of *sisu*, 'to sit'. It has a considerable range of meanings from the specific expression 'to sit down in a canoe', 'to sail' (see next verse), to 'remain, settle' which is the meaning in this verse. ˙

(ix) The opposition which in the free rendering we expressed by 'but' is here contextually given by juxtaposition and the construction of the two sentences.

(x) We have here two interesting constructions: *koupa* is the noun for a stick by which a canoe is moored. *Va-* is a causative or effective prefix. And joined to the noun it means 'to effect mooring'. The repetition of its meaning 'to anchor', 'to make fast', seems to us merely pleonastic; but in native the first clause describes the means, the second the effect. 'By means of mooring, he anchored the canoe.' The repetition of the verb *kammaynaguwa*, 'to go ashore', expresses something like 'after he went ashore he planted', literally 'he went ashore, he was already ashore (and then he planted)'.

(xii) The adverb *mwada*, translated literally by 'perhaps', gives the verb a character of tendency or conditionality. Hence in free translation I added 'he made an attempt perhaps to go'. The last word of this sentence 'they drive off' obviously leaves much unexpressed: 'they drove him off and thus interrupted all his work'.

(xiii) The narrative repetition of the verb *sila*, 'to sit down', 'to get into the canoe', really refers to the duration of the journey. 'He remained in the canoe (for some time) and then he arrived.' The inserted clause about his liking of the village of Bovagise as an explanation of why he bestowed all worldly goods on it is characteristic of native narrative.

(xiv) The meaning of the verb *vagi*, 'to do', which in Trobriand as in many other languages has many uses, is, by the context, here equivalent to 'spoke, addressed'. The verb *wokwo*, 'to be over', 'to finish', has here the meaning of completion 'till there is nothing left'. The verb *katubiyase* means 'to put order into', 'to arrange'. It is used by the natives when they prepare a big distribution or when they pack their worldly goods in moving a dwelling or going on a trip. Here it has got the general meaning: 'to put order into', 'to arrange for'.

(xv) This sentence shows a characteristic sequence of verbs with their contextual implications. 'He planted, it was over, he got into the canoe, he sailed, he went to Nadili.' In the free translation it was necessary to bring out the connecting words or conjunctions to the number of four.

(xvi) The repetition of the verb 'to anchor' and the addition of *wala*, 'just', a strengthening and affirmative adverb translated in the free version by 'indeed', stands in strong contrast to the two following verbs 'they arose, they attacked'. Their opposition has been translated by the English 'but' in the free version. In native, the narrative baldly proceeds to state that he broke 'one nose', that is, one end of the village. To express the relationship between these two sentences, the words 'of the island' have been introduced in the free translation. The expression 'he stand here, one village' refers to the formation of a new island by the action of the hero whose canoe sundered the land from one shore to another. In the free version the contextual implications have been brought out. The last clause 'his bottom his canoe Tudava', or 'the bottom of Tudava's canoe', is a characteristic native apposition giving the cause of a phenomenon. It means really 'formed by the bottom of Tudava's canoe breaking through'.

(xvii) The word 'he run', standing as it does after 'he go to open sea', is a sort of afterthought explanation of why the culture hero went to the open sea. In the following clauses the sentence telling us that the men came round in order to hit, that is to kill, the hero, and the following two clauses in which his new piercing of the land is described, probably express cause and effect, 'since they wanted to kill him, he broke through a passage'.

(xviii) The prefixed verbal modifier in the first verb *bi-* has the rare shade of meaning of strong affirmation. In what exact relation this function stands to the commonest uses, those of future and imperative, is a grammatical problem not to be fully discussed here. Roughly speaking, I think that the emphasis placed on the subjective mode in which the verb is to be taken expresses the desire of the actor, hence the dynamic side of his activity. The noun *valu* means here 'place', 'part of land', in this context obviously 'island'.

(xix) Here the prefixed modifier *ba-* has obviously several meanings. In the first clause it expresses conditional intention, in the second and third a definite conditional future, while at the very end it has a plain future meaning. Only the context allows us to discriminate between these various meanings. *Valu* here refers to the cultivable lands of the people.

(xx) A number of quaint expressions, *o sibu-la*, 'at the bottom of', which means 'somewhere beyond', the bottom being usually the further part of any place. The verb *binibani* is one of those concrete words which can only be translated by a cumbersome complicated English phrase: *bani* is the ordinary word for 'to search'; in connection with fishing it is technically used for only one type of that activity: "to fish for shark with a large wooden hook". The words *kala-yena kwa'u* are to a native quite pleonastic, but they fall, like many pleonasms, within the type of native narrative.

(xxi) There are one or two unusual words here. *Touyo* I think is a variant of *toulo*, 'own', which is usually found in such formations as *ta-toulo*, *toule-gu*, 'own, proper, real', etc., this sentence means, I think, that after it had swallowed the hook the shark swam off and dragged the man in his little canoe to the shore of the land where Tudava lived.

(xxii) The third word, *tolay-gu*, is a somewhat exceptional use of the word *toli*, 'owner'. *Tolay-gu Nadili*, 'owner mine Nadili', 'I belong to Nadili.' The second sentence in this verse explains really the meaning of verse xxi.

(xxiii) The use of the inclusive dual in the middle sentence will be noted.

(xxiv) The characteristic way of using the possessive 'his moon', 'his sojourn of a moon', is a sample of one method of expressing time-reckoning.

(xxv) The anticipatory possessive 'thy wild ginger' is a characteristic native way of expressing intention, 'wild ginger for thee, for thy use'.

(xxvi) The change of subject without any formal indication has to be gathered from the context, but is for one acquainted with native speech unmistakable. The formula 'thou remain, and I shall move off', or some similar expression, is the set native good-bye.

(xxvii) The verb 'to stand up' implies usually both the act of getting up and taking the word. Anyone speaking more or less ceremonially or addressing a departing friend would rise. The verb *kwasu*, 'ritually to bespit', is synonymous with *pulu* or *pulupulu* in contrast to *gi'u*, which means 'to spit ordinarily'. The *bi* in 'he might clean' and 'he might disappear' as well as in 'he might see me' implies a modification of purpose or intention. Translated in the free version by 'so that'. Obviously in English or any European language a number of conjunctions and differences in the mode of verbs would have been used in this direct speech of Tudava. *Valu* occurs twice. In each case the context gives it a clear and concrete meaning. *Valu* when Tudava speaks about the home of the paddler can be translated by 'village', because it obviously refers to a small island with a conspicuous village on it. When Tudava speaks about his own abode, the word 'village' becomes meaningless and we render it in the free version by the indefinite term 'place'. The word 'island' might also have been used. *Simarita* is a synonym of the verb *milakalita* (see next verse) which is a dialectical variant with transposed consonants of the usual verb for 'to clean, to make clean', *milakatile*. In the present context the verbs refer specifically to magic, 'making clean by magic', 'making to appear clearly on the horizon'.

(xxx) and (xxxi) This was spoken in a different tone, as a narrator's commentary, connecting an incident in the narrative to ordinary present-day experience.

42. The following text, which I received as a comment on the Kudayuri myth, is given in free translation in Chapter II (Sec. 5) as an illustration of quarrels arising during the cutting of garden plots.

T. 97. (i) *I-may-se*   *i-lukway-se*   *Mokatuboda:*
they come   they tell   (the elder brother)

"*Bwada-m*   *boge*   *i-takaywa*   *baleko!*"
thy younger brother   already he cut   garden plot

(ii) "*Bwoyne,*   *ba-la*   *ba-gisi!*"   *Lay-la.*
well   I might go I might see he did go

(iii) "*Avaka*   *ku-vagi?*"   *Bwada-la:*   "*Bwoyne,*
what   thou do   younger brother his   well

ku-sisu,   *ba-takaywa*   *uli*   *baleko.*"
thou sit   I might cut down scrub   my   garden plot

(iv) "*Gala,* *gwadi* *yoku,* *tomwaya* *yaygu,* *uli baleko.*"
no   child   thou   old man   myself   my garden plot

(v) *I-vata'i-si,*   *boge*   *i-vagi*   *bwada-la*
they quarrel   already   he do   younger brother his

i-gasisi,   *i-woye*   *tomwaya.*
he fierce   he hit   old man

43. COMMENTARY: (iii) The verb *sisu* is here used in the sense of "remain", "be where you are", "keep off".

(iv) The opposition between *gwadi*, "child", and *tomwaya*, "old man", shows the way in which Kiriwinian gets over its lack of comparative forms in the adjective. "Thou art a child, I am an old man, this is my garden plot" simply means "I am older than you, and this gives me the right to dispose."

(v) The verb "do" is here used in a very specific sense: "to upset", "to bring to an emotional pitch", "to rouse". The juxtaposition of "he roused", "he fierce" conveys the meaning "he was roused to fierceness". The verb "to hit" implies the fact that the blow was lethal. It will be noticed that such words and phrases as were necessary to bring out the implications of this text have been introduced into the free translation.

44. The following statement concerning the effect of magic on the taytu was given me by Towese'i, Bagido'u's younger brother:—

T. 98. (i) *Ta-sapu*   *taytu,*   *boge*   *i-kanukwenu.*
we (i.d.) plant taytu already he recline

(ii) *Iga'u,*   *i-lagi*   *megwa orokaywa,*   *boge*   *i-susine.*
later on   he hear magic above   already he sprout

(iii) *Ta-la*   *o*   *buyagu,*   *ta-liloulo,*
we (i.d.) go   in   garden-site   we (i.d.) walk round

     ta-migamegwa   —   *kumaydona*   *buyagu.*
     we (i.d.) recite magic   all   garden-site

(iv) *Kwaytanidesi*   *yam,*   *titole-la*   *towosi,*
one only   day   himself alone   garden magician

     bi-la,   *bi-megwa.*
     he might go   he might charm

(v) *I-sisu,*   *bi-mwamwa'i,*   *kalatolu*   *bi-la,*
he remain   he might pause   third day   he might go

    i-megwa,   *i-katusakapu*   *sobula.*
    he charm   he make emerge   sprout

(vi) *Bi-liloulo,*   *bi-migamegwa.*
he might walk round   he might recite magic

For free translation, see Chapter IV (Sec. 1). This text presents no special difficulties demanding comment.

45. The following homonymous meanings may be noted in this division:—

1. *la keda*
   1. 'his road'.
   2. 'way', 'manner', 'fashion'.

2. *liku*
   1. 'log cabin'.
   2. 'log' (of *bwayma*).
   3. 'any log receptacle', 'crate'.
   4. 'contents of *bwayma*'.

3. *taytupeta*
   1. 'taytu given in baskets'.
   2. 'harvest gift from man to kinsman'.

4. *tolikwabila*
   1. 'title of headman'—that is:—
   2. 'the eldest member of a sub-clan'.
   3. 'any member of a sub-clan'.
   4. 'any resident in a village'.
   5. 'magician' (when not identical with 1).

5. *urigubu*
   1. 'marriage gift' (gift for sister's husband).
   2. 'taro gardens for sister's husband'.
   3. 'other crops for sister's husband'.
   4. 'all marriage relationship duties'.
   5. 'chief's tribute'.
   6. 'taytu destined for gift to sister's husband'.
   7. 'plot cultivated for sister's husband'.

PART VI

AN ETHNOGRAPHIC THEORY OF THE MAGICAL
WORD

AN ETHNOGRAPHIC THEORY OF THE MAGICAL WORD

In passing to the analysis of magical texts it will be necessary again to engage in general linguistic considerations. Magical formulae differ from other texts considerably, both as regards their intrinsic nature and the place which we have given them in our scheme of presentation. As to its intrinsic nature, the language of magic is sacred, set and used for an entirely different purpose to that of ordinary life. As regards presentation, it was necessary in the course of our narrative account to make the garden magician recite his spells in a rhythmic, elaborated English version of the native text. This was justified because, in native, the language of magic, with its richness of phonetic, rhythmic, metaphorical and alliterative effects, with its weird cadences and repetitions, has a prosodic character which it is desirable to bring home to the English reader. At the same time, just because the language of magic is regarded as sacred, too great liberties must not be taken with it: or at least, such liberties as are taken must be checked against an exact statement of how much is contained in the native original and how much is added by the legitimate process of bringing out implications. This, as we shall see (below, Part VII), necessitates rather elaborate commentaries on each spell. The principles on which these commentaries have been built must be justified, and this is the scope of the present introduction.

Div. I. THE MEANING OF MEANINGLESS WORDS

It follows that those difficulties which we have encountered in the free translation of ordinary texts become much greater here. If, to repeat our paradox (Part IV, Div. II), all ordinary terms which have to be translated are yet untranslatable, this puzzling quality becomes much more pronounced when we deal with words which are avowedly meaningless. For the magician in the Trobriands as elsewhere deals out verbal elements of the *abracadabra, sesame, hocus pocus* type, that is, words the function of which is not 'meaning' in the ordinary sense, but a specific magical influence which these words are believed to exercise. In what way the 'meaning of meaningless words' can be conveyed is a paradoxical problem of linguistic theory which will have to be confronted here, as we have already confronted the puzzle of 'translating untranslatable words'.

Then again while the grammar and structure of ordinary speech presents a complicated task to the translator, the structure of spells—where obscurity is a virtue and non-grammatical formations impart a peculiar and characteristic flavour and value—is even more difficult to handle.

At the same time the elucidation of these difficulties, which the ethnographer has already had to face in the field, is instructive by reason of the wealth of native commentary thereby elicited. These commentaries have to be sifted and made clear and convincing to the reader—a process which leads us directly into a number of theoretical issues. Incidentally also the very strangeness of the magical texts, the very meaninglessness of magical words, brings into relief certain aspects of language which illuminate the Theory of Meaning given in Part IV (cf. especially Div. V) more clearly than does the study of ordinary speech.

The most difficult problem, perhaps, in connexion with magical formulae and, according to our conception of language, the central problem, is that concerning the function of a magical utterance. To us the meaning of any significant word, sentence or phrase is *the effective change* brought about by the utterance within the context of situation to which it is wedded. We have seen how this meaning has to be understood in the active pragmatic speech which passes between a group of people engaged in some concerted task; an order given and carried out, an advice or co-ordinating instruction followed. We have also seen how words of praise or encouragement act, and how they have a dynamic significance. We have enquired into the nature of meaning when speech is used for planning, for education, for narrative or conversation.

Now a magical formula is neither a piece of conversation, nor yet a prayer, nor a statement or communication. What is it? What is the sociological setting of a spell, what is its purpose, what is the function of magical words? In order to elicit the meaning of an ordinary utterance we found that we had to ascertain the social context; the purpose, aim and direction of the accompanying activities—practical, sociable, or generally cultural; and finally the function of the words, i.e. the effective change which they produce within concerted action. But in a magical formula the purpose seems to be imaginary, sociological co-operation non-existent and the rôle of words just to be uttered into the void.

Let us look more closely at the facts, however. When the magician mumbles over some herbs in his hut—is it just an empty monologue? No audience of listeners is supposed to be necessary to the effectiveness of the spell; therefore, according to our definition of meaning, the words would appear to be plainly meaningless. What is the point of his ritually uttered magical comments when, in striking the soil of the garden, he says: "I am striking thee, O soil"? Does he address the land, or his stick, or any people who chance to be present? Or again, on other occasions, does he talk to the herbs, or to a stone, or to one or other of the two saplings, or to spirits which, even if present, are not believed to do anything? When he addresses a spider or a bush-hen, a lawyer-cane or a dolphin, what sort of co-operative act, if any, is involved?

Some of these questions we are in a position to answer. Let us start from the purpose of magic. Imaginary it is from our point of view, but is this a reason for dismissing it as socially and culturally irrelevant? Certainly not. Magic happens in a world of its own, but this world is real to the natives. It therefore exerts a deep influence on their behaviour and consequently is also real to the anthropologist. The situation of magic—and by this I mean the scene of action pervaded by influences and sympathetic affinities, and permeated by *mana*—this situation forms the context of spells. It is created by native belief, and this belief is a powerful social and cultural force. Consequently we must try to place the utterances of magic within their appropriate context of native belief and see what information we can elicit which may help us towards the understanding of spells and the elucidation of words.

All the acts of magic, from the first oblation to the spirits to the last fragment of a banana spell, consist, from the dogmatic point of view, in one type of performance. Each rite is the "production" or "generation" of a force and the conveyance of it, directly or indirectly, to a certain given object which, as the natives believe, is affected by this force. In the Trobriands we have, then, the production and application of Melanesian *mana*, the magical force for which there is no name in our ethnographic province, but which is very much present there in the reality of belief and behaviour (cf. Part V, Div. V, § 5, and Div. VII, §§ 1–5).

Take the principal spell of Omarakana garden magic, which begins with the word *vatuvi* (cf. Part VII, M.F. 2, Ling. Comm. 1, and Ch. II, Sec. 4). The magician, after certain preparations and under the observance of certain rules and taboos, collects herbs and makes of them a magical mixture. Parallel with his actions and in concert with him, the members of the community make other preparations, notably the provision of fish for a gift to the magician and the spirits, and for a festive eating. The magician, after ritually and with an incantation offering some of this fish to the ancestral spirits, recites the main spell, *vatuvi*, over the magical mixture. Let me remind you of how he does this. He prepares a sort of large receptacle for his voice—a voice-trap we might almost call it. He lays the mixture on a mat and covers this with another mat so that his voice may be caught and imprisoned between them. During the recitation he holds his head close to the aperture and carefully sees to it that no portion of the herbs shall remain unaffected by the breath of his voice. He moves his mouth from one end of the aperture to the other, turns his head, repeating the words over and over again, rubbing them, so to speak, into the substance. When you watch the magician at work and note the meticulous care with which he applies this most effective and most important verbal action to the substance; when afterwards you see how carefully he encloses the charmed herbs in the ritual wrappings prepared, and in a ritual manner— then you realise how serious is the belief that the magic is in the breath and that the breath is the magic.

Follow spell after spell and rite after rite and the same type of behaviour, the same dogma, will be found expressed in and documented by every one of them. Take as a second example the other big spell of Omarakana garden magic, Formula 10, which begins with the words *kaylola lola* (Part VII, cf. also Ch. III, Sec. 4). Once more we see that it is chanted directly into the substance to be medicated—the "leaves of covering" (*yayu* and *youlumwalu*). And so with the other rites performed over the gardens. In the rites at *yowota*, for instance, the voice is launched into the 'bad stick' and into the 'good stick', into the soil which is rubbed with leaves and into the soil which is struck with a wand (cf. Ch. II, Sec. 4). Or in the magic of planting; the surface of the taro top from which the new plant is to sprout is impregnated with magic; afterwards a yam tuber and later yet another taro are treated in the same manner (cf. Ch. III, Sec. 4). During the numerous rites of growth magic the voice is made to sweep the soil of each plot and thus to reach the tubers underground, the growing vine and its developing foliage. There is no need to multiply examples. In every act the magician's breath is regarded as the medium by which the magical force is carried. The voice—and let us remember it must be the voice of the accredited and fully instructed magician, and that his voice must correctly utter the words of an absolutely authentic spell (cf. App. I)—"generates" the power of the magic. This force is either directly launched on the earth or the tuber or the growing plant, or else it is indirectly conveyed by the impregnation of a substance, usually herbs, which is then applied to the object to be affected: the earth, the saplings, the *kamkokola* or the harvested taro or yams.

To the Trobriander the spell is a sequence of words, more or less mysterious, handed down from immemorial times and always taught by an accredited magician to his successors; it is received by the first human wielder of the magic from some supernatural agency, or else brought by the first ancestors who came from underground, where they had led an existence in which magic apparently was already in use.[1] The myths about the beginnings of magic are not altogether consistent and sometimes not even clear. Theology, from Australian totemism or Trobriand magical lore to scholastic disputes, modern faculties of divinity and the councils of Christian Science or Theosophy—is always controversial and inconsistent. But on the whole we find in the Trobriands one fundamental belief— that the magic of gardening was first effectively exercised by such cultural heroes as Tudava, Malita, Gere'u and others (cf. Ch. I, Sec. 7), and a much more precise belief that each garden magic has come from underground on the very spot where it is now being practised, or else that it has been introduced to this spot and naturalised there (cf. Ch. I, Sec. 6 and Ch. XII, Secs. 1 and 3). Furthermore, the belief is very strong that supremacy in differential fertility is due to the fact of one magical system being better than the others (cf. Ch. I, Sec. 7). Also the element of luck, whether good or bad, is always accounted for by magic (Ch. I, Sec. 8).

The important point for us is, however, that in whatever manner magic has come into the possession of man, the spell as such has existed from the very beginning of things, *quod semper, quod ab initio*. . . . It is regarded as a specific quality of a relevant aspect of the world. Fertility and the growth of yams matter to man, and cannot be mastered by human forces alone. Hence there is magic, there always was magic, and the magic resides in the spell. When speaking of things sacred and ritual, the Trobriander would fully endorse the truth of *in principio erat verbum*. Though the natives would not be able to formulate it themselves, this is in brief their dogma; and though they also would not be able to tell it simply and in an abstract manner, wherever there is an important human activity, which is at the same time dangerous, subject to chance and not completely mastered by technical means—there is always for the Trobriander a magical system, a body of rites and spells, to compensate for the uncertainty of chance and to forearm against bad luck (cf. App. I).

[1] Compare also *Argonauts of the Western Pacific*, Ch. XVIII, "The Power of Words in Magic", Ch. XVII, "Magic", especially Secs. II to VIII; *Sexual Life of Savages*, Ch. XI, "The Magic of Love and Beauty", Ch. XIV, "A Savage Myth of Incest", and *Sex and Repression*, pp. 83–134 *passim*; *Myth in Primitive Psychology*, Ch. IV, "Myths of Magic".

The native does not pry with any great interest into origins except as they give a general warrant for his beliefs or customs; but he is really interested in the correctness of filiation, of the full and deliberate handing on of spells and rites. Traces of this we find in the mythological references contained in the spells; and still more perhaps in the interest shown in and consideration given to ancestral spirits. These receive oblations (cf. M.F. 1 and 26, Ch. II, Sec. 4), they are taken into the magician's confidence when some of his taboos are ritually lifted (cf. M.F. 26 and Ch. V, Sec. 2).

Div. II. COEFFICIENT OF WEIRDNESS IN THE LANGUAGE OF MAGIC

How far does this dogmatic background help us in understanding the wording of magic? If the main principle of magical belief is that words exercise power in virtue of their primeval mysterious connexion with some aspect of reality, then obviously we must not expect the words of Trobriand magic to act in virtue of their ordinary colloquial meaning. A spell is believed to be a primeval text which somehow came into being side by side with animals and plants, with winds and waves, with human disease, human courage and human frailty. Why should such words be as the words of common speech? They are not uttered to carry ordinary information from man to man, or to give advice or an order. The natives might naturally expect all such words to be very mysterious and far removed from ordinary speech. And so they are to a large extent, but by no means completely. We shall see that spells are astoundingly significant and translatable and we shall also see why this is so.

But the fact remains that unless the reader is forewarned that a great deal of the vocabulary of magic, its grammar and its prosody, falls into line with the deeply ingrained belief that magical speech must be cast in another mould, because it is derived from other sources and produces different effects from ordinary speech, he will constantly be at cross-purposes with the principles according to which the translation of magical utterance has to proceed. If the ordinary criteria of grammar, logic and consistency were applied, the translator would find himself hopelessly bogged by Trobriand magic.

Take the very first formula, for example. This is a direct address to ancestral spirits—a man-to-man communication we might say; hence in parts it is lucid and grammatical. And then comes the sentence: "Vikita, Iyavata, their myth head his." After much consultation with informants and etymological research in their company, I had to conclude that in no sense can these words be set equivalent to any ordinary prose sentence. The meaning of the magical expression is simply the intrinsic effect which, in native belief, it exerts on the spirits and indirectly on the fertility of the soil. The commentaries of the natives, however, reveal the mythological references connected with the names Vikita and Iyavata. Those who are versed in the magical tradition of this spell can interpret the significance of these words and tell us why they are ritually effective.

In what way, then, can we translate such a jumble of words, "meaningless" in the ordinary sense? The words are supposed to exercise a mystical effect *sui generis* on an aspect of reality. This belief is due to certain properties and associations of these words. They can therefore be translated in one sense and in one sense only: we must show what effect they are believed to produce, and marshal all the linguistic data available to show how and why they produce this effect.

To take another example, the exordium of the most important spell, Formula 2, v. 1 :—

> *Vatuvi, vatuvi, vatuvi, vatuvi. Vitumaga, i-maga.*
> *Vatuvi, vatuvi, vatuvi, vatuvi. Vitulola, i-lola.*

The better one knows the Trobriand language the clearer it becomes that these words are not words of ordinary speech. As actually recited in the spell they are pronounced according to a special phonology, in a sing-song, with their own rhythm and with numerically grouped repetitions. The word *vatuvi* is not a grammatical form ever found in ordinary speech (cf. M.F. 2, Ling. Comm. 1). The compounds *vitulola*, *vitumaga*, are again weird and unusual; in a way, nonsense words. Words like *vatuvi* or the root *lola* (M.F. 10, v. 1) are clipped; but there are other words which are compounded, built up, developed, as for instance the words *kayboginega* (M.F. 17, v. 1), *bilalola* (M.F. 10, v. 1), the compounds *siribwobwa'u, bwobwa'u, sirimwadogu, mwadogu* (M.F. 16, v. 1) and so on.

In some formulae we are able to translate the words clearly and satisfactorily after our magically illumined commentator has given us their esoteric meaning. Thus we are told that *gelu* is a magical word for 'bush-hen', in ordinary speech *mulubida*; that *kaybwagina* is a clipped form of *mitakaybwagina*, which is the mystical name for the millipede, known in ordinary speech as *mwanita*. Some of the animals, it is true, are called by their ordinary names. Thus the spider is addressed in Formula 18 by the usual word *kapari*; and so is the dolphin, *kuriyava*, in Formula 27. But even these ordinary words, by association with others, such as *naga* and *nam* (*-m*), not used in common speech, and with proper names of spots which are not comprehensible without a mythological and topographical commentary, are incorporated into a complex prosodic structure, specifically magical in character. We could discover such characteristic structures, usually rhythmical and symmetrical, in almost every formula. Thus in Formulae 17, 19, 21, 25, 27 and 28 we have the enumeration of the same animal, plant or natural object declined through geographical oppositions from north to south or from one topographical point to another.

Again we have in many spells what might be called negative comparison on the pattern "this is not (here the object to be charmed or a part of it is named) . . . but it is (here a pattern or ideal object is named)." Thus, for instance, we have in spell 13, v. 4: "this is not thy eye, thy eye is as the black ant's", or in Formula 16, v. 4: "this is not thy flight, thy flight is as a parrot's", and so on.[1]

---

[1] A succinct enumeration might be useful to the student who wants especially to examine the spells from this point of view. Words used in a specific and unusual manner can be found in M.F. 2, vv. 6–8, where the pause between the verb and the adverb *gala* gives the characteristic meaning of 'begone', 'avaunt', a powerful negation with an exorcistic function. The verbs *ba-yabay-m* (M.F. 2, v. 6) and *tumili-m* (M.F. 2, v. 8) require a special commentary because of their structure. The verbs *a-tabe'u* (v. 4) and *a-givisa'u* (v. 5) are forms never met in ordinary speech. In M.F. 3, v. 2, a number of nominal roots compounded with the prefix *buri-* had to be specifically explained. M.F. 4, v. 2, *a-talilakema* is a queer overcharged compound. M.F. 5, v. 2, *silavila, yomwatewa*, are unusual weird compounds. M.F. 8, v. 1, *luluwa*, far-fetched metaphor; *nukuwalu* and *nukula'odila*, unusual words. M.F. 9, v. 2, *itamala*, not translated, M.F. 9, v. 3, *pudikikita*, translated by etymological hypothesis. M.F. 10, v. 1, *gulugulu*, unusual; v. 4, the compounds with *imduku-* built on magical pattern. M.F. 11, *pwakikita*, unusual compound; *siwakauyo*, untranslatable. M.F. 13, v. 3, and M.F. 14, v. 3, *tavisi-ma, sakapu-ma, -ma* translated only by etymological hypothesis. Also the word *katumyogila* untranslatable. M.F. 13, v. 4, *kapapita, ginausi*, only vaguely translated. Compare also M.F. 12; 15, v. 3; 16, v. 2; 19, v. 4, and 20, for words for kinds of *taytu* or *kuwi*. These words may be ordinary words, since, as I have said in the Linguistic Supplement (Div. III, § 11), I was not able to collect all the names for varieties of crops. But on the whole I think that many of these are not ordinary words. In M.F. 15 the whole of v. 3 is doubtful. M.F. 16: the words of v. 1 have already been mentioned; v. 3: strange compounds of a distinctly magical stamp; vv. 5 and 6: exaggerations difficult to account for, the word *yakanugwalay-gu* really untranslatable. M.F. 17, v. 6: strange magical compounds. M.F. 19: the whole structure of v. 1, several words in v. 3 difficult to translate, the leading word *pwoyliya* not usual and translated by conjectural reasoning; v. 5, *koduwala* only conjecturally translated. M.F. 23, v. 1: *po'isi, pomala* and v. 3: *ko'ulu, kolaluma*, only conjecturally translated. M.F. 24, v. 1: *kilogo*, probable translation. M.F. 25, vv. 3–5, strange condensed grammatical structure, translatable only with commentary.

The same features can be found in any formula: most words can be translated if we know for what reason they are used in the spell. If in Formula 27, for example, we know that the dolphin is big and long as the tubers should become, that its weaving in and out of the rising and falling waves is associated with the winding and interweaving of the luxuriant vines whose rich foliage means a plentiful taytu harvest, we can not only translate the word 'dolphin', but several sentences based on this allusion; above all, we can understand the structure of the whole spell. The same applies to the bush-hen in Formula 21, whose large nest is associated with the swelling round the taytu plant when tubers are plentiful. Again, when we realise that the natives are very much afraid of the bush-pigs which destroy their gardens; when we become acquainted with their beliefs about the homes of the bush-pigs, and furthermore have received a specific commentary on the rites of *pelaka'ukwa* (cf. Ch. III, Sec. 2), the text of vv. 2–5 of Formulae 3 and 7 can be appreciated (cf. also in Part VII the commentary on these verses). Again, the addresses to ancestors are incomprehensible without a knowledge of native belief about spirits. Most mythological allusions have to be interpreted in the same manner, as for instance the invocation to the culture heroes Tudava and Malita (M.F. 10, 22 and 29); references to the obscure women, Vikita and Iyavata (M.F. 1), or to the men Gagabwa and Yayabwa (M.F. 5).

Thus all magical verbiage shows a very considerable coefficient

M.F. 27, v. 4: *dumdum*, not known to me from ordinary speech, is certainly not a usual grammatical form. M.F. 28, v. 3: *tubuga'okuwa, kurabwa'u*, unusual magical compounds. The same holds good for *burokukuwa* and *burokawita*. In M.F. 30 the following words have been left untranslated: *kumgwa'i, ku'uyem, yagesi* and *bibila*, and most of the words in v. 2 (*a*) and (*c*) have only been rendered tentatively. M.F. 31: the words *padudu, pawoya* (v. 1), *rakata'i, lakamawa* (v. 3), the whole of v. 4, the keyword *tagoru* and most of the words in v. 6 (*a*) and (*c*) were left untranslated, while the words *tobisubasuma* and *kapwayasi* (v. 7) were only conjecturally rendered.

References to ancestral spirits are found in M.F. 1, 2, 19, 26, 38, 41 and 42, with a possible addition of 3 and 7. Mythological names are found in M.F. 1, 5, 10, 22, 29 and perhaps 31. Negative comparisons are to be found in M.F. 13, v. 4; 14, v. 4; 16, v. 4; 24, vv. 3, 4. As to the types of prosodic weaving in of words, there are examples in M.F. 2, v. 1; we find the rhythmic opposition of *wa* and *-ma* in M.F. 4, v. 3; 9, v. 1. In M.F. 8 we find repetitive symmetry of simple verbs, the same verb being repeated with the directive suffix *-ke'i*; and with the suffixes *-va'u* and *-mugwa* in M.F. 13, v. 1; 14, v. 1. The opposition of averb coupled with *kwaya'i* and *lala'i* in M.F. 13, v. 2; 14, v. 2. Nouns opposed with *naga* and *-m* are found in M.F. 17, v. 1; 18, v. 1; 21, v. 1; 25, v. 1; 27, v. 1; 28, v. 1. In M.F. 19, v. 1, we have the numerical recital of a magically quantitative noun. In M.F. 22, v. 1, we have the rhythmic play on names. Question and answer are found in M.F. 5, v. 1, and 10, v. 2.

of weirdness, strangeness and unusualness. The better we know the Trobriand language the more clearly and immediately can we distinguish magic from ordinary speech. The most grammatical and least emphatically chanted spell differs from the forms of ordinary address. Most magic, moreover, is chanted in a sing-song which makes it from the outset profoundly different from ordinary utterances. The wording of magic is correlated with a very complicated dogmatic system, with theories about the primeval mystical power of words, about mythological influences, about the faint co-operation of ancestral spirits, and, much more important, about the sympathetic influence of animals, plants, natural forces and objects. Unless a competent commentator is secured who, in each specific case, will interpret the elements of weirdness, the allusions, the personal names or the magical pseudonyms, it is impossible to translate magic. Moreover, as a comparison of the various formulae has shown us, there has developed a body of linguistic practice— use of metaphor, opposition, repetition, negative comparison, imperative and question with answer—which, though not developed into any explicit doctrine, makes the language of magic specific, unusual, quaint.

I should like to add that I do not want to lay too much stress on those words which have proved at our hands completely untranslatable (cf. Note, pp. 220–221). Such words are to be found throughout the spells, but especially in Formulae 30 and 31, and in the formulae of Kurokayva garden magic. Some of these words may have remained untranslatable simply because I did not find a competent and adequate commentator. In order to assist me in the linguistic interpretation of a formula, my informant had both to possess the esoteric knowledge of mythology and magical lore of his own system, and be sufficiently alert, intelligent and perseverant to bring this knowledge over to me. Bagido'u, to whom we owe the translation of Formulae 1–29, united these qualities of a good commentator in the highest degree. Hence the garden magic of Omarakana is the best translated magic in my records, and those words which have remained untranslatable in spite of his assistance and of the excellent opportunities I had to discuss matters with him over and over again, are probably really untranslatable.

The important point, however, is that there is a clear breach of continuity between magical and ordinary speech. Any sample of ordinary utterance or narrative I was always able to translate without any special difficulty. New words and phrases would be defined to me by my informants as 'true speech', *biga mokita*, or as 'the way of talk', *livala la keda*. Both by my informants in the field and by the very structure and character of the formulae, the distinction is unmistakably marked.

Div. III. DIGRESSION ON THE THEORY OF MAGICAL LANGUAGE

Let us rapidly review the main stages of our argument. We started from the observation that magic in all languages and at all times, and certainly in the Trobriands, almost ostentatiously displays words which are avowedly meaningless. Since to us meaning is equal to the function of words within the context of situation, we were led to enquire what the situation of magic really is. Magic produces specific supernatural effects within a world created by magical belief, by means of ritual handling carried out by an accredited magician. Therefore we were led to the conclusion that the meaning of spells consists in the effect of the words within their ritual context. Thus the analysis of meaning in magic must turn on the mystical influences of utterance accompanied by manual acts.

More concretely we found that the magical theology of the Trobrianders declares that there are words of primeval origin which produce their specific mystical effect by being breathed into the substance, spiritual or physical, which has to be influenced. To the Trobriander the very essence of magic lies in the spell. But the spell must be handled by the accredited magician within an appropriate ceremonial. Thus the dogmatic conviction of the Trobrianders places words within a specific mystical context: the words act because they are primeval; because they have been properly handed down by an unbroken filiation of magic; because they have been correctly learnt by the new magician from his predecessor; and because they are carried out by the sociologically determined person, who at the same time observes the necessary taboos and restrictions.

What type of words should we expect from such a magical context? Since meaning is function within the context of situation and the situation of magic is different from that of everyday life, we might *prima facie* expect to find a magical language corresponding to this difference. Add to this the native belief that magic is prehuman in origin, that it existed underground before it emerged with the first ancestors and we should not be surprised if the magical formulae were composed of mere gibberish or nonsense words, concatenated according to a grammar of their own. If a word is believed to be effective, that is, to have a magical meaning, because it has had a different origin, a different history and a different place in language, then obviously its unusual, quaint character is well correlated with this belief. The mysterious and sacred words which are supposed to have a direct hold over reality need not conform to the rules of the grammar and word formations of ordinary speech.

As a matter of fact, the nonsense element in magical wording, the coefficient of weirdness as we have called it, is not overwhelmingly great. Its extent will be clearer when we come to list the words actually in common use included in the spells, and the distortions of such ordinary words.

But let me adduce a few facts which show in a general manner how far the formula really differs from ordinary speech, and how far this is brought out by the natives in their own attitude towards magic. First of all, and using my own linguistic experience, there is no doubt at all that I never had the slightest difficulty in diagnosing whether certain words were uttered as a formula or as an ordinary communication. The magical spell is phonetically different. With very few exceptions it is always chanted in a characteristic sing-song. It is also contextually different, that is, the behaviour of the magician and of those present is different. It is only uttered in full ritual performance; in teaching, that is, when the accredited magician imparts his knowledge to his successor, and at funerary wakes. The noting of an ordinary statement presented certain difficulties, but these were much increased when a formula had to be written down. Magicians as a rule cannot repeat their spells slowly or piecemeal or in an ordinary voice. I usually had to let them run through the whole spell, jotting down words here and there, noting the keyword, interpolating the inventory words and filling out the gaps during the second or third recital. This is also the way in which the spells are taught, that is, a magician recites them time after time, not slowly or in bits, but right through; that is as far as he is prepared to give them. I was told that sometimes the magician, especially when he is "selling" a formula, does not give the full text at once to the purchaser.

Not only was it very much more difficult to note down a formula, but it was always very difficult for me to understand it. Even now, when from my field notes I have to write out, comment upon and translate a spell, the task is incomparably more formidable than the editing of an ordinary text. The process of obtaining comments on magical formulae in the field is also significant. Although I believe that most of the texts of public magic are well known and comprehensible to the members of a community, the ordinary unaccredited person will always refuse to comment upon or inform about magic. In

Omarakana any man, except Bagido'u, his kinsmen or his intimate friends, would immediately give the answer: "This is Bagido'u's magic—we cannot speak about it." It is bad form to trespass on the magician's exclusive field of knowledge. Moreover, even those who would be allowed to speak about magic freely, would often try to put me off by saying: "This is magical speech—we cannot talk about it. There is nothing which meets it" (*gala avaka biboda*, which is equivalent to the statement that such words are untranslatable). Indeed the opposition between *megwa la biga*, 'magic his language', 'the language of magic', and *livala la biga*, 'speech his language', 'the language of speech', that is of ordinary speech, occurred so frequently that it became sacramental and therefore irritating. With every new informant I had to get over the difficulty of making him open up. I had to explain to him that I quite understood the distinction between magical and ordinary speech, and that what I wanted from him was such full commentary as he would give to his matrilineal nephew if he were to teach him this magic. There were in fact a number of defensive phrases: *ayseki gala takateta, megwa la biga*, 'I am ignorant, we do not know, it is the language of magic'; or again, *gala biboda avaka, libogwo*, 'it is not equal to anything, it is old talk'. Or again: *tokunabogwo aybutu otanawa*, 'of old that has been composed beneath (underground)'.

When I finally got a magician to work with me, the commentaries on magical formulae were always much more complicated and also more fruitful. This I have already mentioned. I invariably obtained mythological references, etymologies, parallel sentences. The reader need only look up my commentaries on the words *vatuvi* (M.F. 2, v. 1) or *kaylola* (M.F. 10, v. 1); on the words *dadeda* (M.F. 13, v. 3), *kaybogina* (M.F. 17, v. 1) and *siribwobwa'u* (M.F. 16, v. 1) to have examples of such commentaries.

Thus the coefficient of weirdness is also established by the general way in which magical formulae are uttered, handled, explained and made significant—to the natives as well as to the ethnographer. This coefficient of weirdness we have shown to be correlated with the Trobriand beliefs concerning magic. It corresponds to our view of meaning in magic as a specific emanation from words.

Div. IV. COEFFICIENT OF INTELLIGIBILITY

The emphasis in our argument up till now has been on the strangeness of magical language. I have tried to account for the coefficient of weirdness by correlating it with native magical belief, to exemplify it from the details of magical formulae, and to show how it appears in the general character of magical practice. Yet with all this the net result of our analysis was that magical texts are translatable, that is, that they are intelligible. They are not only intelligible in the sense that we can correlate the strange features of magical language with certain aspects of belief. Side by side with the unusual phrasing, the specific distortions of magic, we find words of common speech; whole sentences or phrases which might have been uttered quite as well in ordinary conversation or narrative; or again, words which have nothing esoteric or mystical about them and expressions where the coefficient of weirdness is almost negligible. Let us briefly survey the facts and classify these elements of intelligibility.

First then, let me adduce a list of phrases which might be used in everyday life. When in an ordinary though persuasive voice the magician informs the spirits that 'to-morrow we penetrate our garden-site' (M.F. 1), he uses a phrase which could be heard on any evening in a Trobriand village. The phrase being quite ordinary is obviously also intelligible and shows no coefficient of weirdness whatever. Let us remember, however, that it receives from the context wherein we find it a sacramental meaning which immediately removes it from the realm of ordinary discourse. Also I have here omitted the last word of this verse—the interjection *kay*—which would be very unusual in everyday conversation. This sentence shows the two-fold character of magical speech. The phrase is intelligible and ordinary, in so far as it has a clear grammatical structure and is composed of words belonging to the everyday vocabulary of the Trobriander. In its full import, derived from the context of speech, the phrases which precede and follow it, the situation in which it is uttered, and the dogmatic setting of belief—the words receive a specific magical meaning. To appreciate the meaning of the sentence, both coefficients—that of intelligibility and that of weirdness—have to be taken into account. It is the duty of the ethnographer to put both sets of fact at the reader's disposal. In Formula 3 we find the expression 'I kick in bottom thine'—a running comment on an action which is no more unusual in the Trobriands than in any other culture. Since, however, a person who kicks another's bottom would not naturally comment upon this action verbally, the phrase though possible is not usual or current in ordinary speech. But beyond this, taken within its context, it has a specific magical meaning. 'I cut thee my garden-site' (M.F. 4, v. 1) belongs to the same type: possible in ordinary converse, grammatical and composed of ordinary words, but unusual. To use it a Trobriander would have to be inspired by a poetical desire to address a garden-site—an occurrence unlikely to be realised. The same might be said of 'I strike thee soil' (M.F. 6,

v. 1) and of several other similar expressions which the reader will find without difficulty.

More ordinary, belonging completely to the speech of everyday life, are the expressions 'he might climb, he might seat himself in high platform' (M.F. 10, v. 2 and M.F. 29, v. 2). They might easily be used in describing the behaviour of any man of rank. The Tro-briander also frequently uses the expression found in Formula 16 (v. 6), 'he copulate mother his' (roughly equivalent to 'damn your eyes'); 'he jump sun', which is the ordinary expression for the sunrise (M.F. 23, v. 6); 'they eat taro' (M.F. 25, v. 4); 'you go, you load our coconut' (M.F. 41, vv. 1 and 3); 'they take a cutting shell; they cut at my banana' (M.F. 44, v. 3) and so on. The whole of Formula 26, 'We might throw away, old man, food old; we might eat again food new', which is the ordinary native phrasing for 'Let us leave on one side the old food, respected friends; let us eat instead the new food'—might easily be heard any evening or morning in the Trobriands, to indicate simply that the food from the previous day should be left and some fresh prepared. But again the ritual context of this spell imparts a different and a mystical meaning. The term *tomwaya*, 'old man' or 'old men', is not a polite form of respectful address, but a designation of ancestral spirits; and the old and new food refers to the crops of the two seasons. In all the sentences quoted there is, over and above the ordinariness and intelligibility of the words, the mystical meaning derived from the context.

Besides these sentences, which might appear in everyday life in an ordinary meaning, we find intelligible phrases and sentences which contain distinctly magical words. We find terms and concepts such as *kariyala*, 'magical portent' (M.F. 10, v. 5; 28, v. 5; and 29, v. 5), *ula'ula*, 'oblation' (M.F. 1, vv. 1 and 2), *kaygaga*, 'wood bad' (M.F. 3, v. 1). Here we might say that the phrase could not be understood outside its magical context; but that once we are acquainted with the concepts, universally known among the Trobrianders and pertaining to their magical universe of discourse, they become intelligible—not by any special esoteric lore of the accredited magician, but as an ordinary part of Trobriand language and culture.

In many spells we find, in the middle part, a long list of inventory words, all or some of which belong to ordinary language. In Formula 2 (vv. 4–8), for instance, some of the inventory words are simple expressions for blights, others are compound words which are used only in magic. In Formula 10 (v. 3) we find such ordinary words as 'soil', *kamkokola*, 'boundary pole', 'boundary of field', 'boundary of plot'; and a whole series of expressions defining the various yam supports, which are used in ordinary speech exactly as they are used in the spell and with the same meaning. In Formula 29 (v. 3) the inventory consists of the ordinary names for the component parts of the yam-house. In Formula 30 (v. 2) we find a few words of ordinary speech, referring also to parts of the yam-house, embedded in a number of compounds with a distinctly magical form. Of course, here again the context in which we find these words and the manner of their recital is completely different from that of everyday language.

Side by side with the technical expressions of magic, such as *kariyala* or *kaygaga* or *ula'ula*, we might have placed compound expressions with a definite magical implication, but having nothing unintelligible in the way in which they are compounded. Expressions such as 'belly of my garden' (M.F. 2, v. 3), 'I might burst open thy passage' (M.F. 1, v. 6); the double negative comparisons, such as 'no eye thine, eye thine a quick insect' (M.F. 13, v. 4), 'no thy flight, thy flight parrot' (M.F. 16, v. 4), 'no eye thine, eye thine morning star' (M.F. 24, v. 4), come into this category. But here already we touch the fringe of the distinctly strange and weird, which we have discussed fully in the previous division. In fact, we see that the coefficient of intelligibility and the coefficient of weirdness are to be found in different proportions, in almost every element of magical speech. Take, for instance, the words which are used ungrammatically or are distorted in their word formation. We find many verbs used without a pronominal prefix: *sakapu* (M.F. 14, v. 1), *tavisi* (M.F. 13), *sayboda* (M.F. 18, v. 3), *karitana'i* (M.F. 22, v. 5). These words contain a significant root, and this is used in the present context with the direct colloquial meaning with which they would be used in ordinary speech. It is important here to realise all the factors of magical reality. When in order to make the sprout emerge the magician says *dadeda sakapu-ma* (M.F. 14, v. 2), and at the beginning of the formula repeats the word *sakapu*, he uses the word ungrammatically. Its function is verbal, but its form is that of a simple root. It could not have been used like that in ordinary language. But the meaning here would be the same as if, in describing the phenomenon which the magician tries to induce, the natives said *sobula bi-sakapu*, 'the sprout will emerge'. Comparing this with such words as *vatuvi* (M.F. 2, v. 1) or *kaylola lola* (M.F. 10, v. 1; M.F. 29, v. 10) we see that, while in the former magical meaning directly parallels ordinary meaning, in the latter the magical 'radiation' or 'emanation' follows very complicated and tortuous lines. But in both cases the integral meaning of the words as used in magic is fundamentally different from their meaning as used in common speech in that their function in the first case is to induce certain phenomena by mystical means, while in the second it is merely to inform another person of what is happening or to assist him in work.

If we were to take words used in a metaphorical manner, we could again establish certain gradations. When in Formula 2 (v. 3) the magician speaks about the 'belly of his 'garden' 'lifting', 'rising', 'reclining', the metaphors are plain. They are nothing more than a slightly exaggerated or poetical description of what is happening. Compare this with the specific and complicated metaphors involved in such expressions as 'millipede he throw, head thine taytu, millipede he throw' (M.F. 17, v. 5); or 'spider cover up, thy open space taytu, spider cover up' (M.F. 18, v. 3); or the derived metaphorical meaning of the expression *pwoyliya* (M.F. 19, v. 1) and *taytu poriyama*, *taytu poriya poriyama* (M.F. 19, v. 4), or the expressions in Formula 23 and Formula 27 (vv. 3 and 4). It is clear that we gradually pass from relatively simple modifications of plain speech to very complicated distortions and rhetorical liberties in the development of indirect or derived meaning.

Exactly as we have accounted previously for the strangeness of some magical expressions, it is necessary here to bring the element of intelligibility into line with magical belief. This will not be difficult. The belief that a word can grip the essence of things absolves the words of magic from the necessity of having ordinary significance. It does not by any means force them into meaninglessness. One of the fundamental tenets of Trobriand magical theology is that the magical word is coeval with that aspect of reality which it has to influence. But the word is always something to be uttered by man. The magical word, therefore, is really an attribute of the relation between man and thing. The magical word, we might well expect, has got some affinity with the name which linguistically defines the relation of man as speaker to the object addressed. Taking the spells as a whole we see that dogmatically they are classed as a language *sui generis*; but still they are part of language. They are chanted by man, and they are chanted at objects and beings, in fact into objects and beings. No wonder, therefore, that at times, as we have seen, these objects or beings are addressed by their ordinary names, at times by a magical appellation. We have met also with a number of associated beliefs which specify certain agencies as being magically effective. Ancestral spirits, the magical predecessors of the magician, vegetable, animal or inanimate realities are very often directly invoked in the spell. We need not finally settle the question whether, in Trobriand magical dogmatics, the various agencies are the ultimate executors of the magical command. I was not able to satisfy myself on this point. On the whole, I think that the natives simply believe that the utterance of the word spider, for instance, sympathetically induces a web-like development of the taytu vine. They assume that the list of ancestral spirits produces a direct effect on fertility and so on. Yet in the commands, invocations and addresses, ordinary speech occurs quite naturally and fits quite well into the context of belief and ritual. Thus when we scrutinise the Trobriand belief in the mystical power of words, we find that the very sources from which this belief is alimented, drive it towards a considerable degree of intelligibility. Trobriand dogmatics impose certain ordinary grammatical forms on the speech and they lead it to the use of common words.

The two coefficients of weirdness and intelligibility co-exist almost down to the minutest detail. They also appear as general characters of magical speech. Even at the beginning, when I found considerable difficulty in taking down and translating spells, certain sentences would leap out of the obscure context and give me a shock by their direct lucidity.

The weirdness consists very largely in artificial form, in the ungrammatical use of certain roots, in reduplications or couplings, in mythological references and concrete topographical allusions. There are magical pseudonyms for objects or animals. There are certain esoteric allusions. But on the whole it is its formal presentation in the spell which gives the magical imprint to the language. The coefficient of intelligibility is found in the fact that even the strangest verbal formations refer directly or indirectly to the matter with which the magic deals. It is found, further, in the fact that, associated with slightly distorted or modified keywords, a long list of ordinary expressions appears. In garden magic the taytu is addressed as taytu and its various parts are enumerated by ordinary terms (M.F. 17, v. 5); so also with the technical apparatus of training and growth (M.F. 18, v. 3). But we need not enlarge on this. The weirdness yields to treatment as soon as we place the spells within their context and develop the general concepts of magic or the special esoteric law which is there as a background to every system. The weirdness becomes explicable and the meaning of meaningless words emerges as their function, based on the multiple mystical associations of a verbal root. On the other hand, the intelligible elements embedded in distortions, associated with magically modified words, disguised by chant, have to be taken not in their ordinary sense, but definitely in their magical function. The translator's task is not made any easier because of this two-fold nature of the spell. On the one hand, even when he meets simple words and ordinary phrases he is not dispensed from the duty of showing how far this language in that context functions magically or mystically. On the other hand, he may not shelter behind such phrases as "the language is archaic" or "the spells are unintelligible to the natives themselves". The esoteric top-dressing may disguise the fact that underneath it there exist associations and linguistic affinities with ordinary speech. The establishment of these is made perhaps more difficult by the esoteric top-dressing, but quite as necessary.

Div. V. DIGRESSION ON THE GENERAL THEORY OF MAGICAL LANGUAGE

So far I have dealt exclusively with Trobriand facts. I have also avoided going beyond what could be immediately documented from our collection of magical data. But obviously there are certain further problems which our theoretical approach raises, and it may be well at least to indicate that I am aware of their existence. The following general considerations on the nature of magical language in its relation to pragmatic speech do not, of course, claim the same degree of ripeness and finality as some of the more limited conclusions established on an exhaustive analysis of our own ethnographic area. But though my argument should not be treated as anything but a suggestive and preliminary statement, I think it better to submit it to prospective field-workers and students of magical facts.

In the first place, then, is it possible for us to venture on some general explanation of why the language of magic has this two-fold character, why the coefficients of weirdness and intelligibility both dominate it. In the second place, the evolutionary or historical problem may have occurred to the reader. Have we to imagine that magical speech starts from sheer nonsense words and emotional sounds, or onomatopoetic reproduction of natural noises, and then develops towards an approximation to ordinary speech? Or should we adopt the inverse hypothesis that magical language at first is strictly utilitarian and rational in function, and gradually develops its weird and incomprehensible aspect? Or is there perhaps a still different genetic assumption to be made?

The answer to both problems is contained in the theory of meaning which has been elaborated in Part IV. We have seen there that language in its inception is both magical and pragmatic. It is charged with a mystical effectiveness and is used as a working tool. By "inception" we mean here, of course, the beginnings of speech in human life, rather than in the life of humanity. In so far as language is used in ordinary life, and for pragmatic purposes, the element of intelligibility comes to the fore. It reaches its maximum in the sociologically set language of drill, of co-operative speech used in economic enterprise. It reaches also its peak of pragmatic effectiveness in the technical terminology of arts and crafts by which the theory of manufacture is handed on from generation to generation and communication is possible between co-operating artisans. In so far as the same words and sentences are used with reference to emotional experiences and crystallised emotional attitudes belonging to the domain of magic and religion, these words and phrases are fraught with a meaning which has no roots in empirical experience or in co-operative activities. There, on the one hand, meaning becomes mystical, and on the other the forms become unusual in so far as they are no more adapted to ordinary communication. Within the linguistic theory of the present book, in which the distinction between "form" and meaning is in the last instance illusory, because form is sound within context, and meaning is the effect of sound within context, the two-fold character of speech has nothing really mysterious or unexpected. Harking back to Division VI of Part IV, we realise that all language in its earliest function within the context of infantile helplessness is proto-magical and pragmatic. It is pragmatic in that it works through the appeal to the child's human surroundings; it is proto-magical in that it contains all the emotional dependence of the child on those to whom it appeals through sound. In the course of long years, during which the pragmatic attitude towards words only gradually develops, the child experiences the power of words and sounds, especially when these are fraught with emotion as well as with the conventional significances of articulation.

Our theoretical approach thus supplies the answer to both questions in one hypothesis, that is, if we adopt the principle that the development of speech in humanity must have, in its fundamental principles, been of the same type as the development of speech within the life history of the individual. This I hold to be the only sound scientific approach to the genetic problems of language as also of other aspects of culture.

The thesis then which I am putting forward here is that the Trobriand phenomenon of a language of magic, within which we find a masquerading of significant speech under the guise of esoteric and mysterious forms, fits into our theory of language. In Trobriand magic we find hardly a single word, the working of which, that is, the meaning of which, could not be explained on the basis of associations, mythological data or some other aspect of Frazer's principle of sympathy. This, I think, is but part of the universal, essentially human, attitude of all men to all words. From the very use of speech men develop the conviction that the knowledge of a name, the correct use of a verb, the right application of a particle, have a mystical power which transcends the mere utilitarian convenience of such words in communication from man to man.

The child actually exercises a quasi-magical influence over its surroundings. He utters a word, and what he needs is done for him by his adult entourage. This is a point of view on which I do not need to enlarge. I think that the contributions of such modern child psychologists as Piaget and Bühler, and of older workers such as William Stern, supply us with a rich material for the confirmation of this point of view. But I have not been able to consult their work in connexion with the writing of this division.

I have also stressed already the fact that this early attitude is partly superseded, but to a large extent confirmed in the further development of the individual. The mastery over reality, both technical and social, grows side by side with the knowledge of how to use words. Whether you watch apprenticeship in some craft within a primitive community or in our own society, you always see that familiarity with the name of a thing is the direct outcome of familiarity with how to use this thing. The right word for an action, for a trick of trade, for an ability, acquires *meaning* in the measure in which the individual becomes capable to carry out this action. The belief that to know the name of a thing is to get a hold on it is thus empirically true. At the same time, it lends itself to obvious distortions in the direction of mysticism. For the genuineness of the process, that is the genuineness of verbal power over things through manual and intellectual control, is the result of a fine balance. On the one hand we have people who are more effective manually than verbally. This is a handicap. The simple mind, primitive or civilised, identifies difficulty of speech and clumsiness and unreadiness of expression with mental deficiency. In the Trobriands *tonagowa* covers idiocy and defective speech; and among European peasantry the village idiot is very often merely a person who stammers or suffers from inability of clear expression. On the other hand the verbal type and the theoretical type of person surpass in mastery of words while they are backward in manual effectiveness. Even within the most primitive differentiation of activities the man who is better at counsel and advice, at talking and bragging, represents what in more advanced communities will become the schoolman, the talmudist or the baboo. This may be an unhealthy development of learning or of a purely consulting or advisory capacity; but it is rooted in something which functions throughout all human work—

I mean the fact that some people must command, advise, plan and co-ordinate.

So far I have been mainly speaking about arts and crafts. Power through speech in the mastery of social relations, of legal rules and of economic realities, is quite as plain. The child who grows up in a primitive community and becomes instructed gradually in the intricacies of kinship, the taboos, duties and privileges of kindred, of clansmen, of people of higher and lower rank, learns the handling of social relations through the knowledge of sociological terms and phrases. The instruction may take place in the course of initiation ceremonies, a great part of which consists in the sociological apprenticeship of the child, boy or girl, youth or maiden, to tribal citizenship. But obviously there is a long educational process between the small infant, who can name and call for the few people of its immediate surroundings, and the adult tribesman or tribeswoman, who must address a score, a few hundred or even a few thousand people in the proper manner, appeal to them through adequate praise, be able to greet, converse and transact business with them. This process again has two sides: experience in "deportment", manners, practices and abstentions, and the capacity to name, describe and anticipate these things, and also to use the adequate words in these relations. Here also the mastery of social aspect and social terminology runs parallel.

If space allowed, I could enlarge on this side of our subject indefinitely. Take, for instance, the problem of law in its verbal and pragmatic aspects. Here the value of the word, the binding force of a formula, is at the very foundation of order and reliability in human relations. Whether the marriage vows are treated as a sacrament or as a mere legal contract—and in most human societies they have this two-fold character—the power of words in establishing a permanent human relation, the sacredness of words and their socially sanctioned inviolability, are absolutely necessary to the existence of social order. If legal phrases, if promises and contracts were not regarded as something more than *flatus vocis*, social order would cease to exist in a complex civilisation as well as in a primitive tribe. The average man, whether civilised or primitive, is not a sociologist. He neither needs to, nor can, arrive at the real function of a deep belief in the sanctity of legal and sacral words and their creative power. But he must have this belief; it is drilled into him by the process whereby he becomes part and parcel of the orderly institutions of his community. The stronger this belief, the greater becomes what might be called the elementary honesty and veracity of the citizens. In certain walks of human life speech may develop into the best instrument for the concealment of thought. But there are other aspects—law, contracts, the formulae of sacraments, oaths—in which a complicated apparatus inviolably based on mystical and religious ideas develops in every community as a necessary by-product of the working of legal and moral institutions and relationships.

This must suffice to establish my proposition that there is a very real basis to human belief in the mystic and binding power of words. We can also see where the truth of this belief really lies. Man rises above his purely animal, anatomical and physiological equipment by building up his culture in co-operation with his fellow-beings. He masters his surroundings because he can work with others and through others. Verbal communication from the earliest infantile dependence of the child on his parents to the developed uses of full citizenship, scientific speech and words of command and leadership, is the correlate of this. The knowledge of right words, appropriate phrases and the more highly developed forms of speech, gives man a power over and above his own limited field of personal action. But this power of words, this co-operative use of speech is and must be correlated with the conviction that a spoken word is sacred. The fact also that words add to the power of man over and above their strictly pragmatic effectiveness must be correlated with the belief that words have a mystical influence.

This sociological explanation of the belief in the mystical power of words is obviously a reinterpretation of Durkheim's theory that mysticism is but an expression in belief of man's dependence on society. But I think that Durkheim's theory is itself a somewhat mystical act of faith—in fact, it is little more than a reformation of the Hegelian doctrine of the Absolute, which embodies itself in the more and more perfectly organised human community. What I am trying to contribute here is a reinterpretation of Durkheimianism in empirical terms. Durkheim's basic conception that a great many phenomena in culture, belief and emotional attitude have to be accounted for by the fact that man is dependent on his fellow-beings and that this dependence produces certain attitudes and leads to certain beliefs, is in my opinion fundamentally sound. Where Durkheim "goes off the rails", so to speak, is in reducing his sound conception to a very narrow formula of the direct emotional experience of the crowd and of the influences of crowd phenomena on the individual. He personified society himself, and he attributed this personification to primitive man. Hence his simple formula that God is society, that the substance of the Absolute is nothing but the feeling of dependence which man, intoxicated by the dionysiac influence of a religiously effervescent crowd concretises into sacred entities and sacred beings. There is no doubt that a *churinga* or a national flag, the cross or the crescent, plays an important part in the crystallising of human attitudes. But to attribute to these phenomena of material symbolisation, which take birth in an orgiastic crowd, the leading part in all cultural process is an extraordinary exaggeration. Durkheim, I think, caricatured his own theory in his biggest work on the Elementary Forms of Religious Belief.

The influence of society, or as I would prefer to say, the influence of culture—that is, of all the institutions found within a community, of the various traditional mechanisms such as speech, technology, mode of social intercourse—this influence works on the individual by a gradual process of moulding. By this process of moulding I mean the effect of traditional cultural modes and norms upon the growing organism. In one way the whole substance of my theory of culture, as I have sketched it out in my article on "Culture" (in the *Encyclopaedia of Social Sciences*), consists in reducing Durkheimian theory to terms of Behaviouristic psychology.

Let me return to the subject in question. Having established the two-fold aspect of linguistic development, the sacred and the profane, the mystical and the pragmatic, within the growth of every individual, we should find within every culture a ready-made distinction and traditional cleavage between these two aspects of human speech. In other words, having started by using language in a manner which is both magical and pragmatic, and passed gradually through stages in which the magical and pragmatic aspects intermingle and oscillate, the individual will find within his culture certain crystallised, traditionally standardised types of speech, with the language of technology and science at the one end, and the language of sacrament, prayer, magical formula, advertisement and political oratory at the other.

Thus if my theory is true, we ought to find in our own culture as well as in any other, these two poles of linguistic effectiveness, the magical and the pragmatic. Is this so? A digression on the modern language of magic would be very tempting, but I can only jot down one or two suggestions. Perhaps the best example of modern magical use of words is what might be called direct suggestion. Monsieur Coué has developed a technique as well as a theory, founded on this phenomenon. I have curative formulae from Trobriand magic which are based on exactly the principles of the Nancy school.

> "It passes, it passes,
>   The breaking pain in thy bones passes,
>   The ulceration of thy skin passes,
>   The big black evil of thy abdomen passes,
>   It passes, it passes. . . ."

Or take one of our formulae of garden magic :—

> "I sweep away, I sweep away, I sweep away.
> The grubs I sweep, I sweep away;
> The blight I sweep, I sweep away;
> Insects I sweep, I sweep away. . . .
>
> I blow, I blow, I blow away.
> The grubs I blow, I blow away;
> The blights I blow, I blow away;
> Insects I blow, I blow away. . . ."

The reader can document this point of view from Part VII without any difficulty.

If instead of analysing the doctrines of Monsieur Coué, which are based on a scientific point of view, we take the beliefs of Christian Science—the main root of which is that by affirming health, welfare, order and happiness generally, you produce them; and by denying them, by allowing evil thoughts to be rampant, you generate disease—we would have a very close parallel to the practices and beliefs of Trobriand sorcery and, I venture to say, of primitive sorcery in general. This subject, however, I must leave for the doctor's thesis of some young anthropologist, eager for parallels between modern and primitive savagery—parallels, which, I venture to foretell, would reward beyond the hopes of intellectual avarice. If we wanted to make an excursion into modern medical quackery, we could analyse the famous electric box and the magical verbiage which surrounded it; we could even attack some of the universal cures by cold water, fresh air, real or artificial sunlight, scrutinising especially the advertisements emanating from such one-track remedies. But here again an indication must suffice.

And this brings me to perhaps the richest field of modern verbal magic, the subject of advertisements. The psychology of advertisement has been widely treated. One of the most prominent psychologists is a professional advertiser—I do not mean self-advertiser, but a member of an advertising firm. The subtle and witty analysis of verbal magic by Miss Dorothy Sayers in her detective story *Murder Must Advertise* would supply ample material for a doctor's thesis written by one who is also professionally connected with the advertising business. The advertisements of modern beauty specialists, especially of the magnitude of my countrywoman Helena Rubinstein, or of her rival, Elisabeth Arden, would make interesting reading if collated with the formulae of Trobriand beauty magic, reproduced in Chapter XIII of *Argonauts of the Western Pacific* and in Chapter XI of *Sexual Life of Savages*.

I smooth out, I improve, I whiten.
Thy head I smooth out, I improve, I whiten.
Thy cheeks I smooth out, I improve, I whiten.
Thy nose I smooth out, I improve, I whiten.
Thy throat I smooth out, I improve, I whiten.
Thy neck I smooth out, I improve, I whiten. . . .

The language of Trobriand magic is simpler, more direct and more honest, but it contains all the essentials of a good advertisement. Some of the formulae might indeed fall within the law of fair advertisement:

One red paint of my companions,
It is sere, it is parched. . . .
One red paint, my red paint,
It is clean, it is buoyant, it is flashing
My red paint.

This phraseology might not be allowed to Monsieur Coty of Paris if he wanted to criticise the lipsticks produced by the Erasmic Co. of London. But similar implications run throughout modern advertisements.

Side by side with advertisement, modern political oratory would probably yield a rich harvest of purely magical elements. Some of the least desirable of modern pseudo-statesmen or gigantic politicanti have earned the titles of wizards or spell-binders. The great leaders such as Hitler or Mussolini have achieved their influence primarily by the power of speech, coupled with the power of action which is always given to those who know how to raise the prejudices and the passions of the mob. Moreover, the modern socialistic state, whether it be painted red, black or brown, has developed the powers of advertisement to an extraordinary extent. Political propaganda, as it is called, has become a gigantic advertising agency, in which merely verbal statements are destined to hypnotise foreigner and citizen alike into the belief that something really great has been achieved.

With this indictment of modern savagery I must close these desultory remarks, which should not be treated as on the same plane with the rest of this contribution. In my opinion the study of modern linguistic uses side by side with those of the magic of simple peoples would bring high rewards. At the very basis of verbal magic there lies what I have elsewhere called "the creative metaphor of magic" (Part IV, Div. VII). By this I mean that the repetitive statement of certain words is believed to produce the reality stated. I think that if we stripped all magical speech to its essentials, we would find simply this fact: a man believed to have mystical powers faces a clear blue sky and repeats: "It rains; dark, clouds forgather; torrents burst forth and drench the parched soil." Or else he would be facing a black sky and repeat: "The sun breaks through the clouds; the sun shines." Or in illness he repeats, like Monsieur Coué: "Every day and in every way it is getting better and better." The essence of verbal magic, then, consists in a statement which is untrue, which stands in direct opposition to the context of reality. But the belief in magic inspires man with the conviction that his untrue statement must become true. How far this is rooted in emotional life, in the power of man to day-dream, in unconquerable human hopes and human optimism, is clear to those who are acquainted with the fact of magic as well as with the theoretical literature connected with it. In another place also I have defined magic as the institutionalised expression of human optimism, of constructive hopes overcoming doubt and pessimism.

I would like to add here that when Freud defines this function of magic as the "omnipotence of thought" (*Allmacht der Gedanken*) and tries to find the roots of magical activities in the human tendency idly to day-dream, this view requires a serious correction—a correction which is contained in our theory here. Because—and this is of the greatest importance—man never runs on the side-track of magical verbiage or of magical activities in that idle day-dreaming which stultifies action. Organised magic always appears within those domains of human activity where experience has demonstrated to man his pragmatic impotence. In the measure as humanity, through developing technique, conquers one realm of activity after another, magic disappears and is replaced by science and technique. We do not use magic in agriculture any more, we do not attract shoals of fish by magic nor improve the trajectory of a high explosive by incantations. Aspects of human activity which have been made subject to the control of physics, chemistry or biology, are treated by systems based on reason and experience. And even in primitive communities we find a clear realisation of those phases in fishing, hunting and agriculture which are mastered by man with his implements, his hands and his brains; where man knows that his thought is impotent, there and there only does he resort to magic. Magic is not a belief in the omnipotence of thought but rather the clear recognition of the limitations of thought, nay, of its impotence. Magic, more especially verbal magic, grows out of legitimate uses of speech, and it is only the exaggeration of one aspect of these legitimate uses. More than that: ritual magic and verbal magic are not mere counterparts of idle day-dreaming. In the affirmation of the hopeful aspect magic exercises an integrative influence over the individual mind. Through the fact that this integrative influence is also connected with an organising power, magic becomes also an empirical force. Freud's conception of magic as a type of vicious megalomania would relegate it to the domain of cultural pathology. Frazer's theory that sympathetic magic is due to a mistaken association of ideas, while it explains one aspect of magic, namely the sympathetic principle which underlies the creative metaphor of magic, still does not account for the enormous organising part played by magic. Durkheim's view that the substance of magic, that is *mana* or magical force, is nothing but society personified, explains one mystical attitude by inviting us to assume another.

In my opinion magic has exercised a profound positive function in organising enterprise, in inspiring hope and confidence in the individual. Side by side with this, magical belief has obviously developed an attitude which exerts disturbing and subversive influences, especially in witchcraft and black magic. In the history of culture every phenomenon, I think, has got its constructive and disintegrating sides, its organising functions and its influences which point towards dissolution and decay. Human cultures do not merely grow and develop. They also decompose, die or collapse. Functional anthropology is not magic; it is not a chartered optimism or whitewashing of culture. One of its duties, in the wider cultural sense, is to show that savagery and superstition are not confined to primitive society. If we have insisted on the "white" aspects of magic side by side with its black aspects, it is rather to bring into relief something which has been less fully recognised and elaborated in anthropological literature and in the practical approach to facts. Apart from Frazer's work on *Psyche's Task* (reprinted as the *Devil's Advocate*), the constructive side of magic has not been sufficiently recognised; and even now, when formulated, it meets with vigorous opposition—remarkably enough from the modern theologian.[1]

Div. VI. THE SOCIOLOGICAL FUNCTION OF MAGIC AS ANOTHER SOURCE OF INTELLIGIBILITY OF SPELLS

In the general digression just concluded, I have laid stress on the organising function of magic. Let me exemplify this on our Trobriand material, and show how this side of magical phenomena directly influences the wording of spells. Let us once more listen to the Trobriand magician while he addresses spirits and animals, plants and soil. The spell in the belief of the natives is a verbal communion

[1] Cf. the criticism of some of my views by Dean Inge in his concluding article in *Science, Religion and Reality* (edited by Joseph Needham).

between the magician and the object addressed. The magician speaks and the objects respond. The words are launched into the things—sometimes even the surrounding world gives the sign that the words have been received by the essence of things: the *kariyala*, 'magical portent', awakens, the thunder rumbles in the skies and lightning appears on the horizon (cf. Ch. III, Sec. 4). But once we understand that while the magician addresses animals and plant agents, while he launches his words towards the soil and the tubers, these words are believed to take effect, then we realise that by this very belief they do have an effect. On whom? Not on the soil and spirits, on the spider and the full moon. This is a native belief which, important as it is, does not directly bind us. But—and this is of the highest importance to the sociologist—they do really produce an effect on the magician himself, on his retinue and on all those who work with him, under him and by him. It is the sociological setting which is of the greatest importance in the study of magic, because it is this indirect effect of the words upon the psychology or physiology of the native organism, and hence upon social organisation, which probably gives us the best clue to the nature of magical meaning. It also furnishes us, in connexion with the data supplied by native belief, with the real answer to the question: What have we to do in translating magical words?

The words which are meant for things that have no ears fall upon ears they are not meant for. It is the influence of magic on the community practising it which moulds ritual and language, which influences the selection of substances, the gestures and the words. We have asked rhetorically whether, in mumbling his incantations over the herbs in his hut, in addressing the spirits, in chanting his spell into a tuber or a sapling or a plot, the magician talks simply in monologue? The answer is now clear. When a man mumbles or chants to himself while at work for his own pleasure, the work would not suffer greatly if he were silenced. But if the magician were to stop in his solitary mumblings a complete disorganisation of the work of the whole community would follow.

The reader who has attentively perused the foregoing descriptive chapters will fully appreciate this and needs no further argument. Throughout our account we saw how, at every step, the magician and his art formed the main organising force in gardening. We have also seen that the *towosi* is the leader, initiating and supervising the successive activities, because he wields the *mana* which ultimately resides in words. But before he can use the words he must be in the right matrilineal lineage, and receive the magic from his predecessor in a socially and ritually correct manner. This process itself presents certain complications into which we need not enter here; but the essentials are that the magician must learn the words accurately, submit to all taboos imposed by his office and be officially approved by his predecessor, usually after the presentation of ceremonial gifts.

How far is all this associated with the words of magic? This question brings us directly to the more elementary one: How far do members of the community at large know the words, and how far are they aware of the spells? The answer to this is that every member of the community is aware of each spell being performed; that down almost to the children they are familiar with the wording of each spell, and regard its recitation as the most important part, not merely in the big ceremonial performance which surrounds it, but in the whole sequence of general activities.

It will be best, perhaps, to illustrate this social, economic and generally cultural context of spells on the first formula which we meet. This formula is uttered in the magician's house, while he offers some particles of food to the spirits. The performance itself seems extremely private, detached from the rest of social activities, and relatively unsuitable to affect either the minds of the natives or to organise their behaviour.

Let us, however, consider what has gone before; first of all the offering of the particles of fish to the spirits has to be prepared. The men have twice gone on special expeditions to the coast in order to procure fish. They offered this fish to the magician as *ula'ula* payment; the word itself, *ula'ula*, which means both 'ceremonial payment' and 'oblation to the spirits', indicates that the offering is to the spirits as well as to the magician. This latter has, on the morning of the same day, gone out to gather the magical herbs from which he will prepare the magical mixture. The men meanwhile have made ready their axes for the ritual benediction of magic which will be uttered over them.

Thus the whole community shares in the preparations for this, the crucial and essential act, the utterance of the two consecutive formulae (1 and 2). The rite itself is, so to speak, the goal of all the previous activities, just as it is the condition of the whole ceremony that is performed on the morrow in the gardens.

After everything has been prepared the magician retires to his house and the other gardeners disperse. It is, moreover, not usual that anybody should be present with him in the house, although a younger brother or matrilineal nephew may assist at the rite, and would so assist at least once or twice when learning the magic.

But while the magician holds solitary communion with the

spirits and later impregnates the herbs and axes with the most important vehicle of magical force, the *vatuvi* spell, the whole community are aware of what is happening under the thatch of the magician's hut. His voice, although he does not shout the words, can yet be heard within a radius of three- or four-score feet or so, so that it reaches the inmates of the nearest houses. They hear him addressing the spirits. They know that he communes with them by the gift and through the words. They are made to realise that now the blessing of the ghosts of those who have once wielded the magic is being invoked. The affirmation of tradition dwells over the whole village. The *towosi* now becomes the representative of a long line of ancestors whom he first addresses as a whole and then enumerates by name. Some of the words uttered by him restate his charter. Some other words again are commentaries upon the importance of the *wasi*, i.e. the complex transaction by which fish is procured; on the *ula'ula*, the gift and the oblation, and on the anticipated magic. "To-morrow we penetrate our garden-site" ("we" embracing the spirits, the magician and the whole community).

And with all this every villager realises that the words which produce such a powerful effect can be uttered by no one except the one who is sociologically determined as the right magician and who fulfils the mystical conditions of correct knowledge and full observance of the taboos.

The analysis of the sociological aspects of the next spell (cf. Part VII, M.F. 2, A), which on this occasion is recited immediately after Formula 1, will show us that here also in the list of ancestors and in the mythological references the magician establishes the traditional charter. Again in the first words of blessing, in the anticipatory affirmations of plenty (v. 3), in the declaration of his magical powers, which he achieves by speaking in the first person and by boldly uttering the affirmations and exorcisms of magic (vv. 4–8), he takes in hand the full fate of the gardens.

I must repeat that the natives are familiar with every spell. Although no unauthorised native would ever dare to utter a magical formula, unless at least potentially entitled by birth to do so, I discovered that there was not a single man in Omarakana who would not recognise a text belonging to his community's official magic. Most of the formula they hear once or even twice every year. To this class belong all those recited in public in the gardens: Formulae 3 to 6, chanted during the public part of the great inaugural rite, and Formulae 10 and 11 recited at the *kamkokola* ceremony. As far as I could ascertain the formulae of growth magic, spoken as they are over each field, are usually witnessed and heard by a considerable number of people, although there is no official attendance. There are, however, other means by which the natives learn to know the formulae. In the first place there are several men in each community who are officially and openly instructed in this magic: besides the garden magician himself, his younger brothers and matrilineal nephews are taught the spells. Very often the older members of the family who, for some reason, do not practice this magic, yet know it thoroughly. Thus in Omarakana, besides Bagido'u, To'uluwa, the old chief, knew the magic quite well though, having a bad memory, he never could recite a spell from beginning to end; so did two or three *tabalu* from the neighbouring village of Kasana'i. Thus Tokolibeba, Kwaywaya and old Mtabalu, when he was alive, knew every word in each formula. In Omarakana old Molubabeba knew this magic and recited it in the presence of his son Tokulubakiki, who once or twice helped me in translating a spell. Besides these, both the younger brothers of Bagido'u, Towese'i and Mitakata, had already learned it. Now every one of these people was quite at liberty to comment privately upon any part of this magic to his relatives or friends. For let us remember that there is no taboo at all on divulging the magic or even reciting it privately and with discretion—provided that you have the hereditary right to do so. Thus the magic percolates, so to speak, so that practically everybody in the village knows it. We know also that there are official occasions on which the practising magician himself will recite the magic aloud, notably during the mortuary vigil over any important person.

We can now approach the real problem before us: how to translate a magical utterance, how to bring home the real meaning of a meaningless, or at least distorted, word. We will start from the point which I have just been making, namely, that the words of magic are familiar to all the community, that they are listened to or that there is at least a keen awareness and appreciation of their utterance. So that in spite of a pretence of privacy and strict mono-poly of use the spell is, in the sense here elaborated, the concern of those for whom it is enacted.

How far does this affect our problem? If each and all the words which form a spell are of importance not merely to the spirits and magical forces, but to the natives themselves, it becomes clear that the verbal substance of the spells is correlated with the mental outlook of the natives. The magician in uttering his formulae speaks on behalf of each gardener. He expresses what each gardener feels, hopes for and anticipates. But magic in its essence, I might almost say in its physiological essence, is the expression of human hope and confidence, of the need of a morally integrated attitude towards the future.

This as we know is fully confirmed by the general theory of magical words here developed; this also agrees with the verbal facts which we have observed. As we have already seen, and as we shall see more clearly in the texts and commentaries which follow, most of the crucial words of Trobriand magic, the key-words of the main part, the leading words which run throughout the whole spell, the initial words which characterise a formula, are words of blessing, anticipatory affirmations of prosperity and plenty, exorcisms of evil influences, and mythological references which draw upon the strength of the past for the welfare of the future. The words which we find in magic are the equivalents of what in personal language we would find expressing the hopes of each individual, his confidence in the power of his magician to see himself and his fellows through a bad season, his conviction that the magic is an ultimate stand-by against adversity.

When in the second formula the magician utters the word *vatuvi*, whatever may emerge from its analysis, this word certainly expresses a general blessing, a blessing which, as determined by its context, is meant to go into the depths, into the body of the earth and become anchored there. This word has been heard for generations in Omarakana and stands to the natives for the value and importance of their agriculture in general and for the special greatness of their own garden magic which, let us remember, is that of the premier community of the Trobriands.

When in the other great formula of garden magic (M.F. 10), he uses as leading word one which expresses the idea of anchoring, very permanently mooring, and repeats this word with the expressions for the fundamental parts of the "magical wall", he again establishes, in this verbal act, the stability of the garden. The same obviously holds good of this spell when uttered with appropriate variations over the storehouses (M.F. 29). In the same way the whole garden is anchored in Formula 23 in the name of the bush-hen, the various parts of the vine being referred to, especially its roots. Thus the affirmation of stability runs through a great many formulae, for the examples here given could be multiplied.

In other spells the magician invokes fertility in general, as, for instance, in the second spell when he bursts into an anticipatory vision of all that the belly of the garden will bring forth; or again when in Formula 5 he foretells the rising of the crops, or in Formula 8 describes, in tensely figurative speech, the flame-like bursting of the garden towards the village and towards the jungle; or in spell 9 when he describes the size of the taro. Growth magic especially is characterised by such hopeful anticipations and affirmations. Each phase of growing and development is stated in an exaggerated manner with repetitions of 'new' and of 'old', of morning and evening, of north and south, of one end of the district and another. The strange exaggerations which we find in a number of formulae—the vomiting from surfeit of taytu, the groaning under the weight of the crops, the death from surfeit—all these express the craving of the gardeners for success, for prosperity, for *malia*, and their belief that by verbal statements all they crave for can be realised. When the magician verbally summons various natural forces to help him, when he uses the negative exaggerations which have been so often mentioned, and speaks about many canoesful of taytu, we meet with the same creative function of speech. To use our former expression, we could say that the creative metaphor of magic dominates throughout the ritual language of Trobriand spells.

It is clear that the words of this type, words which are obviously expressions of strong desire, words the primary function of which is, from the standpoint of individual psychology, to create confidence, to enhance hopes and anticipations, and thus to stimulate people to effort, perseverance and energy, cannot be treated as direct communications or definitions. The mystical words of blessing, of plenty, of stability, and again the strong imperatives of exorcism, must be treated rather as verbal acts which radiate emotional influence, which reproduce feeling, which carry with them a wide system of associations.

The indirect function of such words, then, consists in their influence on the psychology of each individual of the community. But this influence does not remain merely individual. It is one of the powerful elements which contribute towards the integration of the villagers into an effective gardening team.

Thus the fact that the community are aware of the spell and know its wording is the most important clue to the appreciation of the verbalities of magic—that is, if we realise that such a cultural phenomenon as spoken magic is of slow growth, that it is shaped gradually through the various mental and social forces which work upon it; above all, that the ultimate *raison d'être* of its fundamental characters must be correlated with its function. In other words since, in my opinion, the spell plays an important part in influencing individuals in their agricultural work; since it plays this part because of the characteristics which I have just enumerated, I am convinced that we have arrived at an explanation also of the process by which these characteristics came into being.

Let us follow this out a little more in detail in a frankly evolutionary or historical hypothesis as to the origins of magic. The "ultimate origins", as I have said in a previous division, were probably the affirmations of ordinary speech, what we have there called the simplest creative metaphors of magic. These are crystallised into a set formula and chanted with the characteristic emotional intonations of magic. And now comes into being the cultural apparatus of magic, consisting in its sociological side of the leader, who performs the rite and chants the spell, and of the members of the community, who can hear the spell and are aware that magic is being carried out on their behalf. But it is not merely the audience who are aware of the magician; the magician is also aware of his audience. He knows that he is uttering it on behalf of his fellow-workers; he voices their pride in their magic (*da megwa-si*); he shares their belief in its efficacy, for he bears the responsibility of being the leader.

But—and here comes the historically important fact—the psychology of the individual magician is not a circumstance which lies idle and ineffective, separated from his activity as magician. The most important fact is that in each generation the spell, its explanatory comments, its mythological matrix and the whole technique of its recital are in the possession of the magician in office. This official magician has to transmit his formulae with the associated magical lore to his successor. In so doing he acts not merely as a passive receptacle of tradition, he is also the leader of his community, their spokesman, the repository of all their beliefs, hopes, anticipations and strivings. In every generation, therefore, the carrying out of the magic—and that means not merely the recital of the spells, but their explanation and traditional handling—will be influenced by the general attitude of the community towards the spells as part of the magic. This attitude is a controlling force of what a magician thinks and feels, says and does. This controlling force will show its influence above all in the process, repeated generation after generation, in fact, several times within each generation, by which magic is handed over from elder to younger brother, from uncle to maternal nephew, occasionally from father to son.

We can now deal with our conundrum about the meaning of meaningless words in magic. First of all we have been able to establish the fact that these words are meaningless only if we let ourselves be confused by the superficial distortions, by the clipped and unusual style of magic. These elements, as a matter of fact, have a meaning in that they play a part. This part is determined by the typical human attitude towards magical speech. In the Trobriands the belief that spell words belong to a different category is definitely correlated with the coefficient of weirdness which, as we have shown, is more apparent than real. Spells remain meaningless also in so far as we fail to connect them with their ritual context and to place them against their mythology and dogmatics. Above all, and in connexion with the point just made, we have clearly to recognise that, since the function of magical speech is not to communicate ideas or to narrate, the analysis has to be based on a full understanding of the effects which the words produce. The function of a spell, that is its meaning, has to be accounted for first of all in connexion with native belief. We have to establish then what in native belief is the effect which the words and phrases exercise within the traditional universe of magic upon the things or beings to be influenced. In order to bring home this aspect of their meaning the ethnographer has to state all the mystical, mythological and traditional associations of the words.

To the ethnographer, however, the words of magic have another significance, even more important than their mystical effects, and that is the effect which the words of magic produce on human beings. Here the ethnographer can and must go beyond what the natives are able to tell him. He not only has to explore all possible associations, but he has also to treat parts of the magical texts as sociological charters, other parts as forms of suggestion, others again as vehicles of hope and desire. We shall see that in some of the spells the magician establishes his claim to be the rightful successor to the magic, in others he gives evidence of his communion with the spirits, in others he announces his power over animal agents, factors of fertility, pests, blights and bush-pigs. This aspect of verbal magic is an essential part of its sociological function.

All this will be illustrated in the comments on the texts which follow, especially in the comments on the really difficult words of Formula 2. The first word there, *vatuvi*, is obviously one of those expressions which do not refer to any specific object, but magically grip an aspect of the whole situation. *Vatuvi* has no grammatical form. It is neither noun nor verb, though by its etymological affinities it is of a verbal character. An inaugurative word, it is launched freely into the substances to be charmed, the herbs, the axes, the torches and digging-sticks. It has got no context of direct connexion with any specific thing or agency. It has to be taken as a verbal missile of magical power—a conception very much in harmony with the repetitive character of its utterance, whereby it is rubbed into the substance. Incidentally, the manner in which a spell is chanted has to be described in order that we may understand the full meaning of the word.

The word, therefore, will have to be treated not as a precise verbal statement, not as an imperative, nor as the naming of a thing, nor as any definite verbal form, but rather as a word rich in associations and reaching out in many directions. As we shall see, the real etymological identity of this word will define it as connected with *vitawo*, or the prefix *vitu-*, and the word *vituvatu*, 'to institute', 'to set up', 'to direct', 'to show'. We shall also discuss its fortuitous, but magically significant associations with *vatu*, 'coral boulder', 'coral reef', and the more or less real word *va-tuvi*, 'to foment', 'to make heal'.

The meaning of this word consists: (1) in the effect which it is believed to produce; (2) in the manner in which it is launched as regards ritual handling and general cultural setting; (3) in its etymological associations which show the influence which it exercises upon the mind of the magician and upon that of each member of the community; (4) in the possible sociological functions of such a word. In the case of *vatuvi* there is no direct sociological import such as we find in other words, but indirectly, since it is a general blessing and declaration of power, it influences the position of the magician and the relations of the community to him.

With this we are ready to approach the actual task of translating and commenting on spells. We have outlined the chart of the data which are necessary to make a magical text comprehensible. First and foremost, our argument leads us to recognise fully that linguistic analysis is not sufficient without an ethnographic counterpart. We shall, in connexion with every spell, give first a general commentary which, to use our phraseology, contextualises the spell ethnographically. This commentary brings the spell into relation with what has been said in the main ethnographic text. The analysis of the relation between magic and economics given in Appendix I and the argument of Part IV are also to be kept in mind. The second part of the commentary is more especially linguistic, but even there we shall be constantly driven to ethnographic digressions, which account for some of the wider associations of magical meaning.

The main innovation, as far I am aware, in the commentaries here given is the elaborate contextualisation of each spell. This consists of five entries, giving the sociological, the ritual, the structural, the dogmatic and the phonetic description of the spell. Let me briefly justify the division of the material under these headings.

What is of prime relevance in each magical act is its sociological context. Our statement of this (under A of the general commentary) will show how far the words reach the community, how they affect it and how the whole utterance is related to the general economic activity and to the rite of which it is a part. The exact statement of the ritual context (given under B) shows the manner in which manual procedure accompanies and directs the spell. As an introduction to the linguistic analysis of each spell we shall briefly indicate (under C) the manner in which it is constructed. Often each part of it contains a different subject-matter.[1] Now the subject-matter of a formula is closely connected with its "dogmatic context" (given under D), that is, the belief or complex of beliefs surrounding it. I shall state how far the words are launched in an impersonal, fundamentally magical way towards the substance to be affected, how far the magician addresses specific agencies, and what part these agencies play according to native belief in effecting the ends aimed at. The manner in which the magic is chanted will be given under E.

Thus we first begin with what might be called the human, i.e. the sociological, ritual and psychological context of the magic, and then we proceed to its supernatural and dogmatic context; all these aspects being welded as closely as possible.

The second division of the commentary contains a linguistic, i.e. lexicographical and grammatical analysis of the formula. Each word and each phrase will be analysed on the pattern which we have exemplified on the word *vatuvi*. We shall first, therefore, have to define the character of a phrase, expression or word, whether it is an impersonally launched utterance or whether it has a definite grammatical structure, and then we shall give its probable etymology and the more or less fortuitous associations with it.

Words of ordinary speech will be given the fixed meaning as in the texts of Part V. Such words need no special commentary, so that wherever a word is not commented upon the reader can assume that it is translated by the rules of ordinary speech; that it is, in short, a typically intelligible word. When the terms are specific to magic, when they are unique forms found in one formula and one formula only, the English word used in the literal translation is the result of the analysis which will be found in the commentary.

I think that a great deal of what has been here proposed opens the way to an unconventional method of treating magical formulae, and I trust that some of it at least will prove its value in time and be helpful to other collectors and interpreters of magic.

---

[1] The analysis of structure has been included in the first part of the commentary because I have been proceeding on these lines for some time past and have felt it difficult to change. Were I to start again now I would probably place my remarks on the structure of the spell at the beginning of the Linguistic Commentary.

PART VII

MAGICAL FORMULAE

MAGICAL FORMULAE

FORMULA 1
(Cf. Ch. II, Sec. 4)

1. *Da   vaka'ula'ula-si   tomwaya,   la-seyeli — kay!*
   our   oblation   old man   I did put hi

2. *Da   ka'ula'ula-ga   Yowana   —   kay!*
   our   oblation again   (reciter's father)   hi

3. *Nabwoye   ta-sunini   da   buyagu — kay!*
   to-morrow   we penetrate   our   garden-site   hi

4. *Vikita,   Iyavata,   si   libogwo   daba-na.*
   (mythical ancestresses)   their   myth   head his

5. *Ku-bili-se   sigweleluwa,   mwoytatana;*
   you brush away   (an insect)   (a grub)

6. *ba-vasasewo   kam   karikeda   Kaulokoki,*
   I might burst open   thy   passage   (a sea-channel)

   kam   kovasasa   Kiya'u.
   thy   open passage   (a sea-channel)

7. *Ku-vapulupulu,   ku-waya.*
   thou drown   thou get there

GENERAL COMMENTARY

A. *Sociological Context:* this need only be briefly mentioned here as we have already discussed it fully in Part VI (Div. VI). The ceremonial oblation to the spirits marks, as we know, a crucial point in more than one practical activity.

B. *Ritual Context:* the magician utters this spell in his hut, placing some small particles of fish on the hearthstone. This gift to the spirits, which is a diminutive share of the magician's own *ula'ula* reward received from the community, and the words which he addresses to them, are correlated. They establish a sacrificial communion between spirits, magician and community. The words of verses 1 to 3 are associated with the sociological position of the *towosi* and form one of the typical traditional parts of spells.

C. *Structure:* the spell falls naturally into three parts, each related with its dogmatic background (cf. D.). The first three verses are addressed to spirits, the next to mythological agencies and the remainder is an exorcism. The grammar and vocabulary, especially in the first three verses, are regular and simple, obeying closely the rules of ordinary speech.

D. *Dogmatic Context:* I have never been able to satisfy myself completely as to whether the natives believe in the real presence of the spirits or whether the uttering of the words establishes a magically significant continuity with the past. The personal names in verse 4 refer to two mythological women who emerged from the ground in Lu'ebila, the home of the magical system of Kaylu'ebila used in Omarakana. They brought the system with them from underground and were the first to practise it (cf. Ch. I, Sec. 7, and Ch. XII, Sec. 1). The feminine nature of this system is expressed in the ceremony of *yowota*; when he rubs the soil with magical herbs the garden magician (*towosi*) has to sit with legs crossed and buttocks touching the ground, in the position familiar to us from representations of Buddha. This position, called *sipuyatayle*, is adopted only by women. No other *towosi bi-sipuyatayle*, 'would sit like a woman'; he invariably *bi-sinetoto*, 'would squat as men do'. This unusual feature of the Kaylu'ebila system incidentally produces a specific magical effect: the taro of Omarakana does not waste itself in foliage, but grows deeply into the soil and swells into big tubers (cf. Ch. X, end of Sec. 2). In the exorcism (vv. 5, 6 and 7) certain agencies, probably the two mythical personages mentioned in verse 4, and no doubt the ancestral spirits also, are invited to destroy the two principal pests. In verse 6 the garden magician announces that he will open two sea-passages lying to the north-west, somewhere off the village of Laba'i and between the uninhabited island Kiya'u and the island of the spirits, Tuma. This part of the archipelago is always mentioned in magical exorcisms: and blights, diseases and other evil influences are invited to begone in the direction taken by the spirits of the departed after death.

E. *Mode of Recitation:* the spell is spoken in an ordinary voice and not in the melodious sing-song usual in spells.

LINGUISTIC COMMENTARY

1. The magician associates himself with the spirits in sharing with them the food which he has received from the community. Thus he speaks about the oblation as *da*, 'our' (inclusive plural), *vaka'ula'ula-si* (*vaka-*, prefix; *ula'ula*—oblation; *-si*—possessive pronoun plural). The prefix *vaka-* gives the flavour of completion, satisfaction: 'oblation in satisfaction of our (that is, your and my) expectations', 'in payment for our magical services'.

Tomwaya, 'old man'—here contextually plural 'old men'—is the traditional and respectful manner of address, in this case directed towards the ancestral spirits: 'O, old men, the ancestral spirits.'

2. The immediate predecessor of Bagido'u, his father Yowana, is specially mentioned, and the sentence framed in the dual. The

suffix -*ga*, 'again', 'on the other hand', gives a special emphasis, putting the two, Bagido'u and his father, in a separate category. *Ka'ula'ula*, the prefix *ka-* equivalent to *vaka-*.

1. 2. and 3. *Kay*, an interjection, 'hi! hullo!'; it refers in verses 1 and 2 to the oblation and has been freely rendered 'here . . . behold!'. In verse 3, where it is translated 'take heed', it emphasises the invitation to the ancestral spirits to repair to the garden on the morrow and by their presence to bless the work.

3. *Da-* and *ta-*, inclusive plurals, mark the fact that the garden-site belongs to the spirits as well as to the magician and includes them in the morrow's expedition to the garden. *Ta-* puts the verb in the narrative present. In reality, however, this is an exhortation, almost a command. I have translated it in the future in the free version. The final -*si* is here as often, especially in magic, elided.

4. The words 'their myth head his' do not make sense by the usual rules of grammar. In freely translating it 'you fountain-head of our myth (and magic)' I have interpreted the third personal plural pronoun 'their' as meaning in the magician's mouth, the people of the village. But frankly I do not understand this sentence and it may be one of those which has become distorted in the course of traditional handing down. Bagido'u once told me that *dabana* was a personal name and stood for *Modabana*, a mythological wizard who had used this formula. But this commentary does not bring sense to the text and it was not backed up by him on subsequent occasions.

5. *Sigweleluwa* was defined by the natives as 'an insect which feeds on the leaves of coconut, taro and taytu'; *mwoytatana* as a white grub, *wakayla mwanita*, 'the size of a millipede', and similar to the *kakavaku*, the edible white grub which feeds on decayed timber. These are mentioned as representative of all other garden plagues, hence my word 'pest' in free translation. The native word *leria*, 'plague, epidemic', never appears in any spell.

6. *Ba-*, verbal pronoun literally rendered as 'I might', has here a definite sense of futurity and command. A command is also expressed in *ku-*, second personal verbal pronoun; the imperative force being given by the voice and not by the form of the pronoun.

FORMULA 2
(Cf. Ch. II, Sec. 4)

I. 1. *Vatuvi*, *vatuvi* (repeated)
  set right set right

  Vitumaga,   *i-maga.*
  set right groundwards it (goes) groundwards

Vatuvi,   *vatuvi* (repeated)
set right   set right

Vitulola,   *i-lola.*
set right towards moorings   it (goes towards) moorings

2. *Tubu-gu Polu, t. Koleko, t. Takikila, t. Mulabwoyta, t. Kwayudila, t. Katupwala, t. Bugwabwaga, t. Purayasi, t. Numakala; bilumava'u biloma-m, tabu-gu Mwakenuwa, tama-gu Yowana.*

3. *I-gebile lopou-la ulo buyagu;*   *i-tokaye l.u.b.*
he lift belly his my garden-site   he rise

    i-takubila l.u.b.;   *i-gibage'u l.u.b.;*   *i-kabwabu l.u.b.;*
    he recline   he lift-bush-hen-nest   he ant-hill

    i-gibukwayu'u l.u.b.   *i-gibakayaulo l.u.b.*   *i-tawaga l.u.b.;*
    he lift-bend-down   he lift-iron-wood-tree   he lie down

    i-kabina'i l.u.b.;   *i-kabinaygwadi l.u.b.;* — *a-tabe'u!*
    he burgeon   he burgeon (with) child   I sweep away

II. 4. *A-tabe'u,*   *a-tabe'u* (repeated)   *mwoytatana*
    I sweep away   I sweep away   (a grub)

    a-tabe'u, a-tabe'u (repeated); *yokwa'u a . . .; sigweleluwa a . . .;*
    I sweep away   (a blight)   (an insect)

    kimdoga a . . .; kimsuluva a . . .; kimkwataku a . . .;
    tusk-beetle   drilling beetle   underground beetle

    igikalakeluva a . . .; igadaea a . . .; iginumanamile a . . .
    marking-blight   white blight   dew-blight

5. *A-givisa'u,*   *a-givisa'u* (repeated)
   I blow away   I blow away

    mwoytatana a-givisa'u, a-givisa'u (repeated); *yokwa'u a . . .; sigweleluwa a . . .,* etc.
    (*agivisa'u* repeated with all inventory words).

6. *Ba-yabay-m,*   *gala,* etc. (inventory words repeated).
   I might drive thee   begone

7. *Ba-talay-m,*   *gala,* etc. (inventory words repeated).
   I might despatch thee   begone

8. *Tumlili-m,*   *gala,* etc. (inventory words repeated).
   I might lose thee   begone

III. 9. *Ba-vasasay-m*   *kam kwadada*   *Kadilaboma;*
     I might burst open thee   thy shallow passage   (a channel)

10. *kam-malu*   *Laba'i,*   *kam-matu*   *Ituloma;*
    thy village   (a village)   thy boulder   (a boulder)

    im-mwaga   *de'u;*   *im-mwola*   *kwoysakwabu.*
    thy canoe   raft   thy paddle   coconut-leaf-butt-end

11. *Ba-dagay-m,*   *gala;*   *ku-popolu,*   *gala;*
I might stow thee away begone   thou bubble away

ku-vilu'a,   *gala;*   *ku-melela,*   *gala;*   *lu-gu-ta,*   *gala;*
thou whirl away   thou be lost begone sister mine begone

ku-msilay-gu,   *gala;*   *ku-layli-gu,*   *gala;*
shame (of) me begone thou avoid me begone

ku-vatilawa,   *gala.*
thou slink under begone

After the *dogina* (III) the magician returns again to the *u'ula* (I).

A. *Sociological Context:* this formula is undoubtedly the most important in all Omarakana garden magic, for the following reasons: it is performed on several occasions and on each is the essential spell of the complex ceremony in which it occurs; it figures in the two or three most important acts: the grand inaugural rite, the first and second burning, and at harvest; and it contains all the essential elements of Trobriand magic—structural, linguistic and dogmatic. On this, the first occasion of its use, it is chanted immediately after Formula 1, that is, in the presence of the spirits: while outside the villagers, keenly aware of what is passing in the magician's hut, prepare for the next day's ceremony in the gardens. They have previously brought their axes to the magician, and he has prepared the magical substances and inserted them between leaf and axe-blade. The second time, it is recited before the 'great burning' over the torches (Ch. III, Sec. 1). The third time, it is chanted over the axe to be used in the preparatory rite for the *kamkokola* ceremony (loc. cit., Sec. 4); the fourth time, over the axes and digging-sticks to be used in the *basi* or thinning out (cf. Ch. IV, Sec. 3); and the fifth time, it is recited with special solemnity, during the second inaugural harvest rite over the adze, and also over the torches for the first burning of next season's gardens (Ch. V, Sec. 3). The magician always recites the spell alone in his hut, but all the gardeners are aware of his proceedings—some of them can even hear his voice—and the recital is a cause and a condition of all that happens afterwards. This formula is also used for the private charming of axes (Ch. IV, Sec. 4). Thus the spell is recited officially and in the service of the community at least five times, and it may be privately performed even more often.

B. *Ritual Context:* the formula could be described as the indoor spell of garden magic since it is always recited within the *towosi's* hut. More important is the fact that, with the exception of Formula 24, this is the only spell which has the character of delayed ritual action. It does not act directly on the substance (ancestral spirits, bush-pig, vegetation and so forth) to be affected, but on another substance wherein its virtue can be imprisoned and transferred, when the time comes, to its proper object. The other spells expend themselves, so to speak, in the act in which they are uttered. Thus with Formula 1 the virtue of the spell is launched and the magician's part done, when the *towosi* deposits the oblation of fish on the hearthstone. So with the *yowota* spells, they are launched during the act to which they refer, into the substance which they are meant to affect. Not so with this formula. The formula is uttered in the hut over a liturgical object which will only be used on the next day. Its virtue is imprisoned in herbs and round axe-blades which will remain for twelve hours unused and will play their part only on the morrow. On one occasion at least this formula is chanted months before the liturgical instruments impregnated with it will be consumed. I refer, of course, to the charming of the magical torches.

C. *Structure:* the standard tripartite form of the longer spells. It is composed of a *u'ula*, 'foundation' (marked I in the text), a *tapwana*, 'body' (II), and a *dogina*, 'tip', or *dabwana*, 'top' (III) (cf. for these terms Part V, Div. II, § 18). Each of these parts shows a somewhat different character as regards its language and content; each part is chanted or recited differently, and each part fulfils a different function within the magical act. The first part is undoubtedly the most sacred and the most important. The words here are least liable to any, even the smallest, alteration; the chanting is the slowest and most solemn; and the character of the words the most cryptic. The second part, which contains the main body of the spell, is recited more quickly. There is more freedom as regards the order in which the words are uttered, and it is, as a rule, characterised by the combinations of two lists of words. The third part, which often contains mythological references, narrative bits and anticipatory day-dreams, is recited slowly and solemnly, but not with the same careful and religious intonation as the first part. Invariably, moreover, after the last part is recited, the magician returns to the 'foundation' (I), and the formula has to be concluded with that part. For structure, see also below under E.

D. *Dogmatic context:* the most important points will have to be discussed in connexion with the analysis of the inaugural word *vatuvi* (Ling. Commentary, v. 1). The formula is typical of the principle fundamental in Trobriand magic, namely, that a spell is the launching by man of magical power towards the entities or forces which it is meant to affect—in this case the fertility of the garden. This principle dominates its whole verbal character. Certain specific features have to be explained by other beliefs, or perhaps more correctly by the associated functions of magic. Thus the list of ancestors (v. 2, cf. also Linguistic Commentary) affirms the magician's charter, while at the same time the names of those who had so much to do with fertility in the past possess a fertilising influence. The main part—an exorcism directed against pests and blights—is an example of the pragmatic function of words in magic (cf. Part IV, Div. VI). By driving away obnoxious agencies in words the wanted result is achieved. For the dogmatic contents of verse 10, see Linguistic Commentary below and also that to verse 6 of Formula 1.

E. *Mode of Recitation:* I shall try to convey a more precise idea as to how this formula is actually chanted. Verse 1 consists of four lines. The word *vatuvi* is repeated sometimes twice, sometimes four times. It is intoned with a strongly melodious falling cadence. The second line, *vitumaga i-maga*, is recited as a rule once only, giving a sort of prosodic answer to the heavy rhythm of the first line. The third and fourth lines are symmetrical to the first two and they are intoned with an identical melody. The list of ancestors which follows (v. 2) is not spoken with the same loving and careful intonation, but is recited quickly and perfunctorily although, as we have already insisted, it is a sort of magician's charter and is of considerable importance from the sociological point of view. The third verse contains a series of positive assertions or prophesies. It is again chanted energetically and quickly and in a fixed order, though when it is finished the magician may return and repeat some of the phrases. Part I always ends on the word which will become the first key-word of Part II, here the word *a-tabe'u*. This word functions as a link between the first and the second part. At the end of the first part it is invariably intoned slowly, solemnly and distinctly.

The structure of the main part is a litany, in which several key-words are repeated with inventory expressions. At the end of the *u'ula* the magician solemnly and loudly utters the first key-word *a-tabe'u*; he repeats it several times at the beginning of verse 4, at first vigorously, distinctly and solemnly, then in a gradually more perfunctory manner. Then he proceeds to the inventory expressions, which as a rule are spoken more clearly and incisively, following each with the key-word, which is repeated two or three times, producing an effect of rubbing it into every one of the inventory expressions. Whereas the enunciation of the inventory words remains incisive, that of the key-word becomes, towards the end of each stanza, more and more perfunctory. Then, with a return to the solemn manner, the next key-word is intoned, repeated more quickly, and the whole process begins again. The key expressions in 6, 7 and 8 consist of two words each, the second being a vigorous negative pronounced in an explosive, direct manner, almost giving the impression of a strong sweeping gesture. Of the third part, verses 9 and 10 are spoken less melodiously, though 10 has a distinct rhythm of its own. Verse 11 is chanted, and here again the negative punctuates each phrase. After a short pause the magician solemnly returns to the *u'ula*, which is recited till the last intoned word *a-tabe'u* closes the whole spell.

1. The leading word of this spell, *vatuvi*, is a magical form, that is, it has no grammatical setting and is a root never met with in common speech. Its nearest counterparts in ordinary language are the verbs *vituvatu*, 'to put together', 'to give the finishing touches'; *vitawo*, or *vatowa*, 'to step', 'to erect', as a mast is set up in a boat, or as a pole or a *kamkokola* is put up in the garden. The direct commentary given by Bagido'u was: *vatuvi: vitokaye*, '*vatuvi* means to make rise'. Explaining the other associated forms, *vitumaga* and *vitulola*, I was told: *vitumaga: bila wa maga*, '*vitumaga* means it will go into the body of the earth'. The informant added: *maga: pwaypwaya*, '*maga* means earth'. The word *maga* was known to me from ordinary speech as 'the body of', 'the substance of', 'the thickness of'. *Vitulola: bi-sonu 'ga'u i-tokaya*, '*vitulola* means it will sink, afterwards it rise'. The term *vitu-* figures also as formative in the compound *vituloki*, 'to set on the right way', 'to set right'. The verb *vitusi*, which I obtained in one or two texts, but was not very familiar with, means, as far as I could make out, 'to mark', 'to make a sign'. Native commentaries and linguistic comparisons give us what we have called the area of meaning of this word: 'to set up, to erect, to put together, to set right, to set on the right way, to direct'. I doubt very much whether *vatuvi* is etymologically connected with the word *vatu*, 'coral boulder'. But considering the richness with which even fortuitous associations enter into words of magic, it is not impossible that the feeling of strength, depth and stability connected with the term *vatu*, 'coral boulder', 'coral reef', are active in the magical functioning of *vatuvi*. By this I mean that the strength of the 'deeply anchored' coral boulder flavours the more immediate meaning of *vatuvi*, 'setting on the right way, 'setting up', 'showing the way'. Another undoubtedly fortuitous but none the less strong and probably effective association is that between the word *vatuvi* and the root *tuvi*, 'to foment'. The causative prefix *va-* compounded with the root *tuvi* would mean 'to heal', magically to foment', or 'to foster'. This association again undoubtedly plays into the essential meaning of *vatuvi*. As a matter of fact, one or two natives, though not Bagido'u

himself, gave me this explanation of the word when commenting upon the spell.

But to repeat, I do not wish to imply that *vatuvi* may be etymologically connected with the term *vatu*, 'coral boulder', or the verbs 'to set up', 'to inaugurate', or that it might mean 'to heal', 'to foment'. But I think that undoubtedly it covers an area of meaning, primarily derived from the words for 'to institute, to set up', and extending through phonetic and accidental similarity to *vatu* and *vatuvi* and that these also function in the essential magical significance of the word, which as we know (cf. Part VI, Div. VI) is its action on the minds of the natives. It is important to realise that the native commentaries are not to be regarded as correct translations, but rather as free associations suggested to the native by the word mentioned to them. We must remember that the very character of magical words makes it futile to attribute to them a precise and definite lexical meaning, such as we would expect in an ordinary communication or narrative. The present word launched repeatedly at the very beginning of the formula in an impersonal way is meant to convey a general blessing, to exercise a mystical influence. It is a force which emanates from the word to the natives. It is the multifarious associations, the emotional fringe of the word which is believed by them to influence the course of nature, and which through this really influences their own psychology and the organisation of their work. In the free version of this spell I have chosen the expression 'show the way'. This expression renders the indefinite grammatical form of the native word, and covers the variety of meanings which we found associated with it. In the rendering of the whole verse :—

> *Vatuvi, vatuvi, vatuvi, vatuvi,*
> *Vitumaga, i-maga,*
> *Vatuvi, vatuvi, vatuvi, vatuvi,*
> *Vitulola, i-lola.*

> Show the way, show the way,
> Show the way, show the way,
> Show the way groundwards, into the deep ground,
> Show the way, show the way,
> Show the way, show the way,
> Show the way firmly, show the way to the firm moorings.

I have tried to conform to the rhythm of the native words, to reproduce the native repetitions, their antitheses and the characteristic patterning of words. The words *maga*, 'depth, body of the earth', and *lola*, 'mooring stick', have a clear meaning in ordinary speech.

Let us once more define the meaning of *vatuvi* within the context of its strophe and of the whole formula and even of the magical situation: this word conveys a general benediction especially directed towards the depth of the earth; it also implies firmness and permanence of the crops and conveys the idea of going down and rising again.

2. This is a list of ancestral spirits. The first series of names refer to more distant ancestors. It is characteristic that their kinship determination *tubu-gu* is given in the plural. Hence in the free version I have translated them as 'Grandfathers of the name of Polu . . .' and so on. This grammatical form can only be understood by realising two principles, one sociological and one dogmatic. The spell is handed on only in the sub-clans of Tabalu and Kwoynama. The Tabalu are the "owners" of this magic. The sub-clan of Kwoynama has always furnished the privileged wives of the Tabalu chiefs, as well as husbands for Tabalu women. I was told that the name of Namwana Guya'u, literally "her husband of the chief (woman)", hereditary in the Kwoynama sub-clan, expresses this appropriateness. Let us remember that each sub-clan has its body of names, so that probably there were a number of men called Polu, Koleko and so on. The names Katupwala, Bugwabwaga, Purayasi and Numakala can historically be proved to have belonged to reigning chiefs in Omarakana. The last two names are especially framed. Yowana was the father of my informant (cf. v. 2 of M.F. 1), Mwakenuwa his grandfather. The title *bilumava'u biloma-m* is built on the noun *baloma*, compounded first with the suffix -*va'u*, 'new', and secondly with the second possessive pronoun -*m*. Literally it means 'spirit new, spirit thine', so that it means something like 'thy spirit, the new spirit', translated freely 'and thou, new spirit'.

3. This verse is constructed on the repetitive pattern, with the key expression *lopou-la ulo buyagu*, which I have translated in the free version as 'the belly of my garden', i.e. quite concretely. This does not mean, however, that there is a strong feeling of metaphorical allusion to animal or human fertility contained in this expression. In native, *lopou-la*, 'belly his', especially in the form *o lopou-la*, 'in belly his', has become the usual preposition meaning 'inside'. The only expression here which might seem to fit with the fertility idea is *i-kabinaygwadi*,[1] 'to burgeon (with) child'. My informants, as a matter

---

[1] In Part V (Div. II, § 35), I have adopted the meaning 'to grow' for *kabina'i*. Here the verb 'to burgeon' seemed more appropriate. Although I am striving for consistency of 'fixed meaning' in interlineal translation, some such discrepancies are inevitable.

of fact, commented on it in this sense: *taytu latu-la buyagu*, 'taytu is the child of the garden'. 'The belly of the garden', or 'the inside of the garden', refers to the inside of the soil and perhaps to the fertility of the soil. Several verbs in this verse belong to ordinary speech (*gebile, tokaye, takubila, kabina'i, tawaga*). *Kabwabu* is a verbally used noun 'ant-hill': 'it ant-hills', 'it becomes like an ant-hill'. The remainder of the verbs consist of the prefixed formatives *giba-*, *gibu-*, derived from *gebi*, 'lift', 'to make light'. I have rendered them in the interlineal version by direct juxtaposition: 'he-lift-bush-hen-nest', 'he-lift-bend-down', 'he-lift-iron-wood-tree', etc., and in the free translation simply 'grows to the size of a bush-hen's nest', 'rises and is bowed down', 'rises like the iron-wood palm', the translation being a mere adaptation of the native phrases to grammatical English.

4-8. The general structure of this litany shows the repetition of a series of plainly verbal forms in the first person present, *a-tabe'u*, *a-givisa'u*, etc., or in the future, *ba-yabay-m*, *ba-talay-m*, etc.; and one anomalous form *tumlili-m* which has no prefixed personal pronoun. All these verbs designate exorcising actions such as 'to sweep', 'to blow away', 'to drive, dispatch', and 'to lose'. With these are connected nouns, all of which refer to garden pests. On the key-word *a-tabe'u*, not familiar from ordinary speech, I received the following commentary: *a-tabe'u: a-tanevi*, '*a-tabe'u* means I sweep'. *A-givisa'u* is an apophonic variant of *a-yuvisa'u*, from *yuvi*, 'to blow', and the suffix *-sa'u*, signifying completeness, thoroughness, 'to blow away'. Verses 6, 7, 8: I have separated the two words in each phrase by a comma to represent the meaning as well as the manner in which these words were uttered. They were enunciated separately, with a long interval between them and with a strong emphasis on the *gala*. *Ba-yabay-m!—gala!* The word *gala*, as in many similar magical contexts, expresses a definite negative or repulsive function. I have translated it by 'begone'. *Ba-yabay-m* is the transitive future of *yabi*, 'to drive away', the pronominal suffix *-m* of the second person giving it the transitive meaning 'I drive thee away'. *Ba-talay-m*, from *talo'i*, a verb signifying giving a farewell present, is in the same form as the previous verb. *Tumlili-m* was explained to me by the sentence: *kula kusiwa*, 'go, remain there'. Conjecturally I derive the word *tumili-m* from *tamwala*, 'to lose', 'to forget', the future form of which would be *ba-tamwalay-m*, contorted in this magical context into *tumlili-m*. The inventory words are without exception the names of pests and blights. For *mwoytatana* and *sigweleluwa*, see Formula 1, v. 5. *Yokwa'u* is a blight on taro leaves. The nouns compounded of *kim*, 'beetle', and a descriptive or attributive quality word, all refer to the beetle that feeds on the taro tuber. 'The beetle with the tusks, the beetle that drills, the beetle that works underground.' We find the following words compounded with *kim*: *doga* has a plain lexical meaning 'tusk', 'tooth'; *suluva* was explained to me by a manual illustration of the action of boring or drilling (perhaps connected with *sulu*, 'to penetrate, to enter, make holes'); *kwataku* was commented upon: *kwataku: bi-lapwaypwaya*, '*kwataku* means it will go into the ground'. I cannot relate this word to any known roots. The three words with the prefix *igi-*, *iga-* (not to be confused with the verbal form *i-giba*, etc., in v. 3) are derived from *yagi, yagavana, yawesi*, 'leaves'. *Igikalakeluva*, compound of *igi-* and *kalakeluva*, is probably from *kalawa*, 'cycas leaf' (cf. Part V, Div. V, § 18), used for counting and also for fine and intricate designs, the whole compound meaning 'leaf-marks', 'marks on leaves', 'blight on leaves'. *Igadaya* probably from *kadaydaya*, 'whitish', meaning 'leaf whitish', 'whiteness on leaves', 'white blight'. *Iginumanamile* from *numanamile*, 'dew', 'leaf-dew', 'white sparkling blight on leaves'.

9. *Ba-vasasay-m*, 'I might burst open thee', the final *-m* being a possessive affix of the second person, which means 'I burst open for thee'. *Kwadada* was explained to me as *karikeda* or *kwadewo*, 'passage near shore', 'shallow passage'; *kadilaboma*, literally *kadi*, 'road', *la-*, 'his', *boma*, 'taboo', 'sacred place', is the name of a sea-passage near the village of Laba'i.

10. Laba'i is also mentioned here as a village of the pests whose coral boulder is Ituloma, a stone somewhere near Laba'i. The pests are also invited to sail away in an imaginary canoe. Laba'i and the sea-passage here mentioned are to the west or north-west of Kiriwina. The magician thus is 'sending west' the various blights and insects, the English slang expression corresponding as we know already (cf. M.F. 1, D.) to the general mythological tendency of the natives, which we meet in many formulae and in other contexts, to regard the north-west as the direction whither all things to be exorcised must be driven. It is also the direction the spirits of the departed take and whence babies come, the direction of the island of Tuma. Phonetically we note the consonantal assimilation of *v* and *w* into *m* and *mw* respectively in the words *kam-malu, kam-matu, im-mwaga, im-mwola*, which would not occur in ordinary speech.

11. *Ba-dagay-m*—transitive form of *dodige*, 'stow away'. 'I stow thee away (into the imaginary boat mentioned at the end of the previous strophe).' *Ku-popolu* is derived from *polu*, 'to boil', and must not be confused with the verb *pulupulu*, 'to drown', which appears in verse 7 of Formula 1. *Vilu'a*—from *vivilu'a*, 'whirlwind'. *Melela* perhaps from *tamwala*, 'to be lost', 'to disappear' (cf. Commentary on

v. 8 of this formula), obtained by the dropping of the formative *ta-*. The kinship term *lu-gu-ta* exercises magically a strong severing influence, because of the powerful sister-brother taboo. Connected with it is the next term, *ku-msilay-gu*, from the noun *mwasila*, 'shame', here used verbally 'thou be ashamed of me'. *Ku-layli-gu* I can only translate in a conjectural manner on the basis of native information which described this word as 'to avoid'. Concerning the verb *vatilawa*, 'to slink under', my informants said 'as the commoner will do when the chief is sitting on the raised platform'.

FORMULA 3
(Ch. II, Sec. 4)

I. 1. *Da   kaygaga-si   tomwaya!*
     our   wood-bad   old man

  2. *Buriyowa'i,   buriyasila,   burigado'i,   bulakayulo,*
     pig-fighter   pig-high-stone   pig-fence-stake   pig- ?

    burokapatata,   burokapasi'u,   buritolaviya.
    pig-narrow-face   pig- ?   pig-fierce

  3. *Um   laya   tayga-m,   um   kuriga   yeyu-m.*
     thy   sail   ear thine   thy   rudder   tail thine

II. 4. *A-vala   o   sibu-m;   a-vasalay-m,   ku-wa;*
     I kick   in   bottom thine   I dispatch thee   thou get there

    ku-la   o   Ulawola;   ku-uya-ki   tubwalo-m!
    thou go   in   (a village)   thou get there at   back thine

  5. *I-gubu-ki   mata-m;   i-pakay-ki   nano-m.*
     he burn at   eye thine   he refuse at   mind thine

GENERAL COMMENTARY

A. *Sociological Context:* is the same for this and the following formulae, 4 to 6. The magical acts of which each formula is an important part follow immediately one after the other and really constitute one ceremony. On the morning after the oblation to the spirits and the chanting over the axes and herbs connected with it, the magician and all the gardeners repair to the fields. The magical virtue, which has been accumulated on the previous evening and imprisoned round the axe-blades, will now be loosed on the garden-site. The magician is prepared by fasting. His companions have dressed in festive attire and march in a body to the *mile'ula*, the place where the main stile of the garden will be erected, and where the two magical corners of the two main standard plots will gradually come into being. In a series of acts, which are inaugural in the sense that they begin the whole gardening cycle and that they directly lead to a practical activity, spells 3 to 6 will be recited.

B. *Ritual Context:* though the cultural, economic and sociological setting of the four spells is identical, each of them has a ritual context of its own. For the ritual context of the present spell let us hark back to our description in Chapter II (Sec. 4). The magician has gone to the garden holding his magical wand, *kaylepa,* in the left hand and, on his right shoulder, the axe with the medicated leaves round it. Immediately before reciting the following formula he steps to the spot which will become the magical corner of the main standard plot, cuts a small sapling (*kaygaga,* 'bad sapling') with the medicated axe, lifts it up, recites the formula over it and immediately throws it across the boundary belt into the *yosewo,* 'the uncut bush'. This sapling functions as a sort of vegetable scapegoat, representing evil things and things dangerous to gardens, more specifically the bush-pigs, which are the only pests addressed in this formula.

C. *Structure:* as with most of those uttered in the gardens, this spell is short and has got no definite structure. I have divided it into two parts, the first being a compound address, probably to the ancestral spirits and certainly to the bush-pigs, the second an exorcism.

D. *Dogmatic Context:* whether the 'old man', contextually 'old men', addressed in verse 1 are ancestral spirits or the assembled people is difficult to decide. In the free translation I have adhered to the first alternative: 'This is our bad wood, O ancestral spirits.' In verses 2–4 bush-pigs are addressed, *Ulawola* being one of the 'homes' of the bush-pig. *Ulawola: bwalodila si valu, Kuluvitu,* '*Ulawola,* is a village of bush-pigs, near Kuluvitu.' (Cf. also Part V, Div. XI, § 3 where other such places are mentioned.)

E. *Mode of Recitation:* the spell is chanted without a very pronounced melody. It is rather stated in a loud persuasive voice, obviously meant to reach the bush-pigs.

LINGUISTIC COMMENTARY

1. This is a plain grammatical sentence. The only ambiguity which characterises it as magic is the reference to 'old men' (see above D.). 'Our—old men': ancestral spirits. *Kaygaga*—the context defines it as the sapling used to represent bad influences: 'bad wood', 'bad sapling' or 'scapegoat sapling'. Wherever possible I have used in free translation the simplest and most direct word. Here I have adopted the expression 'bad wood' which creates no ambiguities.

2. The titles by which the bush-pig is here addressed are compounds of *buri-, bura-, buro-,* derived from *bulukwa,* 'pig', with those attributes of the bush-pig relevant to the present context: *-yowa'i,*

'fighting', 'the fighter-pig'; *yasila*, by native commentary 'high stone in the *rayboag*' (only occurrence of this word); -*kayulo*, roughly translated by the natives as meaning ugly, perhaps from *ulo*, *ula*, 'decay', 'stench', 'rottenness'. *Kayulo* in this case would mean decaying vegetable and the whole word 'pig attracted by decaying vegetable matter'. In this connexion we may remember that excreta and other stinky matters are taboo in the gardens as they are supposed to attract the bush-pigs (cf. also Part V, Div. VI, § 15). -*kapasi'u*, also not checked with any other context, translated as 'ugly'; -*tolaviya*, 'fierce'.

3. 'Thy ears be thy sail, thy tail be thy rudder', probably to be interpreted as 'may the breath of my magic act as wind in your ears, impelling you to move away, turn your back on our garden and steer yourself away from us'. In the free translation I have kept, however, more closely to the native text.

4. *A-vasalay-m*, probably from *vaysali*, 'to perform a mortuary dance', a form of ceremonial farewell, rendered in both free and literal version as 'I dispatch thee'. 'Thou get there at back thine' is to be interpreted 'go behind' (almost 'get thee behind thee'); in other words, 'return whence you have come'.

5. *Gubu* in *i-gubu-ki* is probably derived from *gebi*, 'to lift', or *gabu*, 'to burn'. I have translated it 'he burn at eye thine', in the sense 'my magic burns thine eye', making it inaccessible to the attractions of this garden. This interpretation is borne out by the native comment: *i-gubu-ki mata-m: i-katupatu matala bwabodila*, 'He burn at eye thine means he closes the eye of the bush-pig.' Thus the meaning of this phrase is simple: 'This magic closes your eyes and makes your inclinations refuse the allurements of the garden.'

FORMULA 4
(Ch. II, Sec. 4)

1. *A-tay-m*   *ulo*   *buyagu.*
   I cut thee   my   garden-site

2. *A-talilakema*   *lopou-la*   *ulo*   *buyagu.*
   I make blossom-with-axe   belly his   my   garden-site

3. *I-guba'i*,   *i-towa;*   *i-guba'i*,   *i-toma.*
   he is lifted   he stand there   he is lifted   he stand here

GENERAL COMMENTARY

A. *Sociological Context:* same as M.F. 3 which it immediately follows. It is in fact a counterpart of the previous magical act.

B. *Ritual Context:* the cutting of the *kayowota*, 'good sapling', which afterwards is inserted again into the soil and is swayed to and fro while the spell is being recited.

C. *Structure:* as with the preceding spell, it is not so much chanted in a sing-song as spoken in a loud and incisive voice.

LINGUISTIC COMMENTARY

1. 'I cut thee my garden-site', uttered as it is while the magician sways the recently cut and good sapling, refers probably to the auspicious cutting of the whole garden.

2. The compound verb *talilakema* is clearly a magical expression. The first component *talila-* is derived from *talala*, *ta-* causative prefix and the root *lala*, 'flower', 'blossom'. The second component is *kema*, 'an axe'. The whole compound was translated in the free version: 'With my charmed axe I make the belly of my garden blossom.'

3. *Guba'i:* from *gebi*, 'to lift', in a transitive-effective form 'to make lift', 'to raise'. 'My garden is made to lift, is raised.' The two words *i-towa*, *i-toma* show the symmetrical opposition of the *w* and *m* forms, the 'there' and 'here' forms.

FORMULA 5
(Ch. II, Sec. 4)

1. *Avayta'u*   *i-silavila*   *o*   *lopou-la*   *Yema?* (repeated)
   which man   he sit-turn   in   belly his   (tabooed grove)

2. *Yaygula'i*   *Yayabwa,*   *so-gu*
   I myself   (mythical magician)   companion mine

   Gagabwa,   *ka-silavila,*   *ka-yobulami,*
   (mythical magician)   we two sit-turn   we two make coconut oil

   ka-yomwatewa   *o*   *lopou-la*   *Yema.*
   we two quick-straight   in   belly his   (tabooed grove)

3. Identical with strophe 3 of Formula 2.

GENERAL COMMENTARY

A. *Sociological Context:* here continues from previous rite, the garden magician does not even rise from his sitting posture.

B. *Ritual Context:* he tears up a handful of weeds and rubs the ground with them, reciting the present formula.

C. *Structure:* very simple. It contains a short exordium in the form of question and answer which we meet occasionally in Trobriand spells. The second part, that is the third verse, is identical with the third verse of Formula 2, i.e. it contains prophetic and creative affirmations about the fertility of the 'belly of my garden-site'.

D. *Dogmatic Context:* we here find mention of two somewhat pale mythological figures. Yayabwa and Gagabwa are said to be *bilibaloma* of this magic, i.e. ancestral spirits who once wielded this magic. Nothing more is known of them and they do not belong to the official lineage enumerated in verse 2 of Formula 2. Yema is an actual tabooed grove between Lu'ebila and Kaybola. The act described in the answer (v. 2) and which places it within the tabooed grove reminds us of the ceremony which forms the first act of the garden cycle of Kurokayva (Ch. IX, Sec. 2). The compound *silavila*, which I translated literally 'sit-turn', is I think not met outside magic. It refers to the posture in which the magician, without getting up, turns round uttering the spell towards all the points of the compass. The meaning of this word would be something like 'magically to bless', and in the free version I have translated it 'we sit down and bless on all sides'.

E. *Mode of Recitation:* the formula is chanted as is usual with question-and-answer phrases. The question is generally repeated twice in a rising cadence. The answer is given in stronger, more positive accents. Then verse 3 is recited with a characteristic repetitive perfunctoriness for the recurring phrase *lopou-la ulo buyagu*, and a stronger more distinct enunciation for the intervening verbs.

LINGUISTIC COMMENTARY

Yobulami, *yo-*, causative prefix, *bulami*, 'coconut oil'; the natives commented: *yagabana taytu makawala ta-putumi*, 'the leaves of taytu we anoint, as it were, with coconut oil'. Hence in free translation 'we anoint it with coconut cream'. *Yomwatewa*, a word which I cannot lexically account for, translated by the natives in the commenting sentence 'taytu shoots grow up quickly and straight'.

FORMULA 6
(Ch. II, Sec. 4)

A-way-m,	*pwaypwaya;*	*ku-tavisi,*	*pwaypwaya;*
I strike thee	soil	thou cut through	soil
kw-iga'ega,	*pwaypwaya;*	*kw-abina'i,*	*pwaypwaya;*
thou shake	soil	thou burgeon	soil
kw-abinaygwadi,		*pwaypwaya* (repeated)	
thou burgeon (with) child		soil	

GENERAL COMMENTARY

A. *Sociological Context:* still remains. It is, however, what follows after this formula—and let us remember that the context frames a spell and a rite on either side—which really matters. The men have been listening to the series of spells in silence, standing in a body at the *mile'ula*. Now that the soil has been struck by the magician, they break into the long-drawn scream *tilaykiki* and then each runs to his own garden plot, and there with his medicated axe repeats part of the ceremony which he has just witnessed. He cuts the *kaygaga* and *kayowota*, throwing the first across the boundary and inserting the other into the ground. Then each man cuts a few saplings on his own garden plot. Let us keep in mind that since each of them uses the axe which has been impregnated with the magical virtue of Formula 2, there is a continuity integrating Formulae 1 and 2 with the present act, which is after all only a part of the compound ceremony in which Formulae 3 to 6 have been uttered. The magician or one of his helpers follows the men and on each plot Formula 5 is recited while the soil is rubbed with the weeds pulled out on the spot.

B. *Ritual Context:* the magician now rises to his feet and performs the eponymous rite of his whole magic, that is, he strikes the soil with his magical wand. As we know, this ceremony is one way of describing the whole office of the garden magician, the magician being very often spoken of as 'the man who strikes our soil'.

C. *Structure:* short and simple. The first phrase is a declaration of what the magician is doing. 'I strike thee, O soil', and the remaining four sentences are imperatives addressed to the soil which is mentioned in each phrase.

D. *Dogmatic Context:* we have, therefore, here a direct communion between the magician and the main object of his ritual activities, the soil, the fertility of which he verbally commands.

E. *Mode of Recitation:* the spell is uttered in a loud commanding voice, each phrase following the other at brief intervals : *A-way-m, pwaypwaya; ku-tavisi, pwaypwaya*, as a separate command. The whole or certain phrases may be repeated.

LINGUISTIC COMMENTARY

The wording here is both simple and regular. The first verb is in the transitive form 'I strike thee', all the other verbs are in the ordinary imperative which in Kiriwinian is marked by stress and context. The change of *ku* into *kw* is the ordinary change which always occurs when the verb begins with a vowel or a *k*. *Ku-iga'ega* = *kw-iga'ega*, *ku-kabina'i* = *kw-abina'i*. The ordinary word *tavisi*, 'cut through', refers here to the sprouting of the crops which have to cut through the soil. Hence in free translation I have put it, 'Open thou up and let the crops through the ground.' The shaking (*iga'ega*) refers to the *kariyala*, 'magical portent', of this spell (cf. Ch. III, Sec. 4).

FORMULA 7
(Ch. III, Sec. 1)

This is identical with Formula 3 with the exception of one single word: instead of *kaygaga-si* in Formula 3, we have in 7 *pelaka'ukwa-si*.

GENERAL COMMENTARY

A. *Sociological Context:* let us remember that we are now on the third day of a compound ceremony. On the first day the wholesale burning, *vakavayla'u*, was carried out and on the second the 'big burning', *gibuviyaka*. Both these acts are based on the main formula of our system, the *vatuvi* spell (M.F. 2), with which the magical torches used in these ceremonies have been charmed (cf. also Ch. V, Sec. 3). Now glancing over Chapter III (Sec. 1), we feel how the wholesale and detailed burning, though carried out by a magician and his immediate helpmates, yet absorbs the attention of the whole community. There is a taboo on the gardens. In the village the gardeners sit and await the return of their official and ceremonial delegate. The gardens must be burnt by the magician or else the whole fertility cycle would be upset. The virtue of the *vatuvi* formula through the the flames and the smoke and the cinders—but only if these are brought into being in the prescribed ritual manner—impregnates the soil and creates fertility. The present formula is also pronounced by the magician alone, or in a small company in the garden, at the magical corner. But the community once more have to wait on its completion; the gardens are again tabooed. The virtue of his voice, though not heard by anybody except the magical powers or agencies, yet affects the consciousness of every gardener who knows the words and who is aware that they are being uttered.

B. *Ritual Context:* consists in the chanting of the spell into a large taro top, right into the surface where it has been severed from the root.

C. *Structure:* almost identical with Formula 3; it is therefore a simple spell.

D. *Dogmatic Context:* does not seem to harmonise with the ritual context at first. Let us, however, examine the one word by which this spell differs from Formula 3. Formula 3 begins: 'This is our bad wood, O ancestral spirits,' and Formula 7: 'This is our dog-dung, O ancestral spirits.' *Pelaka'ukwa* is a compound of *pela*, 'excrement', and *ka'ukwa*, 'dog'—'dog's excrement', 'dog-dung'. In the rite corresponding to Formula 3, the sapling traditionally called 'bad sapling' (*kaygaga*) is thrown into the bush, the meaning of which might be partly to make the discarded sapling a scapegoat, partly, perhaps, to make it representative of the whole garden, impressing thus on the pests that everything grown in this garden is bad. In this formula, the planted taro is named 'dog's excrement'. This derogatory expression may be used to ward off the bush-pigs above all, but other pests and blights also, by making them believe that the crops are not worth touching. The use of names branding human beings and things as disgusting, diseased, weak, is a sort of magical protective colouring well known from ethnographic literature (cf. also Sec. 2 of Ch. III).

E. *Mode of Recitation:* this spell has to be spoken in a soft persuasive voice, right into the cut surface of the taro, and not loudly as is Formula 3.

FORMULA 8
(Ch. III, Sec. 1)

1. *Ku-luluwa,*   *ku-luluwa-ke'i*   *nukuvalu.*
   thou flare up   thou flare up at   direction-village

2. *Ku-butu,*   *ku-butu-ke'i*   *nukula'odila.*
   thou march   thou march at   direction-bush

GENERAL COMMENTARY

A. *Sociological Context:* is identical for the following two formulae. They are both performed on the fourth day. The magician chants the spells alone on the magical corner in the main *leywota* while in the village the gardeners are aware of what is happening; for their gardens are still under a taboo, so that they usually remain at home.

B. *Ritual Context:* this consists for the first spell in the magician squatting at the magical corner and taking the tuber of a *kwanada* yam into his right hand and holding it close to his mouth.

C. *Structure:* it is a short spell.

D. *Dogmatic Context:* it is addressed directly to the *kwanada* and the imperative might be taken as literally a communication from the magician to the yam tuber as representative of the crops in the garden.

E. *Mode of Recitation:* the order is given loudly and peremptorily.

LINGUISTIC COMMENTARY

1. *Luluwa*—the vocabulary meaning is 'to blaze', 'flare up'. A seeming discrepancy was introduced by my informant's comments, which equated this word 'to appear in the village'. This might be perhaps explained by the native commentators' frequent habit of giving the effect of an action and not its equivalent when an explanation was asked for. The growth of the plants is so luxuriant that they

would flare away, i.e. spread towards the village and 'appear in the village'. We have in both lines the two verbal forms, the general and the directed, with the ending *keli*. *Nukuvalu* signifies the end of the *leywota* turned towards the village; *nuku* is an unusual prefix conveying 'direction' (see diagram in Ch. II, Sec. 3).

2. *Butu*, literally 'march', 'move', 'spread'. *Nukula'odila* is the corner of the plot turned towards the bush.

FORMULA 9
(Ch. III, Sec. 1)

1. *Uli*   *pipilawa* (repeated);   *uli*   *pipilama* (repeated);
   taro   swell there   taro   swell here

2. *kapawa*   *uli,*   *itamala*   *kuma;*
   swollen   taro   ?   come

3. *pudikikita.*
   resistant to motion

GENERAL COMMENTARY

A. *Sociological Context:* remains the same.

B. *Ritual Context:* this spell is chanted into another taro top which again is planted at the magical corner, thus making the number of taro magically planted two. After this spell the magician ritually builds a miniature hut and miniature fence of dry twigs, a manual act which does not seem to be connected in any way with the text of this spell.

C. *Structure:* a short spell without any structure; giving rather the impression of a fragment.

D. *Dogmatic Context:* the spell is addressed directly to the object handled in the rite, that is, to the taro top which is mentioned three times by name and to which all the allusions in the spell refer.

E. *Mode of Recitation:* chanted and not spoken, and that in spite of the fact that it is addressed to an object held at very close quarters.

LINGUISTIC COMMENTARY

1. *Pipilawa, pipilama,* the commentary was: *uli pipilawa: makawala kwaypilapada,* 'the *pipilawa* taro is like buttocks'. The root *pipila* is probably connected with *pila*, 'portion', usually 'large portion', the classificatory formative of *pilatala*, 'one portion' (cf. Part IV, Div. III, B.). In any case this word conveys associations of size, in this context growth. Repeated with the suffixes *-wa* and *-ma*, so characteristic of magical symmetry and opposition, it expresses the all-roundness, completeness of the process. Hence in free translation: 'Swell there, O taro, swell here, O taro' (cf. Ch. III, Sec. 1).

2. *Kapawa* was translated to me: *uli kapawa makawala ta'u topwawa, sene kwayviyaka*, 'the *kapawa* taro is like a man with elephantiasis, very big'. Hence in free translation: "O stout taro." *Itamala* I am unable to translate satisfactorily. I received the comment: *itamala kuma: kuma nanakwa*, '*itamala kuma* means come quickly'. The phrase thus conveys the idea of rapid growth; hence in free translation: 'It comes on quickly.'

3. *Pudikikita*, also a word etymologically obscure to me. The native comment was: *pudikikita: kasa'i; biga talivala; sene ikikita megwa pudikikita*, '*pudikikita* means hard (to move); in ordinary speech we say very resistant, in magic we say *pudikikita*'. The prefix *pudi-* is perhaps connected with the root *pada* in *kwaypilapada*, 'buttocks'. In free translation I have rendered it "immovable taro".

FORMULA 10
(Ch. III, Sec. 4)

I. 1. *Kaylola,   lola* (repeated)
   mooring,   to moor

   Kaygulugulu,   gulugulu (repeated)
   boring in,   to bore in

   Kaylola   Tudava,
   mooring   (mythical hero)

   Kaygulugulu   Malita.
   boring in   (mythical hero)

   2. *Bi-sipela   Tudava,   bi-sila'i   o*
   he might climb (mythical hero) he might seat himself in

   tokaykaya:
   high platform

   Avaka   ba-woye'i?   Ba-woye'i   sibulola.
   what   I might hit   I might hit   bottom-mooring

   Bi-lalola!
   he might be moored

II. 3. *Bi-lalola . . .* (repeated); *ulu pwaypwaya bi-lalola, ulo kamkokola bi-lalola, uli kavatam bi-lalola, ulo kaysalu bi-lalola, uli kamtuya bi-lalola, ulo kaybudi bilalola, ulo kaynutatala bi-lalola, ula tula bi-lalola, uri yeye'i bi-lalola, uri tukulumwala bi-lalola, ulo karivisi bi-lalola, uri tamkwaluma bi-lalola, uri kaluvalova bi-lalola, ula kayvaliluwa bi-lalola.*

III. 4. *I-lola   ulu   buyagu,*
   he moor   my   garden-site

   Imdukupolu   ulu   buyagu,
   like stone-buried   my   garden-site

Imdukumaga	*ulu*	*buyagu,*	
like stone-bedrock	my	garden-site	

Imdukumeylosi	*ulu*	*buyagu,*	
like stone-deep-rooted	my	garden-site	

I-lalola	*ulu*	*buyagu,*	*bi-luluvagasi.*
he is moored	my	garden-site	he might be anchored completely

5. *Tudududududu* . . .

Kariyala	*ulu*	*buyagu,*	*i-tututu*	*o*	*bomatu.*
magical portent	my	garden-site	he rumble	in	north wind

GENERAL COMMENTARY

A. *Sociological Context:* in the following two formulae we approach a new ceremony which forms the magical turning-point in the sequence of agricultural events. It is the third big complex rite, the first being the grand inaugural rite and the second the ceremonies of burning and early magical planting. After this last the gardens were cleaned, *koumwala*, divided by the *tula* rods, into squares, *gubwatala*, and planted in a preliminary fashion with such crops as taro, large yams, sugar-cane, peas and pumpkins. Now there takes place the ceremony of the *kamkokola*, after which, as we know, comes the planting of the taytu and the growth of the vine round the supports. The ceremony to which the following two formulae belong creates what we have called the 'magical wall'. The *kamkokola* structure itself is the last word in the completion of the magical corner. Thus the whole performance, the background against which we are to understand the wording of the formula, furnishes the garden for the next stage; changing the bare flat field into a garden bristling with yam supports round which the new plants will twine. It marks the turning-point between the preparatory work in the garden and the real growth of the crops. We have to remember that here again the spells which we shall presently analyse are but a part of the verbal magic of the rite; for the main spell (M.F. 2) also figures conspicuously in it. In estimating the sociological and cultural context of the spells we must bear in mind that the same conditions obtain as in those previously discussed: the whole community has been roused to attention; the garden magician has announced that the gardens will be tabooed; he has imposed this taboo on work by inserting the *kayluvalova* stick on each plot. In addition he keeps the men to their task of collecting *lapu*, the stout poles for supports and for the component parts of the *kamkokola*. Then on the fourth day of the taboo he medicates herbs and axes with the *vatuvi* spell. The villagers will be attentive to the performance and it will influence their minds and mould their relations to the magician and to each other. On the first day when the *kamkokola* are being put up, the virtue of this spell will be imparted to these by rubbing them with the magical herbs and inserting some of the herbs into the hole wherein the upright is planted. On the second day only the formula which we are about to discuss will be actually spoken over the *kamkokola* structure. The leading words of stability and a strong hold upon the ground, its mythological allusions, its enumeration of the essential parts of the magical wall, and of the supports, its optimistic forecast and magical portent, are impressed on those within hearing, while everybody else is aware of the words being uttered over each *kamkokola*.

B. The immediate ritual context of this spell brings us again to the *kamkokola* over which the magician, squatting on the ground close to the structure and with his back to the outer bush, recites it.

C. *Structure:* tripartite, the main part having one key-word only, the root of which appears in the opening words.

D. *Dogmatic Context:* the first part or foundation contains words which are not addressed to any agency, which cannot be regarded as either a communication or imperative or answer and question, but are launched in an impersonal though direct manner towards the garden. As mentioned already the words are words of stability. The two mythological names Tudava and Malita (cf. Ch. I, Sec. 7), well known to all Trobrianders, are mentioned. The last part is in the form of a simple affirmation and is characteristic of creative metaphor. By affirming that the garden is stable like a buried stone, like a stone bedrock, etc., the magician induces strength and stability into his crops. The last sentence refers to the *kariyala*, 'magical portent' (cf. Ch. III, Sec. 4).

E. *Mode of Recitation:* the spell is chanted in a loud voice, since, as we have seen in B, the magician has to launch it over the whole garden plot and should let his breath freely impregnate all the soil thereon. For type of repetition and rhythm, cf. Formula 2, E.

LINGUISTIC COMMENTARY

1. *Lola*—the first thing which strikes us about this word in its present context is that it runs through the whole spell. It appears in the first words of the 'foundation'. It is the last word of the foundation, and the first word of the main part where it is used throughout as a key-word. With this word the third part starts and it reappears towards the end in the penultimate sentence. We shall find one or two more examples of words which thus give the tone to the whole spell; but so far not even in Formula 2 have we met with any comparable phenomenon. I shall call such words 'leading words'.

Lola, 'mooring stick', 'mooring stone' or 'anchor'. The form with the instrumental prefix, *kaylola*, might be translated as 'anchoring stick', but probably here it has rather the abstract verbal sense 'act of mooring'. The naked verbal form *lola* I have here translated by the infinitive 'to moor'; but since in English the anchor or anchoring better expresses the idea of stability, which is the main concept to be conveyed by these words, I have, in the free version, translated it as 'anchoring of my garden'. The addition 'of my garden' is meant to chime on with the assertions of the *dogina*, third part, and to distinguish this spell from Formula 28 of the *vilamalia* (cf. Ch. VII, Sec. 3). *Gulu*: a word which I have not met in ordinary speech. Native comment derives it from *kaliguliguli*, 'to enter by a screwing or drilling movement', 'to bore in'. This refers to the tubers and was rendered in free translation by 'take deep root'. Both words *lola* and *gulu* are—say my native commentators—addressed to the taytu and fit well into the context of this magic, the *kamkokola* structure representing firmness, resistance, magical protection from dangers.

2. Tudava is invited to climb on to the high platform and to preside mystically over the prosperity of the gardens, in the limited sense in which these mythical personalities take part in magical procedures (cf. M.F. 1, D.). The striking refers to the magical act in the same figurative sense in which this word is used in the first inaugurative ceremony (cf. Ch. II, Sec. 4). *Sibulola: sibu*, 'bottom', *lola*, 'mooring stone', literally 'bottom mooring', in free version translated as the 'firmly moored bottom of my taytu'. The expression *bi-lalola* which ends this verse and carries over as key-word of the main part is a reduplicated emphatic form of *bi-lola*. As the natives put it to me: *biga bi-lola, megwa bi-lalola*, 'ordinary speech *bi-lola*, magical speech *bi-lalola*'. This reduplication has the character of what might be called ceremonial emphasis; the magical forms *bi-sila'i* corresponding to the usual *bi-sila*, and *ba-woye'i* to *ba-woye*, are other examples of this.

3. The inventory words enumerated with *bilalola* are expressions denoting various forms of yam support, as well as the ceremonial, decorative and magical elements of the 'magical wall'. They have been fully described in Chapter III (Sec. 4) and Chapter IV (Sec. 1) and linguistically analysed in Div. I, §§ 1–3 (*pwaypwaya*), Div. VI, § 40 (the various terms for yam supports), and Div. VIII, § 20 (*kamkokola*). In the free translation I have kept each native word side by side with its chosen English equivalent so as to mark emphatically the inadequacy of the latter, when it comes to such highly technical and specifically Kiriwinian cultural realities. Thus this part functions harmoniously with the whole spell and with the

rite, towards the strengthening, making firm and steady, of the garden, and especially of the vine supports.

4. The expressions *imdukupolu*, *imdukumaga*, and *imdukumeylosi* are magical compounds. *Im-* from *imile*, 'to become like', a formative often used in magic; *duku* from *dakuna*, 'stone'; *polu*, 'to dive', 'to be immersed, buried'. I am now a little confused as to whether the word should be spelled *polu* or *pulu* (cf. M.F. 1, v. 7 and M.F. 27, v. 4). But the meaning is here definitely that of immersion or drowning. *Maga* was commented upon in this context: *maga: o lopou-la pwaypwaya*, '*maga* means the inside of the earth', that is, underground (cf. Comm. 1, M.F. 2). In this context I have translated it in the free version as 'bedrock'. *Meylosi* I am unable to translate from other contexts; the natives commented: *dukumeylosi: dakuna i-sisu o pwaypwaya*, '*dukumeylosi* means stone that sits in the soil', that is, deep-rooted stone. It has thus been rendered in the free translation. *Luluvagasi*, which was commented upon to me as equivalent to *ikasa'i*, 'it is resistant', is an emphatic form of *lola* with phonetic modifications, the suffix *-vagasi* giving a sense of completeness and permanence; in free translation 'anchored for good and all'.

5. *Tududedu* is the frequently recurring onomatopoeic reproduction of thunder, commented upon in the last sentence of the formula.

FORMULA 11
(Ch. III, Sec. 4)

1.	*Da*	*kamkokola-si*	*yakidasi*	*towosi*		*pwakikita.*
	our	*kamkolola*	ourselves	garden magician		tight (?)
2.	*Da*	*kaybaba-si*	*yakidasi*	*gweguya—siwakauyo.*		
	our	*kaybaba*	ourselves	chiefs	?	

GENERAL COMMENTARY

A. *Sociological Context:* remains the same.

B. *Ritual Context:* the striking of the *kamkokola* pole with the axe which on a previous evening has been medicated with the *vatuvi* spell.

C. *Structure:* very simple, consisting only of two sentences.

D. *Dogmatic Context:* it is a simple impersonal address containing the characteristic magical affirmation.

E. *Mode of Recitation:* spoken in an ordinary voice loudly and emphatically.

LINGUISTIC COMMENTARY

1. *Pwakikita:* compound word of *pwa-*, probably from *pwana*, 'hole, opening', and *kikita*, 'resistant to motion', the same word

which we had in Formula 9 here translated by 'tight', with, however, the same uncertainty which attaches to the translation in Formula 9.

2. The last word, *siwakauyo*, I was unable to translate or receive any adequate commentary upon.

FORMULA 12
(Ch. III, Sec. 4)

Nabugwa,	*nakoya,*	*teyo'u,*
(variety of taytu)	(variety of taytu)	(variety of taytu)

tubaleya;
(variety of yam)

ku-polu	*o*	*lopou-la*	*ulo*	*buyagu.*
thou boil	in	belly his	my	garden-site

Ku-pulupolu	*agu*	*nunula.*
thou boil up	my	corner

GENERAL COMMENTARY

A. *Sociological Context:* I cannot reproduce this exactly. I have not witnessed the ceremony, nor was I aware of its existence until it was mentioned to me by Bagido'u in one of our last sittings when I was reviewing the whole magical scheme of gardening.

B. *Ritual Context:* the formula is uttered over a herb (*kotila*) and some stuff from the bush-hen's nest, and the mixture is buried in the magical corner of the garden.

C. *Structure:* simple, containing a brief invocation to taytu.

LINGUISTIC COMMENTARY

For the different varieties of taytu (*nabugwa, nakoya, teyo'u*), see commentary on Formula 19. *Tubaleya* was defined by the natives as follows: *tubaleya kuvi, sene kavakayviyaka, sene i-kabina'i bwoyna,* '*tubaleya* (is) yam, very big, very he swell good' (i.e. of very good growth). *Ku-polu, ku-pulupolu*—cf. commentary on verse 4, Formula 10.

FORMULA 13
(Ch. IV, Sec. 2)

I. 1.
Tavisi (repeated),	*tavisi-va-u;*	*tavisi* (repeated),	*tavisi-mugwa.*
cut	cut new	cut	cut old

2.
Tavisi	*kwaya'i,*	*tavisi* (repeated),	*tavisi*	*lala'i;*
cut	evening	cut	cut	noon

tavisi (repeated)	*tavisi*	*gabogi;*	*tavisi* (repeated),	
cut	cut	daybreak	cut	

tavisi	*kaukwa'u.*	*Dadeda*		*tavisima.*
cut	morning.	(a plant of vigorous growth)		cut on

II. 3. *Dadeda*   *tavisima* (repeated)*; lakapu d.t.;*
     (a plant of vigorous growth)   cut on   old skin

     imkwitala d.t.;   *katumyogila d.t.*   *taboula d.t.;*
     slow-spreading (taytu)   ?   rotten patch on taytu

     kaypwase d.t.;   *nukunokuna d.t.;*   *tirimwamwa'u d.t.*
     taytu rotten outside   blighted taytu   taytu of heavy growth

III. 4. *Gala   mata-m,*   *mata-m*   *kapapita;*
     no   eye thine   eye thine   (a quick insect)

     g.m.m. kababasi'a;   *g.m.m. ginausi.*
     black ant   (quick thing)

     5. *Ku-yova   taytu* . . . (repeated)
       thou fly   taytu

GENERAL COMMENTARY

A. *Sociological Context:* here once more we find ourselves at a turning-point in the annual run of gardening. The magic of growth (cf. Ch. IV, Sec. 1) happens in a new context and it certainly fulfils a new type of function. Our interest here lies mainly in the question of how the words of the spells function within the new context, i.e. how they are influenced by it and in turn what influence they exercise. Most of the work is done by now, and the gardeners realise that it is for the natural forces of fertility to operate and produce the rich growth of the plant, which is connected with a wealth of tubers. But they believe that magic exercises a favourable and necessary influence, over and above these natural courses of events. This influence the hereditary garden magician is able to exercise on behalf of the whole community. He and he alone can step in now and contribute the most important share that man can contribute. The words of the following spells—for this sociological commentary refers not only to Spell 13, but to Spells 14 and 16, and to 21 as well—fit remarkably well within their context and chime with the cultural function of this growth magic. It can be said that they are launched straight at the growing plant. They are meant to affect the behaviour of the plant, directly through exhortations and commands, but still more indirectly through verbal metaphors and impersonal affirmations. In these spells we have a very clear example of what we might call with Frazer the sympathetic principle, but here expressed not in the ritual but in the wording of magic. But throughout there is a clear indication that the reality on which the words have to act is a growing plant. In Formula 13 taytu is directly addressed by name with a verbal imperative. The first and second verses undoubtedly refer to taytu, and in the third verse we have various kinds of taytu enumerated by name. The 'thou' second person of verse 4 also refers to taytu as our linguistic analysis will show. We have come across (cf. Ch. IV, Sec. 1, and Part V, Div. IX, §§ 6, 8, 10, 13, 14, 16, 17, 22, 24) a number of native statements implying that this magic is heard by taytu; that the taytu reacts to it in a competitive way and that there are important magical effects produced by it. For us, however, it is important that the words here destined for ears which cannot hear are heard by ears for which they are not meant. Each individual gardener is made to feel through the affirmations of this spell, through its exaggerated optimism and anticipations, that all that is in human power to do is being done. Each member of the community realises that the task is once more in the hands of his leader whom he has obeyed so far and to whose organising influence he has submitted. Again the magic, here deeply associated with tradition and chieftainship, asserts its claims and to a large extent fulfils them—not in the way in which the natives believe, but in leadership, power and organising capacity.

B. *Ritual Context:* of these spells is characteristically simple. Going slowly across the gardens, the magician turns to one *baleko* after another and recites these formulae. With a strong voice, clear and resounding, he sweeps the whole garden, letting the words of virtue penetrate into the soil on every *baleko*. In growth magic this context is identical throughout the spells, with the one exception of Spell 16, which will be noted.

C. *Structure:* I have divided this spell into three parts; the middle part shows the characteristic build of a *tapwana*, though it is remarkably short. It will be noted that in this spell, as in Formula 10, we have a leading word, i.e. a word with which the spell begins and which runs right through the first two parts.

D. *Dogmatic Context:* simple (cf. A.). The formula is based on the belief that the plants can listen and hear the magic, that they are affected by the words and this belief is remarkably well and simply documented in the text. One complication, however, remains. In this spell there figures a tree, *dadeda*, which also appears in the next spell. In Formula 16 there is a reference in the first verse to two other trees, the bamboo and the mangrove, and we have the parrot and the rat mentioned in the main part. Formulae 18, 19 and 21 again have, as leading words, the name of the millipede, the word for spider and the word for bush-hen respectively. If we went beyond growth magic we would meet yet another animal, the dolphin (M.F. 27). What are these secondary agencies of magic? Are they regarded, do they function as supernatural beings which are addressed in a religious spirit? Or are they the servants of the magician, commanded by him to act and carrying out his commands effectively? Or what else can they be? Let us answer this with regard to each formula separately. A glance at Formula 13 shows that there are no signs in the wording of any supernatural attitude to the *dadeda* tree. This tree is not a subject of any taboo, and there is no mythological story about it. Its magical influence has been defined to me: *dadeda: ka'i, kaysususina; ta-ta'i, boge bisusine, ta-ta'i, bi-sususina,* '*dadeda* is a tree very intensely sprouting; we cut it, already it sprouts, we cut it again, it sprouts again'. The expression *kaysususina*, with its intensifying reduplication, emphasises the magical significance of *dadeda*. The suffix -*ma* in verse 3 adds a durative flavour to the word: 'cut on', 'cut again and again' (cf.*mesikiya*, 'he is standing for a long time'). The whole expression, therefore—*dadeda tavisima*— would carry the meaning "O *dadeda* tree, continue to cut". Thus the magical influence of the whole key expression of this part would be of the same type as that in all verbal magic. The very mention of this invincibly vital tree induces these qualities in the taytu. In the free translation I have tried to express this by simply juxtaposing the key sentence with the various descriptions of taytu contained in the main part. As to the other agencies enumerated in verse 4, here we obviously have to deal again with a verbal magical influence: a creative metaphor which is effective in the act of being uttered. I have found no indication whatever which would point to a belief in a more immediate agency of insects, birds or plants. I think that exactly as the Trobriander uses the leaves of certain trees, and the garden magician pounds scrapings from a stout heavy coral boulder, or takes stuff from a hornet's nest or a bush-hen's mound and applies this stuff directly as a sympathetic substance, so he also produces a sympathetic effect of growth by mentioning quick animals and quickly growing plants.

E. *Mode of Recitation:* chanted in a clear loud voice which is made to sweep the whole field. The leading word *tavisi* is rubbed in with special insistence.

LINGUISTIC COMMENTARY

1. *Tavisi* from *tavi, ta'i,* 'to cut'. The suffix -*si* probably imparts a durative and intensified action. This formula is described by the natives as *vaguri sobula*, 'to wake up the sprout of the taytu', or *tavisi* or *vavisi sobula*, 'to cut, cut through, the sprout of the taytu' (cf. Ch. IV, Sec. 2 and Part V, Div. IX, § 3). The native commentary was: *tavisi: bisasali, bi-tavisi kala sobula,* '*tavisi* means to break through, so that its sprout might cut through'. The infinitive form might have been translated by 'to cut', but the magical flavour is better rendered by the equally non-committal form 'cut' in interlineal rendering

and "cut through" in the free version. The suffixes -*va'u* and -*mugwa* are oppositions typical of magical spells; *va'u*, 'new', has a perfectly established lexical meaning; *mugwa* means 'previous in time', hence 'early' or 'old' (cf. *kaymugwa*, 'early gardens'). In free translation "cut through anew, cut through of old".

2. The verb *tavisi* is repeated with the times of the day for which the words of ordinary speech are used.

3. The key expression already analysed is here coupled with a series of inventory words describing inferior varieties of taytu, or defective parts or shapes of taytu: *Lakapu:* 'the outer skin' which blisters and peels off, and is an impediment to the sprout, *sobula; imkwitala:* native comment was: *taytu kasa'i bisusina,* 'taytu which is hard in sprouting'; *taboula:* 'a rotten patch on the taytu', taytu marked by such patches—native comment: *boge ipwase, ta-do'u taboula, bi-taka'u bi-tasapu,* 'already it has rotted, we call it *taboula,* we take it (out, sc. out of the *bwayma*), we plant it'; *kaypwase:* described by native informants: *kumaydona boge ipwase, lopou-la-ga bwoyna,* 'all of it already rotted, inside however good'. Such taytu cannot be eaten, but can be planted though it sprouts with some difficulty; *nukunokuna:* 'blight on taytu like pimples'. Native informants say: *ta-kam taytu, pela gala bi-susina,* 'we eat (such) taytu because it will not sprout'; *tirimwamwa'u:* native comment describes this as *taytu sene kasa'i bi-susina,* 'taytu very hard in sprouting'. The word is composed of *tiri* from *tari'a,* 'tide,' 'stream,' *mwamwa'u* reduplicated from *mwa'u,* 'heavy, heavily flowing,' 'heavily growing.' *Katumyogila* was defined to me as a slow-sprouting taytu without further qualification. In the free translation I have mentioned these native names, which do not belong to ordinary speech, side by side with their English translations.

4. *Kapapita* is not known to me from ordinary speech; native comment runs: *mauna, sene nanakwa mitasi, gala ta-loki kateteguna,* 'bird or insect, very quick their eyes, no we get at near'. *Kababasia,* 'the black ants which live underground', invoked in this magic *pela sene nanakwa,* 'because (they are) very fast'. *Ginausi* defined by my native informants as something very quick, but not otherwise identified. Probably a small insect.

FORMULA 14
(Ch. IV, Sec. 2)

I. 1. *Sakapu* (repeated),   *sakapu-va'u;*   *sakapu* (repeated),
emerge   emerge new   emerge

sakapu-mugwa.
emerge old

2. *Sakapu*   *kwaya'i,*   *sakapu* (repeated);   *sakapu*   *lala'i,*
   emerge   evening   emerge   emerge   noon

   sakapu (repeated);   *sakapu*   *gabogi,*   *sakapu* (repeated);
   emerge   emerge   daybreak   emerge

   sakapu   *kaukwa'u.*   *Dadeda*   *sakapuma.*
   emerge   morning   (plant of vigorous growth)   emerge on

Parts II and III as in Formula 13, substituting *sakapu* for *tavisi*.

GENERAL COMMENTARY

Sociologically, dogmatically and structurally, and in every other respect this formula is identical with the foregoing one, the only difference being that the word *sakapu* is substituted for the word *tavisi*.

LINGUISTIC COMMENTARY

Sakapu: a definitely verbal root, translated in the free version by "to come out", is the word used with reference to the mythical act of emergence of the first ancestors of human beings.[1] The verbal change of *tavisi* into *sakapu* corresponds to the function of this formula; whereas the first formula made the taytu sprout, 'cut through its shoot', this one aims at making the shoot come out of the ground. Its name is *katusakapu* or *vasakapu sobula*, 'the making to come out of the sprout'.

FORMULA 15
(Ch. IV, Sec. 2)

1. *Sapi,*   *ba-sopisapi* (repeated)
   brushing   I might brush away

2. *Karivi*   *kam*   *woma;*   *karipusagi*   *kokopa-m;*
   cut open   thy   spent root   split   leaf thine

   i-tobu   *kwaynutay-m.*
   he bend down   stalk thine

3. *Kalakayguya; buyayla ta'u; kalipadaka; namtamata.*
         (names of varieties of taro)

GENERAL COMMENTARY

A. *Sociological Context:* this is a formula of an inaugurative rite, a rite, that is, through which magical sanctification or blessing is bestowed on a new activity. Culturally it fulfils, therefore, a similar function to the inaugurative ceremonies described above. Here

---

[1] Cf. also *Argonauts of the Western Pacific*, Ch. II, and *Sexual Life of Savages*, pp. 418 ff.

again the words, addressed in this case to the plants, reach the ears of the community and affect their minds. The first word in fact is a ritual naming of the activity which the magician inaugurates.

B. *Ritual Context:* a conventionalised repetition of the economic activity which the rite inaugurates. The magician scratches the ground with the digging-stick and uproots a few weeds, uttering the formula.

C. *Structure:* it is a very short spell.

D. *Dogmatic Context:* the first sentence is launched impersonally, the second remarkably enough is addressed to taro.

E. *Mode of Recitation:* uttered in a loud voice which is made to sweep over the garden.

LINGUISTIC COMMENTARY

1. *Sapi:* the impersonal form which I have rendered here by the present participle. The infinitive 'to brush' or the bare word 'brush' might have also been used. The reduplicated form in the repetition puts the magical emphasis. In the free version I have used the English words "I sweep, I sweep away" as fitting better into the context than the verb 'to brush' (cf. Part V, Div. VI, § 21).

2. The words *karivi, karipusagi* are perhaps contracted 2nd person imperative, *kwarivi, kwaripusagi,* since the pronunciation of these sounds sometimes varies slightly. But it is possible also that they are the bare roots of the verb, especially since in the third clause of verse 2 the verb *i-tobu* is used in the third singular. *Karivi,* 'to cut as one cuts a fruit, cut open'. *Karipusagi,* 'to split'. *Woma,* 'spent root' of taro tuber. *Kokopa* which was translated by me as 'taro leaf' is probably the sheathed, rolled up leaf of any plant which grows that way. *Tobu,* 'to bend down', 'to flop down'—in free translation "bow down". When the taro ripens well, the stems of its leaves bend over.

3. This sentence I was not able to translate to my satisfaction in spite of repeated attempts. My native informant insisted that each compound phrase designates the name of a taro variety. *Buyay-la ta'u* means literally 'blood of man'. In the free version I translated it, therefore, "O taro red like blood."

FORMULA 16

(Ch. IV, Sec. 2)

I. 1. *Siribwobwa'u,*   *bwobwa'u;*   *sirimwadogu,*
   frondescent bamboo   bamboo   frondescent mangrove
   mwadogu.
   mangrove

2. *Nabugwa,*   *nakoya;*
   (name of variety of taytu)   (name of variety of taytu)

   ku-sabu   tamu-m;   ku-lulu,   ku-yobilibali.
   thou raise stalk thine thou flare up thou recline

II. 3. *I-gebile   kuvi* (repeated) *i-gibage'u   kuvi;*
       he lift   yam   he lift-bush-hen-nest   yam

   i-gibikumkumula   kuvi;   i-gibakaytalusa   kuvi;
   he lift earth-oven   yam   he lift stump-mound   yam

   i-milakabwabu   kuvi;   i-milidubwadebula   kuvi;
   he like ant-hill   yam   he like grotto   yam

   i-milikaybu'a   kuvi.
   he like coral boulder   yam

4. *Gala   kam   maya'u,   kam   maya'u   kanaga;*
   no   thy   flight   thy   flight   parrot

   Gala   kam   kwaysina,   kam   kwaysina   kokoni;
   no   thy   nibbling (?) thy   nibbling (?) rat

   Gala   kam   tovalala,   kam   tovalala   tovayla'u.
   no   thy   standing up (?) thy standing up (?) thief

III. 5. *Pela   agu   kuvi   i-komki   duri-gu,   i-karigaki*
        for   my   yam   he eat at relative mine   he die of

   ina-gu;   yakanugwalay-gu   tato-gu;
   mother mine   die of surfeit (?)   own-mine

6. *I-kay   ina-la   ta'u;   i-lova   kuvi;   i-to'i*
   he copulate   mother his   man   he throw   yam   he weigh down

   kulugu,   i-towari   kapo'u-gu,   yakakaka . . .
   hair mine   he weigh   shoulder mine

GENERAL COMMENTARY

A. *Sociological Context:* this again is a formula of the magic of growth, so the sociological and cultural context is the same as that of Formulae 13 and 14.

B. *Ritual Context:* this is the only formula of growth magic which is connected with a rudimentary rite: the magician recites it immediately before he puts up the head-stick, *kaydabala*, on each plot. This rite is also the sign that the large supports, the *kayvaliluwa*, may be put in. Thus this formula has also a slightly inaugurative function. But above all it is a magic of growth to make the leaves develop luxuriantly.

C. *Structure:* tripartite, although the second part is by no means a typical *tapwana*. Verse 3 in fact, which we have incorporated in the second part, is very similar to the verse 3 of Formula 2, which we have put there into the first part.

D. *Dogmatic Context:* two plants are invoked at the beginning, but there is no reason to regard this as anything more than sympathetic magic (cf. M.F. 14, A.). The three entities mentioned in verse 4—the parrot, the rat and the thief—are obviously not magical agents, but merely suitable objects for a negative magical simile. The spell refers mainly to yams, although in verse 2 two varieties of taytu are mentioned and directly admonished. The last part contains typical exaggerations which obviously act by mere contagion of words.

Linguistic Commentary

1. *Siribwobwa'u: bwoba'u*, 'bamboo'. *Siri* from *sili*, 'frond', 'frondant', 'frondescent'. *Sirimwadogu:* same formative with *mwadogu*, variety of mangrove exuberant with leaves and fruit. This is a leaf charm and the two trees are among those with the richest foliage in the Trobriand jungle.

2. *Nabugwa, nakoya*, names for two varieties of taytu, literally *na-* from *ina-*, 'mother', *bugwo*, 'a small hillock raised by the bulging of taytu tubers'; *koya*, 'mountain', referring here also to the mound or hillock made by the bulging roots, or else perhaps showing that this variety comes from the southern mountains. In free translation, "O taytu of the hillock, o taytu of the mound." *Sabu* was interpreted to me as equal to *i-tokay*, 'it gets up', rendered by the verb 'to raise'; in free translation "raise thy stalk". *Lulu* abridged form of *luluwa*, 'to flare up, to spread upwards' (cf. also its use in M.F. 8). *Yobilibali*, 'to make horizontal', 'to recline'. Here the vine after growing up is ordered to lie horizontally, probably meaning to form the canopy overhead. All these verbs refer to the growth of the taytu vine and foliage.

3. This verse is built on the same pattern as verse 3 of Formula 2. Half of the verbs are formed by the prefix *gebi-*, 'to lift', 'to raise', 'to rise'. The compounds with *mili-* belong to ordinary speech; those with *gebi-*, *giba-* are magical. And again we have got the bush-hen's nest, the ant-hill, the coral boulder and—absent from verse 3 of Formula 2—the earth-oven, the mound formed round an uprooted tree and a cave. This last probably means that the whole mound formed by the roots of the yam should be substantial like a cave. The returning word is *kuvi*, which does not mean of course that this formula is only directed at the larger species of yams; in verse 2 taytu is indicated, though in verses 5 and 6 the explicitly mentioned crop is again *kuvi*.

4. This verse is built on the typical negative comparison pattern, and can be translated therefore by "the growth should be as the flight of the parrot", and so on. *Maya'u* is alliterated to *kam* and

comes from *vaya'u* which has been equated by my informants to *vayova*, a nominal form from *yova*, 'to fly', hence *vaya'u*, 'flight'. *Kwaysina:* a magical apophonic form of *kasina*, 'nibbling' (?). *Tovalala* I could not translate to my full satisfaction. Some of my informants told me it came from the verb *tovari*, 'to weigh heavily'. Others told me that it was a compound of *to*, 'stand up', *va-* causative prefix, and *lala*, 'to blossom', 'to shoot up'. Hence "the high standing up". Since this latter fits better into the context, I have adopted it.

5 and 6 contain the monstrously exaggerated statements characteristic of some endings of magical spells. "My relative will eat, my mother will die of repletion, I shall die of surfeit." The word *yakanugwalay-gu* is not found in any other context and I have with due reservation to accept the interpretation of my native informants: *ba-kam, ba-karige*, 'I shall eat, I shall die', as its equivalent. *Duri-gu* has been equated by my native informants with *veyo-gu*, 'kinsman', but it is obviously not a modern Kiriwinian form; whether it is related with *dala*, 'sub-clan', *duri-gu* equalling 'member of my sub-clan', I failed to ascertain. *Tura-gu*, 'companion mine', occurs in some of the South Massim languages.

6. The first phrase is somewhat cryptic. My informants were emphatic in saying that it depicts a man (*ta'u*) carrying the yams and groaning, as an expression of mixed admiration and dismay: *i-kay ina-la!*, 'he copulates with his mother!', as he struggles under the weight of the burden. To the present writer, who is a Slav, this, as an expression of admiration or strong emotion, is not so strange as it appears to an Englishman, because Poles and Russians use the expression *yob twayu mat*, 'copulate with thy mother', to express the emotion of wonder or admiration, very much as the Kiriwinians do. The remaining words, stating the heaviness of the burden and including the onomatopoeic *yakakakaka*, confirm the correctness of my informants' interpretation of the first phrase. *I-to'i, i-towari* are variants of the same root meaning 'to weigh down', the second more emphatic than the first.

FORMULA 17

(Ch. IV, Sec. 2)

I. 1. *Kayboginega,*   *kayboginem* (repeated)   *Kabulukwaywaya,*
     millipede   millipede   (a promontory)

   2. *ku-lova* (repeated)   *Kabulukwaywaya,*   *ku-luvake'i*   *Dulata.*
     thou throw   thou throw at   (a cape)

   3. *Kayboginega,*   *Kayboginem* (repeated),   *Dulata*
     millipede   millipede

4. *ku-lova*   *Dulata,*   *ku-luvayumila*
   thou throw   thou throw-fetch-back

   Kabulukwaywaya — *kaybwagina*   *i-lova!*
                        millipede   he throw

II. 5. *Kaybwagina*   *i-lova* (repeated)
       millipede   he throw

   dabwa-m   *taytu*   *kaybwagina*   *i-lova!*
   head thine   taytu   millipede   he throw

   yagava-m   *taytu*   *kaybwagina*   *i-lova;*
   leaf thine   taytu   millipede   he throw

   kam salala   *taytu*   *kaybwagina*   *i-lova;*
   thy fork   taytu   millipede   he throw

   yosi-m   *taytu*   *kaybwagina*   *i-lova;*
   shoot thine   taytu   millipede   he throw

   kam posem   *taytu*   *kaybwagina*   *i-lova;*
   thy aerial root taytu   millipede   he throw

   yawi-m   *taytu*   *kaybwagina*   *i-lova;*
   aerial root thine taytu   millipede   he throw

   kam towabu   *taytu*   *kaybwagina*   *i-lova;*
   thy secondary stalk   taytu   millipede   he throw

III. 6. *Ku-luvalova*   *dabwa-na*   *taytu;*   *ku-yawala d.t.;*
        thou throw   head his   taytu   thou heap up

   ku-luvataulo d.t.;   *ku-yogugoula d.t.;*   *ku-yokopalarita d.t.;*
   thou heap high   thou heap together   thou gather up

   ku-yokulukwala d.t.
   thou like *yokulukwala* creeper

After the *dogina* the magician returns again to the *u'ula*.

GENERAL COMMENTARY

A. B. *Sociological and Ritual Context:* these are identical with the other formulae of growth magic.

C. *Structure:* tripartite, and here we have a real main part with the key-word, uttered at the end of the *u'ula*, carried on to and throughout it. Here also we meet with the phenomenon of the leading word, that is, a word with which the spell starts and which forms the kernel of the key expression. This word here is one of the names by which the millipede is known.

D. *Dogmatic Context:* the main aim of this spell which is called *kaylavala dabana taytu*, 'the throwing (or making) of the head (the foliage) of the taytu', is to produce a rich growth of foliage. The object addressed is the taytu itself. Thus, in the main part, the taytu is referred to by the colloquial second person 'thy head, O taytu', 'thy foliage, O taytu' and so on, and all the inventory expressions refer also to it. Although the structure of verse 6 is not quite as clear, it seems that the imperative refers to the plant, and I have thus translated it in the free version. The animal here invoked is the millipede. It is addressed by the term *kaybwagina*, with slight variants and added suffixes. *Kaybwagina* the natives told me means *mitakaybwagina*, which, as far as I was able to ascertain, is an epithet for the millipede, for which the usual word is *mwanita*. Literally *mita* or *mitu*, 'eye', *kaybwagina*, 'stinking'. This may be "the animal with the stinking eye" or one that makes the eye rot. This latter because if some of the fluid which the millipede emits touches the eye this becomes inflamed and, as the native told me, might even perish. This little animal seems to have a strong appeal to the native imagination, for it is also named in rain magic. The myth on which the rain magic is based tells us that *Bopadagu*, the mother of rain and of its magic, also gave birth to the millipede. In rain magic the little worm is named because of its black colouring (cf. Ch. II, Sec. 7), here because of its quickness. As the natives put it: *tado'u, pela sene nanakwa bi-sakauli*, 'we call on it for it very quickly runs'. Its association with rain, however, probably also makes it valuable in this magic, which indirectly is the magic of fertility. The natives do not seem to believe it is active in producing the foliage of the taytu. In fact, if asked directly they deny it and give the above answer, that it is invoked because of its quickness. Verses 2 to 4 might give us the impression that the millipede is invoked in order to cover the space between the promontory of Kabulukwaywaya near the village of Kuluvitu, and the cape of Dulata which is near the beach of Laba'i, with rich foliage. But here again the phraseology seems to be rather conceived as a verbal simile which should produce a magical effect, rather than as a direct order to the millipede. The construction of the main part proves this almost conclusively. There we have the key expression 'the millipede throws' and in juxtaposition with it the expressions 'thy head, O taytu', 'thy leaves, O taytu' and so on. Such magical juxtapositions are always meant to produce the effect immediately. The inventory words, here the various parts of the taytu, are the objects acted upon. The action of the millipede, its quickness, is the verbal influence which is felt to be active. In the free translation I have said: "Thy head, O taytu, shoots along as the millipede shoots along." I have chosen the verb 'to shoot' in order to obviate the danger of conceiving the word 'to throw' as a transitive verb.

E. *Mode of Recitation:* the formula is chanted loudly, rhythmically, with a pronouncedly melodious intonation.

LINGUISTIC COMMENTARY

1. The suffixes *-ga* and *m* attached to the word *kaybwagina* are probably abbreviations of *naga*, 'now' (the same root as *lagayle*, 'to-day'), and *nam*, a somewhat indeterminate temporal particle. In the free translation I have given these as "here now . . . here ever", but have not rendered them in the interlineal version.

2, 3, 4. The verbs *luvake'i*, *luvayumila* are compounded of the root *lova = lavi* or *la'i*, 'to throw'. The suffix *-ke'i* is the directive 'throw at'. *Yumila* in the compound *luvayumila* is a verb 'to fetch back'.

5. The inventory words enumerated here are all parts of the taytu (cf. Part V, Div. III, §§ 3–8), including the ordinary words for 'head' and 'leaf'. They are all provided with the second possessive pronoun which is either in the form of nearest possession *-m* or the second nearest possession *kam* (cf. Div. XII, §§ 3–7).

6. The *dogina* consists of a series of verbs in the second person imperative, each repeated with the same noun, *dabwa-na taytu*, 'head of taytu'. Whether the imperative refers to the noun juxtaposed is not quite clear. Since the verbs here seem to be intransitive, this view seems likely and I have adopted it in the free translation. The verbs all refer directly to the process of growth which is stimulated by this magic. The meaning of the verbs is at first general: *luvalova*, 'to throw, to shoot up'; *luvataulo*, compounded of *luva*, 'to throw', *taulo*, 'to stand up', 'to heap up'. As the natives put it in commenting on it: *i-vagi sipumtala, bila orokaywa; i-vagi sipumuwela, bila orokaywa*, 'It makes one mop of leaves which goes up; it makes another mop of leaves which goes up.' In other words, 'it heaps one mop of leaves above the other', and so it was translated in the free version. *Sipum-* is a classificatory particle of rare usage applied to clusters of yams and other crops as well as to bunches of leaves. *Kuyawala* (which like most verbs beginning with *ku-* forms its second person singular by the use of its root form) was translated to me: *taytu i-gigupoula*, 'the taytu forms big mops foliage'. *Yogugoula* obviously means also 'to close', *yo-*, formative of leaves, *gugoula*, apophonic variation of *gugula*, 'heap'. *Yokopalarita* was translated *sene bidubadu kuyawala*, 'their many mops of foliage', the word *kuyawala* being used here with a nominal sense. *Yokulukwala* was commented upon: *wotunu ola odila, sene bidubadu kuyawala*, 'creeper in the bush, very many mops (to it)'. This last word therefore sympathetically invites the taytu to form a rich foliage.

FORMULA 18
(Ch. IV, Sec. 2)

I. 1. *Kapari naga, kaparim* (repeated) *Kabulukwaywaya!*
    spider   now   spider   (a promontory)

2. *Ku-sayboda*   *Kabulukwaywaya,*   *ku-saypatu*   *Bomlu'ebila;*
    thou cover up   (a promontory)   thou close up   (sacred grove)

    ku-sayboda   *Bomlu'ebila,*   *ku-saypatu*
    thou cover up   (sacred grove)   thou close up

    Kabulukwaywaya!   *Kapari sayboda!*
    (a promontory)   spider   cover up

II. 3. *Kapari sayboda* (repeated)
     spider   cover up

     Taytu kapari sayboda;
     taytu   spider   cover up

     kam kapulupwalala taytu kapari sayboda;
     thy   open space   taytu spider   cover up

     kam malaga   taytu kapari sayboda;
     thy   bare soil   taytu spider   cover up

     kam libu   taytu kapari sayboda;
     thy   dry twig   taytu spider   cover up

(Then the same phrase is repeated, inserting in the place of the inventory words (*kapulupwalala, malaga*) the following words: *kamkokola, kavatam, kaysalu, kamtuya, kaybudi, kaynutatala, tula, yeye'i, tukulumwala, karivisi, tamkwaluma, kaluvalova, kayvaliluwa.*)

After this the third part, *dogina*, of the foregoing formula, beginning with the words *Ku-luvalova dabwa-na taytu*, is recited. Then the magician returns to the *u'ula* of the present spell, finishing with the words *Kapari sayboda!*

GENERAL COMMENTARY

A. B. *Sociological and Ritual Context:* this spell is symmetrical with the previous one in almost every respect and has the same cultural and ritual context.

C. *Structure:* tripartite, with the real *tapwana* which, incidentally, has a much richer set of inventory words than Formula 17, and with the same *dogina* as that spell, a communistic feature which characterises many cognate spells.

D. *Dogmatic Context:* the taytu is again addressed and the second person runs through the *tapwana* and *dogina*. We could repeat about the spider very much what was said about the millipede, except that this insect has no mythological pedigree. The natives are quite clear that the magical power of the name 'spider', the leading word of the whole spell, is verbal only. "As the spider spins his web, so should the taytu plant make new branches," is a translation I find among my notes of a statement made by the natives. The name of this spell is *kasayboda*: *ka-*, instrumental prefix, *say-*, formative of static completion, *-boda*, 'to cover up', hence 'the covering spell'.

E. *Mode of Recitation:* as are most of these growth magic spells, it is chanted loudly over the gardens.

LINGUISTIC COMMENTARY

1. For *naga*, 'then' (*-m*), see my commentary on Formula 17, verse 1. The geographical compass from Kabulukwaywaya to Bomlu'ebila embraces the north-western shore, Kabulukwaywaya being a promontory east of Laba'i, Bomlu'ebila a sacred grove near the village of Lu'ebila (obviously *bom* stands for *boma*, 'tabooed grove').

2. *Sayboda*: *say-*, formative of static completion, literally 'sit', 'cover'; *saypatu*, 'sit, cover', 'close up'. It really means 'thoroughly to cover', 'thoroughly to close up'.

3. In the main part we have the key-word *kapari sayboda*, 'the spider covers up', repeated in a complex phrase with a number of inventory words. *Kam kapulupwalala taytu kapari sayboda*, 'thy open space, O taytu, the spider covers up': *kapulupwalala* from *pwala*, 'a hole', *kapulu* from *kapwala*, 'covering', 'a hole in the covering', 'a hole in the green surface of the garden'. The expression 'thy open space' means, therefore, 'the open space between thy branches, O taytu'. In the free translation I have tried to combine literal exactness with intelligibility by placing the second in explanatory opposition to the first: "Thy open space, the open space between thy branches, O taytu, the spider covers up." Apart from the first three words—*kapulupwalala*, which has just been explained, *malaga*, which is the space on the ground between the plants, and *libu*, which means the dry twigs separating trees or poles—the remaining words are identical with the list which we find in Formula 10, verse 3, and which has been fully commented on (cf. Part V, Div. VI, § 40; cf. also Div. VIII, § 20). In the free translation I have retained the native words side by side with their English equivalents.

FORMULA 19
(Ch. IV, Sec. 3)

I. 1.
Kaytala	*guluwaga*	*pwoyliya,*
one (w.l.)	my canoe-load	plenty
kwaywela	*guluwaga*	*pwoyliya,*
second (w.l.)	my canoe-load	plenty

kwaytolula g.p.,   *kwayvasila g.p.,*
third (w.l.)   fourth (w.l.)

kwaylimala g.p.   *kaduvatula g.p.,*   *kaduvayyu g.p.,*
fifth (w.l.)   tenth (w.l.)   twentieth (w.l.)

kaduvatolu g.p.,   *kaduvavasi g.p.,*   *kaluvalima g.p.*
thirtieth   fortieth   fiftieth

2. *Ku-ula'i*   *taytu*   *yam,*   *ku'ula'i*   *taytu*   *bogi,*
throw in   taytu   day   throw in   taytu   night

   ku-ula'i   *bi-wokwo.*
   throw in   he might be over

3. *Kam*   *kwoymamalu*   *taytu,*   *kammalu-m;*
thy   fetching back   taytu   fetching back thine

   kam   *kwatatouya*   *taytu,*   *katitoyay-m;*
   thy   hurrying   taytu   hurrying thine

   kam   *kapulupwala*   *taytu*   *kapwalay-m.*
   thy   breaking forth   taytu   breaking forth thine

Taytu   *poriyama,*   *taytu*   *poriya*   *poriyama!*
taytu   plentiful   taytu   plenty   plentiful

II. 4. *Taytu*   *poriyama,*   *taytu*   *poriya*   *poriyama;*
taytu   plentiful   taytu   plenty   plentiful

   nakoya   *poriyama,*   *taytu*   *poriya*   *poriyama;*
   (variety of taytu)   plentiful   taytu   plenty   plentiful

   sakaya p.,t.p.p.;   *nabugwa p.,t.p.p.*
   (variety of taytu)   (variety of taytu)

   kwoyma p.,t.p.p.
   (variety of taytu)

III. 5. *I-kopwoy-m*   *taytu*   *Tokuwabu,*
he hug thee   taytu   (an ancestor of Bagido'u, dead)

   I-vaysali-m   *kaduwala.*
   he mortuary-dance thee   cross-roads (?)

After that the *u'ula* is recited again.

GENERAL COMMENTARY

A. B. *Sociological and Ritual Context:* remain the same.

C. *Structure:* tripartite with a long *u'ula*, a short *tapwana* and a rudimentary *dogina*.

D. *Dogmatic Context:* here again the main background is the same. The taytu is addressed directly in the second verse, and then again in the third, and throughout the main part, verse 4, and in the *dogina* where the second person is shown by the *-m*, possessive pronoun of direct address. The only unusual feature in this spell is its beginning, where the magical name is not that of an animal or plant, but an inanimate object, a canoe, loaded no doubt with yams. The native commentary on the leading word *pwoyliya* (see commentary to v. 1), the name of this spell, *vapuli*, 'making the sprout and making it burst into tubers', the native statement about the aim of this magic (*bivagi bwanawa, bi-ta-basi*, 'it (the magic) will produce young taytu tubers, we shall thin them out')—all fit well into one another. In the last part we have again the characteristic elements of exaggeration, the introduction of the supernatural, and the oblique indirect statement. The taytu is to be so beautiful that Tokuwabu, a mythical personality, or perhaps an ancestral spirit, a previous wielder of this magic (note, however, that his name does not appear on the ancestral list in M.F. 2), is represented as hugging it, blessing it in the next world, and dancing the mortuary dance of affection on the cross-roads. An alternative explanation given to me was that *kaduwala* is not 'cross-roads', but a personal name of another dead hero or magician, in which case we would have "Tokuwabu hugs thee, Kaduwala dances for thee".

E. *Mode of Recitation:* same as in the other formulae of growth magic.

LINGUISTIC COMMENTARY

1. This verse was not clearly analysed by my native interpreters. There can, however, be little doubt that *guluwaga* equals *agu la waga*, or perhaps *gula waga* (*yaygula waga*) and means 'my canoe'. If, as is more likely, it is merely a contraction of *yaygula waga*, this would be a non-grammatical magical form of 'my canoe'. If on the other hand it were *agu*, it would mean 'the food contents of my canoe'. In translating it 'my canoe-load' a compromise has been struck. *Pwoyliya* has been commented upon by the natives: *pwoyliya: megwa la keda; pwelia biga: nani, bi-nanakwa buyagu; boge i-pwelia buyagu*. 'Pwoyliya, the way of magic; *pwelia*, speech (ordinary speech)—(this means) quickly, so that it might be quick the garden; (we say) already it is quick the garden'. Thus the word is equated with 'quickening the garden', 'quick ripening'. In conjunction with the title of this spell, *va-puli*, it is obvious that the words *pwelia* and *puli* are apophonic variants of the same root, *puri, puripuri*, 'to swarm', 'to break forth'. It refers to the action of breaking forth into tubers, producing many small young tubers (*bwanawa*) (cf. D. and also Text 82, in Part V, Div. XI, § 12). Here the word conveys the idea of abundance, fullness, multitude of tubers; and the word 'plenty' seemed most appropriate in conjunction with canoe-load. In the free version I translated this word and its cognates by "plenty", "break forth", "break forth again and again". The long tedious enumeration one

after the other of the canoe-loads of plenty in the *u'ula* magically produces the effect of riches, abundance.

2. *Ku-ula'i* = *ku-ulavi*: *lavi*, 'throw', *ula'i*, a variation of *valavi*, with *va-* causative, 'to throw another', 'to break into tubers', a verb almost synonymous with *puri*. My native informant equated *ku-ula'i* with *kukabina'i*, the ordinary word for 'sprouting, growing'. He added: "The roots of taytu already they penetrate into the soil." The verb *ku-ula'i* is repeated here with a temporal cycle 'night and day until it is done'.

3. A rhythmic invocation to return, to hurry, to break forth quickly. *Kwoymamalu*, *kammalu-* are derived from *kaymali*, 'to fetch back', in free translation "thy return". *Kwatatouya*, the state of being in a hurry, was commented upon by the natives with the expression: *tokatatouya yoku*, 'you are a speeder-up', used when one man complains to another of hurrying. In free translation, "Thy hastening, O taytu, O hasten to us." *Kapulupwala* was commented upon by the adverb *nanakwa*, 'quickly'. It obviously designates haste. I find a further comment written in English "as when a man wishes to get there quickly". I have rendered it in the interlineal version by 'impatience'. There is a possibility, however, that it is derived from *pwari*, *puri*, the same word that we have as leading word in this spell, 'to burst forth'. To do justice to both hypotheses, I have in the free version adopted the second hypothesis "thy breaking forth into a multitude of bunches".

4. The key expression is a compound of the word taytu, which needs no commentary, and the verb *poriya*, which obviously is identical with *pwoyliya*, with the durative *-ma* suffixed (cf. commentary to M.F. 13, v. 3). The key expression here means 'taytu plentiful, taytu plenty plentiful'. In free translation I have combined the meaning of *puri*, 'to break forth', with the idea of plenty in "taytu breaking forth again and again". The key expression is repeated with the list of several varieties of taytu, some of which we meet in other spells (M.F. 16 and 20). All these varieties of taytu are specially hard-growing and difficult to cultivate successfully (cf. Ch. IV, Sec. 2).

Nakoya: described thus by native informants: *nakoya: taytu yagava-na makawala simsimwaya*, 'nakoya (is) taytu leaves his (= whose leaves are) like sweet potatoes' (i.e. leaves as luxuriant as those of sweet potatoes). They also told me that this variety produces small tubers; the seed tuber has to be planted very deeply, but gradually it produces more and more tubers above, till a hillock is raised. *Sakaya:* this seems to be the same type of taytu as last mentioned, the *nakoya*, and so also is *kwoyma*. *Nabugwa* (for literal meaning, see commentary on M.F.

16, v. 2). Native commentary ran: *nabugwa: taytu sene unu'unu o tapwa-la, mtage sene i-kugwo o lumwale-la,* 'the *nabugwa* (is a variety of) taytu (which has) very (much) hair in covering (= outside—on its skin), indeed (but) very (much) he first (rate) in inside' (cf. Part V, Div. III, § 19). The natives also told me that *nabugwa* is a very big taytu which invariably raises hillocks. The main characteristics of these tubers are that they are good to eat and desirable, but difficult of growth; yet, when they thrive, they give good results and produce an effect of richness and wealth by swelling under the surface and making mounds round the stem. I should like to add that all this information must be regarded as based exclusively on native statement, since I was not able to check it by personal observation.

FORMULA 20
(Ch. IV, Sec. 3)

Taytu	*mamalo,*	*ku-mamalu-ga;*
taytu	return	thou return indeed

nakoya	*taytu*	*mamalo,*	*ku-mamalu-ga;*
(variety of taytu)	taytu	return	thou return indeed

nabugwa t.m.,k.;	*sakaya t.m., k.;*	*nonoma t.m.,k.;*
(variety of taytu)	(variety of taytu)	(variety of taytu)

kwoyma t.m.,k.
(variety of taytu)

GENERAL COMMENTARY

A. B. *Sociological and Ritual Context:* remain the same.

C. *Structure:* this is a short formula, the structure of which is definitely that of a *tapwana*, since we have an enumeration of inventory words accompanied by a key-word.

D. *Dogmatic Context:* obviously here the formula is addressed to the taytu which figures in the second person. *Ku-mamalu-ga,* 'thou return indeed'. The name of the spell is *kammamalu,* 'fetching back', and it functions as a reinforcement of the previous formula.

E. *Mode of Recitation:* same as in all growth magic.

LINGUISTIC COMMENTARY

The expression *mamalo, ku-mamalu-ga* refers obviously to the action also defined in the title 'the fetching back, 'the bringing of the taytu'. The root *mamalo* signifies 'return'. *Kammamala* is best known from the words of ordinary speech: *kaymali,* 'to fetch back', also used in the form *kaviyumali.* The form *ku-mamalu-ga*: the second person with the emphatic suffix -*ga* added and the apophonic variation of *mamalo* into *mamalu.* For the varieties of taytu, see Formula 19. *Nonoma* is another variety on which I received no commentary, and which does not appear in Formula 19. Obviously the two lists should be the same, and the omission of one variety from Formula 19 was due to a memory lapse on the part of my informant, Bagido'u. I am, however, reproducing all formulae exactly as they were given to me. Throughout Trobriand magic, as the reader will have noted, the sequence as well as the completeness of inventory words present a considerable latitude.

FORMULA 21

(Ch. IV, Sec. 3)

I. 1. *Gelu*   *naga,*   *gelunem,*   *gelunem*   *o*   *bomatu!*
       bush-hen   now   bush-hen   bush-hen   in   north-east wind

    2. *Ku-lola*   *o*   *bomatu,*   *ku-lake'i*   *wa*
       thou moor   in   north-east wind   thou moor at   in

       youyo.
       south-west wind

    3. *Gelu*   *naga,*   *gelunem,*   *gelunem*   *wa*   *youyo!*
       bush-hen   now   bush-hen   bush-hen   in   south-west wind

    4. *Ku-lola*   *wa*   *youyo*   *ku-lake'i*   *o*
       thou moor   in   south-west wind   thou moor at   in

       bomatu.   *Gelune'i*   *i-lola!*
       north-east wind   bush-hen   he moor

II. 5. *Gelune'i*   *i-lola;*
       bush-hen   he moor

       ula   *taytu*   *gelune'i*   *i-lola;*
       my   taytu   bush-hen   he moor

       kam   *sobula*   *taytu*   *gelune'i*   *i-lola;*
       thy   shoot   taytu   bush-hen   he moor

       kam   *silisilata*   *taytu*   *gelune'i*   *i-lola;*
       thy   underground shoot   taytu   bush-hen   he moor

       gedene-la   *taytu*   *gelune'i*   *i-lola;*
       root-stalk his   taytu   bush-hen   he moor

       kayluwali-m   *taytu*   *gelune'i*   *i-lola;*
       roots thine   taytu   bush-hen   he moor

       kam   *kibwa'u*   *taytu*   *gelune'i*   *i-lola;*
       thy   black surface   taytu   bush-hen   he moor

       kam   *sayada*   *taytu*   *gelune'i*   *i-lola.*
       thy   scratched spot   taytu   bush-hen   he moor

III. 6. *I-lola*   *taytu,*   *i-lalola,*   *i-lolavagasi.*
        he moor   taytu   he moor firmly   he moor definitely

After this the *u'ula* is recited again.

GENERAL COMMENTARY

A. B. *Sociological and Ritual Context:* remain the same.

C. *Structure:* typical tripartite formula with a leading word recurring in the first and second part and in the *dogina*. This latter is very short indeed, consisting only of four words.

D. *Dogmatic Context:* this spell, which is the third in the series directed at the growth of the roots, is called *kasaylola*, 'the spell which definitely anchors the roots', or *talola silisilata*, 'the anchoring of the new root'. The leading word is the name of a bush-hen. Whether *gelu* designates a variety of the bush-hen or whether it is a magical epithet for it I was not able to decide on the basis of the statements I received. It invokes the bush-hen because this bird, when nesting, constructs large mounds in the ground. So far it functions magically in the same way as do the millipede and the spider. But we must also remember that it is from the bush-hen's nest that one of the main ingredients in the standard mixture used with the *vatuvi* formula is taken. The meat as well as the eggs of the bush-hen are taboo to the magician. For the rest this spell is meant for the ears of the taytu which is directly addressed in the second person in the main part and referred to in the third person in the last part.

E. *Mode of Recitation:* is the same as in all growth magic.

LINGUISTIC COMMENTARY

1–4. The bush-hen here again is invoked with the particles *naga* and *-m*, 'now' and 'then', freely translated "here now . . . here ever" (cf. M.F. 17 and 18). In verses 2–4 the bush-hen is invoked with the two winds which, to the natives, form the fundamental opposite points of the compass, the north-east and the south-west.

5. Among the inventory words we have only to mention *kayluwali*, equivalent to *kaynavari*, the ordinary expression for 'roots' in general. *Kibwa'u* was commented upon: *kibwa'u, tapwala taytu bi-bwabwa'u*, '*kibwa'u* we say when the surface of the taytu has become dark'. According to my informants this is a bad symptom, hence in free translation "Thy black blight, O taytu". *Sayada* is the raw spot on the young tuber accidentally scratched during weeding or thinning. It has to be mentioned here because, as the natives say, if such a scratch is not mentioned, the taytu will suffer from this wound, but if the scratch is mentioned, no harm will come of it. In free translation "thy wounded sides". For the other expressions compare Part V (Div. III, §§ 3–8).

6. The short *dogina* simply reiterates the word 'to moor', 'to

anchor', with increasing strength: *lalola* simply reduplicated, and *lolavagasi*, suffix *-vagasi* of circumstantiality and finality. This *dogina* is typical of the simple positive statement characteristic of magic. This is what might be called a 'bare' magical metaphor, in which a simple affirmation of a fact produces the fact. It is important not to imagine such verbal statements as transitive in the direct sense. The magician does not say 'anchor!', nor does he command any agency 'to anchor' the roots of taytu. He merely affirms that the roots are already anchored and that, in the magical universe of discourse, produces the effect of making the roots anchor.

FORMULA 22
(Ch. IV, Sec. 4)

1. *Tudava-tu,*   *Tu-tudava* (repeated)
   (mythical hero)

   Malita-ma,   *Mali-malita* (repeated)
   (mythical hero)

2. *I-pela*   *lilu*   *o*   *Muyuwa;*
   he jump   sun   in   (Woodlark Island)

3. *A-sivilay-m,*   *a-sitaney-m!*
   I sit-turn thee   I sit-sweep thee

4. *A-da'uma*   *buyagu*   *la*   *uri;*   *a-da'uma*   *buyagu*
   I call on   garden-site   his   taro   I call on   garden-site

   la   *taytu.*
   his   taytu

5. *Buribwari*   *karitana'i.*
   fish-hawk   hover

GENERAL COMMENTARY

A. *Sociological Context:* in this and the following spells of private magic the sociological context is obviously very much simpler, The spell is recited by the owner of the garden, or by a paid practitioner on his behalf; the owner is invariably present when the rite is carried out. The reason why I insisted so much on the importance of the sociological and cultural context of public magic is that I wanted to show that this magic, though very often carried out by the magician alone, is yet of such a character and performed under such circumstances that most men know the spell, are aware of its performance, are very keen that it should be properly recited and the rite impeccably carried out, so that the magic may produce its effect. All these conditions are obviously fulfilled here when the person interested either recites or hears the magic.

B. *Ritual Context:* important; it is recited over a basketful of seed yams (*yagogu*) apparently without any manual act to accompany it.

C. *Structure:* simple, though a tripartite structure might be read into it: verses 1 and 2 being the foundation, 3 and 4 the main part, and verse 5 a brief *dogina.*

D. *Dogmatic Context:* we have here the mention of the two mythological heroes, Tudava and Malita (cf. Ch. I, Sec. 7) and in verse 2 a brief reference to the eastern island, Muyuwa (Woodlark Island). The expression *o Muyuwa* really describes the whole eastern archipelago, a part of the world where the traditional exploits of Tudava are most fully described in the relevant myths. Verse 3 shows that here again it is the magician himself (he speaks in the first person) who blesses the crops, and the name of Tudava has only to exercise a sympathetic influence. What the fish-hawk does in this spell is difficult to decide. This bird is often associated with fish magic and perhaps carries implications of plenty.

E. *Mode of Recitation:* the spell is chanted melodiously. The quaint embroiderings on the names Tudava and Malita are repeated several times.

LINGUISTIC COMMENTARY

2. *Pela,* 'to jump', when used with the word 'sun' means 'to rise'.

3. The compounds *sivilay-m, sitaney-m* are built on the ordinary pattern of word formation. The formative *si-,* 'to sit', being often compounded with other words (cf. the unusual compound *silavila* in Formula 5, v. 1). Hence the difference in literal rendering and free translation.

4. *A-da'uma,* apophonic variety of *do'u,* 'to call', with the durative suffix *-ma.*

5. *Buribwari* is the word for fish-hawk, as well as for the painted, carved board of a canoe.

FORMULA 23
(Ch. IV, Sec. 4)

I. 1. *Kalupo'isi,*   *po'isi;*   *kalupomala,*   *pomala* (repeated)
   (magical) cutting   cutting   (magical return)   return

   2. *Kalupo'isi*   *yagogu,*   *kalupomala*   *taytu* (repeated)
   (magical) cutting   seed yam   (magical return)   taytu

II. 3. *I-tokaywo*   *taytu,*   *i-ko'ulu*   *taytu,*   *i-kolaluma*
    he stand up   taytu   he turn round (?)   taytu   he lift-soil (?)
    taytu.
    taytu

4. *I-guba'i tamu-m,*   *kolilami koga-m,*   *kwoyta'uma*
   he raise stalk thine   lift   root thine   push up

   bune-m,   *o lopou-la ula bagula.*
   thy young tubers   in belly his my garden

5. *I-milakaydatutu*   *lopou-la ula bagula;*
   he liken pounding-board   belly his my garden

   i-milakaydawaga   *lopou-la ula bagula;*
   he liken trimming-board   belly his my garden

   i-bisikay-m ginuvavarya   *lopou-la ula bagula.*
   he pierce at mollusc-holes   belly his my garden

III. 6. *Ba-la*   *o valu.*
   I might go   in village

GENERAL COMMENTARY

A. *Sociological Context:* compare commentary to the previous spell.

B. *Ritual Context:* this spell is chanted over seed yams distributed over a square in the gardens.

C. *Structure:* it has no very clear structure, but we have divided it into three parts which can be regarded as *u'ula, tapwana* and *dogina.*

D. *Dogmatic Context:* this spell, as impersonal as any which we have examined, contains the typical statements of magical metaphor, i.e. affirmation uttered about the taytu which is the subject-matter of this spell.

E. *Mode of Recitation:* chanted in a loud voice.

LINGUISTIC COMMENTARY

1. *Kalupo'isi, kalupomala:* the significant part of these words is made up of the verbal roots *isi* and *mala* respectively. The first has the meaning of 'cutting' or 'breaking through', the second of 'returning' (cf. commentary to M.F. 20). The prefixed part *kalupo-* is not so easy to explain, as is natural, since it supplies what might be called the "magical wrapping" of both roots. Two alternatives are possible: (1) it is composed of the instrumental prefix *kay-, ka-,* with the root *lupo, lupi,* 'to lift'. On the magical principle of juxtaposition of roots and of heaping up of meanings the full word would then mean something like 'effective lifting and cutting', 'effective lifting and returning'. (2) On the other hand, and more probably, the word is simply compounded of *kalu,* 'his', and prefix *po-,* connected with *pwa-, pwana,* 'hole'. This word is perhaps etymologically

allied to *pwaypwaya*, 'the ground', but in any case it would add to the root meaning of the word the idea of cutting a hole in the ground, of returning from the ground. Thus we have interpreted the prefix *kalupo-* in free translation: "O crops breaking through from the soil," "O crops returning from the soil." (*N.B.*—I should like to say that the second word *kalupomala* might be simply regarded as compounded of *kalu* and *pomala* standing for *bomala*, 'taboo'. This would be a tempting hypothesis especially as the word *pomala* actually exists in some Oceanic and Indonesian languages. But since *p* and *b* are never equivalent there are not the slightest grounds for treating *kalupomala* as 'his taboo'.)

2. This verse confirms the above interpretation because the cutting through here is associated with the seed yam and the return is coupled with the word for the full crops.

3. The verb *ko'ulu* is probably a variant of *ki'ulu*, 'to lift', 'to turn round'. *Kolaluma* refers, as I was told, to the taytu coming out of the soil.

4. We have here another word, *kolilami*, probably connected with *kolaluma* of the previous sentence, and referring here, as my informants told me, to the soil lifted by the roots of the taytu. This verse is interesting in that the verb in the first phrase is in the third person indicative, in the second we have merely a root, in the third probably an imperative. The natives explained to me the word *kwoyta'uma* as being *megwa la keda*, 'magic his road', 'magical expression'; and said that it corresponds to *kukwa'uma*, *kukwa'u*, *kuma'i*, 'take', 'bring'. Here again it is difficult to decide which is the agency addressed or spoken of. I should say that the natives conceive that there is some magical force which raises the stalk, lifts the root, and pushes up the young taytu tuber, and that this magical force is stimulated verbally.

5. The inside of the garden is here told to become as 'smooth' as the pounding-board, as a trimming-board. Both the idea of smoothness and the comparison are obviously here mere metaphors. Since the spell is recited over the garden when it is still bare and smooth and the smoother it is the better the work and the prospects, we can understand the magical indication. In the last line of this verse the word *bisikay-m* is the directed transitive form of *basi*, 'it pierces at thee', 'it makes holes into thee'. Reference is probably made to the holes produced in thinning. The comparison of the holes thus made with the holes of the *ginuvavarya*, a mollusc which riddles the black, greasy ooze of the mangrove swamp at low tide, is characteristic of the verbal metaphor drawn from sympathetic elements in the animal world.

FORMULA 24
(Ch. IV, Sec. 4)

I. 1. *Taytu   ki'u'i,   ki'u'i* (repeated) *taytu   kilogo,*
      taytu   pluck off   pluck off   taytu   pull out
      kilogo (repeated).
      pull out (?)

2. *Popo'u,   sasoka.*
   earth-swelling (?)   (a fruit tree)

II. 3. *Gala   i-viyaka   tapwa-la   kaga,   i-viyaka   tapwa-la*
       not   he big   main part his   (a ficus)   he big   main part his
       ula   taytu;
       my   taytu

       gala   i-viyaka   tapwa-la   kirima,   i-viyaka   tapwa-la
       not   he big   main part his   (a ficus)   he big   main part his
       ula   taytu;
       my   taytu

       g.i.t.   bwabwaga, i.t.u.t.;   g.i.t.   kaybwibwi, i.t.u.t.;
                 (a ficus)   pandanus

       g.i.t.   kaybu'a, i.t.u.t.;   g.i.t.   vayoulo, i.t.u.t.
                 coral boulder   acacia

4. *Gala   mata-m,   mata-m   kubwana;*
   not   eye thine   eye thine   morning-star

   gala   mata-m,   mata-m   youla'ula.
   not   eye thine   eye thine   (a white flower)

5. *I-guba'i   tamu-m,   kolilami   koga-m,*
   he raise   stalk thine   lift   root thine

   kwoyta'uma   bune-m,   o   lopou-la   ula   bagula.
   push up   thy young tubers   in   belly his   my   garden

6. *I-milakaydatutu   lopou-la   ula   bagula;*
   he liken pounding-board   belly his   my   garden

   i-milakaydawaga   lopou-la   ula   bagula;
   he liken trimming-board   belly his   my   garden

   i-bisikay-m   ginuvavarya   lopou-la   ula   bagula.
   he pierce at   mollusc-holes   belly his   my   garden

III. 7. *Ba-la   o   valu.*
        I might go   in   village

GENERAL COMMENTARY

A. *Sociological Context:* same as that of other private garden magic.

B. *Ritual Context:* recited over a digging-stick used in planting, more especially in thinning.

C. *Structure:* normal. The *dogina* as well as the last verse of the *tapwana* is identical with that of the previous formula.

D. *Dogmatic Context:* the classical one of magic. The taytu figures throughout and is stimulated to prodigies of growth by the exaggerated comparisons juxtaposed. This formula is called *sodayma* or *kabidabida*. In the word *sodayma* the prefix *so-*, probably derived from the word for 'companion', *so-la*, 'companion his', 'the companion spell of the digging-stick'. The alternative name *kabidabida* derived from *bidabida*, 'soil, sod' (cf. Part V, Div. I, § 5), was thus commented upon: *kabidabida: ta-bisibasi, ta-dubwari taytu, deli pwaypwaya*, 'The *kabidabida* spell: we thin out, we cover up the taytu with soil.' Similarly in some other private garden magic recited over an axe, the name *sokema* would mean 'companion spell of the axe'.

E. *Mode of Recitation:* chanted in a loud voice.

LINGUISTIC COMMENTARY

1. *Ki'u'i*, 'to pluck off', a word of ordinary speech. *Kilogo*, probably from *kiligini*, 'to pull out'. This phrase obviously refers to *basi*, 'the act of thinning out', to the plucking off and pulling out of some of the tubers.

2. Mentions two large-size substances the translations of which are tentative.

3. Is built up on the typical negative comparison pattern. It is a magical invocation referring to the taytu tuber; exhorting it to swell to the size of one or other of the three ficus species here mentioned, to the size of the large pandanus, a coral boulder, or an acacia tree. In the free translation I have left "body of my taytu" in order to preserve the flavour of the native spell. Some of the substances mentioned are, as we know from Chapter II (Sec. 4), used in the magical mixture.

4. Is again a negative comparison, built on a simpler pattern.
From 5 to the end the formula is identical with the previous one.

FORMULA 24A
(Ch. IV, Sec. 4)

1. *Le-wa'i* (repeat),   *le-ma'i* (repeat);
   he did move thither he did move hither

   ba-kabi,   *ba-sayli.*
   I might get hold I might place

2. *I-wa'i*   *bugo* *ula* *tula;*
   he move thither mould my boundary stick

i-wawa'i   *bugo   ula   taytu.*
he move and move thither   mould   my   taytu

3. *Bi-kanamo*   *o*   *lopou-la*   *ula*   *bagula.*
   he might recline   in   belly his   my   garden

GENERAL COMMENTARY

A. *Sociological Context:* same as in all formulae of private magic
(cf. M.F. 22, 23 and 24).

B. *Ritual Context:* the spell is recited over a boundary stick,
while this is rubbed into the ground so that it leaves its imprint
(vv. 1 and 2).

C. *Structure:* the magical repetitions in verse 1; the similies in
verse 2, with the crescendo of reduplication in the second phrase;
the typical affirmation of the concluding sentence (v. 3) are patent
in the structure of this simple spell.

D. *Dogmatic Context:* the typical verbal commentary on the ritual
act implies indirectly the aim of the magic—that is, the stability of
the garden. The belief that by rubbing the boundary stick into the
ground and making it sit firmly in its bed the taytu will be induced
to settle firmly in the earth is expressed in verse 2. Verse 3 is a
general impersonal blessing through the affirmation of stability, the
resting and reclining of the garden.

E. *Mode of Recitation:* the spell is chanted.

LINGUISTIC COMMENTARY

1. The roots *wa* and *ma* are among the most hard-worked of
ordinary speech; they describe motion away thither and towards
hither. Here they are probably a verbal expression of the rite—
the rubbing of the *tula* into the ground. Hence in free translation
"move that way, come this way". The words "I might get hold
of, I might place" also probably refer to the manipulation of
the stick.

2. The symmetrical repetition can probably be interpreted: "as
the mould is left by my boundary stick (fast and firm), even more so
(hence the reduplication) is the mould of my taytu (fast and firm)".
Hence in free translation the word of motion *wa* is interpreted by
is effect: "to dig in".

FORMULA 25
(Ch. V, Sec. 2)

I. 1. *Bwato*   *naga,*   *bwatam,*   *bwatam*   *o*   *bomatu!*
      full moon   now   full moon   full moon   in   N.E. wind

   2. *Ku-pipila*   *o*   *bomatu,*   *ku-pipila-ke'i*   *wa*
      thou round off   in   N.E. wind   thou round off at   in

youyo;   ku-pipila   wa youyo,   ku-pipila-ke'i
S.W. wind thou round off in S.W. wind thou round off at

o   bomatu.   Uri   pipila!
in N.E. wind   taro   round off

II. 3. *Uri   pipila* (repeated) *umdu-la   agu uri, uri   pipila;*
    taro round off   rotundity his my taro taro round off at

    sikwaku-la a.u.,u.p.; kwaynuta-la a.u.,u.p.; pusaga-la a.u.,u.p.;
    base of stalk his   top of stalk his   tail of root his

    yaguvane-la a.u.,u.p.
    leaf his

4. *I-koma-si   uri,   i-lugwabi-se   uri,   i-kamilayli-se   uri,*
   they eat   taro they spew   taro they disgusted with taro

   i-gibu-ki   mita-si   uri,   i-pakay-ki   nina-si   uri,
   he burn at eye theirs taro he refuse at   mind theirs taro

5. *i-katupula-ki   tuvata'u,   i-uwa-ki   puputuma.*
   he sunder at (a weed) he fruit at (a weed)

6. *I-milikaydawaga   lopou-la   ula   buyagu;*
   he liken trimming-board   belly his my garden-site

   i-milakaydatutu l.u.b.   i-bisikay-m   ginuvavarya l.u.b.
   he liken pounding-board   he pierce at   mollusc-holes

III. 7. *Ba-la   o   valu.*
     I might go   in village

GENERAL COMMENTARY

A. *Sociological Context:* we have now come to the rites which
immediately preceed the harvest. This is one of the few formulae
which, like the *vatuvi* spell, is chanted in the magician's hut over an
instrument which will not be used until the following day. Here also
the virtue of the spell is carefully preserved, and although no one
is present at its chanting, its words are known and their import
affects the mind of every gardener and that of the whole community.

B. *Ritual Context:* the spell is recited over a pearl shell which is
then wrapped up in dried banana leaf to preserve the magical
virtue, and used on the following day as the implement with which
the first taro is harvested.

C. *Structure:* tripartite.

D. *Dogmatic Context:* the whole wording of this spell, with its
allusions to the full moon, to the roundness of the moon, to swelling
and rounding off, with its direct mention of taro in the key-word
and in the main part, is clearly a taro spell and fits perfectly well
into its ritual and economic context. The leading idea of the spell
is obviously that of fullness and rotundity. I am advisedly saying

leading idea and not word, because the spell begins with the word
bwato (in ordinary speech *bwata*, changed for magical euphony),
'fullness of moon', but in the key-word and in the second verse the
verb *pipila*, 'roundness', occurs. In the compound *yapila* this word is
one of the alternative expressions used with regard to the full moon.
With reference to the prominence of the full moon in this spell I
wish to state emphatically that no moon mythology, no esoteric
ideas about the moon and its influence on the taro are implied. It
is simply used as a magical simile, the mere utterance of its name
being potent in itself. The word taro figures in the key expression
of verse 3 and it recurs repeatedly in verse 4. Verse 4 is characterised
by magical exaggerations, quaint rather than appetising. While
people in the village gorge themselves to disgust and sickness with
taro (v. 4), in the gardens (v. 5) the magic produces no less over-
whelming results. The taro rots, weeds grow out of its roots, and so
on. These two magical sentences express in an extremely telling
manner the Trobriand idea of successful gardening; the ideal of
plenty for its own sake, of plenty so that a surplus may be destroyed
and wasted.

E. *Mode of Recitation:* chanted in a loud melodious voice.

LINGUISTIC COMMENTARY

2. The word *bwata* is passed through the usual rhythmic opposition of *naga* and *-m* and round the compass from north to south.
Bomatu is the north-east wind, but stands for 'north' in general, as
youyo stands for 'south'. I have thus translated them in the free
version.

3. The native comment on the key-word gathered together the
two words *pipila* and *bwato: uri bi-pipila: bi-vagi kwayviyaka, makawala
tubukona wa bwata*, 'the taro might round off—it will be made big,
like the moon at its full'. The inventory words refer to various parts
of the taro. *Umdu-la*, 'the round part', 'the roundness'—in free translation given as "belly of" to avoid the unpleasant taste of a pleonastic
sentence. Of the inventory words, *sikwaku* and *kwaynuta* will be found
in Div. III, § 22. *Pusaga-la*, the part of the taro which 'pene-
trates the soil', which 'splits the soil' (cf. M.F. 15, v. 2). *Yaguvane-la*
is of course the ordinary word for 'leaves', *yagavana*, slightly modified
to balance it phonetically with the third possessive pronoun.

4. The magical boasting of plenty: the people eat, are sick,
become disgusted with taro. The verb *i-lugwabi-se* was translated to
me by *i-lugwabi-se—kasi lagoba, pela sene bidubadu uri*, 'they vomit—
their sickness for very much taro'. The expression *kasi lagoba* is the
usual one of ordinary speech. The following magical expression has

been commented upon: *i-kamilayli-se: i-minayna nina-si*, '*i-kamilayli-se* means mind theirs it is turned'. The expression *i-minayna nanogu* is the ordinary one for strong disgust.

5. *I-katupula-ki* was explained to me as a verb denoting the sundering or splitting of one object by another which grows into it. *Katupula-ki* can be analysed into *katu-*, effective prefix, *pulu*, 'to dive', 'to enter', and the directive suffix *-ki*. *I-uwa-ki* similarly is the directive suffix of *uwa*, 'to fruit'. *Tuvata'u* is a rank weed which grows out of decaying matters. The tubers of taro rot in the gardens and *tuvata'u* grows out of them. *Pututuma*, another rank weed, will bear fruit growing out of rotting taro. The final verses, 6 and 7, are identical with those of Formula 23.

FORMULA 26
(Ch. V, Sec. 2)

Bi-ta-kalavi-se	*tomwaya*	*kala-bogwo;*
we might throw away	old man	food old
bi-ta-kam-si-ga	*kala-va'u.*	
we might eat again	food new	

GENERAL COMMENTARY

A. *Sociological Context:* towards the end of the gardening cycle we find that the magician again gets into touch with the ancestral spirits. The words of this formula bind together the magician's ancestral claims, his main taboo, that on fruit of the new gardens, and the act of harvesting, and sanctifies the sociological duties of relatives-in-law since the food to be offered in oblation and which lifts the taboo must be given by these.

B. *Ritual Context:* fits in well with the sociological function of the spell. The words are spoken while the magician cuts off some of the taro with a shell and breaks off a piece of yam, and lays this small oblation on the hearthstones. Immediately afterwards he partakes for the first time of the new yams.

C. *Structure:* a simple sentence and grammatically constructed.

D. *Dogmatic Context:* the words are addressed directly to ancestral spirits (cf. M.F. 1, D.).

E. *Mode of Recitation:* spoken in the direct persuasive voice of ordinary talk and not in the sing-song of magic.

LINGUISTIC COMMENTARY

The resemblance between *kala-va'u*, 'food new', and *kalavi* the verb for 'throw away' is accidental. The contrast between the old and the new food is expressed by the suffixes *-ga*, 'again', which in this context has the meaning 'on the other hand'. In *bi-ta-kam-si-ga* only the syllable *kam* has the root meaning 'to eat'.

FORMULA 27

(Ch. V, Sec. 3)

I. 1. *Kuriyava   naga   kuriyavam,*
    dolphin   now   dolphin

  2. *kuriyavam   giburokaywo,   kuriyavam   gibutilawa;*
      dolphin   S.E. side   dolphin   N.W. side

  3. *ku-dum   giburokaywo,   ku-dum-ke'i   gibutilawa!*
      thou play (?)   S.E. side   thou play at   N.W. side

     Kuriyava   dumdum!
     dolphin   play

II. 4. *Kuriyava   dumdum . . .*
     dolphin   play

     ulo kaysalu kuriyava dumdum, ulo kaybudi k.d., ulo kamtuya k.d., ula tula k.d., uri yeye'i k.d., uri tamkwaluma k.d., uri kavatam k.d., uri kayvaliluwa k.d., uri tukulumwala k.d., uri kaluvalova k.d., ulo karivisi k.d., ulo kamkokola k.d., ulo kaynutatala k.d.

III. 5. *I-gebile lopou-la   ulo   buyagu;   i-tokaye l.u.b.;*
      he lift belly his my garden-site he rise

     i-takubila l.u.b.; i-gibage'u l.u.b.;   i-kabwabu l.u.b.;
     he recline he lift-bush-hen-nest he ant-hill

     i-gibukwayu'u l.u.b.; i-gibakayaulo l.u.b.;   i-tawaga l.u.b.;
     he lift-bend-down he lift-iron-wood-palm he lie down

     i-kabina'i l.u.b.; i-kabinaygwadi l.u.b.
     he burgeon he burgeon (with) child

  6. *Tomwaya   lagayla   ta-lavi-se   da   okwala-si.*
      old man   to-day   we throw   our   (magical ceremony)

GENERAL COMMENTARY

A. *Sociological Context:* this spell is recited by the magician in solitary communion with the soil of the garden, the villagers indirectly participating in the manner already described (cf., e.g., M.F. 10, A.).

B. *Ritual Context:* the words are chanted over the fields after these have been strewn with leaves, to make the taytu vine droop as it has to do at harvest. The richer the vine and at the same time the more drooping and yielding it is, the better the tubers. With this context and aim the wording of the spell accords well.

C. *Structure:* typical tripartite formula.

D. *Dogmatic Context:* the invocation of the dolphin—whose

magical function is the same as that of the millipede, spider and so forth—transforms, by a daring simile, the Trobriand garden, with its foliage swaying and waving in the wind, into a seascape. The richer the foliage, the more the garden will resemble the undulations of following waves. Bagido'u explained to me by gesture and word that as among the waves the dolphin goes in and out, up and down, so throughout the gardens the rich garlands at harvest will wind over and under, in and out, of the supports. As a matter of fact, after harvest is done and the taytu vines have been cut, there is such a profusion and welter of garlands, wreathes and festoons that it suggests a moving, billowing sea of greenery, especially when towards noon the inevitable trade wind rises in strength and stirs the foliage. Had we incorporated Bagido'u's comments we might have translated the brief sentence *kuriyava dumdum* into "Play, dolphin, there with thy playful winding prances, play". Independently of this there is another associated idea operative in this spell. The dolphin is invoked, the natives say, so that the body of the taytu (*tapwa-na taytu*) might become as big as the body of the dolphin. This point of view, as can be seen, is not expressed in the spell, but was given to me in an independent commentary. The invocation of the dolphin functions in the same manner as the use of the bush-hen's nest and the invocation of this bird, or the ritual use of coral boulder and most of the other substances.

E. *Mode of Recitation:* again chanted loudly, the words sweeping the field.

LINGUISTIC COMMENTARY

1–3. The leading word, *kuriyava*, 'dolphin', is here recited on the ordinary pattern with the words *naga* and the suffix -*m*, and with the opposition between *giburokaywo* and *gibutilawa*, which I was told corresponded to the north-westerly or monsoon direction and the south-easterly or trade-wind direction.

4. The key-word, *kuriyava dumdum*, is repeated with the names of the various supports (cf. M.F. 10, commentary on v. 3, and the references there given). The expression *kuriyava dumdum* was defined to me rather by gesture and extensive commentary than by direct translation. The verb *dumdum* is not a word of ordinary speech. It apparently means the playful undulating motions of the dolphin.

5. This verse is almost identical with Formula 2, verse 3. The one word which is not used there is *i-kolalasi*. *Kolalasi*, I was told, is a slightly changed form of *kaluwali*, 'roots' = *kaynawari* (cf. M.F. 21, commentary on v. 5).

6. Is a perfectly grammatical phrase, *tomwaya*, 'old man', referring of course to the ancestral spirits, the *bilibaloma*.

FORMULA 28
(Ch. VII, Sec. 1)

I. 1. *Kuwa   naga,   kuwam,   kuwam   o   bomatu.*
   rattan now   rattan   rattan   in   N.E. wind

2. *Ku-ma   ku-valola   o   bomatu,   ba-wa*
   thou come   thou moor   in N.E. wind   I might get there

   karikikita   o   kwaybwaga;   ku-ma   ku-valola
   fasten   in S.W. wind   thou come   thou moor

   o   kwaybwaga,   ba-wa   karikikita   o   bomatu.
   in S.W. wind   I might get there   fasten   in N.E. wind

3. *Sibu-gu   binabina,   tubuga'okuwa   kurabwa'u.*
   bottom mine   (a volcanic stone)   ancient dust   soot

II. 4. *I-lola   ula   bwayma,   i-mdukupulu   ula   bwayma,*
   he moor   my   yam-house   he stone-buried   my   yam-house

   i-mdukumaga u.b.,   i-kwoydudubile u.b.,   i-burokukuva u.b.,
   he stone-bedrock   he darken   he interior-darken

   i-burokawita u.b.,   i-lalola u.b.
   he interior blacken   he moored firmly

   Bi-la,   i-loluvagasi.
   he might go   he might be moored completely

III. 5. *Tududududu . . .   kariyala   ula   bwayma   i-tututu*
   (onomatopoeic)   portent   my   yam-house   he rumble

   o   bomatu.
   in N.E. wind

GENERAL COMMENTARY

A. *Sociological Context:* with this spell we are entering on the last lap of Trobriand garden magic, one distinguished by name as well as by context—the magic of wealth, *vilamalia*. The importance of this magic has been made clear in Chapter VII. As regards the sociological and cultural context of the present spell, the magician carries out his work alone or accompanied by a small following only; the villagers keenly aware of his proceedings. As we have seen in Text 24, on which we have commented so fully in Part IV (Div. III and cf. also Ch. V, Sec. 1), it is this magic which comes to the native's mind first when he thinks of the end of an economic disaster and the return of prosperity.

B. *Ritual Context:* prosperity with its necessary concomitants of permanence, firmness, tenacity, form the substance of the magic of *vilamalia* and are expressed in the ritual used and in the object immediately medicated, the *binabina* stone.

C. *Structure:* I have divided this spell into three parts, but in reality the middle part is not a *tapwana* and probably it is just a long one-part spell. The middle part, II, is in fact constructed on the same pattern as the last bit of the foundation in Formula 2 and part of verse 4 in Formula 10.

D. *Dogmatic Context:* is discussed in Chapter VII. It will be remembered that the natives maintain that the magic acts on the human organism while the wording and ritual point to a direct reference to the crops and the storehouses (cf. Ch. VII, Sec. 4). Here we have the invocation of the rattan, "lawyer cane", which, among all vegetable things known to the Trobriander, is the most tenacious. Europeans signalise its singular capacity for grasping and holding in the name lawyer cane. In the last verse we have a reference to the magical portent, the *kariyala*.

E. *Mode of Recitation:* chanted in the ordinary sing-song of magic.

LINGUISTIC COMMENTARY

1. 2. The two points of the compass are determined by the north-east wind and the south-west. That latter, the *kwaybwaga*, rivals the *oyuyo*, south-west wind, as a symbol of the southern side.

3. *Sibu-gu*, 'my bottom', doubtless refers to the taytu, for the *binabina* stone is placed on the floor of the storehouse. The word *∴ bu-na* is often used for the lower part of the tuber (cf. Part V, Div. III, § 2). *Tubuga'okuwa* is derived from *tubwaga*, 'dust' (on the floors); *wokuwa*, denoting completion, antiquity, 'ancient dust'. *Kurabwa'u*, a word which I find only in this context, is probably compounded from *kuria*, 'cooking-pot', and *bwabwa'u*, 'blackness'— 'the old soot forming round the pots' which gathers on the *kuroroba*, 'pot-shelf'. In free translation these meanings have been linked together in the sentence: "My bottom is as a *binabina* stone, as the old dust, as the blackened powder."

4. Is constructed on a standard pattern (cf., e.g., M.F. 2, v. 3) and is almost identical with Formula 10, verse 4, except that yam-house is substituted for garden, and that we have three words (*kwoydudubile, burokukuva, burokawita*) which express darkness—the darkness of the filled interior, this darkness conveying to the natives the idea of riches. *Burokukuva*, *buro-*, prefix probably of *bwala*, 'house', 'interior', *kukuva*, 'obscure'. *Burokawita*, *kawita* being equated by my informants with *bwabwa'u*, 'black'.

5. Is the usual statement about the magical portent of the rite.

FORMULA 29
(Ch. VII, Sec. 3)

I. 1. *Kaylola,　lola* (repeated)
   mooring　to moor

   kaygulugulu,　gulugulu (repeated)
   boring in　　to bore in

   Kaylola　Tudava,
   mooring　(mythical hero)

   Kaygulugulu　Malita.
   boring in　　(mythical hero)

   2. *Bi-sipela　　　Tudava,　　　bi-sila'i*
   he might climb　(mythical hero)　he might seat himself

   o　tokaykaya:
   in　high platform

   avaka　ba-woye'i?　　ba-woye'i　　sibulola;
   what　I might hit　　I might hit　　bottom mooring

   bi-lalola!
   he might be moored

II. 3. *Bi-lalola . . .* (repeated)*; ulu pwaypwaya bi-lalola, ulu ulilaguva b.,*
   ulu bubukwa b., agu liku b., ulo kabisivisi b., ula sobula b., ula teta b.,
   ulu bisiya'i b., ulo kavalapu b., uli kiluma b., ulo kavala b., ulo kaliguvasi
   b., ula kivi b., ula katuva b., ulo kakulumwala b., uli vataulo b., ulu
   mwamwala b.

III. 4. *Bi-lalola!　　　　　I-lola　　ulu　valu,*
   he might be moored　he moor　my　village

   indukupolu　　　ulu　valu,
   like stone-buried　my　village

   imdukumaga　　　ulu　valu,
   like stone-bedrock　my　village

   imdukumeylosi　　ulu　valu,
   like stone-deep-rooted　my　village

   i-lalola　　ulu　valu,　　bi-luluvagasi.
   he is moored　my　village　he might be moored completely

   5. *Tududududududu . . .*
   (onomatopoeic)

   Kariyala　　　ulu　valu　　i-tututu　　o　bomatu.
   magical portent　my　village　he rumble　in　N.E. wind

GENERAL COMMENTARY

A. *Sociological Context:* this is the last spell of the gardening cycle which seals with the seal of prosperity the crops already stored in the yam-houses. Here characteristically we have a spell which is first of all recited by the magician in his hut, and then twice more uttered in public. The magical business has to be carried out by the magician alone; it was, in fact, in connexion with this rite that I first became aware of the strange non-ceremonial, almost technical character of magical proceedings. This convention has a very real significance. It expresses the fact that magic is the expert's task, and emphasises its monopolistic character. On the other hand this highly individualised and specialised social setting of ritual must not obscure the fact that the whole community responds to it in the complex manner on which we have so often insisted. In the case of this and the previous formula many people are actually within earshot; but the words are anyhow familiar, as are all the spells of public magic, to every villager. Its wording documents the continuity of the cycle in that it is almost identical with the principal formula of the *kamkokola* magic (M.F. 10).

B. *Ritual Context:* this spell is first uttered in the magician's hut over some herbs and then in the village. It is chanted into the main storehouse and into the road entry to the village.

C. *Structure:* identical with Formula 10.

D. *Dogmatic Context:* All that has been said about Formula 10 applies here, except that stability refers to parts of the storehouse and not to vine supports and parts of the magical wall. We must remember the curious discrepancy in native belief as expressed in their comments and the purpose of this magic as expressed in the spell (cf. D. of the previous formula).

E. *Mode of Recitation:* uttered in the loud melodious sing-song of the big formulae.

LINGUISTIC COMMENTARY

The first part of this formula is identical with that of Formula 10, but it is placed by context of ritual and by its later parts in the village. Therefore, in the free translation, I added the contexually implied expression "my village", "anchoring of my village". The key-word of the middle part again is the same, expressing the anchoring, firm rooting, but the inventory words refer almost exclusively to the interior of the yam-house. The first word, *pwaypwaya*, has to be understood as the ground of the village on which the yam-house stands, and not as soil in general. One word, and one word only, *ula sobula*, 'my sprout', 'the sprout of my stored-up taytu', refers to something which is not a constructive detail of the yam-house. The other words are explained in Chapter VIII. The last part, verses 4 and 5, is again identical with the last part of Formula 10, substituting the word 'village' for 'garden-site'.

FORMULA 30
(Ch. VII, Sec. 6)

I. 1. *Bibila* (repeated)
   restore (?)

   bibila   kumgwa'i,   bibila   ku'uyem —
   restore   ?   restore   ?

   Tay'uyo   bibila,   bibila!
   conch shell   restore   restore

II. 2. *Ta'uyo   bibila,   bibila*
       conch shell   restore   restore

   This key expression is then repeated on the following pattern:—
   Popoma ta'uyo, ta'uyo bibila, bibila; lukiluki ta'uyo, ta'uyo bibila bibila, etc.

   with a long list of words denoting:—
   - (a) types and aspects of hunger;
   - (b) part of a house or yam-house;
   - (c) parts of the village and its surroundings.

   (a) *popoma, lukiluki, tutubwa'u; kukwaybeta; molubutu; munusauri; nagatugu; nagaluga; nagasauri;*

   (b) *o tatum; o kaykatiga; o kumkumlo; o kaylagila; o kaytaulo; o kavala; o kulumwala; o mitakwabu; wa bariga; wa laba; o kalapisila; o kaukweda;*

   (c) *o bukubaku; o tumkweda; o yagesi; o kadumalaga; o kadamwala; o kovalawa; o kulakola; o luluboda.*

3. *Bibila   kumgwa'i,   bibila   ku'uyem.*
   restore   ?   restore   ?

III. 4. *Gala   kam   yagila,   kam   yagila   Dabwa'i;*
        no   thy   wind   thy   wind   (a N.W. wind)

   gala   kam   karikeda,   kam   karikeda   Kadinaka;
   no   thy   passage   thy   passage   (a sea-passage)

   gala   kam   koya,   kam   koya   Kuyaluya;
   no   thy   mountain   thy   mountain   (hill near Wawela)

   gala   kam   kwabwa'u,   kam   kwabwa'u   Silawotu;
   no   thy   promontory   thy   promontory   (a promontory)

   gala   kam   kovasasa,   kam   kovasasa
   no   thy   open-passage   thy   open-passage

   Kalubaku;
   (a passage between Baymapo'u and main island)

   gala   kam   milaveta,   kam   milaveta
   no   thy   sea-arm   thy   sea-arm

   Kaulokoki.
   (passage between Kayleula and main islaı d)

5. *Lema*   *Kawala,*   *Tuma*
   come (?)   (sea-passage between Tuma and Buriwada)   (island)

6. *Ku-pulupulu,*   *gala;*   *ku-kwariga,*   *gala;*
   thou sink   begone   thou grey hair (?)   begone

   ku-tamwa'u,   *gala;*   *ku-kwariga,*   *gala;*
   thou disappear   begone   thou die   begone

   kw-aliguwaya,   *gala.*
   thou spill   begone

7. *A-tanay-m*   *lopou-la*   *ulo*   *valu;*   *i-polu l.u.v.;*
   I sweep thee   belly his   my   village   he boil up

   i-tokukwa l.u.v.;   *i-tobisubasuma l.u.v.;*
   he darken with plenty   he full of stored food (?)

   i-kapukwapula l.u.v.;   *i-kapwayasi l.u.v.*
   he sweat   he perspire (?)

GENERAL COMMENTARY

A. *Sociological Context:* the cultural context of the next two spells, which belong to the Oburaku cycle of *vilamalia*, is very much the same as the one described for the two previous formulae. The *vilamalia* in Oburaku is if anything more important than in Omarakana. Its performances are more public; it is performed at *isunapulo* as well as at the main harvest, and may also be performed in times of famine.

B. *Ritual Context:* this spell is spoken first into a conch shell, one orifice of which is stuffed with dry banana leaf, after which the open end is laid on a mat, that the virtue may not escape. It is repeated into a conical bag of dried banana leaf, containing wild ginger root. These substances, however, need not retain the magic long, for the magician and his acolytes repair at once to the northern and then to the southern end of the village, where the conch shell is blown and the ginger root chewed and spat upon all the points where a road strikes the village.

C. *Structure:* a tripartite formula of considerable length in which the main part is a typical well-developed *tapwana*, with only one key expression, but a long and very varied list of inventory words. Whether verse 4 and perhaps also 5 and 6 should be included in the *tapwana* or the *dogina* is doubtful. On such points the native informants vary at times in their opinion. On the whole, however, the structure of verses 4–6 is rather that of a *dogina* than a *tapwana*, though in some of the previous spells we have included similarly constructed parts into the body of the spell.

D. *Dogmatic Context:* the leading word, unfortunately not identified beyond doubt, is probably a verbal root. It certainly has a general meaning. The other part of the key expression is the ritual implement of this ceremony, the conch shell. The magic, therefore, does not refer to any animal or vegetable agency, but is throughout an impersonal verbal act. The key expression *ta'uyo bibila, bibila* becomes, if we juxtapose the two English equivalents, 'conch shell, restore, restore'. It should not be understood as an appeal to the conch shell, but rather as a statement something to this effect: "conch shell of restoring", "conch shell of the healing capacity". This spell is uttered into the conch shell, it fills it with this healing capacity, which is then spread over the village by the act of blowing. The conch shell is not a sort of fetish which becomes active, but merely an instrument. Verse 4, though concretely worded, does not make very clear sense, because somehow the geographical orientation does not fit. The first phrase, which means 'not thy wind', 'thy wind' being probably directed to famine and evil influences, is satisfactory. For it consigns famine and evil to the north-westerly wind, which would carry it to the south-east, the place to which this magic is made to exorcise all things undesirable. *Dabwa'i* was translated to me as the north-westerly wind which blows before the rain, that is, the typical mild breeze of the monsoon. In the following phrase, however, we have the evil influences sent to the sea-passage of Kadinaka, which is somewhere to the north-west, and then again to the hill of Kuyaluya, which is the top of a rock to the south-east, and again to the promontory of Silawotu, which is on the coast immediately south of Oburaku, and then to Kaulokoki, which is again to the west. Perhaps this strophe has to be understood in the sense that evil should disperse in every possible direction and leave the village. If this is so, it is exceptional, because usually all things exorcised are sent in one direction only.

E. *Mode of Recitation:* chanted loudly and melodiously.

LINGUISTIC COMMENTARY

1. *Bibila* was defined to me by one of my informants :—

Bibila:	*kidama*	*tay-tala*	*ta'u*	*bi-numata*
	supposing	one (m.)	man	he might be tired

bi-tutubwo,		*ta-bibila,*		*bi-bwoyna*
he might be prostrated		we *bibila* (restore)		he might be good

wou-la.
body his

This definition, which is about the only good one which I received with this spell, seems to fix the meaning of the word as 'to heal', 'to restore', and I have thus translated it. The two magical oppositions, *kumgwa'i*, *ku'uyem*, represent something like 'here' and 'there', 'now' and 'then', but I was not able to analyse them satisfactorily from the linguistic point of view, and in the free version I have in a non-committal way translated them "this way", "that way".

2. This key expression is repeated with three classes of words: (*a*) These I was least able to translate correctly. *Popoma* means 'pot belly', 'a swelling abdomen'. It is the name for a *silami* (type of sorcery), and here it is said to be uttered because a swollen belly is one of the symptoms of starvation. For the word *lukiluki* I could not get anything better than *megwa la keda*, 'the way of magic', 'a magical expression'. It is probably a word denoting some sort of debility, hence in free translation "hunger-exhaustion". *Tutubwa'u* which figures in the above definition text of *bibila* was defined for me: *tutubwa'u: boge i-numata wou-la*, '*tutubwa'u* means already body his he faint'. Hence in free translation "hunger-faintness". *Kukwaybeta* was defined thus: *kukwaybeta: wa molu boge i-kana-kay-gu*, '*kukwaybeta* means (thing which) at times of hunger already overlays me'. Hence in free translation "hunger-prostration". *Molubutu* is obviously compounded of *molu*, 'hunger', and *butu*, 'faint', 'depressed', in free translation "hunger-depression". The word *munusauri* was translated for me by 'just hunger'. It is obviously a compound of *molu* and the root *sauri* or *sawari*, which I think denotes 'drooping'. *Nagatutu*, *nagaluga*, and *nagasauri* are compounds of *naga*, which my informants told me was another word for *molu* and three roots of which *tutu* probably means 'throbbing', *luga* perhaps same as *lugi*, suffix of completion. (*Kaytalugi*,[1] 'to copulate to exhaustion', *komalugi*, 'to eat to repletion'.) Hence in free translation "throbbing famine, utter famine, drooping famine".

(*b*) *Tatum* means probably 'the floor of the house', 'the beaten soil'. *Kaykatiga* is some part of the thatch (I am not certain which). In free translation I put the eaves as a sufficiently general term. *Kumkumlo*, 'earth oven'; *kaylagila*, 'hearthstones'; *kaytaulo*, 'the foundation beams of a house; *kavala*, 'battens' or 'rafters'; *kulumwala*, 'ridge pole'; *mitakwabu*, 'ridge ornament' or 'ornament on ridge pole'; *bariga*, 'shelf'; *laba*, 'board'; *kalapisila*, 'threshold'; *kaukweda*, 'ground fronting house'.

(*c*) This again contains quite familiar terms: *bukubaku*, 'the central place of the village'. *Yagesi* I cannot translate; *tumkweda* is I think the beaten soil of the street, but I am not certain. *Kadumalaga*, 'main road'; *kadamwala*, 'road in between' (small road); *kovalawa*, 'seashore'; *kulakola* was translated for me in connexion with this spell: 'the part of the beach between high- and low-water mark',

---

[1] Cf. *Sexual Life of Savages*, Ch. VII, Sec. 3.

and *luluboda* as the place where the short seaweed grows, probably shallow water. In any case the exorcism of the conch shell starts with definitely evil states of health due to famine, then it is directed to various parts of the yam-house and finally sweeps round the various sites of the village.

3. is a mere repetition of the second part of the opening strophe.

4. is built on the typical negative comparison "not thy wind, thy wind is the north-westerly".

5. Here again the first phrase is not quite clear, *lema* should mean 'it has come'; *kawala*, if it were an ordinary word, would mean 'voice of', 'rumour of'; Tuma is the island of the dead. This would not make very good sense, but my informants insisted that *kawala* is a sea-passage between the islands of Tuma and Buriwada, in which case it makes still less sense. Making a compromise and taking a safe course, I rendered it in the free translation as meaning an exorcism towards the island of Tuma, "Get thee to the sea-passage between Tuma and Buriwada."

6. The typical form of exorcism with the strong negative rendered here as elsewhere by 'begone', drives away famine and evil influences. The word which seems to me least satisfactorily translated is *sosewo*, which means 'grey hair', and here perhaps means 'to get old' and decrepit, for grey hair is to the natives very much associated with unpleasant ideas of decay and weakness.

7. again starts with the exorcistic affirmation of sweeping, making clear, and goes on to the positive statement of prosperity. 'Darkens' refers to the leaves, and 'sweat' to the natives means exertion in gathering food, and probably also in dancing and rejoicing. The word which I cannot satisfactorily translate is *bisubasuma*, which I was told by my informant is a name for a very strong and thick yam support. Perhaps *tobisubasuma* is 'stand up like a garden that needs the strongest yam supports'. *Kapwayasi*, a word which I cannot find in my vocabulary of ordinary speech, was equated by my informants with *kapukwapula*, the ordinary word for 'sweat' (cf. *tokukuva* with *burokukuva* in Formula 28).

FORMULA 31
(Ch. VII, Sec. 6)

I. 1. *Padudu,   pawoya* (repeated).
   ?   ?

2. *Ge'ina-m,*   *ina-m*   *Botagara'i;*
   no mother thine   mother thine   (mythical person)

   getama-m,   *tama-m*   *Tomgwara'i.*
   no father thine   father thine   (mythical person)

3. *Kw-atuvi   rakata'i,   kw-atupusagi   rakamawa.*
   thou break   ?   thou break up   ?

4. *Kumlikiriri, kumliototo, kumlidigadaga, kumlisikwaku, kumriononu, kumriabutuma.*

5. *Ku-la,   ku-gwagwagu,   tududududududu . . .*
   thou go   thou make noise

   ku-roweya.   Tagoru!
   thou go there

II. 6. *Tagoru . . .*
   This key-word is repeated with :—

   (*a*) words which probably describe illnesses or evil influences,
   (*b*) parts or aspects of a yam-house,
   (*c*) parts or aspects of a village.

   (*a*) *rakata'i; rakamawa; rakatuparausi; rakaturidarida; rakatukapita; rabubwalata;*

   (*b*) *ranugwanagula; rakaytaulo; ilapo'u; lakavala; lakulumwala; labubukwa; laleta; lakarivisi; ilosobula; ilaninuva;*

   (*c*) *Latumkweda; layagesi; lakatuposula; lopou-la ulo valu; lakatukupwala; lakulobutubutu; lakatukopita.*

III. 7. *A-tanay-m   lopou-la   ulo   valu   i-polu l.u.v.;*
   I sweep thee   belly his   my   village   he boils up

   i-tokukuva l.u.v.;   i-tobisubasuma l.u.v.;
   he darken with plenty   he full of stored food (?)

   i-kapukwapula l.u.v.;   i-kapwayasi l.u.v.
   he sweat   he perspire (?)

GENERAL COMMENTARY

A. *Sociological Context:* this spell, as are one or two others in Oburaku (cf. also Ch. X, Sec. 1), is recited in the presence of all the gardeners who wait till the mixture and digging-sticks have been impregnated with the virtue of the spell and then carry them, each to his part of the village.

B. *Ritual Context:* the rite is one of impregnation of an intermediate substance, though this is at once conveyed to its final object, i.e. the soil of the village, the houses and the yam-houses.

C. *Structure:* tripartite, with a real *tapwana*.

D. *Dogmatic Context:* almost identical with that of the previous one. Unfortunately I was able to obtain no satisfactory commentary on certain apparently mythological implications such as the names uttered in verse 2 or the words of verse 1.

E. *Mode of Recitation:* chanted in a loud voice.

LINGUISTIC COMMENTARY

1. *Padudu, pawoya*, obviously formed with the prefix *pa-* derived from *pway-*, 'soil' (?), and *-dudu*, which may perhaps stand for the onomatopoeic *dududu* of the *kariyala* (cf. v. 5), and *-woya* which may be the verb 'to hit (magically)'. I am so uncertain, however, about these interpretations, which are entirely the result of my own analysis, that I have neither used them in the free translation nor rendered the words in the interlineal version.

2. is built up on the negative comparison pattern, the names Botagara'i and Tomgwara'i were said to be mythical names. Their symmetrical structure suggests some significance in wording. *Tom-* probably male person prefix, *Bo-* certainly typical female beginning; *gara'i* and *gwara'i* might come from *gwara*, the general Melanesian term for 'taboo', used very seldom in the Trobriands, though some of the yam-houses are called *bwayma goregore*, and the term *gora, gwara* is known in connexion with certain institutions (cf. *Argonauts of the Western Pacific*, pp. 346 ff. and 489). In free translation I have simplified this phrase since I was not able to give any full significance to it.

3. We have here two phrases which consist of a verb and a noun each. These are *kw-atuvi* (second person of *katuvi*, 'to break') and *kw-atupusagi* (second person of *katupusagi*, 'to break into'). As regards the words *rakata'i* and *rakamawa* which head the long list in verse 6, I think that the prefix *ra-* is the third singular personal pronoun. But since I am not able to decide definitely, I have written them without hyphens.

4. Here again I received no help whatever from my informants, and can only venture on one or two indications. The words are probably in the second singular, each having the prefix *ku-*. After this each one of them has the root *-mli-* equals *-mrio-*, or *-mira-*, probably a contraction or alternative of *mili*, 'to be like', 'to become like'. There remains the root in each of them, none of which I can translate, so that our analysis is of little help. The roots *kiriri, ototo*, are quite beyond my comprehension. *Digadaga* may be a reduplicated form of *daga*, 'ladder', which does not explain very much; *sikwaku*—?, *onunu*—?, *butuma*, 'red soil'. The roots may perhaps be some out-of-the-way words for varieties of soil, which would then put them into line with *butuma*, and *digadaga* may be a contraction from *digadegila*, 'light brown, light brown soil'. In that case this whole verse would mean a magical appeal for fertility as referring to the soil. But that is merely surmise.

5. is, with verse 7, about the only verse which makes sense.

Gwagwagu is 'to talk', 'to make noise'. The invitation to go, to make noise, to rumble (onomatopoeically expressed), refers probably to the magic itself, to its force.

6. The key-word *tagoru* I cannot explain with any certainty. The prefix *ta-* may perhaps be a general imperative prefix such as is found in *tage*, 'do not', and which probably exists also in the Polynesian root *tabu*. *Goru* might again be associated with *gwara*. The word would then mean a general prohibition or exorcism. This also fits with the function of the word. Its association first with words probably representing evil influences and then with words denoting parts of storehouses and parts of the village, imply that its meaning is that of undoing, mending and prohibiting at the same time. The verb 'exorcise' is, therefore, the only one which I can suggest, and I have adopted it in the free translation, though in the interlineal rendering the word is left without an equivalent. In (*a*) we find a series of words with the prefix *ra-*, which may be the third person possessive pronoun or may be the verbal pronoun of accomplished past, or may also be some other particle (see above commentary to v. 3). The remaining part of the word represents probably the root meaning. Only one of them can be translated certainly, *bubwalata*, which is a generic description of magic done with intent to harm. *Kata'i = katavi* might be derived from *katuvi*, 'to break', and be connected with *kataulo*, 'illness'; for the other words I cannot even venture to suggest a translation, except that three of them have the formative *katu-*, which has the meaning of 'through', of something which is broken or destroyed. They may, therefore, be names of evil influences or destructive agencies. This again, however, is a mere surmise. The expressions in (*b*) refer to the various structural parts of a yam-house with the exception of *ilo-sobula*, *sobula* meaning the sprout sent out by taytu after it has remained for a few months in the storehouse, which is a sign of plenty. The word *nugwanagula* refers to the sacred stones of a village; the rest can be all found in Chapter VII. Judging by the structure of this verse, the prefix *la-* is the possessive pronoun third singular. (*c*) are parts of the village, most of the words identical with the words found in the previous spell. Three of them, however, I could not translate: *layagesi*, *lakatukupwala* and *lakulobutubutu*.

7. is identical with the last verse of the previous formula and has been fully commented upon. In the free translation the least clear parts have been omitted.

FORMULA 32
(Ch. IX, Sec. 2)

1. *Avay-ta'u*   *i-kavakavala*   *Ovavavala?*
   which man   he bend down (?)   (sacred grove)

2. *Yaygula'i*   *Nasibowa'i*   *a-kavakavala*   *Ovavavala.*
   myself   (the magician)   I bend down (?)   (sacred grove)

3. *Ba-la'i*   *bayse,*   *a-kavakavala*   *Ovavavala;*
   I might carry   this   I bend down (?)   (sacred grove)

   yaygula'i   *Nasibowa'i*   *a-kavakavala*   *Ovavavala;*
   myself   (the magician)   I bend down (?)   (sacred grove)

4. *ba-la'i*   *bayse*   *agu*   *bitumwanaya'i*   *o*   *lopou-la*
   I might carry   this   my   head-basket (?)   in   belly his

   Ovavavala.
   (sacred grove)

5. *Ba-la'i*   *bayse*   *a-kabinaygwadi'a'i,*   *o*   *lopou-la*
   I might carry   this   my growth anew   in   belly his

   Ovavavala.
   (sacred grove)

GENERAL COMMENTARY

A. *Sociological Context:* this and the formulae which follow (33–40) belong to the Momtilakayva system of magic. This spell is recited on three occasions. First in the grove of Ovavavile, when it inaugurates the whole cycle. In order to appreciate the cultural setting of this act, let us remember that the grove is entered by a human being on this occasion only, and then only by the magician, otherwise it is tabooed; and that the very place is associated with ideas of fertility (cf. D.). On the second and third occasions of its use, this spell is chanted over the magical torches, *kaykapola*; those used at the first burning are charmed, as in Omarakana, at harvest-time; those used at the 'big burning', *gibuviyaka*, immediately before this rite. This spell is the one which corresponds most closely to the *vatuvi* (M.F. 2) of the magical system of Omarakana, and all that has been said about the other spell refers to this one.

B. *Ritual Context:* the magician carries a large yam of the species called *kasiyena*, which I think grows wild. This tuber he places on the stone in the grove, a rite which is regarded as an offering to the ancestral spirits, while the spell is uttered. The oblational character of the spell associates it with Formula 1 of the Kaylu'ebila system. The allusion to the object carried, an object which functions as a pledge of fertility (vv. 3–5), probably refers to the tuber. The rite therefore, as well as the spell, binds together a typical act of magic, a rite of somewhat vague ancestor-worship, and a definitely sacred object—the stone in which the tabooed character of the grove is concentrated.

C. *Structure:* starting with a question and answer, this spell does not present any clear structure.

D. *Dogmatic Context:* is clear from what has been said already: the grove which plays a part in ritual, belief and spell, because of its exuberant fertility; the ancestral ghosts, more shadowy even than in the acts of Omarakana; the tuber which is designated as *baloma kasiyena*, 'the *kasiyena* tuber of the spirits'.

E. *Mode of Recitation:* chanted in a loud sing-song.

LINGUISTIC COMMENTARY

1. *Kavakavala* was equated to me by my informants with *kavagine*, 'to bend down', as is done by commoners in the presence of a chief. This is the view I have adopted in translation, both literal and free. Etymologically *kavakavala* seems to me rather to be connected with *kavikavila*, 'lightning'. Considering that lightning, thunder and rain constitute a typical magical portent, *kariyala*, which this act—as the inaugurative rite of the whole system—is emphatically meant to produce, the meaning '(produce) lightning' would fit perfectly well into this context, both of situation and of words. Moreover, as Ovavavala is derived from Ovavavile, probably in magical rhyming to *kavakavála*, this latter word might well be an apophony of *kavikávila*. But since this is my own etymological speculation, I am not adopting it, though I am convinced that I am right and my informants wrong. On either assumption the formula makes clear sense. If I were right, the free translation would run: "Who is it that works the magical portent in the grove of Ovavavala? . . ."

3. *Ba-la'i bayse:* here, as I say, *bayse* probably refers to the tuber, though I could not get a conclusive answer from my informants on this point.

4. Here the *bayse* is more precisely defined as 'my something carried on the head'. My informants equated *agu bitumwana* (the ending *ya'i* is magical) with 'a thing, usually a *peta* (round basket), which is carried (*i-gebila*) on one's head'.

5. *A'kabinaygwadi'a'i:* the *a* is here an abbreviation from *agu*, 'my'; the ending *i'a'i* is again magical. *Kabinaygwadi* is a word which we know already from Formula 2 verse 3. We translated it there, where it functioned as a verbal compound, by 'to burgeon with child'. Here, where it is a noun, I am rendering it in the literal translation by 'growth anew'. Literally it would be 'growth child', 'growth a child', where child stands for something young, new; hence to make sense in English 'growth anew'.

FORMULA 33
(Ch. IX, Sec. 2)

1. *Ko-dali* (repeated).
   thou get together

   Ko-vili (repeated).
   thou twine round

2. *Ko-dali-m,*   *taytu; ko-vilay-m,*   *taytu.*
   thou get together thee   taytu   thou twine round thee   taytu

3. *Tubawa-m*   *waybitu;*   *yagava-m*   *yokwa'oma.*
   fullness thine   (a plant)   leaves thine   (a creeper)

GENERAL COMMENTARY

A. *Sociological Context:* this spell is chanted at the first rite preparatory to the *yowota,* i.e. the inaugural ceremony in the gardens. It
is therefore on this occasion the counterpart of the *vatuvi* spell
(M.F. 2) of the Omarakana system. Here also we have the preparatory buying of fish by the community and preparing of herbs by
the magician. We have also the offering of the *ula'ula* payment
by the men to the *towosi.* Apparently no fish offering is made
to the spirits, the foregoing ceremony in the tabooed grove being
the equivalent and placing the magician in communion with the
ancestors.

B. *Ritual Context:* consists in the uttering of this spell into the
herbs and axes.

C. *Structure:* simple and short.

D. *Dogmatic Context:* direct invocation to the taytu with two
sympathetic plants named in verse 3.

E. *Mode of Recitation:* chanted loudly.

LINGUISTIC COMMENTARY

1. *Ko-dali* probably apophonic form of *ku-dayli; dayli* or *deli,* 'to
range in a row', 'to come together', 'to get together'. Here it probably
refers to the tubers and the leaves of the taytu. *Ko-vili: kuvili, vili,*
'to twine round', referring here to the stalk of the taytu.

2. The same verbs are here repeated in transitive imperative.

3. *Tubawa-m,* a rare probably magical form, derived from the
root *tubwalo-la,* 'back, body'. Here, since it probably refers to the
body of the taytu tuber and conveys the idea of fullness, I have
rendered it interlineally by 'fullness'. *Yagava-m* obviously 'thy leaves'.
Waybitu, a tenacious and prolific plant with very large trunk (?) or
roots or fruit. *Yokwa'oma,* an exuberant creeper with luxuriant
foliage resembling that of taytu.

FORMULA 34
(Ch. IX, Sec. 2)

1. *A-te-m*   *pwaypwaya!*
   I cut thee   soil

2. *Ku-tokaye*   *pwaypwaya;*
   thou arise   soil

3. *guba'uye*   *pwaypwaya;*   *gubagesi*   *pwaypwaya.*
   lift-rise   soil   lift-sag   soil

GENERAL COMMENTARY

This spell is uttered twice on the standard plot in the presence of all the men: at the cutting of the *kaygaga* sapling, and at the striking of the soil with the *kaylepa*. It obviously fits only into the second context.

LINGUISTIC COMMENTARY

3. The two verbs compounded with *guba*, probably from *gebi*, 'to lift'. *Uye* was explained to me in a somewhat unsatisfactory manner, half by gesture and half by words, as equivalent to *i-tokaye*, 'he rise'. It refers here probably to the vine and foliage of taytu. *Gesi*, which means in ordinary speech 'to push away', is meant here to describe the action of the taytu tuber when it sinks deep into the ground, rendered by 'sag'. In free translation I have rendered it "lift and let thy crops sag, O soil".

FORMULA 35
(Ch. IX, Sec. 2)

1. *Semwaraga* (repeated)
   (bush-hen—magical name?)
   Yolumbila (repeated)
   (bush-hen—magical name?)

2. *Gigi-gigila,*   *mwasa-mwasala!*
   laughing (?)   playing (?)

3. *Ba-watay-ma*   *kayga-si*   *a'kwale'i.*
   I might dispute (?)   throat theirs   my garden-companions

4. *Gala*   *kawa-si,*   *kawa-si*   *pulo'u;*
   no   voice theirs   voice theirs   night-jar

   gala   *kayga-si,*   *kayga-si*   *kabwaku.*
   no   throat theirs   throat theirs   (bird)

5. *Ta-ukuwakula-si,*   *ta-lilapwara-si.*
   we cry out at work   we boast about our gardens (?)

GENERAL COMMENTARY.

This short, simply constructed spell is uttered while the magician sways the *kayowota*, 'the good sapling', and again immediately after when he rubs the soil with weeds. The sympathetically invoked bush-hen and the *kabwaku* are well known to us from Omarakana, where the gardeners imitate the latter while planting. The night-jar does not appear in the Omarakanan system. It is a bird of sorcery; it strikes the natives' imagination by its enormous mouth.

LINGUISTIC COMMENTARY

1. I was told that these two words were magical names. The first one being equivalent to *kwaroto*, the ordinary large bush-hen, the eggs and flesh of which are taboo to the magician. *Yolumbila* is the magical pseudonym for *molubida*, the ordinary appellation of the small bush-hen, also tabooed to the *towosi*.

2. These words are probably simply magical reduplications of *gigila*, 'to laugh', *mwasawa*, 'to play'. In this latter the *w* is changed into *l*—a transformation not unusual in Kiriwinian. Rendered interlineally by 'laughing' and 'playing'. In free translation, to cover the repetitions: "O mirthful laughter, O playful playing."

3. *Watay-ma* probably the durative or intensive form (suffix *-ma*) of *watay*, 'to quarrel', 'to dispute'. Whether this means simply 'to vaunt through the throats of my garden-companions' or 'to dispute with my garden-companions' I am not able to decide. In the free translation I have adopted the non-committal translation "I shall cry out with the throats of my companions". Considering that in verse 4 the throats and voices of my companions are extolled by the negative comparison of magic, it is more probable that the re-interpretation of 'dispute' into 'vaunt' is more correct and that my free translation, therefore, renders the meaning adequately.

5. *Ukuwakula* is the name for one of the cries characteristic of garden work. *Lilapwara* was very inadequately commented upon as equivalent to 'brag about one's garden', 'extolling one's crops'. Analysing this word, however (cf. the word *a-talilakema* in M.F. 4, v. 2), into *lila* from *lala*, 'to blossom', and *pwala* perhaps from *pweliya*, 'plenty', the word would be equivalent to 'blossom plenty', or 'blossom in plenty', which vaguely fits into the native explanation.

FORMULA 36
(Ch. IX, Sec. 2)

Uri   dayda'i — dayda'i,
taro   (bracken?)

uri   tarora — tarora,
taro   anchored   anchored

me-lala.
(continuous blossoming)

GENERAL COMMENTARY

This short spell is recited over a taro top. The taro is addressed directly. Its object is to frighten away the bush-pigs. The *towosi* showed some reluctance to give me this magic because if the bush-pigs heard it they would go into the garden.

LINGUISTIC COMMENTARY

Dayda'i was explained to me by my informant as the name of a weed which is very tenacious and never dies. From my own memory I seem to identify the word with the name for 'bracken', but I am not certain. I have incorporated part of the commentary and my reminiscence in the free translation: "O taro tenacious as the bracken." *Tarora* is obviously compounded of *ta-*, an effective prefix, and *rora = lola*, 'to moor, to anchor'. The natives gave me a brief commentary: *tarora: bitalola, bipoula*, '*tarora* is equivalent (to) it might be anchored, it might get strong', in free translation "O taro, anchored firmly". *Me-lala* commented upon as *bimalala, bimatuwo*, '*me-lala* means it might blossom on, it might get ripe'. *Me-lala* is probably compounded of *me = ma-*, the durative prefix (which occurs often in magic), and *lala*, 'to blossom'.

FORMULA 37
(Ch. IX, Sec. 2)

1. *Avayle   litu-la   ay-sitagila?* (repeated)
   who   children his   he cry

2. *Litu-gwa   kwaroto   i-sitagila.*
   children mine   bush-hen   he cry

3. *Basi   uku'uku   bisi-ki   dadam.*
   pierce   (a rank weed)   pierce at   reed

4. *Kw-ali'uli,   ku-rokoupi.*
   thou come at   thou surround

GENERAL COMMENTARY

This brief spell is spoken over a yam.

LINGUISTIC COMMENTARY

1. *Litu-la* is in plural 'his children', the verb ought to be in plural but is in singular. I cannot explain this nor a similar lack of grammar in verse 2. Nor is it clear whether the speaker identifies himself with the bush-hen, saying (in v. 2), "It is the children of me, the bush-hen, that are crying," or else whether he means "The bush-hens, who are my children, are crying." The bush-hen, of course, figures

in this spell because stuff from its enormous spherical brooding-nests (*ge'u*) is used in the magical mixture (cf. M.F. 21, D.). The root *sitagila* in verses 1 and 2 was equated by my informants with *valam*, 'to cry'. *Sitagina* is allied to the word *laytagina* which is used for 'rumour', 'outcry'. Here I have rendered it interlineally by 'cry', in free translation "to cry out". Since my native informants told me that the crying refers to food, I have incorporated this in the free version.

3. The words *basi* and *bisi-ki* do not connect this spell with the activity of that name, 'the thinning out', *basi*. *Basi* is the ordinary word for 'pierce'. *Uku'uku* was defined to me as a rank weed. *Dadam* is a reed growing in the *dumya*. Probably this verse refers to plants of rank growth which break freely through the ground and influence the yams sympathetically.

4. *Kw-ali'uli*, second person of *kali'uli*. *Ku-rokoupi* was equated to me with *kalipatu*, 'to surround', and verse 4 as a whole was said to refer to the bunch of small taytu sprouting from the seed tuber. It is an imperative directly addressed to the plant.

FORMULA 38
(Ch. IX, Sec. 2)

1. *Ne-ku-lalola,*   *ne-ku-lola* (repeated)
thou do moor on   thou do moor

2. *Kway-tala si-lola*   *sa-gwa'i:*
one (r.b.) their anchor   companions mine

   bi-lolakaka,   *lokapwakapwa; ula lola*
he might anchor weakly (?)   anchor feebly   my   anchor

   yaygula'i vatuvi.
myself   set up

3. *A-loli-ma lopou-la ulo buyagu;*   *i-gubakaytala l.u.b.;*
I anchor on belly his my garden-site   he lift-stand up

   i-loluvagasi l.u.b.;   *i-lolamaga l.u.b.;*   *i-kwaydudubile l.u.b.;*
he anchor for good   he anchor bedrock   he darken

   i-lobukayaulo l.u.b.;   *i-lobulatola l.u.b.*
he stand up as the iron-wood palm   he stand up as the foliage interior

4. *Kutorawaya, Torawaya, Wasa'i, Iluvapopula, Tomlawa'i;*
(names of ancestral spirits)

   tubu-gu Mukwa'ina; tubu-gu Uluvala'i;
grandfathers mine   grandfathers mine

   tubu-gu Mwoysibiga; buluma-va'u biloma-m
grandfathers mine   ghost new   ghost thin

   tuwagu Mwagwoyre.
elder brother mine

After this verse 1 is repeated again.

GENERAL COMMENTARY

A. *Sociological Context:* this spell is chanted three times during the performance of the *kamkolola* ceremony. It shows the same context of preparations, taboos and sociological suspense which we have found in the spells of the Omarakana rite. In the case of this spell, however, its publicity is definite and direct; even women and children participate in the rite preceding its third recitation, and, though it is first spoken in the magician's house, at the second ceremony it is chanted for half a day or so over the various fields, so that everybody can hear it. At the third ceremony, the public rite in the gardens, it is chanted over the leaves, which are afterwards handled and used by all individually for their own benefit. Thus the character of the words affects the community in a very forthright manner.

B. *Ritual Context:* this is of course also three-fold. In the first rite a magical mixture is charmed over in the house under the same conditions and with the same precautions which surround every type of magical impregnation. In the second, the magic is launched over the gardens, and in the third it is publicly driven into the *bwabodila* and *kavapatu* leaves.

C. *Structure:* the only spell of the Momtilakayva system which shows any structure, and we have divided it into three parts, although it is by no means a typical tripartite spell, with a regular well-constructed main part.

D. *Dogmatic Context:* the main idea of this spell is stability, and the word *lola*, 'anchoring', the standard word of strength, tenacity and stability, occurs throughout (cf. M.F. 10). The second rite, during which the magician charms each *baleko*, on which the junior magician has previously erected the *kamkokola*, is called by the natives *kilikeli*. The main ceremony which follows is known as *keliviyaka* or 'the great *keli*'. The common root *keli* is connected with *kali*, 'fence'. Thus the erecting of the *kamkokola* is linguistically conceived as the fencing round of the *baleko*. The various elements in the magic, expressing the desire to make things strong, tenacious; and again certain elements pointing to its being connected with the bush-pigs, seem to agree with the assumption that this is the ceremony of the "magical fence".

E. *Mode of Recitation:* each time chanted loudly and distinctly in the typical Trobriand sing-song.

LINGUISTIC COMMENTARY

1. *Ne-ku-lalola*, reduplication of *ne-ku-lola*. *Lola* the root of 'to moor', 'to anchor'. *Neku* probably equal *luku*, second person emphatic

'thou do'. *Ne-ku-lola* would be 'thou do moor', the reduplicated form distinguished in free translation by the addition of 'on' to mark duration or iterativeness.

2. Is a typical depreciative comparison of other people's magical force or entity to the advantage of one's own. *Sa-gwa'i* is a plural, 'companions mine'. The expressions *bi-lolakaka*, *lokapwakapwa*, are depreciative. The first one is probably a verbal form, the suffix *kaka* being defined as signifying 'weakness', rendered literally by the adverb 'weakly'. In the second the prefix *lo-* probably stands for abridged *lola;* suffix *-kapwakapwa*, said by my informants to denote the idea of 'weakness', rendered adverbially by 'feebly'. The second part of this phrase is interesting since it includes the word *vatuvi*. It obviously here has a nominal, perhaps adjectival function, although we have rendered it literally by the verb 'to set up'. Here it denotes 'setting up', 'establishment', 'firmness', 'strong grip', perhaps also a tendency groundwards; a meaning which does not in any way disagree with the analysis of this word in the commentary to verse 1 of Formula 2. In free translation "my anchor is firmness". In connexion with my earlier attempts at determining the meaning of this word, an interesting episode occurred. When I pressed the question as to what this word meant, Nasibowa'i, who was not a good commentator, told me: *vatuvi yaga-la wala ulo kema*, '*Vatuvi* is just a name of my axe.' I was very impressed by this answer and felt that there were unplumbed depths of mystical significance if that word, besides meaning so many other things, could also be the name of the magician's sacred axe. It was only when I understood the language better that it became clear to me that this simply meant '*vatuvi* is just a word which I am using in my magic', because *kema*, 'axe', 'magical axe', is one of the concrete expressions used to designate a magical system. But this is an additional proof that *vatuvi* is a typical word of magic.

3. *A-loli-ma: lola* with the durative or iterative *-ma*, 'I anchor on'. This word and all the remaining ones are coupled with the often recurring phrase 'the belly of my garden'. *Gubakaytala* is compounded of *guba* from *gebi* and *kaytala* probably from *tola*, 'to stand up', "rises and stands up" in free translation. *Maga*, which we have met already in Formula 2, verse 1, and Formula 10, verse 4, and also Formula 29, verse 4, has the meaning of 'bedrock, main part of the earth, of the ground'. The two words *lobukayauli* and *lobulatola* are obviously symmetrical. The latter was equated by my informants with *i-dudubile*, 'it darkens'. It undoubtedly is identical with *yobunatola*, a word which designates a dark interior formed by leaves. *Yo-*, the prefix, 'leafy', *buna* from *bwala*, 'interior'. *Tola*, 'standing up'. The

word *i-lobukayauli* is perhaps a contraction of *lobulakayauli* where *lobula* would be the same as *yobuna*, 'leafy interior', and *kayauli* would be a replacement of the abstract idea of erectness by the concrete expression of the iron-wood palm, hence in free translation "the belly of my garden rises as the interior of an iron-wood palm grove".

4. was said to be all names of *bilibaloma*, 'ancestral ghosts'. The first two have a specially significant appearance, and these are probably names of mythological ancestors which, also probably, show some pronounced etymology.

FORMULA 39
(Ch. IX, Sec. 2)

Yakola,	*ba-yakola* (repeated).		
weeding	I might weed		
Yakola	*lukuvalu'i,*	*yowota*	*lukula'odila;*
weeding	corner-village	making clear	corner-bush
yakola	*lukula'odila,*	*yowota*	*lukuvalu'i;*
weeding	corner-bush	making clear	corner-village
ba-yowota,		*ba-yakola* (repeated).	
I might make clear		I might weed	

GENERAL COMMENTARY

This simple spell, consisting of three short phrases, is chanted while the magician carries out a mimic act of weeding.

LINGUISTIC COMMENTARY

Yakola was equated by my commentators with *pwakowa*, 'to weed'. Its etymology seems to me to be associated with the prefix *yo-*, 'leafy', and *kola* = *kwari*, 'to get hold of', 'to get hold of leaves' perhaps? *Lukuvalu'i* is obviously the same as *nukuvalu* in Formula 8. *Yowota* means 'to make clear' (cf. Part V, Div. VIII, § 9). In the free version I have translated it by "to clear". The name of the ceremony, *yowota*, will be well remembered.

FORMULA 40
(Ch. IX, Sec. 2)

1.	*Kalu-bi-layla,*	*bi-layla* (repeated).
	his going	he might go
	kalu-bi-lutu,	*bi-lutu* (repeated).
	his dropping	he might drop
2.	*Ba-sigutayna'i,*	*ba-pilayma'i;*
	I might make you rise	I might assist you

3. *kay-tala*   *gu-kwa'i.*   *kaukwa'i,*   *kayauli*
   one (w.l.)   my wood   kind of wood (?)   iron-wood palm

   bay-tawu'i   *wokatay-gu.*
   I might set up   on right side mine

4. *Bi-wawota*   *yam, bi-tatayle*   *bogi;*
   he might break through   day   he might cut through   night

   bi-wawota,   *wotaye.*
   he might break through   exchange of fish for food (?)

GENERAL COMMENTARY

Very little can be said about the context of this any more than of the previous formula, because I never witnessed an actual performance of the magic. The spell is chanted over an adze at harvest. Its text roughly corresponds to this aim or function.

LINGUISTIC COMMENTARY

1. The two symmetrical lines are built on the repetition of two verbs, *layla*, 'to go', and *lutu*, 'to come down', 'to drop'. Both have the prefix of futurity. In the first utterance they are, moreover, provided with the prefix *kalu-*, 'his'.

2. The two first verbs, which are provided with the prefix *ba-* of potentiality or futurity, are also used with elaborate endings *na'i* and *ma'i*. These may be only magical distortions, but probably they have some iterative or durative significance. *Ba-sigutayna'i* was translated to me: *bi-basi, bi-guti, bi-la orokaywa*, which means 'it might pierce, it might come out (?), it might go up'. The root *guti*, however, is not quite clear to me; I have rendered it by 'rise'. *Ba-pilayma'i* was explained to me: *bi-ma'i pilatala taytu*, 'it might bring portion of taytu'. The word *pila*, however, conveys the idea of 'assist' so I have rendered it here as 'assist'. Probably these verbs refer to the action of taking out and fetching taytu at harvest.

3. The third word is difficult to translate. It might be simply a magical embellishment of the word *ka'i*, 'tree'. The verb *bay-tawu'i* I translate on my own responsibility as the future of *vitawo*, 'to set up', 'to erect' (cf. M.F. 2, comm. to v. 1). With these provisions the verse makes fairly good sense. "One tree of mine, a fine magical tree, as an iron-wood palm, I shall set up on my right side"—a phrase which perhaps alludes to some of the ceremonial instruments of display used at harvest or on festive occasions; but of what I am not certain.

4. The verb *bi-wawota: wawota* was translated to me as 'the sprouting of new taytu'. But its ordinary meaning is 'to break, to break through', and so I have rendered it here. *Tatayle* was also

said to mean here the sprouting of taytu, probably it is a reduplicated form of *ta'i*, 'to cut', with the emphatic suffix *-la* at the end, rendered as 'cut through'. *Wotaye* is a word with which I am not acquainted, but it was translated in commentary as the name of one type of exchange of fish for food. This verse would then more or less mean "it would be breaking through at daytime, it would be cutting out at night time, it would be breaking through (so as to provide for our exchanges". The breaking through and coming out might, of course, refer to the action of harvesting rather than the growth of the taytu, or else it might be a retrospective magic based on the vague feeling that if the taytu sprouts plentifully it will be good harvest. On the whole this formula is among those which I have least succeeded to translate satisfactorily.

FORMULA 41
(Ch. X, Sec. 3)

I. 1. *Seulo,*   *Milaga'u,*   *ku-lou-si,*
(an ancestral spirit) (an ancestral spirit) you go

ku-didagi-se kada luya-si;
you load   our   coconut

2. *ku-luwaywoy-se   ye'una,*   *bonabona,*
you throw away   (an insect pest) (an insect pest)

silakavaku,   *nukwaybala;*
(a misshapen nut) (a misshapen nut)

3. *ku-didagi-se kada luya-si;*   *lukutukwava,*
you load   our   coconut   (a strong coconut)

ku-mayay-se o du-valu-si.
thou fetch   in our village

4. *Ba-walay-m*   *nuya,*   *ba-ligaweywo*
I might paddle thee coconut I might spill

Nadili!
(Laughlan Island)

II. 5. *Ba-walay-m*   *nuya,*   *ba-ligaweywo*
I might paddle thee coconut I might spill

Nadili: *ye'una,*   *bonabona,*
(Laughlan Island) (an insect pest) (an insect pest)

silakavaku,   *nukwaybala;*
(a misshapen nut) (a misshapen nut)

6. *ba-libuma'i*   *igu-waga sakwabu.*
I might launch (?) my canoe stump of coconut leaf

7. *Ba-dagima'i   agu   nuya,   nudoyoyu,*
   I might load   my   coconut   (a fine coconut)

   lusamaku,   lukutukwava,   lukulawata.
   (a large coconut)   (a strong coconut)   (a white coconut)

8. *Ba-walay-m   nuya,   ba-ligaweywo*
   I might paddle thee   coconut   I might spill

   Koymara'u: *ye'una,* etc., etc.
   (a village on Woodlark Island)   (an insect pest)

The *tapwana* is then repeated (vv. 5 to 7), but instead of Nadili the following localities are named:—
(a) villages on Woodlark Island: Koymara'u (as shown in v. 8), Suloga, Wamwala, Moluweyo'u;
(b) islands in the Marshall Bennett archipelago; Gawa, Digumenu, Kwaywata, Iwa, Kitava;
(c) villages on the east coast of Boyowa: Wawela, Dubwaga, Okayboma, Olivilevi, Moligilagi, Yalumugwa, Kaulagu, Yourawotu, Tilakaywa, Kwaybwaga, Liluta, Kammwamwala, M'tawa, Yuwada,'Kapwani, Idaleaka, Kaybola, Lu'ebila, Laba'i, Kuluvitu and Mwatawa. After this a very short *dogina:*—

III. 9. *I-yali,   i-yapu.*
     he cuts through   he rounds off

     Then the *u'ula* is repeated, the spell ending on verse 4.

A. B. and E. *Sociological and Ritual Contexts and Mode of Recitation:* from the point of view of the cultural context and the relation of the spell to it, we are mainly interested in knowing how far its words directly affect the minds of the whole community. This and the following two spells form part of the rites, which mark the *kaytubutabu* period—an important event which affects everybody, is connected with a definite season, and is imposed in anticipation of dancing, distributions or other festivities in which everybody is keenly interested. The date is fixed publicly. The whole community are then engaged for some time in preparing and trimming the palms and, towards the end, in providing them with the visible signs of the tabooed period. At the same time the magician, who may either be a resident of the village or be specially hired for the purpose from abroad, prepares his magical paraphernalia of the rite. He will receive payments from the members of the community. Thus everybody is aware and intensely interested in the proceedings. The rite itself mobilises the whole village: head-man or chief as well as the commoners are in attendance and the words are chanted publicly and solemnly in a loud voice, right into the substance of the *kaytubutabu.*

C. *Structure:* full tripartite form. The *tapwana* is one of the characteristic main parts in which the key expression is very long and the inventory words, which in such cases are often geographical expressions, consist of one word. The *dogina* is extremely short.

D. *Dogmatic Context:* I obtained no mythological data on this magical system. The spell begins with an invocation to two ancestral spirits or mythological personages who dominate the *u'ula*, since they are invoked to remove the bad coconuts and to import the good ones. The rest of the spell is conducted in the first person, the magician substituting himself for the mythological agencies.

LINGUISTIC COMMENTARY

1. The words *Seulo, Milaga'u* were said to be the names of two men who had lived in Tukwa'ukwa, the village of Tokulubakiki, the present owner of this spell. The two names are significant, *seulo* is the word for 'drizzle, drizzling rain'; *milaga'u* is compounded of prefix *-mila* (like?), and *ga'u*, 'fog'. Whether the association of these two names with moisture, hence fertility, means that they are not names of real people, but of culture heroes connected with fertility magic, I was unable to decide in discussion with my informants.

2. *Ye'una*—the insect producing the black and grey spots on the coconut leaves. Perhaps *ye-*, prefix for leaf, and *ula*, 'decay', *ye'una*, 'the decay on leaves', rather than the insect. The word *mauna*, used for all that flies and moves quickly, may also be used sometimes with unfavourable agencies. Hence in free translation "blighted by black and discoloured leaves". *Bonabona*, 'insect eating the tips of the leaves which cover the coconut, the eyes of the nut' (*matala luya*). Hence in free translation "blighted by their tops being eaten away". *Silakavaku*, 'a dwarfed misshapen coconut', compound of *sila-*, formative prefix of 'branch', and *kakavaku*, 'grub' (?), "malformed" in free translation. *Nukwaybala*—a misshapen coconut of an elongated form, in the free version "grown out of shape". This verse is obviously an exorcism referring to all undesirable and blighted coconuts.

3. *Ku-didagi-se kada luya-si*, 'you load our coconuts', in free translation "load the coconuts fit for us". *Lukutukwava: lukwava* is the ordinary name for water-bottles made of coconut shells. *Lukutukwava* are coconuts good enough to be made into water-bottles, that is, as good as they can be, particularly strong. Rendered in literal version as 'strong coconut', in free translation as "coconuts good for making water-bottles".

4. *Ba-walay-m: wala* from *wola, ulawola*, 'to paddle'. Here a transitive form second person 'I might paddle thee'. In free translation "I shall cast off" in the sense "I shall paddle you off". *Ba-ligaweywo:*

ligaweywo was said to be derived from *laguwa*, best known in the form *kumwaylaguwa* or *kumwaynaguwa*. This means 'to wash ashore', a verb used for the flotsam which is washed ashore, or else for cargo which is unloaded from a boat. This phrase is then repeated with various geographical names.

6. *Ba-libuma'i* is a word which was translated to me by my informants as 'to launch', but I cannot identify it with any known root. But this is not the ordinary word for 'launch'. The other component, the root *libu* which in ordinary speech means 'a dry twig', lends us no assistance. *Igu* is of course an apophony of *agu*. *Sakwabu* was translated to me as the 'butt end of the coconut leaf'. The sentence does not make very good sense. I translated it "I shall launch my canoe (consisting of) the stump of a coconut leaf", following in this the instructions of my native informants.

7. *Ba-dagima'i*, root *dagi*, is obviously from *dodige* or *didagi*, 'to fill, to load'. As regards the various denominations for coconuts, we find first the expression *lukulawata* which was commented upon in verse 3. *Nudoyoyu: nu-*, formative prefix of coconut, *do-?*, *yoyu*, 'coconut leaf'. I cannot really translate *do*. The only possible hypothesis would be that it is a derivative of *dayli* or *deli*, also in the form of *dodeli*, 'to come together', 'to remain together'. It then would mean 'in its clustering together'. It is certainly an expression for a type of fine coconut. *Lusamaku: lu-*, formative prefix of coconut, *samaku* means 'four coconuts', usually intended for a present or ceremonial distribution, hence 'large coconuts fit for ceremonial distribution'. *Luku-lawata: luku-*, prefix, *lawata* refers to the fine whiteish-coloured coconuts of good quality.

9. *Yali* or *yada*, 'to curve, to cut'; *yapu*, 'to round off'. The meaning of this would probably be 'the coconut-buds cut through, the coconuts round off'.

FORMULA 42
(Ch. X, Sec. 3)

1. *Avay-ta'u*   *i-tovivina*   *o*   *bukubaku*
   which man   he stand-turn   in   central place

   gunu-vanu'i? (strophe repeated)
   my village

2. *Yaygula'i*   *Tokulubakiki,*   *so-gu*
   I myself   (the reciter's name)   companion mine

   tabu-gu   *Yaurana*
   grandfather mine   (personal name of grandfather)

   Ka-tovivina   *o*   *bukubaku-na*   *gunu-vanu'i*
   we (two) stand-turn   in   central place his   my village

3. *Me-uwa*   *luya*
   he fruit   coconut

   uwoligilagila   *luya,*
   fruit piled up   coconut

   i-woypwalela   *luya,*
   he fruit-break-forth   coconut

   i-woguduyoulala   *luya.*
   he fruit-bend-feathery branch   coconut

4. *Kawa-la*   *kayo-la*
   speech his   throat his
   Dubwadebula —
   (personal name of the main palm in Omarakana)

5. *Ki-i-i-i-i-i-i-i* (long-drawn *i*).
   (onomatopoeic)

GENERAL COMMENTARY

A. D. *Sociological and Dogmatic Context:* this short spell is chanted regularly over the village every few days while the *kaytabutabu* period lasts. As with magic chanted in the garden over the crops, the magician allows his voice to sweep over the palms which grow between the houses, on the central place and behind the outer ring. The most important part of the whole magic is the chanting of this spell. The words, therefore, the main gist of which is the affirmation of fertility, are deeply relevant to the villagers, who are keeping irksome taboos in preparation for some ceremony or festivity; they fit well into this context, strengthening the people's faith and enhancing their conviction that something real is being done and that all their denials and provisions are being transformed into effective value.

E. *Mode of Recitation:* chanted in a loud voice over the village.

LINGUISTIC COMMENTARY

1. *I-tovivina,* characteristic compound of magical formulae, *to-,* 'to stand', *vivina,* 'turn around', really meaning 'to turn about, to walk about'. *Gunu-vanu'i: gunu,* abbreviation, *yay-gula: gula = guna* in contact with *vanu'i* (= *valu,* 'village', changed into *vanu'i*), the magical equivalent for the usual *ulo valu.*

1. and 2. are the typical question and answer of magical formulae, affirming the ancestral filiation and containing the names of the magician and one of his predecessors, usually the man from whom the magic was obtained.

3. *Me'uwa: uwa,* the ordinary word for 'fruit', 'to make fruit', 'to bear fruit', *me-,* durative prefix. *Uwoligilagila* was translated to me:

"when the fruits pile up, one on top of the other in bunches". Perhaps *uwo-*, prefix of fruit, *ligilagila*, 'basis' (?)—something like 'fruit founded on fruit', 'fruit piled up'. *I-woypwalela*: *woy*, probably formative from *uwa* again, *pwalela*, either 'hole', *pwala*, which does not fit very well here, or some such root as *pwoyliya* (cf. M.F. 19, v. 1), or *puri*, 'to break forth in bunches', which does fit quite well. Thus we have rendered it here 'fruit break forth'; in free translation "breaks forth with bunches of nuts". *I-woguduyoulala*: here again the *wo-*, probably from *uwa*; *gudu*, 'to press down', 'to bend down', thus *iwogudu*, 'fruit pressing down'. *Youlala*: "the top", the young shoots or sprouts of the tree. The whole word might mean. something like "the fruit bending down in the feathery top-branches" Whatever the exact analysis of these words might be, it is a verbal form affirming a successful and prolific production of fruit in the palm.

4. *Kawa-la* means 'his mouth', 'his voice', very often used as 'his speech', 'his act of speaking'; *kayo-la*, 'his throat'; *kawa-la kayo-la* probably means 'the speech of his throat', 'the speech coming out of the throat of Dubwadebula'.

The last sound, *ki-i-i-i*, is onomatopoeic imitation of the high-pitched wail made by the coconuts rubbing against the branches, said by the natives to occur especially when the palm is richly laden with heavy fruit.

FORMULA 43
(Ch. X, Sec. 3)

Gegila	sipisapi	kayo-m	lukumitamata;
lory	cut off	throat thine	coco-green

g.s.k. lukubwebweria;	g.s.k. lukukwaygibu;	g.s.k. lukulawata;
coco-red	coco-brown	coco-white

g.s.k. luku'ama;	g.s.k. lukukwalu.
coco-pale	coco-orange-coloured

GENERAL COMMENTARY

This short formula repeated over and over again in a loud voice over the palms of the village is the last in the cycle and is recited on the eve of the day on which the taboo is finally lifted. One is tempted to interpret this invocation on the scapegoat principle, since the breaking of a taboo would always appear as something dangerous, but my informants were never articulate on this point.

LINGUISTIC COMMENTARY

Gegila is the lory bird, the totemic animal of the Lukulabuta clan. It is tempting to guess at an association between this clan, the first two syllables of which have the characteristic formative of coconut, *luku*, and the coconut palm. Such an association is not admitted by the natives, but this bird certainly seems to stand in some relationship to the palms. *Sipisapi: sapi*, 'to cut', as one cuts a branch or a fruit from a tree. *Kayo-m*, 'throat thine', refers here to the stalk of the coconut.

The nouns at the end of each sentence refer to the varieties of coconut, distinguished here by their colour. I was told that the *lukumitamata* is of a green colour when ripe. The word appears to be compounded from the coconut prefix *luku* and *mitamata*, the normal reduplication of *mata*, 'eye', an etymology, however, which does not fit the comment, and I have adopted as always the opinion of my informants. *Lukubwebweria* is obviously 'red coconut', since *bwebweria* is the ordinary word for 'red'. *Lukwaygibu* from *gibugabu*, 'burning', probably 'brown coconut'. The natives told me that this coconut is *digadaga*, which means anything yellow or blue or any of the greys between white and black. *Lukulawata*, 'white' (cf. M.F. 41, v. 7). *Luku'ama*, also of a pale white colour. *Lukukwalu* was said to be orange, this last definition being given by pointing to some orange-coloured object in my tent.

FORMULA 44
(Ch. X, Sec. 5)

1. *Tomate,*   *bogi*   *ku-yuvayovili,*   *yam*
   dead man   night   thou change completely   day

   ku-pipipila;
   thou grow in size

2. *Usi — kukuva*   *agu*   *usi;*
   banana (kind of fruit)   my   banana

   usi — bowada a.u.;   *usi — yakaulo a.u.;*   *usi — yovila a.u.;*
   banana (kind of fruit)   banana admiration   banana change

   usi — pipila a.u.
   banana size

3. *I-ka'u-se gine'uba,*   *i-tavi-kay-se*   *agu*   *usi.*
   they take (a cutting shell)   they cut at   my   banana

GENERAL COMMENTARY

This is a private spell chanted either by the owner over his own bananas or by a paid specialist. The words, therefore, are heard by the interested parties. The magic has no social or organising significance.

LINGUISTIC COMMENTARY

1. *Tomate*, 'dead man', 'corpse'. This is invoked here because, as the natives explained to me, 'the corpse when the man dies is small. Over-night he swells, next day he bursts. So our bananas should swell and burst'. *Yuvayovili*, reduplication of *yovili*, from *yo-*, effective prefix, and *vili*, 'to turn', 'to change'; for some mysterious reason the change here mentioned is that of mortuary swelling, so my informants assured me. Hence rendered 'thou change completely' and in free translation, with comment incorporated, "make turn and swell". *I-pipipila* from *pila*, 'part', 'large part', 'large portion' (cf. *Uri-pipila* in M.F. 25, v. 3).

2. *Kukuva*, 'a yellow fruit' growing wild, similar to, but larger than the banana. *Bowada* another fruit. *Yakaulo*, 'wonder', caused by the sight of fine bananas. *Yovila* derived from *yovili*.

3. *Gine'uba* = *kayeki*, 'mother-of-pearl shell'. This sentence means 'the bananas are so great that we want to cut them in pieces'. *Tavi-kay-se* from *tavi* = *ta'i*, 'to cut'. *Kay-* directive prefix 'at'.

INDEX

Agriculture: social and cultural setting of, 118, *et seq.*; no abstract term corresponding to, 118

Agricultural activities, word to define, 118; terminology, 15; impossibility of finding English equivalent for, 15, 19, 67; linguistic side of, 18, 21, 49; vocabulary: multiplicity of meaning, 68; technique, 132, *et seq.*

Arden, Elisabeth, *quoted*, 237

Areca-nut, 109, 110, 111; fibre, 110; palm, 108; leaves, 93, 108

Argonauts of the Western Pacific, quoted, 89, 109, 217, 237

Aromatic or decorative herbs, 88

Arrowroot (*bisiya*), 91

Baedeker, 13

Bagido'u, 222, 244

Bagula, 16, 17, 66, 68, 84, 85, 86, 89, 118

Baleko, 16, 20, 27, 28, 66, 68, 82, 83–87; counting of, 125

Baloma, 83

Banana (*usi*), 81, 91; tree, 114; names of varieties of, 114, 115. *See also Usi*

Basi. See Thinning

Bathing, beach used for, 81

Bayse, 30; *Bayse odila,* 80; *Bayse valu,* 79

Beach, 69, 79, 80, 81

Betel-nut, 81

Bida, 80

Bidivalu (soil), 80

Bidubwabwa'u (black soil), 80

Binabina, 71, 82, 151

Bisikola, charm and rite, 161; derivation of word, 161

Bisiya (arrowroot), 91

Black magic, text referring to, 177, 178

Boathouse, 81

Bokavili, 205

Bokaykena (creeper), 115

Boma (taboo), 81

Boma or *Kaboma* (sacred grove), 79, 80, 86, 87

Borogu, 88

Botanical characteristics: expressions referring to, 5, 51, 88; botanical distinctions, terminology for, not scientific, 67; terms: general native description for, 92; place of, in native mind, 7, 92; botanic variations 100, 103

Boundaries: fixing of area, 7, 83; cutting of, 8

Boundary belt, 83

Bracken, 93

Bread-fruit, 115, 119; leaf, 93

Bubwaketa, yam, 115

Buku, Bukula, 31

Bulami, 110

Bulaya, 110

Bulletin of Oriental Studies, quoted, 60, 78

Buraku, fruit tree, 115

Buritila'ulo, 124, 194, 195

Bush, the (*Odila*), 68, 80

Bush-pigs, 48, 178; mythological, 48; home of, 48, 221; fear of, 221

Butuma (red light soil), 82

Buyagu (garden site), 15, 16, 20, 66, 68, 70, 83–87

Bwada-la, 106

Bwanawa, 99

Bwarita (sea), 29, 79

Bwaybwaya or *Bwaybwa'i,* 109

Bwita (tree), 96

Canoe: sea-going, 81; creeper used for lashing canoes, 89

Children and strangers: instruction to, 49, 50; instruction to children in gardening and magic, 61, 62; sources of meaning in the speech of, 62, *et seq.*

Christian Science and Trobriand sorcery, 237

Coconut, 81, 108, 109, 149; leaf girdle tied round trees, 113; leaves, 93, 108, 113; cream, 110; fibre, 110; meat, 110; milk, 110; oil, 110; shell, 110; green, 109; palm taboo, 109

Commentaries, necessity of, 11

Communal working, 8

Concrete expressions, 80

OVERLEAF

particulars of publications
of similar interest
issued by

GEORGE ALLEN & UNWIN LTD
LONDON: 40 MUSEUM STREET, W.C.1
LEIPZIG: (F. VOLCKMAR) HOSPITALSTR. 10
CAPE TOWN: 73 ST. GEORGE'S STREET
TORONTO: 91 WELLINGTON STREET, WEST
BOMBAY: 15 GRAHAM ROAD, BALLARD ESTATE
WELLINGTON, N.Z.: 8 KINGS CRESCENT, LOWER HUTT
SYDNEY. N.S.W.: AUSTRALIA HOUSE, WYNYARD SQUARE

The Social Economy of the Himalayans

by S. D. PANT

Demy 8vo.   *Illustrated*   12s. 6d.

This is a careful and thorough study of the inhabitants of the Kumaon Himalayas, based on nearly five years of first-hand observation and investigation. It gives a detailed account of the Bhotiyas and other peoples, their methods of agriculture, their industries, their trading activities, their recreations, and their religious festivals. It points out how the social and economic life of these peoples has been conditioned by the necessity of moving to higher altitudes in the summer and to the foothills in the winter.

Ubena of the Rivers

by A. T. CULWICK and G. M. CULWICK

Demy 8vo.   *Illustrations and Maps*   15s.

This book was prompted by the eagerness of the Chief Towegale Kiwanga, and many of the Bena royal clan and elders, to have a permanent record of tribal history and custom. Mr. and Mrs. Culwick have lived among them for some years and have the complete confidence of the tribe together with a thorough knowledge of the language and the same training in scientific investigation. The result is a well-balanced picture of the life and outlook of a typical East African Bantu tribe in a period of transition, in which the mythical "dead cake of custom" stands revealed as a living thing, capable of growth and development.

The Folklore of Morocco

by DOCTOR LEGEY

Demy 8vo.   *Illustrated*   12s. 6d.

Doctor Legey has had unique opportunities for amassing data about the superstitions and legends of Morocco during the long period of her pioneer medical work among the natives. She gives a vivid picture of the rites and traditions which still form the mainspring of their daily life, despite the encroachments of French civilization. Divination and fortune-telling; ghosts and demonology and traces of black magic, mingled with bastard Moslem legends; extraordinary cures for extraordinary ills; bird, beast, and plant lore; the propitiatory ceremonies and traditions which accompany each step from birth to death, fill the pages of this fascinating book. It not only forms a valuable contribution to the literature of folk-lore, but should prove of absorbing interest to the general reader. One or two of the photographs used as illustrations have been taken at great bodily risk.

Taming Philippine Headhunters

by FELIX M. KEESING and MARIE KEESING

With an Introduction by THEODORE ROOSEVELT

Demy 8vo.   10s. 6d.

"A mass of information, and is noteworthy for its insight, sympathizing not only with the picturesque tribes but also with the Westernized Philippino."—*Manchester Guardian*
"A serious and carefully written work full of detail, precise and covering all the main problems of the 'Philippine islanders' adjustment to modern and Western conditions."—*Time and Tide*

All prices are net

LONDON: GEORGE ALLEN & UNWIN LTD

CPSIA information can be obtained at www.ICGtesting.com
Printed in the USA
LVOW12s1737150913

352516LV00001B/46/A